JOHN H. TURNER

THE MYTH OF ICARUS
IN
SPANISH RENAISSANCE
POETRY

TAMESIS BOOKS LIMITED

LONDON

SERIE A - MONOGRAFIAS, LVI

I. S. B. N.   84-399-6707-1

Depósito Legal: M. 24.102 - 1977

Printed in Spain by Artes Gráficas Clavileño, S. A.

for

TAMESIS BOOKS LIMITED. LONDON, ENGLAND

CONTENTS

ACKNOWLEDGEMENTS

I wish to express my gratitude to Raimundo Lida for his patient and invaluable guidance since this project was undertaken, and to Stephen Gilman for his frequent advice and encouragement. Thanks are also due to the Bowdoin College Faculty Research Fund for financial assistance. My greatest debts are to Regina Paradis for her careful typing of the manuscript and to Leigh Turner for sound advice and constant understanding.

INTRODUCTION

A cartoon in a recent national magazine depicts Cupid, with his familiar bow and arrows and wings, wearing a double-breasted suit, two-tone shoes and dark glasses standing on a busy street corner. With a cigarette dangling from the corner of his mouth he is surrounded by the garish perversity of New York's 42nd Street. The figure is quite recognizable as the Roman god of love but in context it has more to say about contemporary values than it does about ancient Rome. The myths endure and are infinitely renewable—their very continuity provides us with perspective on the contexts in which they are invoked.

One of the most familiar and eternal of these myths is that of Icarus who flew too near the sun and perished in the sea. This story has always fascinated men but there seem to have been periods when its appeal was particularly intense. To the French romantic poets the sublime but fatal flight seemed peculiarly appropriate and they made the figure of Icarus their own.[1] In the early twentieth century the figure Icarus was used symbolically in a philosophical argument between the biologist Haldane and Bertrand Russell.[2] In our own day, as recent popular culture clearly shows, the idea of flight still has a strong appeal and the figure of Icarus is still familiar, even though the technological problem is, in a sense, solved. Indeed there now exists a computer program designed to identify Icarian imagery[3] and, according to the psychologist Henry Murray, an "Icarus complex".[4]

But perhaps the age which most took the figure of Icarus to its heart was that of the Renaissance, a time of ambitious idealism. This

---

[1] Maurice Shroder, *Icarus; the Image of the Artist in French Romanticism* (Cambridge, Mass., 1961).

[2] J. B. S. Haldane, *Daedalus, or Science and the Future* (New York, 1924); Bertrand Russel, *Icarus, or the Future of Science* (London, 1926).

[3] Daniel M. Ogilvie, *Psychodynamics of Fantasized Flight*, unpublished dissertation, Harvard University, 1967, especially chapter III, "Folktales and a Dictionary".

[4] Henry A. Murray, "American Icarus", *Clinical Studies of Personality*, Vol. II of *Case Histories in Clinical and Abnormal Psychology* (New York, 1955), pp. 615-641.

book documents the fascination of that age with the story of the flight and fall of the legendary young Greek, particularly in Spain where the appeal of the story was greatest. One might, perhaps, suppose that the men of the Renaissance expressed unfailing admiration for a young man who dared to fly too high and became immortal in his dying, yet Breughel's famous depiction of his fall should counsel caution. In Breughel's painting the calamity of Icarus' fall is reduced to a tiny splash in the corner of a picture in which the rest of the world goes about its business. We shall look for patterns in the portrayal of Icarus in the hope of wresting from the experiment some tentative observations about the tenor of the age that produced them. We shall follow the figure of Icarus as it is picked up by Renaissance poets and its fortunes in Spain, where there are more than enough documents to make such an undertaking rewarding.

I begin by examining the role of Icarus in previous literature, in the writers, both poets and collectors of myths, in classical literature and the Middle Ages. Then the attitudes of Renaissance scholars and translators are considered before the study of the poetic texts themselves. I shall restrict myself mainly to poems in Spanish, although the search for sources leads us into Italian poetry and there are some French poems in the tradition which are so well known that we cannot ignore them. The vogue of Icarus imagery in Spain is unparalleled, I am persuaded, in other countries. In all of Shakespeare, for example, the myth is only referred to in two plays.[5]

The story of the permeation of the ancient gods and heroes into Western European culture is already known in its broad outlines, thanks to the work of such men as Gilbert Highet and Jean Seznec.[6] Their lack of knowledge of the Spanish tradition has been partially amended.[7] José-María de Cossío's book on *Fábulas mitológicas en España*[8] deals only with longer narrative poems and does not, therefore, refer to the same material as we shall be dealing with. As far as our particular myth is concerned, little is written. Gallego Morell has writ-

[5] *Henry IV, part I*, IV, 6, 11. 55 ff. and IV, 7, 1. 16; *Henry VI, part III*, V, 6, 1. 21.

[6] Gilbert Highet, *The Classical Tradition* (Oxford, 1949); Jean Seznec, *The Survival of the Pagan Gods* (New York, 1953).

[7] María Rosa Lida de Malkiel, "Transmisión y recreación de temas grecolatinos en la poesía lírica española", *Revista de Filología Hispánica*, I (1939), pp. 20-63; "Perduración de la literatura antigua en Occidente", *Romance Philology*, 5 (1951), pp. 99-131; "La tradición clásica en España" (review of Highet), *Nueva Revista de Filología Hispánica*, 5 (1951), pp. 183-223.

[8] Madrid, 1952.

ten on versions of a closely related myth, that of Phaethon.[9] Pablo Cabañas has commented on a few sonnets dealing with the story of Icarus.[10] Joseph Fucilla has been the only scholar to write at any length on the myth that concerns us.[11]

[9] "El mito de Faetón en la literatura española", *Clavileño*, 37 (1956), pp. 13-26, and 38 (1956), pp. 31-43, also published as a book by the Consejo Superior de Investigaciones Científicas, Madrid, 1961.
[10] "Icaro o el atrevimiento", *Revista de Literatura*, I (1952), pp. 453-460.
[11] "Etapas en el desarrollo del mito de Icaro, en el renacimiento y en el siglo de oro", in *"Superbi colli" e altri saggi* (Rome, 1963), pp. 54-84.

Chapter I

THE CLASSICAL TRADITION

As an introduction to the study of the myth of Icarus in Renaisance poetry, I wish first to examine the treatment of the story in classical literature and in the Middle Ages. This background will provide constant reference points in the later chapters. The story of the flight of Icarus from the labyrinth of King Minos on Crete and his subsequent fall into the sea has an archetypal simplicity that has long appealed to the imaginations of men. Daedalus, Icarus' inventor father, is mentioned in the *Iliad* (18, 592) as is the Icarian Sea (2, 145), although Homer does not refer to the source of its name.[1] Many of the early accounts of Icarus' fate are etymological, that is they are concerned with the events that lead to the naming of that part of the Aegean Sea which was called the Icarian or of an island, still called Ikaria today. The names are said to commemorate the death of a young Greek who fell there from the sky and was drowned. Such brief accounts are to be found in Strabo's *Geography* (14, I, 19) and in Arrian's *Anabasis of Alexander* (VI, 20, 5).

Five classical collectors of myths record the story of the escape from Crete, though they do not agree on the details. Three of these versions, one early, that of Palaephatus, the others late, one by the Roman Hyginus (fab. 40)[2] and the other by Zenobius (iv, 92)[3] give only the barest outline, but Apollodorus of Athens (*Epitome* I, 13-14) and the Sicilian Diodorus (IV, 7-9) go into more detail. From the former we learn of Daedalus' advice to his son about flying too high or too low. He warns him that any deviation from the middle path will cause the sun of the sea to dissolve the glue with which his feathers are held in place. In Diodorus, who recounts the story and then apolo-

---

[1] No specific references will be given to works which can be found in many standard editions. In most cases the edition consulted was that of the Loeb Classical Library.

[2] *Hygini fabulae,* ed. Mauricius Schmidt (Jena, 1872), p. 69.

[3] In Andreas Schottus, *Adagia Graeca* (Antwerp, 1612), pp. 110-11.

gizes for its fantastic nature, this glue becomes the more familiar wax, something on which all later accounts agree; this change probably accounts for his other, less imitated, variant, that Daedalus warned only against flying too high and arrived safely in Italy by keeping his wings wet. All four mythographers agree on a point which is to be essential for the poets we shall study, that Icarus' death conferred immortality upon him in the naming of the sea into which he fell, although only Diodorus mentions the island also.

There have come down to us several rationalizing interpretations of the story, in the spirit of Euhemerus, all of which involve the idea that flight is a metaphor for great speed and that the myth refers to the invention of sails. Pliny the elder, in his Natural History (7, 56), is more specific, crediting Icarus with the invention of sails and his father with that of the masts and yards. Although Palaephatus grudgingly records the traditional story for posterity —he is as skeptical of its historical truth as Diodorus— he is clearly much more interested in telling us that what in fact happened was that Icarus perished in a great storm while sailing to freedom. Diodorus, a great admirer of Euhemerus, reports that Icarus and his father escaped from Crete in boats provided by Pasiphaë. According to this version, Icarus died as he was disembarking on the island to which he gave his name. Pausanias, in his *Description of Greece* (Boetia, XI) writes that, when father and son were escaping in boats, Deadalus used a sail to outrun the pursuing galleys of King Minos. Icarus, a less skillful sailor, fell into the sea and was drowned, and his body was carried by the tide to the shores of a nearby island, thereby giving names to both the sea and the island.

The story of Icarus' flight and fall is recounted sometimes as an edifying parable about the dangers of ambition. Dio Chrysostom refers to the story twice in this way. On one occasion (Discourse 71) he compares the ambitious person to Daedalus, whose rashness in inventing such an unnatural device was punished by the death of his son. On the other (Fourth Discourse on Kingship) he likens the arrogant ruler to Icarus, soaring in constant peril of disaster. In Lucian also, the death of Icarus exemplifies the hazards of ambition. In two of his dialogues, *The dream* and *Essay in Portraiture,* the impetuosity of young Icarus is contrasted with the prudence of his father and the reader is cautioned to fly low and keep his wings damp. In this Lucian clearly follows the lead of Diodorus. In the former's essay on astrology he considers Daedalus to have been a master of this occult art. He "practised it constantly himself and taught it to his son," but because Icarus was young and reckless, he "let his mind carry him into the zenith," made errors and "was precipitated into a sea of unfathomable perplexities." In all these cases pride is seen to lead to a fall.

One of Lucian's works actually commemorates Icarus in its title. *Icaromenippus* takes the form of a conversation between Menippus, who claims to have returned from a flight to heaven, and an incredulous friend. When the latter asks how his friend escaped the fate of Icarus, Menippus glibly replies that he did so by avoiding the use of wax in the construction of his wings.

The story of Icarus attracted a large number of Latin poets. At the beginning of the sixth book of the *Aeneid*, for example, Virgil describes his hero arriving at Cumae and finding there a temple to Apollo on whose doors is depicted the story of the labyrinth and the minotaur. Daedalus would have recorded his son's fate here too, except that his grief prevented it.

> tu quoque magnam
> partem opere in tanto, sineret dolor, Icare, haberes;
> bis conatus erat casus effingere in auro,
> bis patriae cecidere manus (VI, 30-33).

> (you too would have a great share in such a work,
> Icarus, were it not for the grief; twice the attempt
> was made to express your fall in gold, and twice the
> father's hands fell).[4]

Horace refers to Icarus several times in his *Odes*. In a well known poem in which he seems to prophesy his own immortality, he feels confident that he will though fly posterity "more famous than Daedalian Icarus" ("Daedaleo notior Icaro," *Odes* II, 20). In another ode (III, 7) the poet consoles the maiden Asterie who complains that the man she loves is as deaf to her weeping as the rocks of Icaria, suggesting the heedlessness associated with the rocks as well as their literal insensibility. Elsewhere, in a much quoted passage, Horace warns a fellow poet of the dangers of emulating the high lyricism of a poet like Pindar:

> Pindarum quisquis studet aemulari
> Iule, ceratis ope Daedalea

---

4 Except where otherwise indicated, the translations are my own.

nititus pinnis vitreo daturus
   nomina ponto (IV, 2).
(whoever strives to emulate Pindar, Jullus, rests
on wings joined with wax by Daedalian art und will
give his name to a sea).[5]

But Ovid is without doubt the classical poet most attracted by the
figure of Icarus and to whom we owe most of the symbolism associated
with the myth. He tells the story at length twice, first in his *Art of Love*
and later, in greater detail, in the *Metamorphoses*. It is this latter
version that provides the inspiration for the vast majority of all modern
evocations of the myth.

Daedalus interea Creten longumque perosus
exsilium tactusque loci natalis amore
clausus erat pelago. "terras licet" inquit "et undas
obstruat: et caelum certe patet; ibimus illac:
omnia possideat, non possidet aera Minos".
dixit, et ignotas animum dimittit in artes
naturamque novat. nam ponit in ordine pennas
a minima coeptas, longam breviore sequenti,
ut clivo crevisse putes: sic rustica quondam
fistula disparibus paulatim surgit avenis;
tum lino medias et ceris adligat imas
atque ita conpositas parvo curvamine flectit,
ut veras imitetur aves. puer Icarus una
stabat et ignarus sua se tractare pericla,
ore renidenti modo, quas vaga moverat aura,
captabat plumas, flavam modo pollice ceram
mollibat lusuque suo mirabile patris
impediebat opus. postquam manus ultima coepto
inposita est, geminas opifex libravit in alas
ipse suum corpus motaque pependit in aura;
instruit et natum "medio" que "ut limite curras,
Icare", ait "moneo, ne, si demissior ibis,
unda gravet pennas, si celsior, ignis adurat:
inter utrumque vola. nec te spectare Booten

---

[5] An interesting gloss on this passage is provided by Gilbert Highet's remarks on
slavish imitation:

With the best available wax, and selected high-grade feathers, they
construct artificial wings, launch themselves off into the azur air in pursuit
of Pindar, the Theban eagle, and fall into the deep, deep bog of bathos
with a resounding flop. *(The Classical Tradition*, p. 242).

aut Helicen iubeo strictumque Orionis ensem:
me duce carpe viam!" pariter praecepta volandi
tradit et ignotas umeris accommodat alas.
inter opus monitusque genae maduere seniles,
et patriae tremuere manus; dedit oscula nato
non iterum repetenda suo pennisque levatus
ante volat comitique timet, velut ales, ab alto
quae teneram prolem produxit in aera nido,
hortaturque sequi damnosasque erudit artes
et movet ipse suas et nati respicit alas.
hos aliquis tremula dum captat harundine pisces,
aut pastor baculo stivave innixus arator
vidit et obstipuit, quique aethera carpere possent,
credidit esse deos. Et iam Iunonia laeva
parte Samos (fuerant Delosque Parosque relictae)
dextra Lebinthus erat fecundaque melle Calymne,
cum puer audaci coepit gaudere volatu
deseruitque ducem caelique cupidine tractus
altius egit iter. rapidi vicinia solis
mollit odoratas, pennarum vincula, ceras;
tabuerant cerae: nudos quatit ille lacertos,
remigioque carens non ullas percipit auras,
oraque caerulea patrium clamantia nomen
excipiuntur aqua, quae nomen traxit ab illo.
at pater infelix, nec iam pater, "Icare", dixit,
"Icare", dixit "ubi es? qua te regione requiram?"
"Icare" dicebat: pennas aspexit in undis
devovitque suas artes corpusque sepulcro
condidit, et tellus a nomine dicta sepulti (VIII, 183-235).

Daedalus all the while in Crete was pent,
Hating the isle and his long banishment.
Longing for home, but sundered by the sea:
"Let Minos close the seas and lands", said he:
"The skies are open: we will travel there;
Though he owns all, he does not own the air."
And speaking so, he let invention range,
Exploring arts unknown, and sought to change
Man's very nature.—Feathers large and small
He set in rank, from smallest up to tall.
(A slope tree-fringed, or rustic pipe, looks so,
With straws unequal in a slanting row.)
The craftsman, fastening these with threads of flax
At base and center, sealed the joints with wax;

And bent the finished fabric, copying
The slight curvation of the natural wing.
Young Icarus with beaming face stood by
And pressed the golden wax to pliancy,
And snatched at feathers by the breezes blown,
Handling his own destruction, had he known.
Play-hindered thus, the wondrous work went on:
The final touch was given; the task was done.
The inventor's living weight the balance tried;
The rocking pinions take the air, and ride.

He winged his son, and warned him not to stray,
Upward or downward, from the middle way:
"Above, the fear of singeing fire is seen:
Below, the clogging wave: so fly between.
Not by Boötes let your course be laid,
Nor Helice, nor bright Orion's blade:
Look to your leader." Thus he schooled his son,
While fastening the strange equipment on.

With toil and talk the old man's hands were set
A-trembling, and the father's cheeks were wet.
A kiss he gave, the last that Icarus knew;
Then rose, wing-borne, and took the lead, and flew;
And like the bird, that from the nest on high
Leads forth her tender brood upon the sky,
With backward glance, and fears for him alone,
He watched the boy's flight, and maintained his own;
And thus as coach, encourager, and guide,
Taught Icarus the skill by which he died.
Anglers with trembling rods, and shepherds bowed
On staves, and plowmen stooping as they plowed,
Looked up to see them pass, with awe-struck eye,
And thought them gods, since none but gods could fly.

Delos was left, with Paros, in the rear:
Before them Samos, Juno's isle, drew near
To leftward; while Lebinthus on the right
And honey-stored Calymne came in sight.
The boy, his heart with risk and rapture high,
Forsook his guide, aspiring to the sky,
And soared aloft: through nearness to the sun
The wax, that bound the wings, began to run;
The fastings flew: he flapped bare arms in air,
And lacking oarage, got no purchase there;
And calling on his father, down he came,

And perished in the sea that bears his name.
What could the father, now no father, do,
But cry: "O Icarus, Icarus, where are you?
Where, Icarus, where? What quarter of the sky
Must I explore?" He saw the plumes drift by;
And cursed his craft; and in the land they call
Icaria now, gave Icarus burial.[6]

Ovid also refers to the story on several other occasions. In the *Fasti* (IV, 284), there is a brief etymological reference, but in the *Tristia* there are two more interesting passages. In lines reminiscent of Horace's warning about literary ambition quoted above, Ovid cautions the book he is writing to be content with being read by ordinary folk:

Ergo, cave, liber, et timida circumspice mente
    ut satis a media sit tibi plebe legi.
dum petit infirmis nimium sublimia pennis
    Icarus, aequoras nomine facit aquas (I, 1).

(Therefore be careful, my book, and look all around with timid heart, so as to be satisfied with being read by common people. When he tried on weak wings to go too high, Icarus gave a name to the sea.)

Again in the *Tristia*, Ovid appeals to the example of Icarus as he warns of the perils of ambition:

quid fuit, ut tutas agitaret Daedalus alas,
    Icarus inmensas nomine signet aquas?
nempe quod hic alte, demissius ille volabat;
    nam pennas ambo non habuere suas.
crede mihi, bene qui latuit bene vixit, et intra
    fortunam debet quisque manere suam (III, 4).

(Why was it that, though Daedalus flew on safe wings, Icarus marks the vast sea with his name? Doubtless because he flew high and the other flew lower for both had false wings. Believe me, he who hides lives well, and one ought to remain within one's place assigned by Fortune.)

In an epigram defending the writing of simple poetry, Martial decries the pretentious filling out of poetry with mythological allusions. Icarus is on the list of examples of often used myths.

---

6 Traslation by A. E. Watts, *The Metamorphoses of Ovid* (Berkeley, 1954), pp. 170-2.

ille magis ludit qui scribit prandia saevi
   Tereus aut cenam, crude Thyesta, tuam,
aut puero liquidas aptentem Daedalon alas
   pascentem Siculas aut Polyphemen ovis (IV, 49).
(He is more frivolous who writes of the dinners of savage
Tereus or your supper, bloody Thyesta, or of Daedalus applying
liquid wings to the boy, or of Polyphemus grazing on Sicilian
sheep.)

Excessive use of mythological imagery is an ever present danger, apparently. [7]
Seneca, like Martial born in Spain, refers to Icarus twice in his tragedies. In his *Oedipus,* the chorus draws a lesson from the story that we have already found in Ovid, "quicquid excessit modum,/pendet instabili loco."

> Gnosium regem timens
> astra dum demens petit
> artibus fisus novis,
> certat et veras aves
> vincere as falsis nimis
> imperat pinnis puer
> nomen eripuit freto;
> callidus medium senex
> Daedalus librans iter
> nube sub media stetit,
> alitem expectans suum
> (qualis accipitris minas
> fugit et sparsos metu
> conligit fetus avis),
> donec in ponto manus
> movit implicitas puer
> comes audacis viae.
> quicquid excessit modum
> pendet instabili loco (892-910).

---

[7] The universality of this tendency to refer to the myth of Icarus when discussing the pretentious use of mythology is attested to by this short passage from a story by the Brazilian Machado de Assis. He is giving advice in a story entitled "Education of a Stuffed Shirt" on how to "dress up one's style":

> You can use any number of expressive tropes: the Lernean Hydra, for example, Medusa's head, the sieve of the Danaids, the flight of Icarus, and others that Romanticists, Classicists and Naturalists employ without loss of reputation when they need them. *"The Psychiatrist" and Other Stories* (Berkeley, 1973), p. 116.

(Fearing the Cretan king, while madly seeking the stars, trusting to new arts, he tries to surpass real birds. The boy gives too great orders to his false wings and took the name from the sea. The clever old Daedalus, balancing a middle course, took his stand beneath the middle cloud waiting for his winged son, just as a bird avoids the threat of a hawk and assembles its offspring scattered by fear. Until the boy, his companion in the bold journey, waves his hands entangled in the sea. All that exceeds the measure, hangs in a perilous place.

The peril of ambition is also the theme of a passage from the chorus at the end of Act III of *Hercules Oetaeus*.

> Medium caeli dum sulcat iter:
> tenuit placidas Daedalus oras
> nullique dedit nomina ponto,
> sed dum volucras vincere veras
> Icarus audet
> patriasque puer despicit alas
> Phoeboque volat proximus ipsi,
> dedit ignoto nomina ponto (687-697).

(While he ploughs the middle way of heaven, Daedalus held to calm regions and gave no name to the sea, but since Icarus dares to surpass true birds and the boy looks down on his father's wings and flies very close to Phoebus himself he gave a name to an unknown sea.)

Although there are different interpretations and versions of the story in classical writers, generally speaking Icarus is a symbol of overconfidence, either childish or ambitious, while his father is either the inventor of unnatural devices, punished by the death of his son, or, alternatively, an example of prudence, the middle way. It is the obverse of this coin, the boldness of the flight and immortality conferred in the naming of the sea that attracts the poets of the early Renaissance, although there is later a return to a more "classical" view of the myth as we shall see.

The Medieval Tradition

Early Christian writers on classical mythology appear to have been most interested in the major figures, the gods who seemed potential rivals to their own. I have been unable to find a reference to Icarus in the Church Fathers. There are brief, almost identical accounts of the story in two of the Vatican Mythographers, which add, as if to explain how it was that Daedalus was able to get wax and feathers in prison, that he bribed the guards of the labyrinth.[8] Isidore of Seville seems to be the first Christian writer to tell the story in his *Etymologies*. He first mentions Icarus in the section dealing with islands (XIII, 16, 8) and later when he comes to the Icarian Sea (XIV, 6, 26). The latters takes its name, according to the Bishop, from the fall of Icarus while the name of the island derives, in the tradition of Palaeplatus, from his shipwreck. Johannes Tzetzes, the twefth century Byzantine polymath also gives the outline of the story in his *Chiliades* (I Hist. 19).

A major concern of Christian writers is, of course, to present the mythical tales as morally edifying. Some of the explanations offered by Christian apologists are quite fanciful. The *Ovide moralisé,* for example, tells us by way of explanation of the story of Icarus that Daedalus represents God, the only true inventor, creator of all things, and that Icarus' predicament is that of man who has to follow the Father to Heaven. Before ascending into heaven, God offered us advice as to the way we may follow Him. We must put on two wings, one of them the love of God and the other that of our fellow man. With these it is important not to fly too low and become too attached to the things of this world, nor too high in pride in what is ours only by His grace. Those who "volent trop bassement, / ce sont cil qui mauvesement / metent lor amor en ce monde" while "cil que trop hautement vole / c'est cil que par orgueil s'afole / et cuide comme malsenez / des biens que Diex le a donnez." Either extreme will have the same consequence:

> Pour bien qu'il face, en tel propos,
> Ains versera dampnablement
> Ou puis d'enfer parfondement.
> En enfer ert sa sapulture...[9]

A coeval works, attributed to Thomas de Walleis but believed to be by Petrus Berchorius, retells the stories from Ovid and appends moral commentaries to each of them. These reflections on the Icarus story are entirely different. It is first suggested that the story contains a

---

[8]   Georg Heinrich Bode (ed.), *Scriptorum rerum mythicarum latini tres...* (Celle, 1934, facsimile ed. Hildesheim, 1968), I, 17 and 116.
[9]   *Ovide moralisé* (Wiesbaden, 1966), III, p. 147 ff.

worthwile lesson for children, that they should always obey their parents. Or, the author continues, we may take Daedalus as an image of the poor sinner exiled in the labyrinth of human experience. He must make for himself wings of contemplation on which he may flee the abysses of the world and regain his eternal abode in heaven.[10]

When lyric poetry is reborn in Europe, in twelfth century Provence, the image of Icarus is not long in reappearing. Several versions of a love poem by the troubadour Rigaud de Barbezieux mention Icarus or Daedalus in a context that makes the effort to fly not only arrogant but sacrilegious. This may be because some texts have "lo Magus" (Simon the Magician) instead of "Ycarus."

> Ben sai qu'Amors es tan granz
> Que leu me pot perdonar
> S'eu falhi per sobramar
> Ni renhei com Ycarus
> Que dis qu'el era Jhesus
> E vole volar al cel outracuidanz;
> Mas Deus baisset l'orgolh e lo sobranz;
> E mos orgolhs non es res mas amors; [11]

The poet hopes that Cupid will forgive him if, like Icarus, he flies too high, for his lover's pride is innocent. The parallel between the lover's boldness and Icarus' fate, made here for the first time, is destined for a long history.

There is a brief reference to the story in the *Flamenca*, a widely read romance of the thirteenth century. The story is apparently familiar enough that the author can refer to it, along with others ancient and modern, as being told as part of the entertainment after a banquet. [12] There is also a brief mention of the story of the flight in the *Romance of the Rose* (II, 5196-9).[13] In Dante's *Paradiso* we hear of "quello / che, volando per l'aere, el figlio perse" (VII, 125-6), Icarus' death being seen as the father's punishment for defying the natural order. But in the *Inferno* Icarus occurs to the poet as expressive of his own feelings. As he flies through the sky on the back of the mythical monster, Geryon, he looks down at the earth and imagines the fear that

---

[10] Consulted in French translation, *La Bible des poetes...* (Paris, 1520), f. 80 r.
[11] *Les Chansons du troubadour Rigaud de Barbezieux*, ed. Joseph Anglade (Montpellier, 1919), p. 61.
[12] *The Romance of Flamenca*, ed. Marion E. Porter (Princeton, 1962), p. 62.
[13] *Le Roman de la rose*, ed. Félix Lecoy (Paris, 1968), v. I, p. 160.

Icarus must have felt and considers it comparable to, though not greater
than, his own.

> Magior paura non credo che fosse
> quando Feton abbandonò li freni,
> per che 'l ciel, come pare ancor, sicosse;
> ne quando Icaro misero le reni
> sentì spennar per la scaldata cera,
> gridando il padre a lui "Mala via tieni!"
> che fu la mia, quando vidi ch'i era
> nell' aere d'ogni parte, e vidi spenta
> ogni veduta fuor che della fera (XVII, 106-114).

In a passage of his *House of Fame* which may owe something to Dante,
Geoffrey Chaucer describes being swept through the air by an eagle
and he also compares his flight to that of Icarus. No one was ever so
high, he says,

> Ne eek the wrechche Dedalus
> Ne his child, nyce Ykarus,
> That fleigh so highe that the hete
> His wynges malt, and he fel wete
> In myd the see, and ther he dreynte.
> For whom was maked moch compleynte (II, 919-24).[14]

Although the poets of the sixteenth century will not take flights as
literal as these, both Chaucer and Dante anticipate later evocations of
Icarus in their identification of the protagonist's situations with the
plight of Icarus. Dante is also the first to link the myths of Icarus
and Phaethon, treated quite differently by classical poets.[15] They are
destined, as we shall see, for an extremely fecund association.

In Boccaccio's *Amorosa visione,* Fortune includes Icarus' fate in a
recital of spectacular reverses. In this case the fall is seen as the result
of not heeding Daedalus' advice.

> Appresso vedi que' che con sottile
> maestero del padre uscì volando
> del Laberinto, che tenendo vile
> miseramente ciò ch'amaestrando

---

[14] *The Works of Geoffrey Chaucer,* ed. F. N. Robinson (Boston, 1957), p. 290.
[15] See the early pages of Robert Vivier, *Les Frères du ciel, quelques aventures
poétiques d'Icare et de Phaéthon* (Brussels, 1962).

il padre gli avea detto, per volare
troppo alto, in giu, le sue reni spennando,
   ora si cala, e appresso affogare
più là il vedi ne' salati liti;
questo avien de' non savi seguitare.[16]

In the *Confessio amantis,* John Gower provides us with our second Icarus in an amorous context. The lover's confessor introduces the story of the escape from Crete by telling us the moral he thinks it illustrates:

In hih astat it is a vice
To go to lowe, and in service
It grieveth forto go to hye,
Wherof a tale in poesie
I finde...[17]

Then he follows Ovid's account of the flight and fall in the *Metamorphoses* and finally the confessor relates the fable to the condition of the lover:

And lich to that condicion
Ther fallen ofte times fele
For lacke of governance en wele,
Als wel in love as other weie.[18]

Icarus is once again the symbol of the dangers of overconfidence.

One would expect perhaps that in Petrarch, the source of so much of the imagery of the poets we are going to discuss, Icarus might appear as an expression of the high aspirations and dangers involved in the campaigns of love. In lines like the following, the amorous adventure is seen as a flight, both exhilarating and frightening:

Pace non trovo, e ho da far guerra ;
e temo, e spero, ed ardo, e son' un ghiaccio,
e volo sopra 'l cielo, e giaccio in terra ;
e nulla stringo, e tutto 'l mondo abbraccio.[19]

[16] *Opere minori in volgare,* ed. Mario Marti (Milano, 1971), v. III, pp. 335-6.
[17] *The English Works of John Gower,* ed. G. C. Macaulay (London, 1900, reprinted 1957), I, p. 329.
[18] *Ibid.,* p. 330.
[19] *Canzoniere,* ed. G. Contini (Turin, 1964), p. 186.

and

> Volo con l'ali dei pensieri al cielo...[20]

Yet the name of Icarus appears nowhere in Petrarch's writings. It is not until the fifteenth century that one of his admirers, Jacopo Sannazaro, writes the sonnet that fires the imagination of a host of poets in his own country and others, particularly in Spain.

---

[20] *Ibid.*, p. 451.

Chapter 2

THE SCHOLARLY VIEW

Before considering the poems which are the principal focus of this study, I shall examine another aspect of the context in which they were written. The poems are one manifestation of the Renaissance fascination with the classical world, and mythology in particular. The sixteenth century saw the publication of a vast number of works dealing, in one way or another, with classical mythology. With the access of printing there began a stream of editions, translations, commentaries, manuals and encyclopedias, so that, as Jean Seznec puts it "the knowledge of mythology became so diffused that it took on the character of a veritable invasion." [1] I shall limit my remarks to the more popular of these works, especially those that deal directly with the myth that interests us and were published or widely read in Spain.

It is not my intention to suggest that any of these works was a source for the poets. In fact, it seems that in the particular case of Icarus, the poets received little or no direct inspiration from the works of the popularizers. The question of the role of the manuals is treated in some detail by Seznec, who concludes that they may have influenced painters, sculptors and organizers of displays of pageantry, but the little he has to say about poets, in the case of Ronsard, for example, is inconclusive. [2] He seems forced to the position that, though the poets, like all learned men, had the manuals on their desks, they were the source of occasional information rather than direct inspiration. José María de Cossío suggests that translations and commentaries were sometimes a source of "interpretaciones, imágenes y metáforas." [3] There is perhaps some reason for believing this to be true in the case of the longer, narrative poems to which he mostly refers. But in the case of the short lyrics, some of them epigrams, with which we are largely concerned, the narrative facts of the story are seldom as important as the development of one key image, often derived from another poet.

[1] Seznec, p. 219.
[2] Ibid., pp. 307-309.
[3] *Fábulas mitológicas en España* (Madrid, 1952), p. 38.

In his whole work Cossío does not adduce one example of direct influence. The poets could, after all, read the poetry of the classics in the original and found inspiration there or in other poets.

But the enormous popularity of these works cannot be ignored, and even if they do not often appear as direct sources of poetic images, they can still help us in our investigation. They are the product of the same period as the poems we shall study and reflect attitudes toward mythology and images of mythological figures with which the poets must also have been familiar. To be sure, the poets and the popularizers were writing for different purposes, but it will be useful to have the background of what the writers on mythology and their readers thought about the myth of Icarus during the period under discussion.

The original source for most of the details of the Icarus story is Ovid's *Metamorphoses*. This work had been known in Spain as early as the late thirteenth century since parts of it found their way into Alfonso X's *General estoria*.[4] Though Juan Ruiz's knowledge of Ovid, in the fourteenth century, seems to have been limited to the *Art of Love*, the fifteenth witnessed the establishment of the *Metamorphoses*, the "libro mayor de Ovidio", as one of the most popular works of antiquity. The *cancionero* poets were familiar with it and at least two of them, the Marqués de Santillana and Gómez Manrique, owned manuscript translations.[5] In 1494 the first printed version appeared, in Catalan,[6] but the sixteenth century was several decades old before the mention of the first Spanish printed translation, apparently the "libro de las fábulas de Ovidio en romance",[7] in the will of Fernando de Rojas. This was followed, some forty years later, in a decade of intense scholarly activity, by three others, one of them incomplete.

---

[4] Alfonso el Sabio, *General estoria*, ed. Antonio Solalinde et al. (Madrid, 1930-1961). The story of Icarus and Daedalus is in the *Segunda parte*, I (1957), pp. 420-422. The date of the *Ovide Moralisé* has usually been put in the XIVth century, but Solalinde, based on parallels between the French work and the *General estoria*, posits an earlier date in: "La fecha del *Ovide Moralisé*, RFE, VIII (1921), 285-288.

[5] Rudolph Schevill, *Ovid and the Renascence in Spain* (Berkeley, 1913), pp. 68-69 and 81. A list of Gómez Manrique's library can be found in *Cancionero de Gómez Manrique*, ed. Antonio Paz y Meliá (Madrid, 1885), II, p. 332 ff.

[6] Ovidio, *Transformacions* (Barcelona, 1494). According to Clara Louise Penney's catalogue of *Printed Books in the Hispanic Society of America* (New York, 1965) the translator of this version in prose is Francesch Alegre.

[7] "El testamento de Fernando de Rojas", *Revista de Filología Española*, XVI (1929), pp. 366-388.

The annotator (don Fernando del Valle Lersundi?) suggests (p. 387) that this is probably Bustamante's translation. Theodore Beardsley, in his *Hispanoclassical Translations* (Pittsburgh, 1970), gives 1543 as the date for this translation, apparently assuming the work in Rojas' library to be a manuscript. Stephen Gilman is sure, however, that Rojas owned no manuscripts.

The first printed translation of *Metamorphoses* in Spanish is that of Jorge de Bustamante, published sometime before 1541.[8] This version remains the most popular, even after the appearance, beginning in 1580, of three others. It was reprinted sixteen times in less than a century, a record which makes it the most printed translation of a classical work after the fables of Aesop.[9] The work is unique in several important ways among Spanish printed translations of Ovid: it is in prose; it is a very "free" translation even by sixteenth century standards; it appeared anonymously;[10] and it contains no allegorical or learned commentary.[11] Bustamante's work as popular in both senses of the word: it appealed apparently to a large reading public and made no pretence of great learning.

It is clear that there was no such thing as an attempt to translate literally in the Renaissance, even if such an ideal were practical.[12] Except in the special case of biblical translation, it occurred to nobody to expect a translation to be faithful to the letter of the original. Bustamante's French contemporary, Etienne Dolet, who was burned

---

[8]   The edition consulted is: Ovidio, *Las metamorphoses, o Transformaciones repartidas en quince libros y traduzidas en castellano* (Anvers, en casa de J. Steelsio, 1551). This edition is anonymous. For details of other editions and their locations, see Beardsley, pp. 35-36.

[9]   Beardsley, p. 107. Bustamante's translation was printed sixteen times between 1543? and 1664, while Aesop's *Fables* had thirty-two printings in the years 1488 to 1682. Without more information about the number of volumes per printing it is difficult to assess accurately the relative popularity of works of the period.

[10]   In some editions the author is identified in an acrostic which reads JORGE DE BUSTAMANTE, NATURAL DE SILIOS.

[11]   The Antwerp editions of 1595 and 1599? include the "Allegorías" published by Pérez Sigler with his translations, many of which are taken almost literally from Anguillara's translation.

[12]   The best pages on the complex subject of translations in the Renaissance in Spain are in J. Richard Andrews' work on Juan del Encina *(Juan del Encina; Prometheus in Search of Prestige* [Berkeley, 1959]). Pages 33-53 deal with the attempt to understand the quite different aims and aesthetics of translators of the period, concerned with bringing the work alive for their contemporaries, much more than with fidelity to the original in the way we understand it today. There are a number of general works on different aspects of early translation, but very little is relevant to Spain or Italy. Some of the more useful ones are: Paul Herbert Larwill, *La Théorie de la traduction au début de la renaissance... entre 1477 et 1527* (Munich, 1934); Flora Ross Amos, *Early Theories of Translation* (New York, 1920); Frédéric Hennebert, *Histoire des traductions françaises... pendant le XVIe et le XVIIe siècles* (Gand, 1858); Theodore Savory, *The Art of Translation* (London, 1957), especially the chapter "Translation Through the Ages", pp. 37 ff.; and perhaps the best book on the subject, although it deals only with England, Eric Jacobsen, *Translation, a Traditional Craft* (Copenhague, 1958). One of the weaknesses of most these books is that they are based on prefaces and prologues and, as Jacobsen points out (p. 140), these must be carefully compared with what the translators did in practice. There is a "Critical Bibliography of Works on Translation" in *On Translation*, ed. Reuben Brower (Cambridge, Mass., 1959), which purports to cover the period from 46 B. C. to 1958. However, the period until 1576 is represented by only four works.

as a heretic for one of his translations, advises against translating "mot pour mot".[13] Felipe Mey, another translator of Ovid, admired an Italian translation precisely because it was "tan agena de la letra".[14] These men were writing, after all, for a reading public to whom the original was inaccessible and for whom, therefore, the details of Latin style were irrelevant. Their task was to present the essence and the spirit of the original in as contemporary a way as possible. It is for this reason that Dolet insists that the translator have complete command, not only of the original language, but also of his own. As Felipe Mey says later in his prologue: "es cosa cierta que la mayor parte de la gente no tiene cuenta si está fielmente traducido, sino en si le da gusto el libro por otras circunstancias."

Bustamante's translation is not only in simple prose but it is so free that Rudolph Schevill in his study of Ovid's influence in the Spanish Renaissance was prompted to say of it that "no translator of a noted classic has ever proceeded in a freer manner, no translation has ever been a greater fraud than this, if judged only from the standpoint of Ovid's text".[15] The Spanish wanders very far from the Ovid original, not merely in details, but also in the transposing of whole stories from one part of the poem to another. One may regret, with Schevill, the author's freedom with Ovid's text, but it is impossible not to admire the vigor and simple elegance of the prose style and the obvious delight in the stories that infuses the whole work.

The author's unscholarly approach and his enjoyment of Ovid's stories without drawing any moral implications may explain, as Schevill suggests, the fact that the work was at first issued anonymously. It may be that what the critic calls the "unnecessary expansion of certain salacious passages"[16] made it even more desirable for Bustamante to conceal his identity. But both his refusal to moralize and his freedom with the text must have contributed to the work's great popularity.

---

[13] Etienne Dolet, *La Manière de bien traduire* (Lyon, 1542), reprinted in *Babel*, I (1955), pp. 17-20. His five requirements for a good translation are these: (a) "qu'il est besoing et nécessaire à tout traducteur d'entendre parfaictement le sense de l'autheur", (b) "que le traducteur ait parfaicte cognoissance de la langue de l'autheur qu'il traduit: et soit pareillement excellent en la langue en laquelle il se mect à traduire", (c) "qu'en traduisant il ne se fault pas asservir iusques a la que l'on rende mot pour mot", (d) "il te fault garder d'usurper mots trop approchans du Latin, et peu usitez par le passé", and (e) "l'observation des nombres oratoires: c'est asscavoir une liaison et assemblement des dictions avec... douleur".

[14] Ovidio, *Del Metamorphoses*, trans. Felipe Mey (Tarragona, 1586), "prólogo al lector", pages unnumbered.

[15] Schevill, p. 152.

[16] *Ibid.*, p. 19.

When Erwin Panofsky compares a medieval translation of Ovid with a sixteenth century version, he opposes the medieval writers' tendency to use the stories as vehicles for their own allegorization or moralization and the Renaissance discovery that a good story can "stand up on its own" and may have as many different interpretations as readers.[17] The Renaissance meant that the classics could again be read and enjoyed rather than merely consulted as authorities. Maria Rosa Lida writes about this change:

No existe en la Edad Media la conciencia de una nueva época histórica; el pensamiento antiguo, sus *loci communes*, sus esquemas verbales viven llenos de sentido, no como reliquias que hayan de mantener cuidadosamente su forma original. Precisamente porque siguen siendo actuales varían y crecen, desarrollando conforme a los nuevos gustos el caudal greco-romano; cuando se produce la excisión entre presente y pasado, que aparta a la antigüedad y la muestra tan remota y ejemplar como la Edad de Oro, es que ha llegado el Renacimiento. Sobre la continuidad de cultura que caracteriza la Edad Media, el Renacimiento reanuda consciente y directamente la dependencia de los modelos antiguos, sello que presta nobleza a su arte.[18]

In other words it was paradoxically the distance from the classics that permitted the writers of the Renaissance to get so close to them. The Medieval defensiveness bred by proximity prevented what Seznec calls the "immediate intuition of antiquity" (p. 224) that the Renaissance implied. It is in this sense, I think, that Schevill says of Bustamante's work, that "no version... could better reflect the spirit of the age in which it was written" (p. 152).

The Icarus story in Bustamante's version is really a paraphrase of Ovid. Many of Ovid's touches are reproduced in elegant, simple Spanish prose—Icarus playing all unknowing with the feathers that will cause his death; the fishermen and the shepherds looking up in awe as the two men fly overhead. But the translator leaves some things out and in other places adds his own embellishments. The details of the making of the wings are completely omitted, yet instead we are

17 Erwin Panofsky, "Renaissance and Renascences", *Kenyon Review*, VI (1944), p. 201 ff.

18 "Transmisión y recreación de temas grecolatinos en la poesía lírica española", *Revista de Filología Hispánica*, I (1939), p. 20.

offered the following new explanation for how Daedalus happened to come by so many feathers in captivity:

... y para ello, disimulando su propósito, a todos los amigos que le venían a consolar, rogaba que le trujesen muchas plumas de todas suertes, así pequeñas como grandes, fingiendo hacer cosas maravillosas dellas: de las cuales después de traídas hizo dos pares de alas... (f. 127r).

Bustamante leaves out the names of the constellations mentioned by Daedalus in his warning to his son, as well as the names of the islands over which they flew, presumably feeling that these details were not pertinent to his prose narrative. He was telling the story, not reproducing Ovid. Some details inspired the translator to expand considerably Ovid's Latin. When Daedalus cries out in anguish at his son's misfortune, Ovid has "Icare, dixit, ubi es? Qua regione requiram Icare".[19] This becomes in the Spanish "Hijo Icaro, ¿dónde te buscaré? O ¿qué será ahora de mi afligida vejez, habiendo perdido la lumbre y contentamiento que contigo en ella pensaba tener?", a passage which is extremely reminiscent of Pleberio's lament at the end of La Celestina: "¿Adónde hallará abrigo mi desconsolada vejez?" etc.[20]

Bustamante makes no effort to follow the events exactly as Ovid presents them. At times one has the impression that he did not work from the Latin at all, although until another source is found, we must assume that he did. There is a curious confusion in his version that may be merely an oversight or the result of his attempt at conciseness. Ovid and all the translations I have seen have Daedalus trying out his own wings before returning to earth and giving his advice to his son. Bustamante has them both take off ("fueron bien altos de la tierra") before Daedalus delivers his advice and apparently before he has affixed his son's wings.

Although the translator avoids moral commentary on the fate of Icarus—he neither praises nor blames him—there is, to be sure, in the prologue, the conventional disclaimer about the underlying morality of these pagan stories:

me resta ahora decir, lo que tan excelentes filósofos y poetas, como Hesíodo, Horacio, Menandro, Ysopo, Lucio Apuleyo,

19 Metamorphoses, VIII, 11. 231-232.
20 Fernando de Rojas, La Celestina, ed. M. Criado de Val and G. D. Trotter (Madrid, 1965), p. 295.

Cebetes y otros diversos y graves autores, y especialmente Ovidio, tuvieron en inventar estas ficciones, que no fue otro sino mostrar a los hombres muchos avisos y astucias para más sabia y prudentemente vivir...

This prologue is, for Cossío, evidence of the translator's "temperamento tradicional" (p. 42). He considers Bustamante's translation a work of transition between the Middle Ages and the Renaissance. Yet the prologue, seen in the light of the actual translation, seems more of a concession to traditional morality than evidence of personal conviction.

Given the extremely close cultural ties between Spain and Italy at this time, it is impossible to omit reference to the two well known Italian translations of the *Metamorphoses*. Lodovico Dolce's *Transformationi* was published in 1554 and Giovanni Andrea Anguillara's *Metamorfosi* in 1571.[21] These were the first translations in verse, both being in octaves. They were widely read and referred to in Spain—Cossío (p. 47) even suggests that Anguillara may have been more popular than any Spanish translation. Both of these versions were, in the spirit of the times, quite free, Anguillara's particularly so. Dolce does not even respect Ovid's division of the work into fifteen books. His translation has thirty cantos of between sixty and one hundred octaves each.

Dolce appeared, like Bustamante, in several early editions without allegorical commentary, although after 1568 some editions appeared with short notes on the moral significance of some of the stories, so short as to seem almost a concession to the mood of the times. After this time almost no version of Ovid's work appears without some kind of moral commentary. In Dolce the story of Icarus and Daedalus is fairly wordy and, since it spans cantos 17 and 18, includes two transitional stanzas in which the author reflects upon the story he is telling and compares it to the story of Phaethon, so frequently associated with Icarus in the imaginations of the poets, as we shall see. These are the two stanzas in question:

> Non è tanto da noi lontano segno,
> se ben vista mortal non l' assegura;
> che non vi s'erga, e aggiunga il nostro ingegno,

---

[21] Lodovico Dolce, *Le Trasformationi tratte da Ovidio...* (Venice, 1554 and 1568, 1570, etc.). *Le metamorfosi di Ovidio, ridotte da Giovanni Andrea dell' Anguillara ottava rima... con l'annotationi di Giuseppe Horologgi* (Venice, 1571). This edition calls itself the fourth. Dates of earlier editions appear to be uncertain.

con l'ali, che gli da l'alma natura.
Ma chi di gir tropp' alto fa disegno,
sciocco, la morte sua cerca e procura:
già vi diede Fetonte un chiaro esempio;
hor d'Icaro vel dà l'acerbo scempio.
    Che non sì tosto le cerate piume
a se stesso sicuro il padre mise,
ch 'egli seguendo il pueril costume,
bramoso di volar a lui s'assise.
Vede, come 'l fanciul di sè presume,
e come a punto il suo camin divise,
Dedal gli va insegnando, come suole
pietoso padre, e dice tai parole.[22]

It is natural to want to fly high but we must resist the temptation.
Icarus is presented as overeager even while his father is still putting
the finishing touches on the wings. His father's words of warning are,
as much as anything, a reaction to his son's impatience. There is also
a curious omission in Dolce's version. He makes no mention of Icarus
giving his name to the sea into which he fell or to the island on which
he was buried. This detail is of paramount importance in the poetic
treatments of the myth. For the poets, as for Ovid, the young man's
immortalization in the sea is the tempting counterpart to his tragic
death.

Anguillara's translation contains no digression such as that in Dolce
but even without it, is extremely lengthy (132 lines compared to Ovid's
53). The story is retold with great attention to detail but with complete
disregard for Ovid's text. Within the canon of the age it is surprising
that this version should have been admired. Allegorical interpretations
accompany each myth, the work of one Horologgi. Some of these
allegories were destined to be reproduced several times, usually without
credit being given for their source. Pérez Sigler, whose Spanish version
we shall now discuss, is the first such case.

In 1580, after almost forty years, during which Bustamante was
reprinted eight times, Ovid's Metamorphoses were again translated into
Spanish, this time in verse. Antonio Pérez Sigler's version[23] is composed
in octaves and in verso suelto. The verse is undistinguished, perhaps
because the author tries to follow Ovid too closely. In the case of the

[22] Dolce, Le trasformationi di Ovidio (Venice, 1553), p. 175.
[23] Los quince libros de los Metamorphoseos de el excelente poeta latino Ovidio,
tr. Antonio Pérez Sigler (Salamanca, 1580).

Icarus story all of Ovid's details are reproduced and yet the result is no more than a shadow of the original. Ovid's concise lines expressing Daedalus' warning to his son are expanded into this halting octave:

> Por medio el aire Ícaro conviene
> volar, que mucho al mar nos acercando
> la pluma pesará que nos sostiene
> y quitará la fuerza de ir volando,
> si muy alto subir acaso aviene
> la cera el sol fogoso regalando
> despegará la pluma, y desta suerte
> cayendo nos darán las aguas muerte (f. 178 r).

While this does convey the literal sense of Ovid, it is rather heavy and pedestrian. At the end of each book the allegorical sense of the myth is explained. In this case this has been translated word for word from Horologgi. This is the message of Icarus:

> El vuelo de Dédalo y su hijo significa que cuando el deseo de las cosas altas es refrenado de la razón y prudencia, no excede los términos alzándose más de aquello que piden sus méritos, por lo cual llega el hombre después del curso desta vida al deseado fin: como sabiamente hizo Dédalo, mas los que a semejanza de Ícaro quieren alzarse más que debrían, transportados de un desreglado deseo, vienen después a caer en las miserias del mundo, figurado por las ondas del mar con infamia y daño irreparable (f. 201 r).

Icarus was drowned as a punishment for overstepping those elusive bounds which are supposed by moralists to be self-evident and immutable. The prudent course flown by his father is praised as it commonly, but by no means always, is. In the seventeenth century it is common to see Daedalus' flight condemned too. For one French emblem writer of the seventeenth century, for example, Daedalus is "tout à fait exécrable" for his attempt at flight.[24]

Cossío comments on the allegorical interpretations of Pérez (or Horologgi): "Pese, pues, a sus modelos, y a las fábulas y traducciones existentes cuando Pérez Sigler emprende su empresa, parece pesar sobre el traductor una preocupación moralista, que por entonces casi era anacrónica" (p. 45). This raises an interesting question. It is strange to

---

[24] Jean Baudoin, *Recueil d'emblèmes divers* (Paris, 1638), I, p. 355.

call a tendency to comment on the moral significance of myths anachronistic, when this is precisely the period when the tendency toward allegory, which had never died out, is being revived again. Rabelais' mockery of empty allegorizing is sometimes assumed to be characteristic of his age:

> Croiez vous en vostre foy qu'oncques Homere, escrivent l'*Illiade* et *Odyssée,* pensast es allegories lesquelles de luy ont beluté Plutarche, Heraclides Ponticq, Eustatie et Phornute, et ce que d'iceulx Politian a desrobé? Si le croiez, vous n'aprochez ne de pieds ny de mains à mon opinion, qui decrete icelles aussi peu avoir esté songéez d'Homere que d'Ovide en ses *Metamorphoses* les sacremens de l'Evangile, lesquelz un Frere Lubin, vray croquelardon, s'est efforcé demonstrer, si d'adventure il recontroit gens aussi folz que luy, et (come dict le proverbe) couvercle digne du chaudron.[25]

But Seznec points out that this is not true:

> It is readily assumed that most of Rabelais' contemporaries shared this attitude of his. In fact one of the essential differences said to exist between the Middle Ages and the Renaissance has to do with this very matter. Whereas the medieval cult of ancient literature was not disinterested, but looked to the classics for moral sustenance and studied them only in their "Christian" aspects, the Renaissance, free from such scruples, is thought to have looked on classical literature as a source of pleasure, aesthetic as well as sensuous. As a logical consequence, it must have wished to banish allegory, which hid or disguised the real figures of the gods... But the jeers of Rabelais were no more effective than the diatribes of Luther in checking the moralizations of Ovid. Already numerous in France and Italy at the beginning of the [sixteenth] century, towards its close they had spread all over Europe (pp. 95-96).

The moralists of the Counter-Reformation found in allegory, as those of the Middle Ages had done, the way to reconcile the great popularity of the stories of the pagan gods with their desire to inculcate their own teachings. As a result, despite attacks, like that of Malón de

---

[25] François Rabelais, *Gargantua,* ed. Ruth Calder and M. A. Screech (Genève, 1970), pp. 15-16.

Chaide,[26] against all kinds of imaginative literature, classical mythology continued to be widely published and read, although always accompanied by edifying explanations of the moral truths expressed. In Spain it almost seems, based on the late date at which most of the mythographical works start to appear, that the Counter-Reformation is a guiding force behind the popularization of mythology.

Before discussing the last Spanish translation of our period, mention must be made of an incomplete version published in 1586.[27] Felipe Mey is the author and publisher of this translation of the first seven books of the *Metamorphoses* which is, like the Italian versions, completely in octaves. He intended to complete his work and add "una declaración de todas las fábulas"[28] but this was never done. Presumably because the work was never finished, it was never reprinted and seems to have enjoyed a great deal less popularity than the others. Menéndez y Pelayo refers to it only in passing[29] and Schevill has almost nothing to say of it.

The last translation in our period (the last until 1841), that of Pedro Sánchez de Viana,[30] was published in 1589 and not reprinted until the twentieth century. It has traditionally been regarded as the most successful version, artistically speaking, though Bustamante continued to be reprinted into the seventeenth century. Ticknor called it "one of the happiest translations made in the pure age of Castilian literature"[31] and Menéndez y Pelayo, mediating between this extreme and that of the one severe critic of Sánchez, says that "entre las varias traducciones de los Metamorphoses de Ovidio que se hicieron en el siglo XVI, merece, sin duda, el primer lugar, la que trabajó el licenciado Pedro Sánchez de Viana".[32] He qualifies this praise in words that the contemporary reader might well agree with: "Entendía Viana al poeta de Sulmona, cuyo espíritu en parte reproduce y en parte no menor deslíe y echa a perder con excesivas amplificaciones." Sánchez' was a serious undertaking in more than one sense. Not only are the stories told with great attention to detail, which can sometimes become tedious, but

[26] Fray Pedro Malón de Chaide, *La conversión de la Magdalena*, ed. Félix García (Madrid, 1947-1957), Prolog.

[27] Ovidio, *Del Metamorphoses*, trans. Felipe Mey (Tarragona, 1586).

[28] "Prólogo al lector", pages unnumbered.

[29] Marcelino Menéndez y Pelayo, *Biblioteca de traductores españoles*, IV, in *Obras completas* (Madrid, 1953), vol. 57, p. 233.

[30] Ovidio, *Las Transformaciones...*, trans. Pedro Sánchez de Viana (Valladolid, 1589).

[31] Ticknor, *History of Spanish Literature* (Boston, 1863), II, p. 588 n.

[32] Menéndez y Pelayo, *Biblioteca*, IV, p. 232.

the book is also supplemented by a mass of learned and allegorical
commentary written "con erudición copiosísima y no siempre opor-
tuna," [33] to quote don Marcelino once again.

Sánchez follows Ovid's text extremely closely, and if his translation
seems long it is partly because he is willing to sacrifice succinctness to
sonority. Here is the octave in which he presents Daedalus giving Icarus
his final words of advice:

> Ícaro mío, yo te mando y ruego,
> que vayas por el medio con tu vuelo.
> Si vuelas bajo, humedecidas luego
> tus alas causarán mi desconsuelo.
> Si alto, quemarátelas el fuego
> con el ardor vecino al claro cielo.
> Huye el bajero aire, y el supremo
> vuela por medio, guarte del extremo (95v & 96r).

He also reproduces Ovid's touching detail of the father's trembling
hands as he affixes the wings to his son: "Tembláronle las manos, y
ya dados / los besos a su hijo postrimeros, / en vuelo fueron ambos
levantados" (96 r). Sánchez' version is indeed "happier" than those of
his predecessors. Here are parallel passages from Ovid, Pérez and Sánchez, which evoke Daedalus in the act of making the wings:

> dixit et ignotas animum dimittit in artes
> naturamque novat. nam ponit in ordine pennas,
> a minima coeptas, longam breviore sequenti,
> ut clivo crevisse putes: sic rustica quondam
> fistula disparibus paulatim surgit avenis.
> tum lino medias et ceris adligat imas
> atque, ita conpositas parvo curvamine flectit,
> ut veras imitetur aves (*Met.* VIII, 188-195).

> Dijo: y mete su ingenio en las ignotas
> artes con que renueva la natura:
> porque poniendo en orden muchas plumas,
> y comenzando en una muy pequeña,
> iban creciendo luego de una en otra,
> cual suele poco a poco levantarse
> la fístula con cañas desiguales,
> y con hilo y con cera las atando
> vino a hacer unas alas muy perfectas

---

[33] *Ibid.,* p. 234.

y compuestas, despúes las dobla un poco
por imitar las verdaderas aves: (177v).

y en su arte
en tal necesidad halló acogida.
Renovó la natura, pues reparte
las plumas en su orden de manera
que a la menor en la más baja parte
se sigue la que un poco mayor era.
Y que en el monte habían así nacido,
cualquiera sospechara que los viera.
Con desiguales cañas ha crecido
la rústica zampoña desta suerte,
de do procede el desigual sonido.
Y para que a volar mejor acierte,
con lino las de en medio, y las bajeras
con cera aprieta y al momento advierte
que para que parezcan ser de veras
es menester doblarlas tanto cuanto,
para imitar las aves verdaderas (Sánchez f. 95v).

Sánchez is more wordy, perhaps, but a finer poet than the earlier translator and, in the end, closer to Ovid. He is also careful in his rendering
of the Latin, in Cossío's words, not to obstruct its course "con observa-
ciones o consideraciones agenas al espíritu del original" (p. 51).

Sánchez took his work seriously. The enormous length of the commentaries that he appended to his work and the breadth of erudition
they attest to, show that, for him, the traditional justification of the
prologue is more than a convention. His prologue tells the reader that
"aun debajo de maravillosa máscara y cobertura las adorna de manera,
que allende de un incomparable fruto que se saca de tanta y tan varia
lección, es increíble el gusto y contentamiento del ánimo, el deleite
de los sentidos que un bien acondicionado ingenio recibirá de semejante poesía." Accordingly a separate volume is appended to the actual
translation "con el comento y explicaciones de las fábulas: reducién-
dolas a filosofía natural y moral y astrología e historia." Sánchez is as
good as his word; every story in the *Metamorphoses* is given an allegorical meaning or several, and sometimes a euhemeristic interpretation
as well. Sánchez offers the explanation of Palaephatus, available in
French and Latin early in the century,[34] that the discovery of Daedalus

---

[34] Palaephatus appeared in French as *Le Premier livre des narrations fabuleuses*
at Lyon in 1558. It was published in Latin as early as 1505 according to Seznec
(p. 225).

was the use of sail, that their "flight" was a metaphor for great speed, and that Icarus died because he was an inexperienced sailor.

It is in the allegorical interpretation offered by Sánchez that we can listen most directly to his voice. Icarus "no tuvo mucha memoria de los preceptos paternales... (como los más mozos suelen) y contento con el nuevo ejercicio, pensó dar consigo en el Cielo." [35] Even in his translation he had described Icarus' departure from the *via media* in these words: "y con intento / de visitar el cielo cristalino, / cuyo deseo concibió al momento / con ala presta toma su camino / más alto," which makes Icarus' action the result of a conscious decision. That Sánchez is impatient with Icarus' impetuosity becomes clear when he makes his final moral statement about the significance of the myth:

> Y también es muy de tener en la memoria, que para pasar esta miserable vida con menos peligros es lo mejor amar las gentes la medianía, porque muy mayor es una caída de los que la fortuna lleva al cuerno de la luna, que mil trabajos que padezca un pobre, y de lo uno y lo otro se escapa el discreto que sabe trabajar hasta adquirir un mediano estado, y se sabe conservar en él sin necesidad, ni sobresalto de la caída que suelen dar los muy ricos, y levantados, tras el rastro de los cuales anda muy de ordinario la carcomiente envivida (f. 161r).

Here is the ascetic moralist at work. In Cossío's words,

> no estamos ante un espíritu transido de renacentismo, desinteresado y satisfecho con el comercio y disfrute de la resucitada antigüedad, sino con un castellano de los que nuestros accéticos llamaban "sustanciales" a quien no le parecía suficiente una aspiración meramente artística y ajena a toda preocupación moral, como la que sintieron poetas italianistas del tipo de Garcilaso, por ejemplo (p. 51).

The meaning of the myth, for Sánchez, is that, in order to protect oneself from a hostile world, one should avoid extremes, keep to the middle of the road and thereby escape misfortune. The view that Icarus' mistake was the transgression of the ideal of *aurea mediocritas* is implied, of course, in Ovid's "Medio... ut limite curras," (*Met.* VIII, 203) but the moralizing tone of Sánchez' explanation of the sense of

---

[35] *Libro de las anotaciones sobre Ovidio,* bound in the same volume as the translations, f. 160v.

the myth is a long way from Ovid. This view makes Icarus nothing more than a negative model of conduct, a view that we shall find in poetry, particularly in the seventeenth century.

Aside from translation, there is another genre dealing with mythological material which contributed to the store of information and attitudes about the classical myths. These are the manuals or compendia, similar to medieval *summae,* the earliest and best known of which is Boccaccio's *Genealogia Deorum,* which does not mention the myth that interests us. The sixteenth century mythological encyclopedias of Giraldi, Cartari and Natale Conti [36] enjoyed great popularity and were translated into all the languages of Europe. They contained information about how the classical heroes and gods should be represented and what their special attributes were. Some, like Cartari's *Images of the Gods* were particulary aimed at providing painters and illustrators with iconographical information, while others, like Pérez de Moya's *Filosofía secreta* in Spain, were more concerned with elucidating the moral truths expressed in the stories. Conti, whose work is most often referred to by Spanish mythographers, mentions the narration of the story in Ovid's *Art of Love,* and tells the story as if Icarus were simply a disobedient son: "verum Icarus... parum ea referre ratus neglectisque; utilibus, paternis, ac salubribus admonitionibus, captus suavitate volandi, altiora loca expetivit" (p. 776). He goes on, in his role as scholar, to offer another explanation of the name of the Icarian sea, based on the name of Icarius, reputed to be the inventor of wine.

Pérez de Moya's *Filosofía secreta,*[37] the first Spanish manual of mythology, was published in 1585. The stories of the classical myths are told briefly and then to each one are appended "declaraciones," often euhemeristic as well as moral. In his prologue the author explains the function of fable as "debajo de una honesta recreación de apacibles cuentos, dichos con alguna semejanza de verdad, inducir a los lectores a muchas veces leer y saber su escondida moralidad y provechosa doctrina." Mythology is "una habla que con palabras de admiración significa algún secreto natural, o cuento de historia..." [38] His

---

[36] Lilio Gregorio Giraldi, *De deis gentium varia et multiplex historia in qua simul de eorum imaginibus et cognominibus agitur,* etc. (Basel, 1548); Natale Conti, *Mythologiae sive explicationis fabularum libri decem* (Venice, 1551); Vincenzo Cartari, *Le imagini colla sposizione degli dei degli antichi* (Venice, 1556). For details of further editions, see Seznec, pp. 279-280.

[37] Juan Pérez de Moya, *Philosophia secreta donde debajo de historias fabulosas, se contiene mucha doctrina provechosa a todos estudios, con el origen de los ídolos, o dioses de la gentilidad* (Madrid, 1585).

[38] *Filosofía secreta,* ed. Eduardo Gómez de Baquero (Madrid, 1928), I, p. 7.

work is largely derived from other contemporary works. His narration of the Icarus story is taken almost word for word from Bustamante, another monument to that work's great popularity. The first part of his "declaración" is, once again, Horologgi's allegory, already printed with Anguillara's translation and translated by Pérez Sigler. The other part of his commentary is as follows:

> Por esta fábula nos quisieron los poetas dar muy excelente doctrina, de que en todas las cosas amemos el medio, porque en esto consiste la virtud, y que guardemos el consejo de los padres y huyamos de la soberbia, si no queremos despearnos y anegarnos en el mar deste vano mundo, lo cual haremos amando la humildad, que no tiene caída.[39]

Again we are given the view of the ascetic moralist who appeals to the authority of the church fathers. Icarus is here a symbol for the vanity of overweening ambition, an entirely negative example.

The other important mythological manual in Spain was published in 1620 with the title *Teatro de los dioses de la gentilidad*.[40] The title derives from the analogy which the compiler, Baltasar de Victoria, explains in his prologue: on the stage all the players, however lowly their estate or appearance, contribute equally to the morality expressed in the drama.[41] It is a much more scholarly undertaking than Moya's. It ranges over classical literature, classical and medieval mythography, the church fathers, as well as the contemporary authorities and even contemporary literature. Garcilaso's sonnet XII is mentioned, as are two references to the myth in Ovid, Diodorus Siculus, Alciati and a passage from Virgil which describes Daedalus' successful flight.[42] The attitude of the work's compiler towards the story of Icarus is both explicit in his commentary and implied in an octave, presumably by Victoria himself, which tells the story of Icarus' fall:

---

[39]   *Ibid.*, II, p. 151.
[40]   Baltasar de Victoria, *Teatro de los dioses de la gentilidad* (Salamanca, 1620). This is the first part of the work. Part two appeared in 1623. The first edition contains an "aprobación" by Lope de Vega himself, in which he describes the book as "Lección importantísima a la inteligencia de muchos libros, cuya moralidad envolvió la antigua filosofía en tantas fábulas para exornación y hermosura de la poesía, pintura y astrología, y en cuyo ornamento los teólogos de la gentilidad... hallaron por símbolos y heroglíficos la explicación de la naturaleza de las cosas."
[41]   Emilio Orozco Díaz's, *El teatro y la teatralidad del barroco* (Barcelona, 1969), is interesting for the light it throws on the way the metaphor of the theatre seems to inform much of the life of the early 17th century.
[42]   *Aeneid*, VI. 11, 1-17.

> En tanto que levanta el presto vuelo,
> con flacas alas aquel mozo insano,
> intentando subir al santo Cielo,
> salió burlado el pensamiento vano:
> su cuerpo le cubrió el cercano suelo,
> y el nombre se quedó en el mar insano,
> y el ejemplo a los hombres deste hecho,
> que les sirva de ejemplo, y de provecho.[43]

The sky which attracts Icarus is now "santo Cielo" which would seem to make Icarus' crime one of sacrilege. His end is seen as an example to all men. If we are in any doubt as to the moral to be learned, it is made clearer: "Solas las desgracias... se guardaron para el desgraciado de su hijo Ícaro, que con su locura, y con su caída dio escarmiento a los hombres, y a las aguas el nombre." The flight of Icarus is treated as if it were a simplistic parable counseling the avoidance of any venture involving risk.

In other countries, too, the story of Icarus is discussed and commented upon. For Sir Francis Bacon, for example, "it is an easy and familiar parable." He continues:

> The path of virtue goes directly midway between excess on the one hand and defect on the other. Icarus, being in the pride of youthful alacrity, naturally fell a victim to excess. For it is on the side of excess that the young commonly sin, as the old on the side of defect.

So far this is the familiar interpretation of the middle way between two extremes, but Bacon goes on to explain the Renaissance weakness for a figure whom moralists seem to condemn in this way:

> And yet if he was to perish one way, it must be admitted that of the two paths, both bad and mischievous, he chose the better. For sins of defect are justly accounted worse than sins of excess; because in excess there is something of magnanimity—something, like the flight of a bird, that holds kindred with heaven; whereas defect creeps on the ground like a reptile.[44]

Another genre that reflects the Renaissance fascination with classical mythology is the Emblem book. Beginning in 1532, with Andrea

---

[43] *Teatro de los dioses de la gentilidad* (Barcelona, 1702), I, pp. 628-9.
[44] Francis Bacon, *Works*, ed. Spedding, Ellis and Heath (Boston, 1891), XIII, 157-8.

Alciati's *Emblematum libellus,* these books presented incidents from mythological and other sources in the form of woodeurs, each followed by an epigrammatic verse and a longer prose commentary explaining their allegorical significance. The relationship between these books and poetry is complex. On the one hand they appear to bridge the gap between the mythographers and the artists, in the attempt to provide edification ("emblema es pintura que significa aviso debajo de alguna o muchas figuras") as well as a source of information and inspiration for painters, sculptors and poets. In the last century Henry Green wrote a book in which he made a case for the influence of the emblem writers on Shakespeare.[45] Yet we must remember, as Mario Praz points out, in one of the few works in this little studied field, that we should be wary of attributing too much importance to them.

> We touch here upon a serious difficulty, (says Praz in establishing the influence of emblem writers upon literature). The allegorical way of thinking was pervasive and habitual during the XVIIth century, and the emblematical image had great vitality. Coincidences of subject and treatment do not necessarily imply a priority of the emblematist to the poet; rather, as emblem writers drew upon ancient historians, apologues, proverbs, etc. for their compositions... many cases of *rapprochement* between their works and literary passages prove illusory: their similarity is caused by a common source.[46]

In our particular case this idea seems to be borne out. Alciati's work, which remained ever the most popular work in the genre and was widely read and quoted in Spain by scholars and commentators (Herrera, Victoria), sees in Icarus a symbol of the rash astrologer.

> Icare, per superos qui raptus et aëra, donec
>   In mare praecipitem cera liquata daret,
> Nunc te cera eadem, feruensque resuscitat ignis.
>   Exemplo ut doceas dogmata certa tuo.
> Astrologus caveat quicquam praedicere: praeceps
>   Nam cadet impostor dum super astra volat.[47]

---

[45]   Henry Green, *Shakespeare and the Emblem Writers* (London, 1870).
[46]   Mario Praz, *Studies in Seventeenth Century Imagery,* 2nd edition, expanded (Rome, 1964), p. 206.
[47]   Andrea Alciati, *Emblemata* (Antwerp, 1692), p. 223 (Emblem 103).

This idea has a precedent in Lucian's dialogue *Astrology* (cf. p. 15) but to my knowledge the image of Icarus as false seer never occurs in poetry, though the idea of punishment for rash or foolish behavior is of course common. Although many of the sonnets that we shall study read almost like descriptions of emblems, and at least one of them actually is, it seems that the emblem tradition contributed little to the image of Icarus that inspired the poets.

In this chapter we have considered some of the more significant works in the mythographic tradition in Spain in the sixteenth and early seventeenth centuries. While it is dangerous to draw any grandiose conclusions from a brief review of such a complex field, some observations are worth making: the early translations (Bustamante and Dolce) were without commentaries, while later editions, even of the same works, had them; earlier works tended to be less concerned with exactness in the rendering of the stories as told by the classics, while later volumes referred to ever more sources and translated more literally; with the trend towards greater erudition, there is a change in the direction of harsher moral judments of some of the gods and heroes. These trends parallel the change that takes place in the arts, with the gradual devaluation of the figures of the Greco-Roman pantheon, but the two phenomena are not necessarily causally related. Seznec sums up some of these trends eloquently:

> the sixteenth century, as it advances, is forced to avow the disaccord which it thought had been successfully hidden [between pagan beliefs and Christian morality]. An era of crisis and reaction then dawns. The gods no longer arouse the same sentiments. Zeal is succeeded by admiration grown reticent and overscrupulous; intoxication with beauty, by a cold archaeological interest, by scholarly curiosity. From being objects of love, the gods are transformed into a subject of study ... But at the same time, since the gods cannot be excluded from art, poetry, or education, a compromise consists in presenting each of the gods as an edifying symbol. Thus the allegorical method dear to the Middle Ages flourishes again with new vigor. All mythology is nothing more —or pretends to be nothing more— than a system of ideas in disguise, a "secret philosophy" (pp. 320-321).

In our particular case the search for edifying truths leads to an ever more severe judgment of Icarus' rashness and eventually to his and his father's condemnation for defying the natural law. Such will also be the kind of evolution we shall document as we follow the fortunes of Icarus as a poetic image. His portrayal will be "increasingly erudite and diminishingly alive, less and less felt but more and more intellectualized" (Seznec, p. 321). The difference is that, since the poets do not set out with the moral or pedagogical concerns of many of the writers in this chapter, they are freer in their choice of interpretations. The result is a much greater variety, including the burlesque, for example, and the trend, or return, toward moralism, when it comes, is even clearer.

Chapter 3

ICARUS REDISCOVERED BY THE POETS

In the *cancionero* poets of Spain's fifteenth century, the names of the classical gods and heroes begin to appear frequently and there is an occasional reference to Daedalus as the archetype of the artist. But Icarus is mentioned scarcely at all. Since these poets are writing within the conventions of courtly love, many of the feelings and dilemmas which will be associated in the sixteenth centruy with Icarus, are already present, but the appropriateness of the figure of Icarus occurs to no one.[1] This is in part because in none of these poets is there the intense fascination with classical mythology or the sense of their immediate and personal relevance that characterize the poets of Garcilaso's generation and after.

Juan de Mena, the poet who incorporated most mythological material into his poetry, refers to Icarus in his *Laberinto de Fortuna* but without identifying with his fate. From the crystal palace of the goddess

---

[1] These are a few examples from Foulché-Delbosc's, *Cancionero castellano del siglo XV* (Madrid, 1915): "Pues el que está más subido / más la caída recela" (Gómez Manrique, II, 40),

> Mi cautivo pensamiento
> tan alto subió a volar,
> que el más ciego entendimiento
> verá ser atrevimiento... (Soria, II, 258);

and in Jorge Manrique, the lover's daring is compared to that of Lucifer, in much the same way that later poets will compare it to Icarus':

> ¡Qué amador tan desdichado
>   que gané
> en la gloria de amadores
> el más alto y mejor grado
>   por la fe
> que tuve con mis amores!
> Y así como Lucifer
> se perdió por se pensar
> igualar con su señor,
> así me vine a perder
> por me querer igualar
> en amor con el Amor. (II, 245.)

Fortune the poet looks down upon the world. After casting his eyes over most of the known world, he at last considers the Greek islands, among which he sees Icaria.

> e vimos las islas Heolias estar,
> Icaria, a la cual el náufrago dio
> de Ícaro nombre, que nunca perdió,
> el mal governado de sabio volar.[2]

The only function of this parenthetical reference to the myth is that of reminding the reader of the origin of the island's name. Schevill says of Mena's use of mythology that "the references to stories or ideas to be found in Ovid are chiefly of that purely academic, erudite nature which reveals little that is inspired" (p. 72). The use of mythological names and figures as "puro artificio poético," as Antonio Alatorre calls it, is quite different from what we shall see in the following century.[3]

In what may be an echo of Juan de Mena,[4] Daedalus as the symbol of the daring artist appears in the acrostic verses at the beginning of *La Celestina*.

> No hizo Dédalo cierto a mi ver
> alguna más prima entretalladura...[5]

The theme of the fall from Fortune lies behind much of this work and, as Professor Gilman points out,[6] it is present also in these verses. It is expressed in the metaphor of the flying ant:

> como hormiga que deja ir,
> holgando por tierra, con la provisión:
> jactóse con alas de su perdición:
> lleváronla en alto, no sabe donde ir.[7]

The metaphor flight expresses the idea of the danger involved in such an artistic venture. In comparing the view of Fortune implicit in *La*

---

[2] Juan de Mena, *Laberinto de Fortuna*, ed. John G. Cummins (Salamanca, 1968), p. 59, ll. 413-416.

[3] Antonio Alatorre (Tr.), *Las heroidas* (Mexico, 1950), p. 54.

[4] Cf. Mena, ed. cit., pp. 92-93:

> y él de una silla tan rica labrada
> como si Dédalo bien la fiziera. (ll. 1135-6.)

> se falla tuviesse pintadas de mano
> nin menos escultas entretalladuras... (II. 1149-50.)

[5] Rojas, *La Celestina*, ed. M. Criado de Val and G. D. Trotter (Madrid, 1965), p. 10.

[6] Gilman, *The Art of "La Celestina"*, pp. 129-130.

[7] *La Celestina*, ed. cit., p. 7.

Celestina with that which underlies Breughel's famous depiction of the fall of Icarus, Gilman finds that both works convey the "unconcern of the spatial universe to man's fall." Yet, although the theme is similar, and Calisto, in his defiance of social order and fall is an Icarian figure, Icarus himself does not appear in Rojas' work.

We must go to Italy in order to find the beginnings of the fascination with the figure of young Icarus as a symbol of one of man's essential predicaments. The earliest example I have found is in prose, in the dialogue *De libero arbitrio* by Lorenzo Valla (1405-1457). Two men discuss man's role in the universe. One of them is young and impetuous, while the other is older and more cautious. Lorenzo, the older man, says:

> One may be endowed with nobility, another with high office, another with wealth, another with genius, another with eloquence, another with none at all. Nevertheless, no level-headed person who is aware of his own efforts would think of mourning because he himself does not have these things. Besides, how much less ought he to mourn because he lacks the wings of a bird which no one has?

To which Antonio replies:

> To be sure, I admit that what you say is true, but somehow I am so impatient and greedy that I cannot control the impulse of my mind. For I hear what you have said about the wings of a bird, that I should not regret it if I don't have them; yet why should I forswear wings if I could possibly attain them by Daedalus' example? And indeed how much finer wings do I long for? With them I might fly not from the prison of walls but from the prison of errors and fly away and arrive not in the fatherland, which breeds bodies as did Daedalus, but in the one where souls are born.[8]

Antonio wishes to follow Daedalus' example, although he does not refer to himself specifically as Icarus. Here, for the first time, the flight of Daedalus has become something more than a moral example; it is a symbol into which the young man can pour all of his yearning after Platonic ideals of transcendence. The later poets will express their

---

[8] Translated by Charles Edward Trinkaus, Jr., in: *The Renaissance Philosophy of Man,* ed. Cassirer, Kristeller and Randall (Chicago and London, 1969), pp. 158-159.

efforts to transcend their humanity by their perseverance in love and
their flights of inspiration. The impulse that is expressed, for example,
in Fray Luis de León's "¿Cuándo será que pueda / libre de esta prisión
volar al cielo," is already present here, expressed in terms of the flight
from Crete.

The Italian Precedents

The earliest extant poem to celebrate Icarus' flight is Italian, the
work of Jacopo Sannazaro in the late fifteenth century.

> Icaro cadde qui: queste onde il sanno,
> che in grembo accolser quella audaci penne;
> qui finì il corso, e qui il gran caso avvenne
> che darà invidia agli altri che verranno.
>
> Aventuroso e ben gradito affanno,
> poi che, morendo, eterna fama ottenne!
> Felice chi in tal fato a morte venne,
> c'un sì bel pregio ricompensi il danno!
>
> Ben pò di sua ruina esser contento,
> se al ciel volando a guisa di colomba,
> per troppo ardir fu esanimato e spento;
>
> et or del nome suo tutto rimbomba
> un mar sì spacïoso, uno elemento!
> Chi ebbe al mondo mai sì larga tomba? [9]

In striking contrast to the conclusions of the medieval moralists who
had seen in Icarus only a warning against extreme flights of ambition,
Sannazaro glorifies Icarus' venture and points out, as will many poets
who follow, that in his death Icarus was assured of immortality by
giving his name to the sea into which he fell.

Ariosto refers to the myth more than once. The following stanzas
from a longer poem tell of the poet's fear that his attempt to sing the
praises of such great beauty as his beloved's will be as great a venture
—and as perilous— as the flight of the young Icarus, dazzled by the
sun's beauty.

---

[9] Iacopo Sannazaro, *Opere volgari*, ed. A. Mauso (Bari, 1961), p. 195.

Tacer debbo e vorrei; ma pur mi sento
inebriato d'una tal dolcezza
che, mentre di lei penso, il cor contento,
anzi beato, sale a tanta altezza,
ch'a mal mio grado canto, e non pavento,
mortal, a dir d'un'immortal bellezza;
anzi con l'ale de'pensieri al cielo
mi porta il mio desir, la gioia e'l zelo.

Ben temo ch'io farò come chi suole
alla vista del sol perder il lume;
e che mi debbia alfin questo mio Sole,
come d'Icaro avenne, arder le piume;
ma non posso non far quel ch'Amor vuole;
altrimente convien ch'io mi consume,
anzi ch'io mora; e se morir se deve,
morte, di lei parlando, è dolce e lieve.[10]

The poet's unfitness to sing such exalted themes will recur in later poems. Ariosto also evokes the image of Icarus in a sonnet, this time comparing the folly of his amorous thoughts with the young Greek's flight:

Nel mio pensier che così veggio audace,
timor, freddo com'angue, il cor m'assale;
di lino e cera egli s'ha fatto l'ale,
disposte a liquefarsi ad ogni face.

E quelle, del disir fatto seguace,
spiega per l'aria, e temerario sale:
e duolmi ch'a ragion poco ne cale,
che devria ostargli, e sel comporta e tace.

Per gran vaghezza d'un celeste lume
temo non poggi sì, che arrivi in loco
dove si accenda, e torni senza piume.

Saranno, oimè! le mie lagrime poco
per soccorrergli poi, quando nè fiume
nè tutto il mar potra smorzar quel foco.[11]

[10] Lodovico Ariosto, *Lirica*, ed. Guiseppe Fatini (Bari, 1924), p. 278.
[11] Ariosto, *Poesie varie* (Florence, 1824), p. 147.

The association between the tears of grief the lover will shed when his intentions come crashing down in flames and the water into which young Icarus fell is a detail that later poets will echo.

In both of the texts just quoted, there are elements not normally associated with the Icarus story. Both accounts have Icarus' wings actually catching fire, whereas classical accounts agree that his fall was caused by the melting of the wax used in their manufacture. The suspicion that the figure of Phaethon, traditionally depicted as hurtling through the sky in flames, is present in the poet's mind is reinforced by the mention of the river in the penultimate line. Phaeton is supposed to have fallen into the Po at the end of his flight.

Another image commonly evoked along with that of Icarus is the Phoenix, which dies a victim to a great light but is reborn. In this sonnet by Tommaso Castellani, the lover, borne aloft on more daring wings than those made by Daedalus, exhorts his wings to fan the flame that both attracts and frightens.

> Avventurate, ma più audaci piume
> de quelle, già che vanamente alzaro
> Icaro verso il ciel; onde mostraro
> esempio a chi salir troppo presume;
>
> se'l caso averso per men caldo lume
> a lor avenne. or voi, ch'un sol più chiaro
> scalda con raggi ardenti, qual riparo
> vieta, che tanto ardor non vi consume?
>
> Ma quel, ch'ad altri nuoce è sol radice
> del vostro ben; però movete el vento
> per accrescer la fiamma, che vi giova.
>
> Onde poi quella nostra alma fenice
> le gran forze d'Amor; l'altrui tormento
> nel proprio ardor, se stessa e voi rinova.[12]

Her passion may be harmful to others but it is the breath of life to him. The energy of love constantly renewing itself, suggests the image of the Phoenix, reborn from its ashes.

In a sonnet by Annibale Caro the images of Icarus and the Phoenix

---

[12]   Tommaso Castellani, *Rime diverse* (Venice, 1549), Vol. I, p. 51. Also published in Fucilla, "Etapas...", p. 56.

are more explicitly linked. The poem in question is a series of *sestinas,* rhyming *nido, piume, core, fiamma, mondo,* and *foco.* The Phoenix is the image that sustains the poem through twelve and a half stanzas. But in one stanza the figure of Icarus appears:

> Icaro già nell'acqua, io nella fiamma
> lasserò del mio ardir memoria al mondo,
> all'alto mio sperar ben degno nido.
> Che si dirà: costui sospinse il core
> tanto verso una luce, che nel foco
> strusse la cera, e 'ncenerió le piume.[13]

Icarus gave his name to a sea. Caro's lover will leave his name in the flames of his love. In both this poem and the preceding one the theme of pleasure derived from the harshness of the beloved's response is treated. This almost masochistic delight in abject submission, an essential convention of courtly love, finds particularly effective expression in Icarus' and Phaethon's fascination with the very source of their own peril.

It is Tansillo's evocations of Icarus that are the most frequent source of inspiration for the Spanish poets. This is his best known and most often imitated sonnet in the tradition:

> Amor m'impenna l'ale e tanto in alto
> le spiega l'animoso mio pensiero,
> che d'hora in hora sormontando spero
> a le porte del ciel far novo assalto.
>
> Temo, qualhor giù guardo, il vol troppo alto,
> ond'ei mi grida, e mi promette altero,
> che se dal nobil corso io cado e pero,
> l'honor fia eterno se mortal è il salto.
>
> Che s'altri, cui disio simil conpunse,
> dià nome eterno al mar col suo morire,
> ove l'ardite penne il sol disgiunse,
>
> il mondo ancor di te potrà ben dire,
> questi aspirò ale stelle e s'ei non giunse
> la vita venne men, non già l'ardire.[14]

---

[13] Annibale Caro, *Rime* (Venice, 1757), p. 95.
[14] Luigi Tansillo, *Il Canzionere* (Napoli, 1926), Vol. I, p. 4.

There is another version of the sonnet, in which the identification with
Icarus becomes more complete, in that, in the final tercet, the poet
attributes eternal fame to himself. As well as changing the word 'nobil'
in line 7 to 'superbo', Tansillo ends his sonnet in the other version thus:

> ancor di me le genti potran dire:
> "questi aspirò alle stelle, e s'ei non giunse.
> la vita venne men, ma non l'ardire." [15]

Where Sannazaro had apostrophized the young flyer, Tansillo, iike
Dante, sees the youth as a self-image and draws an analogy between his
own feeling and those that he imagines Icarus to have had. This is
the sonnet that seems to have had the greatest impact in Spain, as we
shall see. It was imitated many times, translated and given prose commentaries, the most famous of these by Giordano Bruno. Both this
sonnet and the following one are quoted by Bruno in his *Eroici furori* [16]
as expressions of the kind of heroic love which ignores suffering and
human limitations and seeks consummation in the realm of infinite
good and beauty. In the other sonnet the lover again identifies with
Icarus and perceives the danger implicit in such an identification; if
Icarus died, so can he. The lover again consoles himself, though, with
the thought that, even if he dies, he will be immortalized too.

> Poi che spiegate ho l'ale al bel desio,
> quanto per l'alte nubi altier lo scorgo,
> più le superbe penne al vento porgo,
> e d'ardir colmo verso il ciel l'invio.
>
> Nè del figliuol di Dedalo il fin rio
> fa ch'io paventi, anzi via più risorgo:
> ch'io cadrò morto a terra, ben m'accorgo;
> ma qual vita s'agguaglia al morir mio?
>
> La voce del mio cor per l'aria sento:
> "ovi mi porti, temerario? china,
> che raro è senza duol troppo ardimento."

---

[15] *The Oxford Book of Italian Verse* 2nd ed. (Oxford, 1952), p. 202.
[16] For some critical reactions to the philosophical interpretation of Tansillo's
sonnet in Bruno's work, see Giordano Bruno, *Opere italiane*, ed. G. Gentile (Bari, 1908),
p. 343 (note), Benedetto Croce, "Per un famoso sonetto del Tansillo", *La critica*, VI
(1908), pp. 237-240, and the reply to Croce by M. Valgimigli, in *Giornale storico
della letteratura italiana*, LIII (1909), pp. 176-178 and J. C. Nelson, *Renaissance
Theory of Love; the Context of Giordano Bruno's "Eroici furori"* (New York, 1958),
p. 226-7.

"Non temer," rispon'io, "l'alta rovina;
poichè tant'alto sei, muori contento,
se'l ciel sì illustre morte ne destina!" [17]

We shall refer to this poem on more than one occasion at later stages in our investigation. Tansillo also wrote a madrigal in which he evokes the figure of Icarus as an example of someone who dared all in a worthwhile cause.

S'un Icaro, un Fetonte
per troppo ardir già spenti il mondo esclama;
quel che perder di vita, elli han di fama,
di me, farfalla pargoletta e frale,
qual fia la gloria tra' più vaghi augelli,
ch'ebbi ardir di spiegar le piccol'ale
al gran splendor de gli occhi e de' capelli,
ove Amor vinto regna,
e col volo cercai morte sì degna?
Qual pregio udendo dire:
ogni farfalla, spenta in sul gioire,
intorno a picciol lume morir suole,
puest'ebbe morte per gioir nel sole.[18]

Here other images enter the picture. The myths of Icarus and Phaethon are equated here, as in Dante. The image of the butterfly, attracted to the very flame that must kill it, appears also as an expression of the lover's situation. Here the tradition of the butterfly as a metaphor of the frailty of human life—for the Greeks the butterfly was a symbol for the human soul—joins the developing tradition of Icarus as the ill-fated lover.[19] Both Phaethon and the butterfly will be associated with Icarus frequently in Spanish poems.

[17] Tansillo, *op. cit.*, pp. 5-6.
[18] *Ibid.*, p. 164.
[19] Cf. Petrarch:

Come talora al caldo tempo sole
semplicetta farfalla al lume avezza
volar nagli occhi per sua vaghezza,
onde aven ch'ella more, altri si dole;

(*Rime*, ed. N. Zingarelli [Bologna, 1963], p. 818.)

Dante: "angelica farfalla, / che vola alla giustizia senza schermi", (*Purg.* X, 121-122). For a study of the image of the butterfly in Elizabethan poetry, particularly Edmund Spenser, see D. C. Allen, *Image and Meaning* (Baltimore, 1960), Chapter 2, "Muiopotmos, or the Fate of the Butterflie", pp. 20-41.

A contemporary of Tansillo, Onorato Fascitello, wrote the following
sonnet in which the lover asserts his identity with Icarus and again the
parallel with the butterfly is made:

> Icaro io son, che con cerate piume
> m'innalzo al Sol del vostro immenso onore,
> qual semplice animal che per costume
> vola alla luce, ove s'incende e muore.
>
> E temo che non strugga e non consume
> la cera del desire ei troppo ardore,
> sì sono ardenti i rai del vostro lume;
> onde caggia nel mar del proprio errore.
>
> Debili vanni ho certo a sì gran volo;
> ma chi frena el desio vago di farsi
> eterno in grembo della vostra gloria?
>
> Dirassi almen dopo mill'anni ch'arsi
> le penne ardite per seguirvi solo:
> e fia di me nel mondo alta memoria.[20]

The idea, in the first quatrain, that the beloved's beauty and reputation
are the sun to which the lover-as-Icarus is attracted is a case of another
tradition, that of the beloved's beauty compared to the sun, being
pulled into the complex of images around the story of Icarus. In
line 11 the word "grembo" recalls the second line of Sannazaro's
"Icaro cadde qui..." In the earlier work Icarus fell into the lap of the
ocean. Here, the scene of the disaster that may bring glory is, more
literally, the lap of the lady he loves.

Some years later Torquato Tasso, too, writes a sonnet in the same
tradition. Here again Icarus and Phaethon appear side by side. They
appear, as in some Spanish sonnets, one in the first quatrain, one in
the second:

> Se d'Icaro leggesti e di Fetonte,
> ben si come l'un cadde in questo fiume
> quando portar da l'oriente il lume
> volle e di rai del sol cinger la fronte,

---

[20] Published by Michele Ricciardelli in (Il mito de Icaro e la correlazione",
Romance Notes, VIII (1967), p. 287.

e l'altro in mar, che troppo ardite e pronte
a volo alzò le sue cerate piume;
e così va chi di tentar presume
strade nel ciel per fama appena conte.

Ma chi dee paventare in alta impresa,
s'avvien ch'Amor l'affide? e che non puote
Amor, che con catena il cielo unisce?

Egli giù trae da le celesti rote
di terrena beltà Diana accesa,
e d'Ida il bel fanciullo al ciel rapisce.[21]

The fates of Icarus and Phaethon counsel caution, but the lover is consoled by the thought that Cupid is his guide. If Love could bring Diana down to earth and take Ganymede up to Olympus, he can surely help this young lover. Such confidence in Love's benevolence is far from universal.

These lines by Giovanni Battista Guarini, also from the latter half of the sixteenth century, express at first sight a view of Icarus very similar to those we have seen.

A voi, Donna, volando
l'amoroso mio cor da me si parte,
vago di riveder gli amati Soli;
ma non sò' con qual arte
o d'Icaro, o di Dedalo sen voli:
sò ben ch'al caldo lume
poria perder le piume, e poi la vita.
Ma segua ove l'invita
suo...[22] ò sua gioia,
pur che Dedalo giunga, Icaro moia.[23]

At the end we realize that something quite different is happening. The lover's heart flies away and the poet cannot tell whether it is flying daringly like Icarus or more cautiously like his father. He knows that there is danger but he refuses to try to hold back his heart because, even though the Icarus in his heart's venture may die, his more prudent

---

[21]   Torquato Tasso, *Rime* (Bologna, 1900), p.345.
[22]   Printed thus, with a word missing.
[23]   Giovanni Battista Guarini, *Rime* (Venice, 1598), f. 64v.

side may win through. This is reading of the symbolism of the father/
son relationship that, so far as I know, is not encountered elsewhere.

This review of some of the Italian versions of the Icarus myth
makes no pretence of being exhaustive—even if every extant poem could
be found, we would still probably have very little idea of what seems to
have been an immensely rich tradition. It will serve, though, as
background when we study Icarus in Spain, and it may also contribute
something to the study of a very complex question, the nature of the
literary relations between Spain and Italy at this time. It seems, from
this evidence, that the two traditions evolved independently after the
initial impulse provided by Sannazaro's poem. Some images occur in
the Italian poems that we do not find in Spain and a great many
original variations on the theme are played in Spain without parallels
in Italian poetry.

Garcilaso de la Vega

Icarus appears first in Spanish lyric poetry in Garcilaso's impeccable
sonnet XII. The lover considers his situation, torn by hopes and fears,
and perceives a parallel between his plight and that of Icarus and
Phaethon:

> Si para refrenar este desseo
> loco, imposible, vano, temeroso,
> y guarecer de un mal tan peligroso,
> que es darme a entender yo lo que no creo,
>
> no me aprovecha verme qual me veo,
> o muy aventurado o muy medroso,
> en tanta confusión que nunca oso
> fïar el mal de mí que lo posseo,
>
> ¿qué me á de aprovechar ver la pintura
> d'aquel que con las alas derretidas,
> cayendo, fama y nombre al mar á dado,
>
> y la del que su fuego y locura
> llora entre aquellas plantas conocidas,
> apenas en ell agua resfrïado? [24]

The identification of an emotional dilemma with the adventures of
these two mythological figures goes back to Dante and to other, more

[24] Garcilaso de la Vega, *Obras,* ed. Elias Rivers (Madrid, 1964), p. 14.

immediate, sources like Ariosto, and recurs in Torquato Tasso, as we have seen. Both Sannazaro's "Icaro cadde qui..." and Tansillo's "Amor m'impenna l'ale..." have been called sources for Garcilaso's sonnet.[25] If we look at the structure of the poem, we must reject Sannazaro's influence, since the only similarity between the two works is that both, in some way, deal with the myth of Icarus. Structurally they are very different. Tansillo's sonnet is closer to Garcilaso but even here the differences are considerable. In "Amor m'impenna l'ale..." the lover finds solace in the thought that Icarus, who also aimed high, gained immortality in his dying. For Garcilaso Icarus and Phaethon are clear warnings to desist—they tend to curb his desires ("refrenar este desseo..."). In Tansillo the lover persists because of the example of Icarus, in Garcilaso despite it. Structurally, Tansillo's other sonnet, "Poi che spiegate ho l'ale...", is closer to the Spanish work. In that sonnet the lover's heart is warned by the contemplation of Icarus' fate and at first tries to call him back, but at the end, as in Garcilaso, the lover asserts his intention to persist, despite the risk. One might also point out that the pairing of Icarus and Phaethon does not occur in either sonnet but rather in the madrigal (see above, p. 46). Garcilaso's sonnet was written in 1535, when he and Tansillo were together in Naples, so we may assume some contact between them, but it is impossible to say with any certainty which single poem provided the immediate inspiration to the Spaniard.

In Garcilaso, as in Tansillo and Ariosto, the lover sees the parallel between the fates of Icarus and Phaethon and the perilous course upon which he has embarked. His own instincts also warn him that he is in danger and yet he is powerless to desist. How then, are mere pictures or, as Herrera suggests in his commentary, pictures in words, that represent the moral views of others, going to deter him? Herrera, in his *Anotaciones,* tells us what the Phaethon story meant for his generation: "algunos significan la fábula moralmente contra los que presumiendo subir con temeraria osadía más alto que lo que pueden sus propias fuerças, al fin caen en tierra".[27] Garcilaso's lover, in common with Rojas' Calisto and other men of the Renaissance, considers and

---

[25] Another image that seems to have contributed to the popularity of the myth of Icarus is the traditional one of the lover who is as wax in the hands of the beloved. Cf. Garcilaso: "Si a vuestra voluntad yo soy de cera..." (*Obras,* ed. cit. p. 22.)

[26] Lapesa suggests that there are in Garcilaso's sonnet "algunas reminiscencias" of Sannazaro's sonnet (*Trayectoria poética de Garcilaso* (Madrid, 1968) 2nd ed., p. 156). Fucilla points out ("Etapas...", p. 52) that the closer source is Tansillo.

[27] *Garcilaso de la Vega y sus comentaristas,* ed. Antonio Gallego Morell, 2nd ed. (Madrid, 1972), p. 348.

rejects the moral commonplace—the higher you fly, the further you fall—and asserts his own, tragic, autonomy.

There is no doubt about the immediate source of this sonnet by Gutierre de Cetina:

> Amor mueve mis alas y tan alto
> las lleva el amoroso pensamiento
> que de hora en hora subiendo siento
> quedar mi padecer más corto y falto.
>
> Temo tal vez mientras mi vuelo exalto;
> mas llega luego a mí el conocimiento
> y pruébase que es poco en tal tormento
> por inmortal honor mi mortal salto.
>
> Que si otro puso al mar eterno nombre
> do el soberbio valor le dio la muerte,
> presumiendo de sí más que podía,
>
> de mí diran: aquí fue muerto un hombre
> que si al cielo llegar negó su suerte,
> la vida le faltó, no la osadía.[28]

It is a close imitation, almost a translation, of Tansillo's "Amor m'impenna l'ale..." The contemplation of the example of Icarus offers the consolation of immortality as compensation for an untimely death. Cetina has imitated the version of the Italian sonnet which employs the first person in the final tercet, the version in which the identification with Icarus is more complete.

In both the Italian and Spanish sonnets, it is the lover's thoughts that lead him on. It is an established topos of the Petrarchan tradition that the lover is not in control of his destiny. He is the victim of young Cupid's darts which affect his will. The tradition of the lover as victim of his own thoughts goes back certainly as far as Petrarch —"Volo con l'ali del pensiero al cielo..." It continues in Tansillo— —"l'animoso mio pensiero"—and becomes a constant image of Renaissance and baroque poetry, often associated, as we shall see, with the image of Icarus as the lover's thoughts.

Tansillo's "Amor m'impenna l'ale..." enjoyed great and lasting popularity. Translations of it appeared in two works published in the

---

[28] *Obras*, ed. Hazañas and la Rúa (Seville, 1895), p. 17.

New World in the seventeenth century. The first is by Diego d'Ávalos y Figueroa:

> Alas me pone Amor, y tanto en alto
> me levanta mi honroso pensamiento
> que por horas espero y aun intento
> a las puertas del cielo dar asalto.
>
> Miro la tierra y temo de lo alto,
> mas quién me esfuerza dice tan contento,
> que si falta el efecto en tal intento,
> da gloria eterna ser mortal el salto.
>
> Porque si aquel que igual tuvo el deseo
> dio tal renombre al mar do fue su muerte,
> manifestando el sol su desvarío;
>
> cantará de ti el mundo su trofeo:
> —éste ha querido levantar su suerte,
> y faltóle la vida mas no el brío.[29]

The other translation appears in Lugo y Dávila's *Teatro popular,* a collection of exemplary stories which appeared in 1622. Tansillo's poem is still being referred to and translated as late as this. Tansillo's poem is introduced by Ricardo, the young hero of one of the stories, who is defending his decision to dress as a woman in order to further his love suit. In the face of criticism, he defends his apparently unworthy behavior thus:

> Y para que no me replique el maestro, que bien sé de mucha erudición y letras, hallará razones; digo que aunque conociese con evidencia ser lo peor lo que pretendo seguir, ya no me hallo en estado para volver atrás mi resolución, de más que basta emprender las cosas arduas, aunque no se consignan: pues en atropellar el peligro está la bizarría de ánimo: tenga paciencia para oír este soneto del Tansillo que traduje, y hace a mi propósito:
>
> Amor pluma a mis alas da, y tan alto
> las bate mi animoso pensamiento,

---

[29] Diego de Ávalos y Figueroa, *La miscelánea austral* (Lima, Perú, 1603), f. 78 v. The poem is reprinted by Fucilla in *Estudios sobre el petrarquismo en España* (Madrid, 1960), p. 232.

que de hora en hora remontado siento
dar al cielo a las puertas nuevo asalto.

Temo cuando caeré, y vuelo más alto,
donde amor grita, y del prometer siento,
que si en el noble curso pierdo aliento,
será eterno el honor, si es mortal salto.

Que si otro con deseo semejante
dio nombre eterno al mar con su caída,
donde el sol desasió las plumas bellas,

De mí el undo dirá, y es justo cante,
si no llegó, aspiró a las estrellas,
no el brío le faltó, faltó la vida.[30]

In another sonnet by Cetina, Cupid again sweeps the lover off his feet:

Amor me tira y casi a vuelo lleva
por do mi presunción hizo la vía,
tan alta va mi loca fantasía
que las nubes pasar volando prueba.

The lover is more critical of his ambition this time—it is a mad fantasy to want to soar higher than the clouds. Once again, as in Garcilaso, Icarus' example is of no avail:

No espero que yo el fin de Ícaro mueva
la dura obstinación de mi porfía,
pues veo que el ardor que la desvía
él mismo la rehace y la renueva.[31]

Icarus' warning cannot help because, in one of those paradoxes so dear to Petrarch and his followers, the very heat that deters him is the source of the energy that stimulates his ambition. A similar idea is expressed in the sonnet by Castellani that we looked at before:

Ma quel, qu'ad altri nuoce è sol radice
del vostro ben; però movete il vento
per accrescer la fiamma, che vi giova.

[30] Diego de Lugo y Dávila, *Teatro popular* (Madrid, 1622), ff. 144r and 144v.
[31] *Obras*, ed. cit., p. 16.

The very flames that are harmful to others are the source of the lover's joy. The self-renewing aspect of the power of love suggests the image of the Phoenix in Castellani and we shall find these two images linked in Spain also.

The image of the lover's throughts having wings is so frequent that it is sometimes hard to be sure if the myth of Icarus is alluded to specifically or not. In the following sonnets by Francisco de Figueroa, the lover's thoughts are chided as if they were Icarus flying too high, but there seems to be no specific reference to the myth.

> ¿De dónde ahora tan osados bríos?
> bajad las alas, vanos pensamientos,
> menos rebeldes a mis mandamientos
> y más humildes, pues al fin sois míos.

> No es tiempo ahora para andar baldíos
> en mar tan alto con contrarios vientos;
> gozad la libertad, vivid contentos,
> si no queréis volver mis ojos ríos.

> Mas id gloriosos donde os llama el cielo,
> ricos de suerte y bienaventuranza,
> que sólo con el alma gozo y veo;

> id donde distes, con tan alto vuelo,
> gloria a la pena, fuerza a la esperanza,
> vida a la muerte y alas al deseo.[32]

> Tan alto ha puesto amor mi pensamiento
> y tan sobre las nubes se ha encumbrado,
> que huelgo de vivir desesperado
> por solo imaginar contentamiento.

> Tendrá alguno por loco atrevimiento
> haber tan alto el vuelo levantado,
> pero éste no sabrá que haber osado
> es mucho donde hay tal merecimiento.

[32] Francisco de Figueroa, *Poesías* (Madrid, 1943), pp. 144-145.

Si la pena y dolor que se recibe,
recibe el hombre en ver do nace,
el cuerpo con tormentos se deshace;

mas el alma bien empleada lo recibe,
así aunque muriera do alegre vivo,
sólo por ser de vos gracia cautivo.[33]

"Su tema y desarrollo tienen una estrecha afinidad con el célebre so-neto de Tansillo: 'Amor m'impenna l'ale...'" says Fucilla of the second sonnet.[34] Yet all references to Icarus are omitted and, if we did not have the Tansillo sonnet to compare it with, there would be no way of knowing that there was any connection with Icarus.

In a sonnet by Manuel de Portugal we can see the process of iden-tification with the fate of Icarus very clearly. In the quatrains the flight and fall of Daedalus' son are narrated:

Rompiendo el aire junto al alto cielo
Dédalo con su hijo caminaba.
Soberbio el mozo viendo que volaba,
deja su padre y alza más el vuelo.

Febo derrite el ala y quema el pelo,
y cuanto más el mozo se acercaba
así bajaba cuando a lo alto estaba
hasta morir en el profundo suelo.

And then, in the tercets, the poet applies the image to himself as the lover:

Yo que unas alas desta misma suerte
de amor y de esperanza había tejido,
tanto subí que pude así quererte.

Mas fue tu resplandor tan encendido
que el alma derritió, y así mi muerte
no fue si no de haber tanto subido.[35]

---

[33] *Ibid.*, p. 151. Also printed previously in Eugenio Mele and Angel González Palencia, "Notas sobre Francisco de Figueroa", *Revista de Filología Española*, XXV (1941), p. 339, with the note "Debe de haber erratas de copia en los dos tercetos". In fact, lines 10, 12 and 13 do not scan and line 14 is very obscure.

[34] Fucilla, "Fuentes italianas de Francisco de Figueroa", *Clavileño*, 16 (1952), p. 7.

[35] Manuel de Portugal, *Poesía española*, Ms 756 in the Biblioteca Nacional in Madrid, published by Fucilla in "Etapas...", p. 68.

The idea that Icarus' hair is burned by the sun (line 5), which appears in no other version of the myth, is a detail more appropriate to the myth of Phaethon, from which it may be derived by association. We shall have occasion later to return to the theme of contamination of one myth by another.

This sonnet by Francisco de Aldana is, at first, as full of reckless defiance as Garcilaso's:

> ¿Cuál nunca osó mortal tan alto el vuelo
> subir, o quién venció más su destino,
> mi clara y nueva luz, mi sol divino,
> que das y aumentas nuevo rayo al cielo,
>
> cuanto el que pudo en este bajo suelo,
> oh estrella amiga, oh hado peregrino,
> los ojos contemplar que de contino
> engendran paz, quietud y recelo?

The lover considered his act of daring to look into his beloved's eyes as an act of supreme audacity, analogous to the attempt to fly. The beloved is identified as the sun, the source of the light of his life. This contributes to the parallel, so far only implicit, with the ill-fated flight of Icarus. The idea that the lover must overcome his destiny is a particularly intense expression of the grandeur of his passion, comparable to Tansillo's hope to "a le porte del ciel far novo asalto" But in the tercets the tone changes suddenly:

> Bien lo sé yo, que Amor, viéndome puesto
> do no sube a mirar con mucha parte
> olmo, pino, ciprés, ni helado monte,
>
> de sus ligeras alas diome presto
> dos plumas y me dijo: "Amigo, ¡guarte
> del mal suceso de Ícaro o Faetonte!" [36]

The lover's exaltation in the contemplation of such rare beauty gives way to fear as Cupid offers him two feathers (one each for Icarus and Phaethon?—there are traditionally no feathers involved in the Phaethon story) and warns him of the risk he runs. The traditional image of the lover's wings is seen ironically. Cupid is portrayed as mischievously

---

[36] Francisco de Aldana, *Poesías,* ed. Elías Rivers (Madrid, 1957), p. 7.

taunting his victim in a way reminiscent of the way Góngora portrays him offering his blindfold as a bandage to Angélica. The whole story of Icarus' flight and fall is here reduced simply to a "mal suceso," like the "caso averso" of Castellani. The myth will be evoked by ever more indirect allusion.

There are few cases where the image of Icarus occurs in traditional Spanish meter, especially in a serious context. One of the exceptions is this poem by Hurtado de Mendoza:

> Pensamiento mío,
> no me deis tal guerra,
> pues sois en la tierra
> de quien sólo fío;
>
> que si en tal altura
> no vais poco a poco
> quedaré por loco
> y vos por locura.
>
> Con alas deshechas
> vais dando ocasiones
> que vuestras canciones
> se vuelvan endechas...
>
> Honrada y dichosa
> es vuestra subida;
> pero la caída
> muy más peligrosa.
>
> ¿Qué buen fin espera
> quien va sin recelo
> subiendo en el cielo
> con alas de cera?
>
> De vuestros antojos
> vencido el volar
> daréis nombre al mar
> que han hecho mis ojos.
>
> Y al luto después
> traerás en venganza
> por mí, y la esperanza
> y yo por los tres... [37]

The lover addresses his thoughts in the conventional expression of powerlessness to control his fate, and warns his heart that this flight of fancy may lead to a fall. The contemplation of the example of Icarus lead Garcilaso and Cetina to a proud assertion of their determination to persist despite, or even because of, the dangers. In these lines Icarus is clearly a more persuasive warning. He is so for Aldana too, but the tone of this lament by Mendoza is quite different from anything we have seen so far. In Garcilaso there is a transition from the consideration of the dangers to the anticipation of the fame to be won by overcoming them. Here there is a clear movement from glory to defeat—*altura - locura, canciones - endechas, subidas - caída,* etc. The dangers outweigh any honour to be gained. Icarus falls here into a sea of tears, an idea that is implicit in Ariosto (see p. 51) and that we shall see again.

Icarus, then, can inspire fear or admiration; he can seem to offer death or immortality. These are the two extremes of the range of emotional attitudes associated with the myth. Hurtado's poem is unusual in this period for its extremely gloomy tone, although as we go on we shall discover many similar reactions to the story of Icarus.

Hernando de Acuña begins his incomplete translation of Boiardo's *Orlando innamorato* with these lines:

> No los atrevimientos levantados
> de Ícaro, y Faetón, que al fin cayeron;
> ni los fieros Gigantes abrasados
> por lo que contra el cielo acometieron:
> ni casos semejantes ya cantados,
> que viven en historias y no fueron;
> mas las armas, amor, y el varón canto,
> que fue del mundo admiración y espanto.[38]

Here, in order to point up the particular importance of his subject, Icarus, Phaethon and the Giants are all thrown together as examples of daring punished by death. This is an early sign of the total condemnation that Icarus will inspire in some poets in the seventeenth century. In a sonnet, however, Acuña reserves moral judgement on Icarus and is content to recount the story of his flight and fall without drawing any parallels or conclusions.

---

[38] Acuña, *Varias poesías,* ed. Elena Catena de Vindel (Madrid, 1954), p. 377. Boiardo's poem begins quite differently, without the references to Icarus and Phaethon and without the echo of Virgil in the line "mas las armas, amor y el varón canto".

Con Ícaro de Creta se escapaba
Dédalo, y ya las alas extendía,
y al hijo que volando le seguía
con amor paternal amonestaba,

que si el vuelo más alto levantaba,
la cera con el sol se desharía,
y en el mismo peligro le pondría
el agua, y su vapor si más bajaba

Mas el soberbio mozo y poco experto,
enderezóse luego al alto cielo,
y ablandada la cera en el altura,

perdió las alas, y en el aire muerto
recibiéndole el mar del alto vuelo
por el nombre le dio la sepultura.[39]

In contrast with the Icarus condemned above for his great boldness, here he is merely, as in Ovid, an inexperienced youth who acts unwisely and suffers the consequences.

Before continuing the study of the tradition in Spain, we shall turn aside to consider the fate of Icarus in France.

---

[39] *Varias poesías*, ed. cit., p. 361.

Chapter 4

ICARUS AS HERO

The myth of Icarus had its vogue in France too, althought its career there was less brilliant and more short lived.[1] It came to that country along with the rest of the Petrarchist tradition, naturalized by the generation of the Pléiade. There was some reluctance to accept in France the uncritically heroic image of Icarus presented by the Italian sonneteers, from whom poets on both sides of the Pyrenees derived their inspiration. The "classicist" reaction to the more extreme manifestations of this tradition, when it came, was focused in part on the excessive use of mythological imagery, so it is not surprising to see Icarus at the center of the debate—his image had after all been associated, at least since Horace, with bold or risky poetic endeavors. But before this reaction, even as early as the manifesto of the Pléiade, *La Deffence et illustration de la langue françoyse*, Du Bellay had called French a "langue si pauvre et nue, qu'elle a besoing des ornementz et (s'il faut ainsi parler) des plumes d'autruy," using the image of borrowed feathers apologetically, as if he thought it affected. On another occasion, less self-consciously, he says of hard work and suffering that "ce sont les esles dont les ecriz des hommes volent au ciel."[2] In similar vein, in one of the poems of *Les Regrets*, he asks:

> Aveque la vertu je veux au ciel monter.
> Pourrois-je au ciel monter aveques plus haulte aelle?[3]

The figure of Icarus must have been closely associated in DuBellay's mind with the Petrarchist tradition for him to turn it "contre les pe-

---

[1] Guy Demerson, in *La Mythologie classique dans l'oeuvre de la "Pléiade"* (Geneva, 1972), for example, only mentions Icarus four times.
[2] Joaquim du Bellay, *La Deffence et illustration de la langue françoyse*, ed. Henri Chamard (Paris, 1904), pp. 67 and 198-9.
[3] Joachim du Bellay, *Les Regrets et autres oeuvres poétiques*, ed. M. A. Screech (Geneva, 1966), p.265.

trarchistes," as he does in a satirical poem of that title. "L'un meurt
de froid, et l'autre meurt de chault, / L'un vole bas, et l'autre vole
hault," he complains. The image recurs in the final lines:

> Si toutefois Pétrarque vous plaist mieux,
> je reprendray mon chant mélodieux,
> et voleray jusqu'au sejour des Dieux
> d'une aele mieux guidée.[4]

While the tradition is still quite new in France, its most conventional
expressions are being criticized in terms of one of the myths so central
to it, that of Icarus.

Étienne Jodelle, another member of the Pléiade, mentions Icarus
along with Phaethon and Prometheus in his *Cléopâtre*, referring briefly
to Icarus' naming of a sea.[5] But it is in the poetry of Pierre de Ronsard
and his younger rival for court favour, Philippe Desportes, that the
myth of the flight from Crete comes into its own for a brief period in
French poetry. What is probably the earliest sonnet in the familiar
tradition in French is number CLXVII of Ronsard's *Amours,* a conventional plea for caution to the lover's thoughts. It is a translation of
Ariosto (see p. 51).

> Ce fol penser pour s'en voler plus hault,
> apres le bien que haultain je desire,
> s'est emplumé d'ailles joinctes de cire,
> propres, à fondre aux raiz du premier chault.
>
> Luy fait oyseau, dispost de sault en sault,
> poursuit en vain l'object de son martire,
> et toy, qui peux, et luy doys contredire,
> tu le vois bien, Raison, et ne t'en chault.
>
> Soubz la clarté d'une estoile si belle,
> cesse, penser, de hazarder ton aisle,
> ains que te voir en bruslant desplumer:
>
> car pour estaindre une ardeur si cuizante,
> l'eau de mes yeulx ne seroit suffisante,
> ny suffisants toutz les flotz de la mer.[6]

---

[4] Joachim du Bellay, *Divers jeux rustiques,* ed. V. Saulnier (Geneva, 1947),
pp. 77 and 82.

[5] Etienne Jodelle, *Oeuvres complètes,* ed. E. Balmas (Paris, 1965-8), II, p. 116,
11. 723-4.

[6] Pierre de Ronsard, *Les Amours,* ed. Henri and Catherine Weber (Paris, 1963),
p. 107. Subsequent references will be to pages of the same edition.

The most famous—infamous, for some—sonnet in the French tradition is that which opens Philippe Desportes's *Amours d'Hippolyte*. This bold poem, which Ronsard seems to have taken as a personal affirmation and almost as an *art poétique* on the part of the younger poet, seems to mark the beginning of a rather intense period of interest in the myth, in the work of both poets. Many of the following treatments of the myth Ronsard may owe inspiration to that famous poem, although this is only obvious in a poem I shall treat later.

The next sonnet by Ronsard appears to derive, if not from Desportes, then from the same sources, Sannazaro and Tansillo. It too begins a sequence of sonnets, those addressed to Astrée, a lady to whose celestial beauty the poet is fatally attracted:

> Dois-je voler emplumé d'esperance,
> ou si je dois, forcé de desespoir,
> du haut du Ciel en terre laisser choir
> mon jeune amour avorté de naissance?
>
> Non, j'aime mieux, leger d'outrecuidance,
> tomber d'enhaut, et fol me decevoir,
> que voler bas, deussé-je recevoir
> pour mon tombeau toute une large France.
>
> Icare fit de sa cheute nommer,
> pour trop oser, les ondes de la mer:
> et moy je veux honorer ma contree
>
> de mon sepulchre, et dessus engraver,
> *Ronsard voulant aux astres s'eslever,*
> *fur foudroyé par une belle Astrée* (p. 373).

Ronsard reworks some of the ideas implicit in the Italian sources in his own way, referring, as he so often did, to his own fame. Tansillo seems to be the inspiration for the beginning and the end of the sonnet, although lines 8 and 10 are very reminiscent of Sannazaro's "Chi hebbe al mondo mai si larga tomba" and "Per troppo ardir fu esanimato e spento."

Elsewhere Ronsard makes a personal adaptation of traditional material in as interesting a way. He uses a contemporary argument about classical philosophy to tempt the woman he loves to a less platonic relationship. Icarus is brought forth as a symbol of the folly of the delight only in the spirit.

> Vous aimez l'intellect, et moins je vous en prise:
> vous volez, comme Icare, en l'air d'un beau malheur:
> vous aimez les tableaux qui n'ont point de couleur.
> Aimer l'esprit, Madame, est aimer la sottise (p. 407).

It is Philippe Desportes, in this respect the French Herrera, who is most often inspired by the story of Icarus. In one of his elegies he regrets the blindness of his amorous infatuations:

> Helas! je connoy bien que j'ay trop entrepris,
> et qu'un aveuglement a saisi mes esprits,
> que mon vol est trop haut, et que ceste arrogance
> d'Icare ou des Geans attend la recompense.[7]

In another poem the coin is reversed. He pushes aside his regrets at his situation and finds consolation in the thought that, even if he dies, the instrument of his demise is of celestial beauty:

> Je ne me plains du vol que j'ay tenté,
> jeune Dedale, aux perils temeraire;
> quoy qu'il en soit, j'auray de quoy me plaire,
> fondant aux rais d'une telle beauté.[8]

In the same book he appeals once again to the image of Daedalus' son, this time without mentioning him by name. He complains of Love's harsh treatment of him:

> Il croist de jour en jour sans espoir mon martyre;
> il me fait voller haut sur des ailles de cire,
> puis me fait trebucher, quand je vay m'elevant.[9]

In *Les Amours de Cléonice*, there is a curious sonnet which Malherbe censures severely for what he considers the gratuitous confusion of two myths, those of Icarus and Phaethon:

> J'ay dit à mon Desir: Pense à te bien guider,
> rien trop bas, ou trop haut, ne te face distraire:
> il ne m'escouta point, mais jeune et volontaire,
> par un nouveau sentier se voulut hazarder.

[7] Philippe Desportes, *Élégies*, ed. Victor E. Graham (Genève, 1961), pp. 50-1.
[8] Desportes, *Les Amours de Diane*, ed. Victor E. Graham (Genève, 1959), I, pp. 67-8.
[9] *Ibid.*, p. 156.

Je vey le ciel sur luy mille orages darder,
je le vey traversé de flamme ardente et claire,
se plaindre en trebuchant de son vol temeraire,
que mon sage conseil n'avoit sceu retarder.

Apres ton precipice, ô Desir miserable!
je t'ay fait dedans l'onde une tumbe honorable
de ces pleurs que mes yeux font couler jour et nuit:

et l'Esperance aussi ta soeur foible et dolante,
apres maints longs destours, se voit changée en plante,
qui reverdît assez, mais n'a jamais de fruit.[10]

Although Icarus is unmentioned, the echo of Daedalus' advice to his son is very clear in the opening lines. Moreover, the tomb in line 10 recalls Sannazaro's Icarus sonnet and its imitations. The idea that the sea will consist of the lover's own tears is at least implicit in Ariosto and echoed in Hurtado de Mendoza. Malherbe is right that, at the end, the sister who becomes a waterside plant is clearly a reference to the sisters of Phaethon who were turned into poplar trees beside the Po. His criticism of the imagery, while perhaps justified by the rigors of logic, seems severe to a modern reader, and would have applied to a great many earlier poets, even the greatest of them.

Just as Ronsard had feared the fierce beauty of Astrée, so Desportes, like Herrera, expresses his trepidation before the suns of his loved one's eyes:

Mes yeux sont assez clairs pour lire en vos beautez
L'irrevocable loy de ma mort asseurée,
Et pour voir que trop haut mes desirs sont portez,
Ayans l'aile tardive et foible et mal cirée,
Pour voir qu'à vos Soleils leurs cerceaux se desfont,
Et que tout mon espoir comme neige se fond.[11]

By far the best known Icarus sonnet in France, though, is Desportes's version of Sannazaro's "Icaro cadde qui..."

Icare est cheut ici le jeune audacieux,
qui pour voler au Ciel eut assez de courage:

---

[10] Desportes, *Cléonice, Dernières amours,* ed. Victor E. Graham (Geneva, 1962), p. 11. Malherbe's annotations are on the same page.
[11] *Ibid.,* p. 56.

icy tomba son corps degarni de plumage,
laissant tous braves coeurs de sa cheutte envieux.

O bien-heureux travail d'un esprit glorieux,
qui tire un si grand gain d'un si petit dommage!
O bien-heureux malheur plein de tant d'avantage,
qu'il rende le vaincu des ans victorieux!

Un chemin si nouveau n'estonna sa jeunesse,
le pouvoir luy faillit mais non la hardiesse,
il eut pour le brûler des astres le plus beau.

Il mourut poursuivant une haute adventure,
le ciel fut son desir, la Mer sa sepulture :
est-il plus beau dessein, ou plus riche tombeau? [12]

As if he took this poem personally, Ronsard countered with an opening poem to his second book of sonnets for Hélène in which an old man defends his powers and mocks the folly of youth. He does so at the same time as parodying the younger poet's fascination with certain heroic myths:

Lecteur, je ne veux estre escolier de Platon,
qui la vertue nous presche, et ne fait pas de mesme :
ny volontaire Icare ou lourdaut Phaethon,

perduz pour attenter une sottise extrème.
Mais sans me contrefaire ou Voleur, ou Charton,
de mon gré je me noye, et me brusle moymesme (p. 419).

The word "volontaire" seems to be a direct echo of Desportes.

The edition of Desportes that contains Malherbe's written commentaries is a document as priceless as Herrera's *Anotaciones*. One of his most frequent criticisms of Desportes' poetry is his exaggerated, sometimes confused or obscure, use of mythological imagery. Malherbe's common sense is offended by several of the references we have just seen to the myth of Icarus. He strikes out the line "D'Icare ou des Geans attend la recompense," [13] without saying why. "Jeune Dedale" is im-

---

[12] Desportes, *Les Amours d'Hippolyte*, ed. Victor E. Graham (Geneva, 1960), pp. 11-12.
[13] Malherbe's comments may be found in the notes to the above cited editions of Desportes' poetry.

precise enough to arouse his anger: "Je croy qu'il veut dire *Icare* par *le jeune Dedale;* mais cela ne se peut deffendre, veu que le succes de Dedale et d'Icare, en meme dessein, furent différents (sic), car Dedale ne fut pas temeraire." The final lines of the sonnet "J'ay dit a mon Desir…" infuriated Malherbe. "Ce sonnet est bourru si jamais il en fut. Il fait allusion a la fable de Phaeton et de ses soeurs changées en peupliers, mais à quelle fin, et à quel propos, je ne sçay." His critical spirit responds also to the passage beginning "Mes yeux sont assez clairs…" He crosses out the word "asseurée" and then goes on to complain about the expression "mal cirée." He asks "Quand elle seroit cirée le mieux du donde, ne fondroit-elle pas? C'est un inconvénient qui suit la matière et non la forme."

Petrarchist poetry cannot long sustain such logical scrutiny and the poetry of the seventeenth century restricts its use of mythological reference to a few familiar figures, amongst whom the daring Icarus seems not to find a place. When, almost a century after Desportes, Molière recalls the story of Icarus—at the beginning of *Le Malade imaginaire*— it is in a pastoral interlude peopled by figures of antiquity. The god Pan reproaches the shepherds for their daring attempt to sing the praises of their King. In this setting, their venture is analogous, once again, to that of the young Greek of old who ignored his father's warnings.

> Laissez, laissez, Bergers, ce dessein téméraire
>   Hé! que voulez-vous faire?
>   Chanter sur vos chalumeaux
>   ce qu'Apollon sur sa lyre,
>   avec ses chants les plus beaux,
>   n'entreprendroit pas de dire?
> C'est donner trop d'essor au feu qui vous inspire,
> c'est monter vers les cieux sur des ailes de cire,
>   Pour tomber dans le fond des eaux.[14]

Fernando de Herrera

Icarus seems to have held a particular fascination for Fernando de Herrera. The traditional theme of love as a heroic exploit in which the lover must prove his fortitude, tenacity and immunity to suffering

[14] Jean Baptiste Molière, *Oeuvres complètes,* ed. R. Jouanny (Paris, 1962), II p. 763.

merges with the convention of the beloved's beauty as a source of an
attraction that affords as much danger as delight. The theme of daring
(osadía, atrevimiento) is ubiquitous in Herrera's poetry and is often
associated with the peril of the fatal charms of a lady whose literary
name is Luz or Lumbre. The lover in Herrera's poetry often feels himself to be the protagonist in a drama of mythical proportions, and
Prometheus, Phaethon and Icarus are evoked in comparisons. There
can be few expressions of such monumental despair as the sonnet "Subo
con tan gran peso..." [15] or another poem based on the parallel with
Prometheus, in which the lover speaks or surpassing Prometheus'
feat—"mi grande afán al suyo exceda." [16] Nor have many poets expressed such rapture at emulating the flights of Icarus and Phaethon as
is expressed in this splendid sonnet:

> Dichoso fue el ardor, dichoso el vuelo
> con que, desamparado de la vida,
> dio Ícaro en su gloria esclarecida
> nombre insigne al salado y hondo suelo,
>
> y quien despeñó el rayo donde el cielo
> en la onda del Erídano encendida,
> que llorosa lamenta y afligida
> Lampecie en el hojoso y duro velo.
>
> Pues de uno y otro eterna es la osadía
> y el generoso intento, que a la muerte
> negaron el valor de sus despojos.
>
> Yo, más dichoso que la alta empresa mía,
> que en el olimpo me encumbró mi suerte
> y ardí vivo en la luz de vuestros ojos. [17]

The lover persists in flying to the heart of the blinding light of his
lady's beauty. Icarus and Phaethon flew towards the sun but the heat
forced them to fall. This ambitious lover endures the heat that attracts
him and finds fulfillment in burning alive in the fire of the beloved's

---

[15] Fernando de Herrera, *Poesías,* ed. Vicente García de Diego (Madrid, 1962), p. 55.
[16] *BAE,* XXXII, p. 332.
[17] Herrera, *Rimas inéditas,* ed. José Manuel Blecua (Madrid, 1948), p. 89.

eyes.[18] What greater joy could there be for the Petrarchan lover than this self-immolation? in another sonnet Herrera expresses a similar idea:

> ¡Oh, si pudiera acrecentar la pena
> y avivar más el fuego que me inflama,
> para daros debidos los despojos! [19]

The lover wishes to be burned alive so that his ashes can be offered as a sacrifice on the altar of his beloved's beauty. A similar idea occurs in the Icarus sonnet by Castellani, in which the lover also thinks of his daring as surpassing that of Icarus (see p. 52). The self-perpetuating energy of love is seen here as the Phoenix, an image that is more than once associated with that of Icarus.[20]

In another sonnet the sun which attracts the lover-as-Icarus is his beloved's golden hair.

> ¡Oh vos, que al sol vencido, prestáis fuego,
> en quien mi pensamiento no medroso
> las alas metió libre y perdió el vuelo! [21]

In this case the dazzling beauty of her hair, which is so bright that it lends light to the very sun, proves overpowering and Icarus falls. He does so too in these lines in which the lover compares his fate with those of Icarus and Phaethon once more:

> Vuelo tan alto, que con rayo fiero
> o con el ardiente sol fuera impedido
> si no me diera aliento mi Luz pura;
>
> mas ya que muero como siempre espero,
> ni en mar seré ni en río sumergido;
> que el mundo me será la sepultura.[22]

---

[18] A similar image occurs in a sonnet by Lope:

> Aquí tan loco de mirarla estuve,
> que de niñas sirviendo a sus safiros,
> dentro del sol sin abrasarme anduve.

> (Obras poéticas, ed. Blecua [Barcelona, 1969], I, p. 97.)

[19] BAE, XXXII, p. 262.

[20] Cf. Herrera:

> Ardo todo, y en fuego al fin deshecho,
> me rehago en su llama, y siempre crece
> con el ardor la fuerza y la porfía.

> (BAE, XXXII, p. 282.)

[21] Ibid., p. 279.

[22] Ibid., p. 279.

The lover welcomes death if that is the price of glory, but in his death he will outshine his mythical forerunners. As Icarus fell into a sea and Phaethon into a river, the whole world will be this man's memorial. A similarly grandiose thought informs this stanza at the end of a poem which considers the death of Phaethon:

> Si quiere Amor que del cielo
> encendido bajo muerto,
> lugar pequeño es el suelo [33]
> para tanto desconcierto. [24]

The whole sky could not contain the crash of the tragic climax of such a love.

Perhaps Herrera's finest sonnet on the daring of love symbolized in the flight of Icarus, is this one:

> ¡O cómo buela en alto mi desseo,
> sin que de su osadía el mal fin tema!;
> que ya las puntas de sus alas quema,
> donde ningún remedio al triste veo.
>
> Que mal podrá alabarse del trofeo
> si, estando ufano en la región suprema
> del fuego ardiente, en esta vanda estrema
> cae por su siniestro devaneo.
>
> Devía en mi fortuna ser exemplo
> Dédalo, no aquel joven atrevido
> que dió al cerúleo piélago su nombre.
>
> Mas ya tarde mis lástimas contemplo;
> pero si muero, porque osé, perdido,
> jamás a igual empresa osó algún hombre. [25]

As in Garcilaso's sonnet, the lover is unable to follow the advice that he sees implicit in the fall of Icarus. Daedalus is here considered a positive example for his caution and good sense but for the lover caution is no virtue.

It is difficult to trace precisely the impact of the Icarus tradition

---

[23] The text has "cielo", surely an error for "suelo".
[24] *BAE*, XXXII, p. 342.
[25] Herrera, *Poesías*, ed. García de Diego, p. 90.

on Herrera's poetry. His verse is so full of daring hopes and dreadful disappointments that it is hard to be certain where the myth is alluded to specifically. The image of the lover soaring toward the source of the light of his life is central to Herrera's personal mythology. Icarus and Phaethon are often evoked indirectly, by allusion to a detail from the tradition. Other myths seem sometimes also to be implied. There is apparently no direct allusion in these lines to the myth of Icarus.

> Subí sin procurallo hasta el cielo;
> que se perdió en tal hecho mi osadía.
> Cuando me aventuré me vi en el suelo.[26]

yet the theme is clearly essentially that of the myth. In the following lines the poet's soul flies upward inspired by the fire of the beloved's beauty:

> Fulgor divino, lúcida centella,
> por quien libre mi alma en alto vuelo,
> las alas rojas bate y huye el suelo,
> ardiendo vuestro dulce fuego en ella...[27]

The irresistible consuming fire of love is one of the constants of Herrera's imagery and his lover continually finds himself a complacent victim of it. Nothing could indicate how deeply his poetry is imbued with the spirit of the myths of Icarus and Phaethon than the palinode sonnet with which he prefaced his edition of *Algunas obras:*

> Osé i temí: mas pudo la osadía
> tanto, que desprecié el temor cobarde.
> Subí a do el fuego más m'enciende i arde
> cuanto más la esperanza se desvía.

With regard to his own poetic career, the poet speaks of himself in the same imagery—the daring flight, the fear, the self-renewing energy that attracts and repels. In the final tercet the poet has acknowledged the error of his ways but concludes, as does the lover, that the only honorable course is to persist in his venture, like Icarus ignoring his father's warnings:

[26] *Ibíd.,* p. 108.
[27] *BAE,* XXXII, p. 294.

Sigo al fin mi furor, porque mudarme
no es onra ya, ni justo que s'estime
tan mal de quien tan bien rindió su pecho.[28]

Gabriel Celaya very plausibly suggests that in Herrera, as to some extent in all these poets, the role of poet and that of lover are not very different.[29] The love of the sonneteer is, to some extent, a convention. His love is a poetic attitude. In the following passage from a *canción* the roles of poet and lover appear together:

Jamás alçó las alas alto al cielo,
de rosados colores adornado,
mi tierno i amoroso pensamiento,
que de vos ¡o Luz mía! no olvidado
temiese nombre dar al ancho suelo,
del cerúleo Neptuno hondo assiento,
como aora que el blando y dulçe aliento
del manso Amor, que favorable espira,
temo para cantar la gloria vuestra
si a la alma no me inspira
la lumbre que a subir al cielo adiestra;
porque para estimar tanta belleza,
no ay espíritu igual a su grandeza.[30]

Both his love and the expression of it are doomed to be inadequate, as Icarus' flight was doomed to failure. Herrera's *canciones* often include an expression of the poet's inadequacy to sing the exalted theme he has undertaken, the traditional *petitio humilis*.[31] Sometimes the object of the poet's awe is his beloved. At others it may be a figure at court. The following lines are from a song in praise of don Alonso Pérez de Guzmán, duke of Medina:

Antes pensara, alçando osado el vuelo
por la immensa región de vuestra gloria

---

[28] *Poesías*, p. 16.
[29] Gabriel Celaya, *Exploración de la poesía* (Barcelona, 1964), pp. 15-88.
[30] *Rimas inéditas*, ed. cit., p. 114.
[31] The image of the artist as having wings occurs in the fifteenth century, too. Here is an interesting case of a parallel made between the artist and Phaethon:

El niño Feronte [for Fetonte?], sin seso regido,
tomó grande empresa con simplicidad,
así yo, ilustre señora, vos pido
que me perdonéis con humanidad.

(Iohan de Andújar in Foulché-Delbosc, *Cancionero*, II, p. 215.)

sin perder el dichoso atrevimiento,
entre los puros astros que orna el cielo
con cercos de lumbroso movimiento
vuestra insigne memoria
entrelazar, negando la victoria
del claro nombre al tiempo desdeñoso;
mas, aunque el valor vuestro y su grandeza
no admiten de mis versos la rudeza,
y de Ícaro el suceso peligroso
me vuelva temeroso,
y el riesgo a que me obligo atento veo,
no puedo contrastar a mi desseo.[32]

On another, similar occasion the myths of both Icarus and Phaethon come to mind as expressions of the enormity of the task in hand:

Vuestro valor ecede soberano
al más claro i ecelso entendimiento,
i ciega vuestra luz resplandeciente
los ojos d'el umano sentimiento.
Yo (aunqu'el osado amor me da la mano)
temo d'el hondo Pado la corriente,[33]
i el mar que dentro siente
d'el atrevido joven la caída.[34]

The river and the sea conjure up the two daring rivals of the sun, whose fate the poet, on his flimsy wings, fears to share. Love, often mischievous or malicious, here lends the poet a hand in the task of expressing such great passion. Torquato Tasso expressed the same confidence in Cupid's aid—"Ma chi dee paventare in alta impresa, / s'avvien ch'Amor l'affide?" (see p. 57).

The image of the artist in flight and therefore in danger, often associated with Icarus as it will be so frequently amongst French poets of the nineteenth century,[35] seems to have enjoyed a particular vogue with the translators of Ovid, near contemporaries of Herrera. Pérez Sigler speaks in his prologue of his inspiration in terms of having been given wings. The image of flight also informs one of the dedicatory sonnets to the same translation.

[32] *BAE*, XXXII, p. 315.
[33] "Pado" from Latin Padus = Po.
[34] *Poesías*, p. 259. Cf. also *BAE*, XXXII, p. 276.
[35] See Maurice Shroder, *Icarus; the Image of the Artist in French Romanticism* (Cambridge, Mass., 1961).

Pérez, yo llamo en mi socorro al cielo,
y si la eternidad tiene guardado
valor que nunca se verá menguado
cuanto a la fama le durare el vuelo,

del tesoro inmortal descubra el velo
y abra su seno el que con pecho osado
quiere alcanzar lo que a ninguno es dado
de cuantos hombres han pisado el suelo.[36]

Pérez's admirer wishes the high and danger-fraught exploit to be recognized, as Icarus' is remembered.

At the beginning of the incomplete Mey translation, Ovid's opening lines are expanded to include the metaphor of the poet as Icarus:

Cuerpos en nuevas cosas trasformados
desde el origen y principio humano
siguiendo de uno en otro encadenados
hasta le edad felice de Octaviano,
mis versos cantarán, si levantados
del suelo fueron por la hermosa mano
que pues tuvo poder de trasformarme,
podrá para volar las alas darme.

Que de otra suerte corto es todo vuelo
para llegar adonde yo deseo,
si mi pesada pluma barre el suelo,
y deja atrás las nubes el deseo
que de ensalzaros tengo sobre el cielo
a vos que de la tierra alzáis trofeo,
perlado Augusto, y le ponéis tan alto
que en alabaros todo verso es falto.[37]

The wings on which this Icarus would fly consist of only one feather, the poet's quill, a conceit that recurs, for example, in these lines "de incierto autor" in *Flores de poetas ilustres*:

Tomé la pluma con celo
de celebraros en suma;
mas ¿quién con sola una pluma,
podrá volar a ese cielo? [38]

---

[36] Introductory pages to Pérez Sigler translation.
[37] Prefatory pages to Mey translation.
[38] *BAE, XLII*, p. 9.

In Aldana's sonnet (see p. 65), Cupid offered the lover two feathers with which to fly. Here the poet has to try to fly with only one.

Cervantes, too, composed a sonnet on the theme of Icarus, as the lover this time. It is recited by Cardenio in *La entretenida*. It begins with the traditional evocation of the lover's aspirations flying upward on fragile wings:

> Vuela mi estrecha y débil esperanza
> con flacas alas, y, aunque sube el vuelo
> a la alta cumbre del hermoso cielo,
> jamás el punto que pretende alcanza.

Cervantes' Icarus is aware from the start that he cannot emulate the feat of Icarus, in strong contrast to Herrera's lover who claims to have reached the source of the fatal attraction. In the second quatrain the lover makes the comparison between his ambition and that of Icarus:

> Yo vengo a ser perfecta semejanza
> de aquel mancebo que de Creta el suelo
> dejó, y, contrario de su padre al celo,
> a la región del cielo se abalanza.

Here the allusion to Icarus is largely to his disobedience, which has not been an aspect of the story much stressed before. The poem ends with the certainty that, like Icarus, the lover will be immortalized in the death that his love will surely bring about.

> Caerán mis atrevidos pensamientos,
> del amoroso incendio derretidos
> en el mar del temor turbado y frío;

> pero no llevarán cursos violentos,
> del tiempo y de la muerte prevenidos,
> al lugar del olvido el nombre mío.[39]

But Cervantes cannot long maintain this level of conventional idealism and immediately after reciting these lines, Cardenio turns to the *gracioso*, Torrente, and asks: "¿Comes? Buena pro te haga; / la misma hambre te tome."

[39] Cervantes, *La entretenida* (Act 1), in *Obras completas*, ed. Schevill and Bonilla (Madrid, 1918), III, p. 14.

There is also in Cervantes an interesting prose passage, in *La Galatea,* in which Icarus is used as a pejorative image for lovers who have
only themselves to blame if they continually set their sights too high.
Lenio has complained in a long poem of being treated harshly by
Love. Tirsi, who is older and more learned responds at great length
to the effect that, if lovers are unhappy, they may have only themselves
to blame, for "habría de considerar primero adónde levantaron la fantasía, y si la subieron más arriba de lo que su merecimiento alcança,
no es maravilla que, cual nuevos Ícaros, caigan abrasados en el río de
las miserias, de las cuales no tendrá la culpa Amor, sino su locura".[40]
Tirsi takes one of the favorite images of the courtly love tradition and
turns it against the excesses of some courtly lovers. This is the first
time that Icarus is used as such a clear warning. Cervantes examines
the tradition of the lover who deliberately aims too high and, with
his usual common sense, questions it. Others who follow will treat it
even more critically.

In these early manifestations of the fascination with the figure of
Icarus in lyric poetry we have had to do largely with an Icarus who
symbolizes the noble aspirations of a man who, as lover or artist, sets
out to transcend his humanity and gain immortality in an act of
supreme daring. In the poetry of Spain written during the empire of
Charles V and the early years of the reign of Philip II, a spirit of
adventure and ambition leads to an image of Icarus as an example of
noble courage ill-fated but motivated by an understandable, and even
admirable, ambition for a great goal. To be sure, the view of Icarus
as vain and misguided is not absent but so far it has been outshone
by the glorious portrayal of Icarus as the hero who challenges his fate
and wins immortality. This image will become much more complex
and will even change radically in the poets we shall discuss in the
following chapters.

---

[40] Cervantes, *La Galatea,* ed. Juan Bautista Avalle-Arce (Madrid, 1961), II, p. 66.

Chapter 5

ICARUS MOCKED

One of the marks of the great poet is, I suppose, the ability to breathe new life into established tradition. A good part of the genius of Luis de Góngora seems to lie, not in the discovery of any new theme nor in the use of original techniques, but rather in the ability to emulate and outdo his predecessors within the canon that they had consecrated. Part of the heritage that came down to Góngora was the frequency of allusion to classical mythology, a convention that was, at Góngora's hands, vitally enriched yet critically altered. The same inventive genius that created sublime effects along quite traditional lines, led also to parody. Góngora's images—"serpiente de cristal", "mariposa en cenizas desatada"—involve a startlingly personal freshness of vision. With inimitable wit he explores irreverently all the possibilities inherent in the tradition, whether they lead to the most lofty idealism or to the bitterest skepticism.

The myth of Icarus seems to have exercised a particular appeal for don Luis. Perhaps there was something in his poetic career or his private life, both marked so persistently by ambition and disappointment, that encouraged this, but of all the poets of the period none has found the figure so fascinating and so suggestive. In the work of Herrera and Villamediana, to be sure, one can find frequent references to the myth, but not the range of attitudes to it nor the ingenious complexities that it inspired in Góngora. In a poetic world expressed in a language of tensions between ambition and fear, vanity and humility, rivalry and flight, the myth of the bold but ill-fated flight of Icarus seems to hold a special place.

Some of Góngora's evocations of the myth are conventional enough. The young Greek was for Herrera and others sometimes the symbol of the artist risking all for his art. So too in don Luis, as the following *décima* shows:

> Por más daños que presumas,
>   vuela, Ícaro español,

que al templo ofreces del Sol
en poca cera tus plumas.
Blanco túmulo de espumas
haga el Betis a tus huesos;
que tus gloriosos excesos,
si de mi Musa los fías,
los venerarán los días
en los álamos impresos.[1] (Millé 152)

Unlike the poet addressed by Horace (*Odes* IV, 2), this artist, a fellow *andaluz,* is exhorted to ignore the dangers of flying too high and think instead of the immortality that may be his. Góngora seems to assure his fellow poet that, if he follows his own Muse, he will be sure of fame.

Icarus is not the only mythological figure in the poem. The traditional association between Icarus and Phaethon influences Góngora as he interweaves the two myths here. The river into which this Icarus runs the risk of falling suggests the convergence of the two stories and by the time we come to the poplars in the last line, Icarus seems to have metamorphosed into Phaethon. The mingling of more than one myth—not always deliberate, perhaps—becomes gradually more common, as we shall see, and is intimately involved with another trend, the reduction of mythological figures from the foreground to the background. A great many of the early evocations of Icarus were narrative, reproducing the outline of the story as told by Ovid. Now, as the story is becoming more familiar, more may be taken for granted and the trick is to refer to the character or story as succinctly or elliptically as possible. The figures of mythology appear fleetingly, or in miniature, rather than occupying center stage.

Don Luis' best known work in the Icarus tradition is this one, writen when he was twenty-three years old:

No enfrene tu gallardo pensamiento
del animoso joven mal logrado
el loco fin, de cuyo vuelo osado
fue ilustre tumba el húmido elemento.

Las dulces alas tiende al blando viento,
y sin que el torpe mar del miedo helado

---

[1] Góngora, *Obras completas,* ed. Millé (6th ed. Madrid, 1967). All references to Góngora's work will be to this edition. Short poems will be identified in the text by number and longer works by page.

tus plumas moje, toca levantado
la encendida región del ardimiento.

Corona en puntas la dorada esfera
do el pájaro real su vista afina,
y al noble ardor desátese la cera;

que al mar, do tu sepulcro se destina,
gran honra le será, y a su ribera,
que le hurte su nombre tu rüina.[2] (Millé 241)

Like the previous poem, this sonnet is an exhortation to self-confidence.
The person addressed is to ignore, as the *persona* of Garcilaso's sonnet
XII had done, the dangers exemplified in the story of Icarus and think
instead of the glory to be earned, even posthumously. The adventure
—and it is not clear whether the theme of this poem is amorous or
artistic—may lead to disaster but it will confer immortality.[3]

As in many previous poems in the same tradition, Icarus is not
mentioned by name. He is referred to elliptically in the second line
and the remainder of the poem tells the familiar story as if the young
person addressed were himself Icarus. The use of ellipsis is carried to
extremes. The sea is "húmido elemento", a synecdoche fairly common
in Góngora.[4] Another elliptical expression presents the sun by a further
reference to mythology, "dorada esfera / do el pájaro real su vista
afina", an allusion to the traditional belief that the eagle, sacred to
Jupiter, could look at the sun without being blinded. So Icarus' nemesis
is a gilded sphere on which the royal bird hones its sight! One allusion
is built upon another as Góngora skillfully creates a complex image
from fragments of others.

---

[2]   In the case of the sonnets, I have used the text of Biruté Ciplijauskaité (*Sonetos
completos*, Madrid, 1969). This sonnet appears on page 131. Ciplijauskaité's reading
"tiende" in line 5 is clearly better than Millé's "tienden". In line 9, "puntas" is a
term from falconry meaning, according to Alemany "parada o vuelta que da el hal-
cón cambiando de dirección en su vuelo". The interlocutor of the poem, as an eagle,
is to crown the sun by making these turns about it.
[3]   Ciplijauskaité points out (p. 131) that several epigraphs indicate the possibility
that the poem was addressed to don Luis Gaytán de Ayala, a poet. It is possible that
the poem is an exhortation to artistic daring, though Robert Jammes (*Études sur l'oeuvre
poétique de Luis de Góngora*, Bordeaux, 1967), treats it as a love sonnet (p. 361).
[4]   There is already a tradition for this synecdoche associated with Icarus. Cf. Sannazaro's sonnet (p. 50), in which Icarus falls into "un mar sì spacïoso, uno elemento",
Alemany lists several cases of Góngora's using the image of a liquid or diaphanous
element to refer to the sea or the air. Cf. also p. 91 of this chapter: "bien que todo
un elemento / de lágrimas urna es poca".

The sonnet is enormously rich in allusions. In a reversal of the usual formula "nombre al mar ha dado...", "puso al mar eterno nombre...",[5] Góngora would have his interlocutor steal the name of the sea into which he falls and the shores nearby. Góngora recalls the tradition that few poets before him refer to, the naming of the island of Ikaria. There is also a rather obscure precedent in Latin literature for the idea of Icarus' stealing the name from the sea, in Seneca's *Oedipus*—"nomen eripuit freto" (see p. 20). To the traditional imagery of the protagonist suspended between his high goal and possible disaster, poles represented by the sun and the sea, don Luis adds an observation that accentuates even more strongly the agony of the situation. In line 6 the sea is referred to as "el torpe mar del miedo helado". The source of the threat is seen as fear itself made concrete. The real danger to the young man is his lack of confidence, an interpretation of the story that a modern psychologist might well accept.

The tradition of the lover as victim of the headiness of his own thoughts goes back certainly as far as Petrarch—"Volo can l'ali del pensiero al cielo..." it is continued by Tansillo (see p. 53) and becomes a constant commonplace of Renaissance poetry. The opening lines of the play *Las firmezas de Isabela* show that Góngora follows the lead of his predecessors:

> ¿De qué seno infernal, oh pensamiento,
>   o, por dónde has venido,
> si de tus alas torpes huye el viento? (Millé, p. 709)

Marcelo's thoughts here are gloomy and thus borne on clumsy wings. Elsewere, it may be the sighs of the lover that fly to his loved one, as in the *romance piscatorio*. "En el caudaloso río..." (Millé 5). In the hope of seeing the woman he loves, the fisherman rows nearer to the shore but is careful to avoid frightening her.

> Y aunque el deseo de verla,
> para apresurarle, arma
> de otros remos la barquilla
> y el corazón de otras alas,
> porque la ninfa no huya,
> no llega más que a distancia
> de donde tan solamente
> escuche aquesto que canta... (Millé, p. 47)

---

[5] Cf. Garcilaso's sonnet XII and Cetina's "Amor mueve mis alas..." (see p. 60).

His heart flies to her side as he approaches and he addresses his sighs in a manner very reminiscent of the by now familiar apostrophe to the amorous thought:

> Volad al viento, suspiros,
> y mirad quien os levanta
> de un pecho que es tan humilde
> a partes que son tal altas. (Millé, p. 47)

Sometimes the flight of Icarus, now also a commonplace, seems to under-lie a related image. Here the "otras alas" as well as the "partes tan altas" (with the play on the word "partes"?) suggest a high, dangerous flight, though there is no evidence to prove a direct reference to Icarus.

In the *romance* "Minguilla la siempre bella..." (Millé 84), Gil's love for the beautiful shepherdess is expressed in terms of clear though indirect allusions to the flight of Daedalus' son:

> Gil desde sus tiernos años
> aras le erigió devoto,
> humildemente celando
> tanto culto aun de sí propio.
> Profanólo alguna vez
> pensamiento que, amoroso,
> volando en cera atrevida
> nadó, en desengaños loco. (Millé, p. 231)

In the context of a love between two people with such rustic names as Gil and Minguilla, the altars and rites of such an ideal love are out of place. The illusion of this ideal love is created only so that it can be spoiled by the intrusion of a daring thought, the breaking of the spell of courtly love by the thought of profane, or physical, attraction. Gil's bold thought falls like Icarus in this case the fall leads only to a swim in the nearby Tagus. In this context the reference to the world of Ovidian mythology is incongruous, gently mocking Gil's pretensions to courtly love while at the same time the juxtaposition Gil/Icarus must detract from the stature of the myth. In some of Góngora's poems Icarus is often in much less exalted company than in the works of previous poets. This has the effect of making his image more complex, more flexible, but the high idealism attached to many earlier evocations is attenuated by more frivolous or less flattering associations.

The subject of the devaluation of mythological imagery will concern us more directly in due course.

In the *canción* "Qué de invidiosos montes...", once again the lover's thoughts don wings in order to fly to the beloved's side. At the end of the first stanza, in which the poet expresses sadness at the distance between him and his lady, he says: "el noble pensamiento / por verte viste plumas, pisa el viento." Góngora wittily sees the wings this lover's thoughts will fly upon as the plumes of fashion. The theme of vanity is always dear to Góngora; this thought is noble and must dress accordingly.

In the *letrilla* "Hágasme tantas mercedes..." (Millé XXXIII) the poet begs his thoughts not to fly too high nor to leave the confines of his room. They must be humble and remain secret. This is the refrain:

> Hágasme tantas mercedes,
> temerario pensamiento
> que no te fíes del viento,
> ni penetres las paredes.[6] (Millé, p. 424)

In the first stanza the poor lover appeals to the personification of his dangerous thoughts by recourse to the cautionary tale of Icarus:

> Pensamiento, no presumas
> tanto de tu humilde vuelo,
> que el sujeto pisa el cielo,
> y al suelo bajan las plumas:
> otro barrió las espumas
> del Mediterráneo Mar,
> pudiendo mejor volar
> que tú ahora volar puedes.

The second stanza presents another warning, in the shape of Acteon who, because of rashness induced by Eros, was torn to pieces by his own hounds. Once again, as in previous examples, two myths are woven together.

In the *letrilla* "¡La vaga esperanza mía..." (Millé 164), the refrain is similar to that of the *letrilla* just discussed:

---

[6] In the case of the *letrillas*, though using Millé numbers for reference, I shall use the text of Robert Jammes (*Letrillas de Luis de Góngora*, Paris, 1963). "Hágasme tantas mercedes..." is on page 25 and "La vaga esperanza mía..." on page 13. Jammes considers the former authentic, while for Millé it belongs to the "letrillas atribuibles".

¡La vaga esperanza mía
se ha quedado en vago, ay triste!
¿Quien alas de cera viste,
cuán mal de mi Sol las fía? (Millé, p. 361)

This time it is the lover's hopes that are reminded of the potential
hazards of setting their sights too high. As in Herrera the danger lies
in a lady whose poetic name is Sol. In the verse the story of Icarus
underlies the narration of the lover's hopes, drowned, as in Hurtado's
endechas, in his own tears:

Atrevida se dio al viento
mi vaga esperanza, tanto,
que las ondas de mi llanto
infamó su atrevimiento,[7]
bien que todo un elemento
de lágrimas urna es poca.[8]
¿Qué dire a cera tan loca,
o a tan alada osadía?

The butterfly has a long history as an image in lyric poetry. The
idea of the butterfly attracted fatally to the flame which is his undoing
is obviously very close to the essence of the story of the fall of Icarus,
as we have already seen in the case of the sonnet by Fascitello.[9] Góngora has a particularly fine sonnet in the butterfly tradition, in which
there is evidence of contamination by the story of Icarus.

Mariposa, no solo no cobarde,
mas temeraria, fatalmente ciega,
lo que la llama al Fénix aun le niega,
quiere obstinada que a sus alas guarde:

pues en su daño arrepentida tarde,
del esplendor solicitada, llega

---

[7] In this line as in line 8 of the sonnet "Icaro de bayeta..." (see p. 92), the
tradition that Icarus gave honour to the sea into which he fell by conferring his
name upon it is turned round and the falls of these flyers will bring discredit on
the sea into which they fall.

[8] See note 4 above. Also cf. *Polifemo* 1. 492, "urna es mucha, pirámide no poca".
In each case a cataclysmic death is referred to by means of the reference to the
funeral urn, in one case presented as too small to contain the catastrophe and, in
the case of the rock that killed Acis, bigger than is necessary.

[9] See Don Cameron Allen, *Image and Meaning* (Baltimore, 1960) chapter 2:
"Muiopotmos, or the Fate of the Butterflie" (pp. 20-41).

a lo que luce, y ambiciosa entrega
su mal vestida pluma a lo que arde.

Yace gloriosa en la que dulcemente
huesa le ha prevenido abeja breve,
¡suma felicidad a yerro sumo!

No a mi ambición contrario tan luciente,
menos activo sí, cuanto más leve,
cenizas la hará, si abrasa el humo. (Millé, 372)

In her edition of Góngora's sonnets, Biruté Ciplijauskaité (p. 236) refers us to Herrera's "La incauta y descuidada mariposa..." [10] The comparison only reinforces the impression, not just of don Luis' originality, but of the identification in his mind between this image and that of Icarus. The moth falls to a liquid grave in the wax of the candle and its fall is characterized in terms reminiscent of the traditional attitude to Icarus' flight, Tansillo's "l'honor fia eterno se mortal e il salto (see p. 53). Again, is "mal vestida pluma" merely a gongoresque expression of the fragility of the insect's wings or is there perhaps also a reminiscence of the unnatural wings that Daedalus made for his son?

Thus far Góngora's variations on the theme of Icarus as a symbol of man's fate have remained fairly conventional. In the tradition of Garcilaso and Cetina, Icarus has been the image of the daring but ill-fated lover or artist borne aloft on Cupid's wings or those of his Muse, or he has symbolized the boldness of the lover's thoughts, although we have already seen some evidence of the gradual devaluation of the myth in its evocation in non-courtly and ironic contexts. But in the work of don Luis we can also find a broadening of the range of applications of the myth and a diversification of the contexts in which it appears. One of the most striking examples of a brilliantly original evocation of the myth is a remarkable satirical sonnet. To mourn the death in 1611 of Queen Margaret, the wife of Philip III, the city of Écija built an elaborate catafalque which Góngora celebrates thus:

Ícaro de bayeta, si de pino
Cíclope no, tamaño como el rollo,
¿volar quieres con alas a lo pollo,
estando en cuatro pies a lo pollino?

---

[10] Herrera, *Rimas inéditas*, p. 59.

¿Qué Dédalo te induce peregrino
a coronar de nubes el meollo,
si las ondas que cl Betis de su escollo
desata, ha de infamar tu desatino? [11]

No des más cera al Sol, que es bobería,
funeral avestruz, máquina alada,
ni alimentes gacetas en Europa.

Aguarda a la ciudad, que a mediodía,
si masse Duelo no en capirotada,
la servirá masse Bochorno en sopa.[12] (Millé 315)

Here is Góngora at his derisive best. The iconoclastic opening taunt, "flannel Icarus", emphasized by the accented initial syllable, leads into a complex of pejorative references characterized largely by the contrast between the sublimity of the flight of Icarus and the grotesque pretentiousness of the edifice. The monument is Icarus in its vanity but earthbound in its bulk and mundane in its materials. It tries to be a bird (a chicken!) but is an ass in its ponderousness. Instead of conferring immortal fame on the waters into which he falls, this Icarus will only bring discredit ("ha de infamar") on the anyhow shallow waters of the Guadalquivir, if indeed he manages to get off the ground. Again the context in which the myth is evoked has the effect of devaluating it.

In *Las firmezas de Isabela* a young man who is to be married is seen as an unwilling Icarus, "que entre rayos y entre olas, / si no se quema las plumas, / a fe que no se las moja" (Millé, p. 730). Lelio is

---

[11] See note 8 above.

[12] This sonnet raises some problems of interpretation. An index of its difficulty is that Alemany lists no fewer than 9 words *(rollo, pollino, meollo, escollo, gacetas, masse, Duelo, capirotada, Bochorno)* as having unique or unusual applications in this sonnet. The gist is clear, I think, although details like the edifice being described as "Cíclope" are obscure. Ciplijauskaité tells us (p. 180) that "el rollo de Écija era una gran columna de granito universalmente conocida". References to it may also be found in the *Diablo cojuelo* (Madrid, 1922), p. 150 and in Delicado's *La lozana Andaluza* (Madrid, 1871), p. 320. In lines 3 and 4, Góngora plays on the semantic difference that now separates the cognates *pollo* and *pollino*. (The Latin word *pullus* meant the young of any species.) In line 8, Millé has "desata han de...", which is evidently an error. "Meollo" means, according to Alemany, "la parte más elevada", so lines 5 and 6 seem to ask why this monument makes so much smoke with its candles when its foolishness will only discredit the river (as the wax flows into it?). The word "capirotada" is a pun on a cooking term, a sauce rather like a *sofrito* and "capirotado", meaning wearing a cape, as if in mourning. For further thoughts on this sonnet see Brockhaus, *Góngoras Sonettendichtung* (Bochum, 1935), pp. 144-145.

not yet burning up with ardor for the lady in question—he has not
even met her—but he is determined to take no risks of any kind. This
Icarus needs no warnings about the perils of love. He already considers
marriage "la más estrecha mazmorra / que tiene Argel" and so he
asks permission of his father to leave the city. Icarus is reduced to
the level of the reluctant bridegroom. We have come a long way from
Tansillo and Garcilaso.

In the same play Góngora gives us our first female Icarus. Violante,
hurt by her supposed rejection by Marcelo and piqued by a suggestion
of Tadeo, the *gracioso*, that she has already given herself to the man
she loves, defends herself haughtily:

> La bien nacida mujer
> de honrada peca y altiva;
>   y orillas del mar espera
> sus ruinas, sin cuidar
> si no diere nombre al mar,
> que el suyo en las ondas muera. (Millé, p. 767)

Violante is Icarus in her pride and self-respect. Just as Icarus' flight
could be a sin for some, she talks of the sin of her pride. In a brilliant
inversion of tradition, she cares little if her pride will not make her
immortal. She, as a woman, must avoid fame even if this means
obscurity.

Perhaps the most ingenious Icarus of all occurs in the same play.
Emilio is showing Galeazo the wonders of Toledo ("ciudad metrópoli
de España) and Galeazo osks: "¿Y aquél quién es, que con ocado vuelo / a la casa de el rey le pone escalas?" To which Emilio replies:

> El Tajo, que hecho Ícaro, a Juanelo,
> Dédalo cremonés, le pidió alas,
> y temiendo después al Sol el Tajo,
> tiende sus alas por allí debajo. (Millé, p. 776)

The reference is to the ingenious scheme of the Italian architect Jua-
nelo Turriano [13] to raise the waters of the Tagus, by a system of locks,
to the level of the city of Toledo. Góngora sees the river, in its vain
effort to rise upwards toward the city, as Icarus, doomed to failure.

---

[13] See Quevedo, *Buscón*, ed. Américo Castro, note on page 95 and Conde de Ce-
dillo, *Toledo en el siglo XVI* (Madrid, 1901), pp. 93 and 150.

The myth that we have seen so frequently as an isolated image in shorter poems, is tightly woven into the fabric of Góngora's masterpiece, *Soledades*.[14] Images of flight, as elsewhere in his work, are common in the poem—Cupid, Hymen, Phaethon, Daedalus, even Dido, and the birds and insects all have wings. Flight is used as a metaphor for unusual speed—the wind flies (II, 184), as does a boat (II, 46), and even the pilgrim himself is said, at the beginning of the poem, to scale a cliff that would daunt the very birds (I, 49-51). Flight and feathers are also associated with the pride and vanity that are constant preoccupations of the poem. *Soledades* contrasts the innocent simplicity of an idealized rustic existence with the vanity and greed of life at court. One of the commonest interpretations of the myth of Icarus, that pride comes before a fall, is the overt message of several short scenes, but is also at the very heart of the poem, expressed persistently in the symbol of Icarus' rash flight.

The first reference to the myth is made by the pilgrim himself. He has fallen, like Icarus, into the sea as a result of a flight from imprisonment, but he survives to reach a deserted shore. He climbs a cliff and is led by a distant light, at one point seen as a nocturnal sun (I, 76), to the encampment of some goatherds. This is part of his rapturous apostrophe to his new surroundings:

> No a la soberbia está aquí la mentira
> dorándole los pies, en cuanto gira
>   la esfera de sus plumas,
> ni de los rayos baja a las espumas
>   favor de cera alado. (I, 129-33)

At the center of the young man's statement of the major theme of the poem, appears the figure of Icarus falling headlong as in contemporary woodcuts, expressing the precarious nature of favor at court, dependent on self-serving flattery and deceit, and subject to sudden changes of fortune. Dámaso Alonso's prose version of these lines is more specific than the poem:

> ni se dan aquí las espantosas caídas de los validos
> que, nuevos Ícaros, vuelan con alas de cera y,
> arrimándose a los príncipes, con el mismo calor de los

---

[14] The importance of the image of Icarus in *Soledades* has already been treated by L. J. Woodward in "Two images in the *Soledades* of Góngora", *Modern Language Notes*, LXXVI (1961), pp. 773-785.

> rayos del poder se les funde a veces la cera y desde
> la altura, van a caer al mar de la desgracia...[15]

The pilgrim is invited to a wedding and, as part of the festivities, he witnesses an athletic contest, in which one of the competitors is identified with Icarus.

> ...Bien que impulso noble
> de gloria, aunque villano, solicita
> a un vaquero de aquellos montes, grueso,
>   membrudo, fuerte roble,
> que, ágil a pesar de lo robusto,
> al aire se arrebata, violentando
> lo grave tanto, que lo precipita
> —Ícaro montañés— su mismo peso,
> de la menuda hierba el seno blando
> piélago duro hecho a su rüina. (I, 1002-11)

These games are the innocent pastime of simple country people. The flight of the athlete is not motivated by greed or excessive ambition, rather, ironically, by a "noble" desire for winning and so he falls without harm into the soft grass. This Icarus asserts rather than denies his humanity.

In *Soledad* II, the pilgrim is amongst fisherfolk on the seashore. References to the story of Icarus continue, the first in this part being the evocation of one the nets the fishermen use:

> recurren no a las redes que, mayores,
> mucho océano y pocas aguas prenden,
> sino a las que ambiciosas menos penden,
> laberinto nudoso de marino
> Dédalo, si de leño no, de lino,
> fábrica escrupulosa, y aunque incierta,
> siempre murada, pero siempre abierta. (II, 74-80)

Here it is Icarus' ingenious father, who created the labyrinth from which they were escaping, whom Góngora recalls. Shortly afterward comes the well-known passage where the young man himself makes the analogy between his situation and that of Daedalus' son. He has escaped from a prison ("... me fuerza a que huya / de su prisión..." II, 134-5)—the metaphorical prison of courtly love. He sees the object of

---

[15] *Soledades,* ed. Dámaso Alonso (3rd ed.), p. 121.

his devotion, in a tradition we recognize immediately, as so dazzlingly beautiful that his attraction is dangerous.

> Audaz mi pensamiento
> el cenit escaló, plumas vestido,
>   cuyo vuelo atrevido
> —si no ha dado su nombre a tus espumas—
>   de sus vestidas plumas
> conservarán el desvanecimiento
> los anales diáfanos del viento.
>
> Esta, pues, culpa mía
> el timón alternar menos seguro
>   y el báculo más duro
> un lustro ha hecho a mi dudosa mano,
>   solicitando en vano
> las alas sepultar de mi osadía
> donde el sol nace o donde muere el día. (II, 137-50)

The myth is familiar enough to Góngora's readers that he can refer to it concisely and give it an original twist that reinforces the vanity of the exploit. This fall will live on, not in the name of a sea, but blowing in the wind. The image is still present a few lines later, when the rejected lover says that his great love deserves to have as its memorial "urna suya el océano profundo" (II, 163). When the old fisherman reminisces about his life at sea and upon the dangers of navigation, he refers to the sea as granting to those who die in it, including the greedy colonizers of the New World, no more than "túmulos de espuma" (II, 406).

Soledad I ended with a sporting scene and it is no accident that Soledad II does also. The difference between them is so great, though, that some have thought the hawking sequence out of tone with the rest of the poem. Robert Jammes, for example, says:

> Quant à la promenade en barque du lendemain elle nous éloigne tout à fait du sujet. Cette cinquième journée jure avec les précédentes: nous quittons les huttes des chevriers ou les cabanes des pêcheurs pour aller vers un ostentatoire palais de marbre et c'est une très aristocratique chasse au faucon qui est longuement décrite: ce long passage n'a plus rien à voir avec les Soledades proprement dites, et la réapparition, à la fin, d'humbles chaumières autour desquelles picorent des volailles, ressemble à un remords tardif de Góngora.[16]

[16] Jammes, Etudes, pp. 583-4.

L. J. Woodward points out quite correctly that, if this scene is different from the others in the work, the difference is quite deliberate. Góngora prepares the change meticulously [17]. The horn, which heralds the appearance of the band of hunters, is "ronca" (II, 710), "duro son" (714). The prince who leads the hunt is, in contrast to the sturdy countrymen, "en miembros no robusto" (810). The hawks are "escándalo bizarro / del aire" (753-4) or "infestador... / de las aves (772-3). This invasion of the idyllic countryside by the pomp of the court is clearly decried by the poet. If we need the point made more clearly, this passage also contains within it a short parable about the hunter who is himself hunted:

> galán... valiente, fatigando
>   tímida liebre, cuando
> intempestiva salteó leona
>   la melionesa gala,
>   que de trágica escena
> mucho teatro hizo poca arena. (766-71)

Most importantly, though, as Woodward sees clearly, the details of the hunt offer a fascinating parable in themselves. Briefly what happens is this: after the death of the flycatcher, a crow appears, greedily hiding a snail whose shell the poet compares to a ruby. The bird calls together a flock of other crows who darken the sky so that an owl thinks it is night, opens its eyes and spreads its wings. The crows are attracted to the gold in the twin suns of the owl's eyes and they fly toward them. One of the birds is punished for its greed and becomes the ball in a fatal game of tennis, losing its feathers and finally expiring. The crow flies toward the gold of the sun, loses its feathers and falls to its death. The parallel, in a poem whose theme has elsewhere been underlined by reference to the myth of Icarus, is obvious.

On several important occasions and in smaller details, the symbolism of the myth of Icarus is worked into the complex imagery of *Soledades*. He appears as a conventional symbol of overweening ambition and as the bold but ill-fated lover. The   references are often oblique, even cryptic, and are often connected with other stories, those of Phaethon or the Phoenix. In lines like the following, it seems that Góngora has Icarus in mind as well as the Phoenix, since it is the sun which burns the feathers of the mythical bird.

---

[17] See p. 95, n. 14.

> Este, pues, Sol que a olvido lo condena
> cenizas hizo las que a su memoria
> negras plumas vistio... (I, 737-9)

The sources of Góngora's references to the Icarus myth and of his attitudes to it, are to be found in accessible poetic traditions. In his hands a convention like that of the lover who emulates the boldness of Icarus, takes on abundant new life. And even where don Luis seems to break most sharply with tradition, creating original, sometimes startling new associations for the myth—making Icarus a river or a woman—he is merely taking innovation a logical step further along a familiar path. He plays the old tunes in a new way and fresh tunes upon traditional instruments and in conventional modes. The question whether the novelty of Góngora's poetry is "the natural consequence of an evolution which began with the classical Renaissance style of Garcilaso de la Vega, dominant in the sixteenth century," or "the indecorous result of an eccentric litorary heresy," [18] implies a false dichotomy. His poetry is a natural, though brilliantly original, development of the tradition to which he was heir, but this does not mean that his critics are mistaken when they see something radically new in it. As Andrée Collard expresses it, "los ataques contra la 'nueva poesía' no apuntaban tanto a la intensificación de recursos estilísticos (cultismo y concepto) de tradición renacentista, y presentes en la literatura española antes de Góngora, como a la manera, discrepante y orgullosa, con que Góngora los utilizaba." [19]

Góngora's scandalous innovation was the arrogant freedom with which he handled traditional material, a freedom that has come to be prized by many modern readers. It may be that great originality was responsible in part for what seems, with exceptions of course, to be a decline in lyric inspiration in the seventeenth century. He was certainly not a bad example but perhaps his very brilliance dazzled and deterred his successors. Or perhaps it is, as T. E. Hulme suggests, that "each field of artistic activity is exhausted by the first great artist who gathers a full hervest from it." [20] It is tempting to cast Góngora's effect on the Spanish Petrarchist tradition in this light. His was surely a hard act to follow.

[18] Elías Rivers, "Introduction" to *The Solitudes of Luis de Góngora*, trans. Gilbert F. Cunningham (Baltimore, 1968), p. xv.
[19] Andrée Collard, *Nueva poesía, conceptismo, culteranismo en la crítica española* (Madrid, 1971), p. ix.
[20] T. E. Hulme, *Speculations* (New York, 1924), p. 122.

Chapter 6

ICARUS CHIDED

The rehabilitation of the gods and heroes of classical antiquity, though its effects are still evident today, was in a sense short-lived. By the early years of the seventeenth century attitudes to mythology are clearly changing. The almost pagan celebration of the old stories gives way to a more sober vision in which there is room for irony, disapproval and even flat condemnation. This change has its roots in a more profound axiological evolution whose complexities, for Spain at least, Stephen Gilman goes a long way toward explaining in his "Introduction to the Ideology of the Baroque in Spain." [1] He attributes the development of the new dominant ideology to the attempt to implement the reforms envisioned by the Church at the Council of Trent. He sees a transition from a philosophy based on Neo-Platonic ideals, with their emphasis on the possibility for personal transcendence (reflected in the writings of philosophers like Pico and Ficino and in the works of the mystics) to one based on a faith in a divinely-ordered system offering fulfillment only in the hereafter (expressed in the writings of the ascetic moralists and in the sermons of the preachers). In Gilman's words, "asceticism rejected philosophies of *voluntad* and love, philosophies leading the individual to a personal solution of the problem of existence, in favor or stoic reliance on *entendimiento* and disdain" (p. 93), bringing about a return to the dogmatism of the Middle Ages which, despite the apparent revolution of humanism, had never lost much ground.

We have seen that Icarus represented for the poets one of the basic dilemmas of the human condition, the tension between the desire for personal self-fulfillment and the often disastrous consequences of such efforts. The spokesmen for a return to a more traditionally Christian world-view simply denied the existence of such a dilemma and, in their

---

[1] *Symposium*, I (1946), pp. 82-107.

allegorical and rationalizing commentaries on the ancient myths, attempted to reduce the heroes of mythology, with their potential for providing ideals in conflict with the teachings of the Church,   to human—and even less than human—terms.[2] Mythology again began to be, as it had been for the writers of the Middle Ages, a source of Christian morality. Since we are dealing with artists, whose prime concern need not be moral, and largely with love poetry, we should not expect to see the change in attitude complete or exclusive of other views, but, in most cases, Icarus is, for the poets we shall consider in this chapter, a negative model for conduct, a source of "escarmiento."

Velázquez's portrait of Mars is one of the clearest examples of the same process manifested in the art of painting. Fierce Mars is reduced, in the words of José López-Rey, to a man with a "flabby torso ., uncouth, dull and quite human features," a victim of rather "unheroic weakness." Velázquez achieves a "masterful scaling down of a god to a human shape—and a worthless one at that".[3] This critical view of the mythological figures, who had been treated with such respect by artists not too many years before, is also part of a general trend toward realism, in the sense of an emphasis on the less attractive aspects of human life, so that portraying the folly of the gods and heroes has the impact of a "double-edged parody of the false world of fable and of sinful human ways." López-Rey wrote those words (p. 44) about another mythological painting by Velázquez, the "Triumph of Bacchus," which was so far from a conventional treatment of the subject that it has been traditionally known as "Los borrachos."

Returning to poetry, we must also take into account, when talking of the baroque poets, the important developments in style concomitant with the ideological changes we have been discussing. These developments have in recent years traditionally, though not always precisely or usefully, been labelled culteranismo, the persistent use of a highly conventionalized language rich in neologism and latinism, the latter both syntactical and lexical; and conceptismo, a propensity for complex and highly intellectual metaphors, or "conceits." These tend to mean, as we look at mythological poetry, an ever increasing complexity of allusion (sometimes leading to obscurity), partly out of a belief that

---

[2] This had the dual advantage of exploiting the literary fashion for pedagogical ends and of disarming a potentially dangerous rival system of values at the same time.
[3] José López-Rey, Velázquez, a Catalogue Raisonné of his Oeuvre (London, 1963), p. 73. The introductory essay to this work appeared, slightly altered, as Velázquez's Life and World (London, 1968).

such complexity enhances art [4] and partly because of the constant necessity for originality within an already extremely conventional tradition. This trend toward greater obliqueness of reference may account for Fucilla's finding that, in the seventeenth century, "las versiones [del mito de Ícaro] que aparecen... son pocas y esporádicas." [5] What this means is that evocations of the kind we have seen in Garcilaso, Cetina and others, in which there is a sustained reference to, and even narration of, the events of the story as traditionally told, become less frequent. What happens is that, as the myth becomes more familiar it may be evoked by a simpler, often less direct, allusion—to feathers, to wax, to the sea as a tomb. Icarus continues as a source of inspiration, appearing in an even greater variety of contexts and guises and embodying, in many cases, ideals quite different from those he represented for the poets of earlier generations.

Lope de Vega

Icarus still appears, for example, as he did in Herrera, as the humble poet expressing his awe at the great task he has undertaken. We see him in this role in Lope de Vega, a prolific, if not always precise, user of mythological references. In the dedicatory sonnet to doña Leonora Pimentel which introduces La Filomena, the poet, in the dual role of lover and artist, expresses his inadequacy in language whose syntax is as complex as any Lope ever criticized in Góngora.

> Las plumas abrasó rayo febeo
> del que miró su luz, águila humana,
> lince infeliz, por sendas de oro y grana,
> jamás tocadas de mortal deseo.

> No menos alto el pensamiento veo
> que me conduce a vos, oh soberana
> deidad, oh sol, que mi esperanza vana
> Dédalo mira, y teme Prometeo.

---

[4] There are many texts that attest to this tenet, among them there is the famous letter of Góngora in which he defends his obscurity as a worthwhile intellectual exercise and talks of the inadvisability of casting pearls before swine (Millé, pp. 894-898), and Luis de Carrillo y Sotomayor's Libro de la erudición poética (ed. Manuel Cardenal Iracheta, Madrid, 1946).

[5] Fucilla, Etapas..., p. 83.

> Si de mis alas el incendio culpa
> vuestra sangre real y entendimiento,
> dulce ambición de gloria me disculpa;
>
> que, cayendo del sol mi pensamiento,
> vuestro mismo valor tendrá la culpa,
> y el castigo tendrá mi atrevimiento.[6]

Icarus is evoked in the first quatrain in one of those periphrases which are becoming more common, this time involving two legendary creatures, the eagle, credited by popular tradition with the ability to look unharmed at the sun, and the lynx which was believed to be able to see through material objects. Icarus is an "águila humana" in setting his sights on the sun and, when his daring leads to tragedy, "lince infeliz." The familiar parallel is then made between the flight of Icarus and the lofty aspirations of the poet—"no menos alto el pensamiento veo / que me conduce a vos..." In his hopes he is like Daedalus, the artificer of flight, the artist supreme, but his fears suggest the image of Prometheus who was punished for reaching a forbidden goal. Icarus is just one element in a complex of mythological and other allusions whose theme is that of the superhuman nature of the poet's undertaking. The idea of the burning of Icarus' wings, which is not present in Ovid or the translations, appears to be the result of the continual linking of the myth of Icarus with that of Phaethon, whose fall did involve flames. The frequency with which Icarus is said to fall in flames suggests contamination by the imagery of the other myth.

In another poem by Lope, Icarus and the eagle appear together, along with other images. This is the second quatrain of the sonnet "Al sol que os mira, por miraros, miro...:"

> Águila soy, a salamandra aspiro;
> este Dédalo Amor me está animando;
> pero anochece y, como estoy llorando,
> en el mar de mis lágrimas expiro. (p. 58)

Many traditions come together here, The idea of the Icarian Sea composed of the lover's tears recalls the *endechas* of Hurtado de Mendoza (see above, p. 66). The image of the lover given wings by Cupid is not new either, although the succinctness of "este Dédalo Amor" is an

---

[6] Lope de Vega, *Obras poéticas* I, ed. José Manuel Blecua (Barcelona, 1969), p. 575. Subsequent references will be to the same edition.

original touch. Icarus is once again the eagle in his aspiration to contemplate the radiant beauti of his beloved, but here he longs to be
a salamander, and thus survive the heat of the source of the light that
blinds him. Here one thinks of Herrera's remarkable "ardí vivo en
la luz de vuestros ojos" (see above, p. 76), or of Lope's own expression
of the idea that self-immolation is the ultimate tribute to the beloved:

> Aquí tan loco de mirarla estuve,
> que de niñas sirviendo a sus safiros,
> dentro del sol sin abrasarme anduve. (p. 97)

Similar in its acceptance of suffering is this tercet, in which the reference to wings in an evocation of Phaethon is inappropriate, his flight
being in his father's chariot.

> Subí, Faetón, subí; llegué, abraséme;
> mas donde el alma salamandra vive,
> ¡qué importa, Lope, que las alas queme! (p. 857)

These two closely associated myths appear confused more than once.
In this octave, from La Filomena, the myth of Phaethon expresses the
artist's fears of his inadequacy, although the image of the artist's quill
in the last line belongs more properly to the Icarus tradition.

> Clarísima Leonor, si castigarse
> merece un amoroso atrevimiento,
> mi musa puede en piedra transformarse,
> por este de Faetón mayor intento;
> pero pudiendo, quien se atreve, honrarse,
> a vuestro celestial entendimiento,
> no es mucho que abrasar mi amor presuma
> en tanto sol tan atrevida pluma. (pp. 747-48)

Lope continues, too, the tradition of the lover led into temptation
by his thoughts. In the following sonnet the image of Icarus is linked,
in a conceit that we have already seen, with the butterfly.

> Cayó la torre que en el viento hacían
> mis altos pensamientos castigados,
> que yacen por el suelo derribados,
> cuando con sus extremos competían.

> Atrevidos, al sol llegar querían
> y morir en sus rayos abrasados,
> de cuya luz, contentos y engañados,
> como la ciega mariposa ardían.
>
> ¡Oh siempre aborrecido desengaño,
> amado al procurarte, odioso al verte,
> que en lugar de sanar, abres la herida!
>
> Pluguiera a Dios duraras, dulce engaño:
> que si ha de dar un desengaño muerte,
> mejor es un engaño que da vida. (p. 82)

In contrast, though, to other poems in this period and later, the poet's cry is not one of thankfulness for deliverance from the deceit and vanity of love's snares, but instead a plea that such a delightful deception should continue.

Here are Icarus and the butterfly side by side again, but in a very different context. The following lines are from *La Filomena;* they are part of the denigration of Torres Rámila:

> Luego se le ofreció la portentosa
> fábrica de ignorantes, que la fama
> diciendo mal presumen que se adquiere,
> y tiñendo la pluma latinosa
> en el ageno honor, lució la llama
> al torno de la débil mariposa,
> Ícaro de su luz, sol que en que muere,
> quedando más ardiente y vitorosa;
> que el envidioso ciego
> de añadir combustible sirve al fuego. (p. 625)

The complexity of these lines by Lope needs elucidation. Rámila thought to earn praise by defaming someone else ("tiñendo... honor"); he is "débil mariposa" and Icarus in his presumption and he is consumed in the fire of the reputation he sought to destroy, which burns the brighter for the fuel that his futile attempt provides.

The figure of Icarus is becoming less and less the focus of attention and more often part of a complex of complementary images as we saw in the last chapter. Icarus is less the center of the picture and more a part of the background. The figures of mythology, as they become more familiar, leave the foreground and become part of the stock of images, fragments from which more complex images are built. Mythology is gradually evolving as part of the language instead of part of the theme (*significante* rather than *significado*, in Dámaso Alonso's application of Saussure's terminology to literature). The heroes of myth become little more—or less—than figures of speech, terms of reference to a gradually developing system of values, whose precise significance is made clear only in the particular context.

The poets of the seventeenth century had, by and large, a different view of Icarus than that of their predecessors. While for Garcilaso and his followers Icarus had presented a challenge which they accepted gladly, for Bartolomé de Argensola the contemplation of Icarus counsels caution and leads finally to resignation to a humble, earthbound existence. After recounting the story of the escape from Crete, he ends with these lines by way of moral deduction:

> Pasó el viejo, y un templo fundó en Cumas;
>   cayó el rapaz, y con el nombre suyo
>   intituló sus trágicas espumas.
> Por esto, no te admires si me excluyo
>   del tráfago, y me apelo a mi retrete,
>   donde a mi soledad me restituyo.
> Donde si la fortuna me acomete
>   con cuanto poseyeron Craso y Creso,
>   no habrá prosperidad que me inquiete.
> Mi pensamiento, ya no como preso,
>   sino como consorte y grato amigo,
>   reprueba los que vuelan con exceso;
> y en la continuación de estar conmigo,
>   no es fácil de creer de su grado
>   sigue el mismo dictamen que yo sigo.[7]

The example of Icarus has taught the poet here to avoid the *tráfago* of life with its constant excesses and lead an uninvolved, contemplative life. Far from being a glorious figure Icarus is merely one more bad example to avoid. As in Góngora's *Soledades*. Icarus is motivated by greed in his flight toward the sun, being reduced simply to "el rapaz".

In a sonnet entitled "a un privado" Bartolomé presents Icarus in an even more unflattering light:

---

[7] *Rimas de Lupercio y Bartolomé Leonardo de Argensola*, ed. José Manuel Blecua (Zaragoza, 1950-51), II, p. 77.

¿Hasta cuándo, Babel, piensas que el cielo
ha de sufrir tu loco atrevimiento?
Detén el curso, enfrena el pensamiento,
que muy grande caída da un gran vuelo.

Ya tu desdicha pronostica el suelo,
que sabe que no dura lo violento;
y la ambición es un dañado intento,
por más que encubras su amoroso celo.

Escarmienta en las plumas abrasadas
del sin consejo Ícaro atrevido,
por quien fundó su padre un templo en Cumas; [8]

o en quien, por ver sus glorias levantadas,
con sus caballos y ellas sumergido,
se vio el Po soberbio en las espumas.

The ambition of a pretentious young courtier is presented in terms of both Phaethon and Icarus, the latter's flight being reduced to "loco atrevimiento" and ambition described categorically as "un dañado intento." Icarus stands here not for an unrealistic or particulary daring aspiration but for ambition in general. The word "escarmienta" (line 9), a favourite of moralists of the time, is particulary appropriate in contemporary evocations of the myth.

Icarus has most often symbolized the hopes and fears of the lover confronted with the object of his adoration. A major variation on this theme has been the artist in contemplation of his medium, particularly in Herrera. Now, in this sonnet by Francisco de Pacheco, the figure of Icarus stands for the feelings of the artist in relation to his patron.

Osé dar nueva vida al nuevo vuelo
del que cayendo al piélago dio fama,
príncipe excelso, viendo que me llama
el honor de volar por vuestro cielo.

Temo a mis alas, mi subir recelo
¡oh gran Febo! a la luz de vuestra llama;
que tal vez en mi espíritu derrama
esta imaginación un mortal hielo.

---

[8] The references in these poems and in Juan de Arguijo's "Osaste alzar el temerario vuelo..." (see p. 110) to a temple at Cumae derive from the opening of the sixth book of Virgil's *Aeneid*.

Mas promete al temor la confianza
no del joven la muerte, antes la vida
que se debe a una empresa gloriosa;

y esta por acercarse a vos se alcanza;
que no es tan temeraria mi subida,
puesto que es vuestra luz más poderosa.[9]

The poet is ambitious and he considers his ambition a new flight of
Icarus *(Nuevo* is used in line one in its literal sense and also in the
sense of unwonted, unique, dangerous, etc.) This Icarus hopes not to
die but rather to derive life from the energy of this sun, more powerful
than Phoebus. The life he hopes for is artistic life, even the life of
fame, but it is also, in this context, simply a matter of daily sustenance.
The yearning for immortality gained by a courageous exploit which
the Renaissance tradition associated with the myth of Icarus is here
reduced to a plea for patronage.

Lupercio Leonardo de Argensola was also inspired by the image of
Icarus, and once again the lesson learned is rather grim.

De la horrenda prisión terrible y dura
huye el que dio renombre al mar muriendo,
y en la región del aire vago hendiendo,
en la del fuego halló su desventura.

El de Delo en herirle se apresura,
y las fingidas alas encendiendo,
el temerario joven fue cayendo,
y Neptuno le dio la sepultura.

Así mi pensamiento procuraba
huir de la prisión del niño ciego
por no estar en la tierra o mar seguro.

Mas, viéndome volar, abrió su aljaba,
y una flecha tiró de tanto fuego,
que dio en el mar con mi soberbio muro *(Rimas,* I, p. 282-3)

Icarus' escape from the labyrinth is evoked, without mentioning him
by name, and then the lover makes the conventional analogy with his
own situation, in this case, his attempt to flee from the prison of love.

---

[9] *BAE,* XXXII, p. 370.

own situation, in this case his attempt to flee from the prison of love. Just as the flight of Icarus ended in tragedy, so does the lover's vain effort at escape from Cupid's power. The attempt is an act of *atrevimiento* which leads naturally and inescapably to an unhappy ending. In another sonnet by Lupercio, which begins in a similar way, the poet warns Lisandro of the danger in the eyes of the beautiful Laura:

> En sus ligeras alas confiado
> (dícelo así la fama), sale huyendo
> el atrevido Ícaro, subiendo
> do el sol ardiente a nadie ha perdonado.
>
> Pagó su atrevimiento el desdichado,
> y a Apolo el gran Neptuno obedeciendo,
> en sus soberbias olas sumergiendo
> sepultura le dio en el mar salado.
>
> ¿Es menos poderoso el sol ardiente
> que sale de los ojos soberanos
> de Laura bella? Di, Lisandro amigo.
>
> ¿Pues dó subes tan alto? Passo, tente,
> y no llames los dioses inhumanos,
> si te dieren de Ícaro el castigo. (*Rimas,* I, p. 260)

Once again there is a feeling of futility. Man is pitted against a hostile world which demands payment ("pago") for each act of daring committed against it. In lines reminiscent of the words Cervantes put into the mouth of Tirsi in *La Galatea* the poet tells his friend that he has only himself to blame for an unhappy end if he persists in aiming so high. There is no mention of the immortality traditionally associated with Icarus' drowing, which is seen here as the price of defying the natural law. The lover, if he is not more cautious, will meet the same end.

An even more frankly moralizing version of the myth is told by Juan de Arguijo:

> Osaste alzar el temerario vuelo,
> Ícaro, vanamente confiado
> en mal ligadas plumas, y olvidado
> del sano aviso, te acercaste al cielo,
>
> donde el ardor del que gobierna Delo,
> deshaciendo tus alas, despeñado

te arrojó al mar, a quien tu nombre has dado,
y él sepultura a ti en el hondo suelo.

Por más cierto camino el sabio viejo
de tal peligro discurrió seguro,
y a Febo dedicó el cumano templo.[10]

¡Oh, si seguir supieras su consejo,
que no quedara en tu castigo duro
de las rendidas alas el ejemplo! [11]

The youthful impetuosity of the son is contrasted with the wisdom and circumspection of the father. The final tercet is merely an admonishing apostrophe to the vain young man. As in Bartolomé de Argensola's poem, the sun is personified as an agent of retribution, leaving it quite clear that Icarus' death is regarded as the castigation of an error, the restoration of the natural order, and not merely as the consequence of an act of overconfidence or youthful rashness.

Francisco de Quevedo

But if Arguijo makes a distinction between the folly of Icarus and the prudence of his father, Francisco de Medrano, in a poem on the perils of navigation, a popular theme since classical times, implies that even Daedalus is guilty of overstepping the bounds prescribed for human endeavor. "... Osó romper, dicen, el viento / con ambicioso vuelo, / negado al hombre..." writes Medrano, adding "y a Dios, de furias lleno infernales, / mal enojar osamos".[12] This is one of the commonplaces particularly dear to baroque writers, and found in classical poetry also, that the history of man has been a succession of dangerous inventions, beginning with Prometheus' and including Daedalus'. There is, of course, a similar tendency in the Judeo-Christian tradition dating back to the original sin of pride in the Garden of Eden. Quevedo expresses a similarly gloomy view of the history of human progress, beginning

---

[10] See note 8 above.
[11] Juan de Arguijo, *Obras completas*, ed. R. Benítez Claros (Santa Cruz de Tenerife, 1968), p. 53.
[12] *BAE*, XXXII, pp. 348-49

this time with the mythical beginning according to the story of Deucalion and Pyrrha: [13]

> El hombre, de las piedras descendiente
> (¡dura generación, duro linaje!),[14]
> osó vestir las plumas;
> osó tratar, ardiente,
> las líquidas veredas; hizo ultraje
> al gobierno de Eolo;[15]
> desvaneció su presunción Apolo,
> y en teatro de espumas,
> su vuelo desatado,
> yace el nombre, y el cuerpo justiciado,
> y navegan sus plumas.[16]
> Tal has de padecer, Clito, si subes
> a competir lugares[17] con las nubes.[18]

The history of mankind is exemplified in the myth of Icarus who tried to reach too far and brought unhappiness upon himself. Man's ambition and his continual acts of daring, such as the attempt to cross the seas, have led to the state in which he now finds himself.

This is not the only time that the figure of Icarus appears in the poetry of the mercurial Quevedo, to whom sudden changes of fortune, as in *La hora de todos,* are apparently so fascinating. He begins his "Canción a la muerte de don Luis Carrillo", with these lines which evoke the calm before the storm, the period of serenity shattered by the young poet's death. His demise is considered in terms of a shipwreck, in turn expressed as an Icarian flight.

> Miré ligera nave
> que, con alas de lino, en presto vuelo,
> por el aire süave
> iba segura del rigor del cielo
> y de tormenta grave.
> En los golfos del mar el sol nadaba

---

[13] Deucalion and Pyrrha, the Greek counterparts of Noah and his wife, scattered rocks upon the ground after the flood had subsided and thus repopulated the earth.

[14] Even in the context of the "Sermón estoico", Quevedo cannot resist the pun on "duro", hard in the sense of obdurate and also because of being descended from the stones of Deucalion and Pyrrha.

[15] Icarus, in his flight, offends Aeolus, the ruler of the winds.

[16] Even the feathers, in their "navigation" upon the sea, suggest daring.

[17] According to the *Diccionario de Autoridades,* one of the meanings of "lugar" is "empleo, dignidad, o puesto elevado".

[18] Francisco de Quevedo, *Obras completas* I, ed. José Manuel Blecua (Barcelona, 1963), p. 131.

> y en sus ondas temblaba,
> y ella, preñada de riquezas sumas,
> rompiendo sus cristales,
> le argentaba de espumas,
> cuando, en furor iguales,
> en sus velas los vientos se entregaron
> y, dando en un bajío,
> sus leños desató su mismo brío,
> que de escarmientos todo el mar poblaron,
> dejando de su pérdida en memoria
> rotas jarcias, parleras de su historia. (p. 316)

As in the previous poem, Icarus' flight is connected with sailing. The word "lino", which is one of the materials that Ovid tells us were used in the manufacture of the wings, contributes, by the association with the materials of sails, ingeniously to the association. Perhaps, too, the "rotas jarcias, parleras de su historia" are a distant echo of the feathers that, in *Metamorphoses* VIII, Daedalus saw floating on the sea where his son fell.

Don Francisco also makes a contribution to the tradition of the lover's thoughts flying on flimsy wings, a tradition in which, as we have noted, the myth of Icarus seems often to be implicit.

> Atrevido pensamiento,
> no me pongas en peligro,
> que, para ser venturoso,
> no basta ser atrevido.
> Si subes por levantarme,
> mirad que presto me rindo,
> pues para quien no descansa
> lleváis muy largo camino.
> Tras vosotros va el deseo;
> y yo, que a ratos le sigo,
> tropiezo en los desengaños
> y retírome a mí mismo.
> Porfiáis con la esperanza;
> yo con la razón porfío;
> que ésta me vuelve al atajo
> y ella os alarga el camino.
> Si a las aras de Fortuna
> queréis ir en sacrificio,
> moriréis tan malogrado

> como fuisteis bien nacido.
>   Poco aventura a perder
> quien se ve ya tan perdido,
> y sólo temo en mi daño
> que me habéis de dejar vivo.
>   Encogé un poco las alas,
> estad a cuentas conmigo,
> que ya de experimentado
> soy en mi mal adivino.
>   Mirad que es mucho mejor,
> en un caso como el mío,
> ser de cobarde sagaz,
> que de osado arrepentido. (p. 478)

The last two stanzas of the *romance* are more disillusioned than most instances we have seen. Long experience has taught this lover that discretion is the better part of valour. "Encogé un poco las alas", he says, echoing Tansillo's "china…" (see p. 54) and Lupercio's "Passo, tente…" see p. 110). He has suffered so much in love that he has "caído en la cuenta" and is now prepared to be a coward, instead of once again vaunting his great courage.

The tradition of Icarus as a symbolic expression of the *petitio humilis* also continues in Quevedo. As with Herrera we frequently find the image in the introductory lines to a *canción*. At the opening of Quevedo's hymn to the stars, for example, the poet apologizes for his inadequacy thus: "A vosotras, estrellas, / alza el vuelo mi pluma temerosa…" (p. 428) and his *canción* "a la señora doña Catalina de la Cerda" opens with these lineas:

>   Dichosa, bien osada, pluma ha sido
> la que atreve su vuelo
> a vos: no emprendió más quien buscó el cielo,
> y a menos luz cayó desvanecido.
> Confieso por menor aquel intento
> y éste por más glorioso atrevimiento (p. 327).

As in Góngora, so in his great enemy, Icarus appears sometimes in ironic guise. At the end, this time, of a *canción* in celebration of a lady devoted to the cult of Bacchus, Quevedo bids farewell to his song with these words:

>   Que así vayas convino,
> canción, porque seas della recebida;

> y si te ves subida
> como el que al mar Icario de alto vino,
> recoge el vuelo y haz que más no suba,
> porque no pongas nombre a alguna cuba (p. 658).

The traditional *despedida* becomes a caution not to fly too high because, in this case, a fall might lead to the ignominy of conferring one's name on a wine-cask. The parody is double-edged; the mention of Icarus mocks the lady by virtue of the inappropriateness of such a sublime image but at the same time the image is devalued by this same incongruity, for images, like men, are known by the company they keep.

In one of the many diatribes against his arch-enemy from Córdoba, Quevedo uses the image of Icarus against Góngora. In the first tercet of the sonnet "¿Socio otra vez? ¡Oh tú, que desbuedelas..." he writes:

> Merlinocaizando nos fatiscas
> vorágines, triclinios, promptuarios,
> trámites, vacilantes icareas [19] (p. 119).

Quevedo calls Góngora's use of these scandalous words, some of which are accepted in modern Spanish, hesitant flights of Icarus ("icareas"). Within this context Icarus' adventure clearly means for Quevedo an empty and presumptuous flight of fancy, a vain display of erudition.

One of Quevedo's most celebrated sonnets, "En crespa tempestad del oro undoso..." also contains a reference to Icarus, as well as to four other myths, Hero and Leander, the Phoenix, Midas and Tantalus. This is the second quatrain, in which the reference to Icarus occurs:

> Leandro, en mar de fuego proceloso,
> su amor ostenta, su vivir apura;
> Ícaro, en senda de oro mal segura,
> arde sus alas por morir glorioso [20] (p. 496).

The tendency to build complex images out of references to several myths, which we have seen in Lope and which is characteristic of some of Góngora's most elaborate poetry, reaches its culmination in

---

[19] Merlin Coccaio is the pseudonym of Teófilo Folengo (1496-1544), author of a poem in maccaronic verse entitled *Baldus. Fatisco -ere* means in Latin a) to crack open, crumble, fall apart and b) to become weak, to weaken. Quevedo not only uses it as a first conjugation verb but also transitively and with a double object.

[20] Once again Icarus' wings are said to burn, as in Lope's "Las plumas abrasó rayo febeo...", indicating contact with the Phaethon story.

this sonnet which A. A. Parker has analyzed. He calls it "un ejemplo perfecto... de la tensión barroca" because of the way the poet's emotions are expressed and refined in the play of these different images.[21] Icarus is here no more than one of the symbols of the instability of human life as felt by the lover beset by hopes and fears.

In a sonnet by Francisco de Medrano the traditional theme of Icarus as the ardent suitor is given a new variation.

> Estaba de mi edad en el florido
> abril, que fruto asaz me prometía,
> y de mi Flora en el regazo un día
> vi reposar al niño Amor dormido.
>
> Las alas que tan alto lo han subido,
> por no bajar, abandonado había;
> yo, que de celos y de invidia ardía,
> tenté con ellas usurparle el nido.
>
> Volar tenté; mas, de la luz medroso
> de tus soles, ¡oh Flora!, mudé intento,
> con el fracaso de Ícaro avisado;
>
> que es mal valor tal vez ser temeroso,
> y no siempre fortuna da al osado
> favor, ni quiere el gusto ser violento.[22]

The lover sees Cupid resting in his beloved's lap and, burning with jealousy, tries to steal his wings. But the attempt to fly reminds him of the fate of Icarus and, chastened, he concludes, in an inversion of a Latin proverb, that fortune does not always favour the brave.

A sonnet by Martín de la Plaza also concludes that the perils of love outweigh the promise of happiness.

> ¿Adónde, temerario pensamiento,
> subes ligero a penetrar la esfera,
> si componen tus alas lino y cera,
> y es fuego al que te acercas elemento?

---

[21] Alexander A. Parker, "La agudeza en algunos sonetos de Quevedo", *Estudios dedicados a don Ramón Menéndez Pidal*, III (Madrid, 1952), p. 353. Cf. also Manuel Durán, on this sonnet, in "Manierismo en Quevedo", *Actas del Segundo Congreso Internacional de Hispanistas* (Nijmegen, 1967), p. 305.

[22] *BAE*, XXXII, p. 345.

Tu perdición en tu atrevido intento
conoce; teme y tu altivez modera;
si no, precipitado ya te espera
en las ondas cerúleo monumento.

Inclina el vuelo, pensamiento loco,
no te opongas al sol que miras ciego
en unos ojos por quien lloro y canto;

que si abrasados vuelves, es muy poco
el alto mar, para templar tu fuego,
que mis ojos te dan de amargo llanto.[23]

Many traditional images occur again. For Martín de la Plaza, too, the idea that Icarus falls into the sea in flames seems to derive from association with the myth of Phaethon. Again the sea is the lover's tears and the line "Inclina el vuelo..." once more recalls Tansillo's "China..." (see p. 54). As in Herrera's "lugar pequeño es el suelo / para tanto desconcierto" (see p. 78), here in the last tercet Icarus' (and the lover's) demise is such a catastrophe that it could not be contained in a whole element, a view completely opposite to that expressed in Breughel's painting, where Icarus' leg is scarcely visible in a corner.

But though the prevailing tone of the poems we are now discussing is pessimistic,[24] seeing Icarus as a warning instead of as an incentive to adventure, the older tradition, inspired by Tansillo and his early imitators, continues too, particularly, as we shall see, in Villamediana. In continues, too, in the pastoral novels, in one of the last of which, Suárez de Figueroa's *La constante Amarilis,* this sonnet appears:

Dédalo al hijo incauto con recelo
vuelve a mirar, ya de su fin presago;
y él sin temor rompiendo el aire vago[25]
levanta más el temerario vuelo.

Al fuego llega, y se convierte en yelo,
porque haciendo en sus alas fiero estrago
precipita y se anega; justo pago
de quien se atreve al resplandor del cielo.

---

[23] *Cancionero antequerano: 1627-1628* (Madrid, 1950), pp. 61-62.
[24] Gilman, in his "Introduction...", writes about the "increasing pessimism" of the writers of the Golden Age (p. 90).
[25] Cabañas (p. 457) omits "él". The pronoun is necessary, however, to signal the change in subject, without which the syntax is extremely awkward.

> De esto ¿qué me decís, o pensamiento?
> ¿Osáis tocar en la mayor altura?
> ¿Adónde vais? No echéis por donde os guío.
>
> Mas no, mejor hacéis, subid sin tiento,
> que si os perdéis por corto de ventura,
> por falta no de generoso brío.[26]

Daedalus is seen, for the first time, at the moment in which he turns round to make sure his son is following safely (Ovid, *Met.* VIII, 1. 216). Then the grammatical subject changes and we see Icarus flying recklessly upward until he falls victim to the sun's rays and earns what the poet calls his just reward for defying the heavens. But, despite this harsh judgment of Icarus' flight, Menandro, who recites the sonnet, exhorts his thoughts to persist for, though Fortune may fail them, their noble spirit will not.

Villamediana

The importance of the myth of Icarus in the work of Juan de Tarsis, count of Villamediana, has already been noted. Frances Harlan, in her unpublished edition of the sonnets,[27] refers to the frequency of the image and Juan Manuel Rozas, in the introduction to his recent edition of some of the poems, describes the whole of his early poetry as written "bajo el signo de Ícaro." [28] With Herrera and Góngora, Villamediana stands out as one of the poets whose work most often expresses the ambitions and fears of the lover in terms of Prometheus, Phaethon and particularly Icarus. Perhaps the most sublime expression in Spanish of the lover's flight seen through the myth of Icarus is this sonnet:

> De cera son las alas, cuyo vuelo
> gobierna incautamente el albedrío,
> y llevadas del propio desvarío,
> con vana presunción suben al cielo.
>
> No tiene ya el castigo, ni el recelo
> fuerza eficaz, ni sé de qué me fío,

26   Suárez de Figueroa, *La constante Amarilis* (Madrid, 1781), p. 293.
27   Frances Harlan, *The Sonnets of Villamediana*, unpublished dissertation (New York University, 1949).
28   Villamediana, *Obras*, ed. Juan Manuel Rozas (Madrid, 1969), p. 17.

si prometido tiene el hado mío
nombre a la mar, como escarmiento al suelo.[29]

Mas si a la pena, Amor, el gusto igualas
con aquel nunca visto atrevimiento
que basta a acreditar lo más perdido,

derrita el sol las atrevidas alas,
que no podrá quitar al pensamiento
la gloria, con caer, de haber subido.[30]

The lover takes flight on wings of love, accepting his fate, heeding neither the fear of punishment nor the instinct for caution. Once again death is not too high a price for the glory he seeks. The final lines seem to me the finest expression of this feeling that is linked with Icarus first in Tansillo. This joyful acceptance of suffering, required by the conventions of courtly love—a "despairing and tragical emotion", in C. S. Lewis' words [31]—is reminiscent of Garcilaso's lines "no me podrán quitar el dolorido / sentir si ya del todo / primero no me quitan el sentido".[32] Both passages voice a "romantic" attachment to great emotion, even if that passion proves fatal, as perhaps it did in real life for Villamediana.

Although the willing acceptance of suffering is such a traditional aspect of the role of the Petrarchan lover, for whom acceptance as a suitor would in a sense mean defeat, one of the distinctive features of Villamediana's erotic poetry is his insistence on the lover's almost complete ambivalence about the outcome of his exploit. Defeat is anticipated with as much excitement as the slim possibility that his love might be requited. The final lines of the following sonnet, which is apparently addressed to Icarus (line 4), seem frankly masochistic in their apostrophe to death. Of course, the image of love itself as a kind of death is already established in the tradition, reflected in versions "a lo divino" such as Saint John's "que muero porque no muero".[33]

¡Oh volador dichoso que volaste
por la región del aire y la del fuego,

[29] In Rozas' edition this line begins "hombre...", possibly an error.
[30] Villamediana, ed. Rozas, p.79.
[31] C. S. Lewis, *The Allegory of Love* (New York, 1958), p. 3.
[32] *Obras completas*, ed. Elías Rivers (Madrid, 1964), p. 79.
[33] San Juan de la Cruz, *Poesías completas*, ed. Dámaso Alonso (Madrid, 1959), p. 53.

y en esfera de luz, quedando ciego,
alas, vida y volar sacrificaste!

Y como en las de Amor te levantaste,
tu fin incauto fue el piadoso ruego
que te dio libertad, pero tú luego
más con el verte libre te enredaste.

Efectos de razón, que aquellos brazos
soltando prenden, y, si prenden, matan
con ciegos nudos de eficaz misterio.

¡Oh muerte apetecida, oh dulces lazos,
donde los que, atrevidos, se desatan
vuelven con nueva sed al cautiverio! (p. 105).

The imagery of the following sonnet is based on the myth of
Icarus too:

Si con mayor peligro que escarmiento
olímpicos alcázares escalas,
nieguen, Amor, las plumas de tus alas
el ser de cera al sol, de nieve al viento.

Présteme ya tu soberano aliento
esperanza que infundes, fe que exhalas,
y archiven cuanto animas, cuanto igualas
piélagos del diáfano elemento.

Ya fugitiva luz de astros errantes,
conduzca osado el peligroso vuelo,
donde, aun cayendo, gloria me colijo.

De ansias menos felices que constantes,
el golfo, si de gracia es mar el cielo,
inmutable sea, fiel, mi norte fijo (p. 151).

This is a difficult sonnet, complicated by the division into two parts,
in tension, of lines 1, 4, 6, 7, 11 and 12, and perhaps also by a mutilated
text.[34] The poet addresses Cupid and begs that the wings he provides

---

[34] Rozas (p. 151) mentions some of the textual problems without resolving them.

not be defenseless before the heat of the sun which might melt the wax or before the winds which could blow away the feathers, which are as light (or white?) as snowflakes, of which they are made. He begs him to bear him up on breezes of hope and he wants the waves of the sea ("diáfano elemento") to record the exploit that Cupid exhorts him to. He wishes to be led on toward the stars, where, even though he may die, he will find glory. The last lines are quite obscure but they seem to express the desire that the sea ("golfo") of anxieties remain ever his guiding light.

Images of flight pervade Villamediana's erotic poetry as they do Herera's. Occasionally, as in the sonnet that follows, the imagery of the Icarus myth seems to underly the sense, although the mythological figure never quite appears.

> Tan peligroso y nuevo es el camino
> por donde lleva Amor mi pensamiento
> que en sólo los discursos de mi intento
> aprueba la razón su desatino.
>
> Efecto nunca visto y peregrino,
> enloquecer de puro entendimiento
> un sujeto incapaz del escarmiento,
> ciego por voluntad y por destino.
>
> Amor no quarda ley, que la hermosura
> es lícita violencia y tiranía
> que obliga con lo mismo que maltrata.
>
> Su fin es fuerza, y esperar locura,
> pues es tal por su causa el ansia mía
> que de mí que la tengo se recata (p. 78).

Several words recall poems in the Icarus tradition. The last line echoes Garcilaso's "fiar el mal de mí que lo posseo" (see above, p. 58), for example, while the general structure of the sonnet, based on the image of the lover's thoughts led astray by love and threatened by tragedy, is almost identical to many sonnets we have seen in which there are specific references to Icarus.

In two of the sonnets we have just referred to, the poet insists on the role of the lover's intellect in his involvement in the perilous flight of love ("aprueba la razón su desatino...", "enloquecer de puro entendimiento", "efectos de razón"). In the tercets of yet another sonnet the lover's reason is again affected by the power of love.

> cuando ya las razones y el instinto
> pudiera de mí mismo defenderme,
> y con causa fundada en escarmiento;
>
> en otro peligroso laberinto
> me pone Amor, y ayudan a perderme
> memoria, voluntad y entendimiento (p. 87).

The tripartite division of the soul inherited by the philosophers of the Renaissance from medieval psychology, leads to discussions of the roles of the three in the afflictions of love. John Charles Nelson, who has studied the theory of love in the Renaissance, distinguishes an evolution in attitude marked by transition from a view of love as affecting merely the will to the position adopted by Giordano Bruno and echoed here by Villamediana, that the intellect is also caught up in the lover's quest for the ideal.[36] In the early Renaissance, the poets spoke of themselves as slaves to their passions, unable to control their will, but they usually maintained intellectual detachment—they could understand and talk about what was happening to them. In Villamediana, all the faculties of the soul are involved in submission to the tyranny of love. It is from this point in the development in the theory of love that Sor Juana Inés de la Cruz can go on and apply the imagery to her own quest for enlightenment through her intellectual activities, which she expresses also through the image of Icarus, as we shall see in the next chapter.

---

[35] John Charles Nelson, *Renaissance Theory of Love; the Context of Giordano Bruno's "Eroici furori"* (New York, 1958), pp. 197-199.

Chapter 7

THE FALL OF ICARUS

The flight of Icarus as a symbol for high endeavours doomed to spectacular failure was short but, as we have seen, artistically highly productive. That image, the embodiment of the highest aspirations of the courtly lover and the neo-Platonic artist in their struggles to reach the realm of the ideal, is now becoming less frequent. It is tarnished by incongruous, grotesque and moralistic associations, as well as by the burlesque treatments that began with Góngora. In the seventeenth century, the awe in which Icarus was almost universally held by the poets of the early sixteenth century seems to turn to criticism and even censure. Classical mythology loses respect as a source of symbols for man's capacity for greatness and becomes instead a system for teaching Christian morality; references to mythology, even in poetry, tend to become demeaning or disparaging. Icarus, Phaethon and other Promethean symbols are more often reminders of mortality than intimations of immortality.

One of the factors contributing to the devaluation of the myth of Icarus is the more general discredit into which the conventions of courtly love were falling. The traditional expressions of a highly idealized passion now appear side by side, as in Quevedo, with the grossest and most cynical declarations of skepticism.

Moralists like Malón de Chaide were not the only writers to level strong criticism at the extreme expressions of passion in erotic literature. One of the poets who had strong opinions on the subject was Bartolomé Cairasco de Figueroa who, in his *Definiciones morales,* wrote a *canción en esdrújulos* against "aquellos paralíticos, / tan pobres cuan lunáticos, / que tienen el ciego amor en su probática".[1] The insistence on the *esdrújulo* endings is, of course, an appropriate gesture in a poem aimed against the conventions of a kind of poetry which, like the use of *es-*

---

[1] Cairasco de Figueroa, *Definiciones poéticas, morales y cristianas. BAE,* XLII, pp. 498-99.

drújulos, was always associated with Italy. These servants of Cupid are, according to Cairasco "a Dios no muy católicos", a sentiment shared by the author of the *Conversión de la Magdalena*. A *licenciado* Dueñas wrote a reply to Cairasco in the same form, in which he expressed complete agreement with him, vituperating against "el indómito ciego" who "al ánimo católico / le vuelve casi herético". This tirade against the blinding power of love, which is slightly reminiscent of Calisto's complaints against Cupid in *La Celestina*, culminates in a familiar image:

> y llegan los negocios a tal término,
> que ya cualquiera pícaro
> .quiere volar y vuela más que Ícaro.[2]

As he seemed to in France, Icarus has come to symbolize, for detractors, the essence of the erotic literary tradition, with its implications of lack of judgment and disinterest in conventional morality. The image has been so frequently associated with the figure of the lover that it can be used critically without elaboration. The idealized rhetoric of love is so pervasive now, according to Dueñas, that every man on the street can think himself the victim of a great passion that leads him to forget all else, including his religion. For Dueñas, as for Malón de Chaide the passion of love, here symbolized in the flight of Icarus, is a threat to morality. When the moralist employs the imagery of the Petrarchans against them, he willingly contributes to the devaluation of these images, in this case most notably by the use of the rhyme *Ícaro / pícaro*.

Gracián in his *Agudeza y arte de ingenio* inveighs against the slavish imitators of Góngora. "Algunos, "he says," le han querido seguir. como Ícaro a Dédalo; cógenle algunas palabras de las más sobresalientes..., incúlcanlas muchas veces de modo que a cuatro o seis voces reducen su cultura".[3] Don Luis, the paragon of the artistic ideals advocated in Gracián's work which Batllori calls "exaltación de la agudeza sobre la imitación",[4] is a new Daedalus, an inventor, while many of those who came after him, without the genius to emulate his achievements, are like Icarus—they fall short. For both Gracián and Dueñas, although from different points of view, Icarus represents the follower of fashion instead of the true artist. For Gracián the followers of Góngora debased

---

[2] *BAE*, XLII, p. 499.
[3] Baltasar Gracián, *Agudeza*, ed. Evaristo Correa Calderón (Madrid, 1969), II, p. 251.
[4] Miguel Batllori, *Gracián y el barroco* (Rome, 1958), p. 113.

art by relying on the originality of another, while Dueñas regrets the imitation of poetic conventions because they are, of themselves, pernicious. For both writers the figure of Icarus has pejorative connotations.

But imitation is still of the essence of the poetic tradition with which we are concerned,[5] so Juan de la Cueva, in his *Ejemplar poético*, makes careful distinctions between different kinds:

> Unos imitan del sermón romano,
> otros hurtan, y otros puramente
> traducen de otra lengua en castellano.

The imitation of the classics and the translation of modern writers is "lícita, y licencia permitida / al ingenio más alto," but to the plagiarist Cueva issues a stern warning, involving once again the image of Icarus:

> mira que ese furor icáreo intenta
> en ese vuelo tu mortal ruina
> y abatimiento, en vez de honrosa cuenta.[6]

Icarus is now, instead of the image of the artist challenging the cosmos in his effort to express the ineffable, the symbol of the derivative versifier. The plagiarist, because he follows in the steps of the great artist, but without his talent or training, just as Icarus followed Daedalus, is condemned.

The fiction of the uniqueness of the experience expressed in identification with the fate of the son of Daedalus is destroyed by referring to him in the plural as Soto de Rojas does. In the first lines of a sonnet with the epigraph "Díjole que no le hablase, que ella le miraría," the poet addresses a lady who has been so cruel that she has caused the downfall of many Icaruses.

> Fénix, después que vuestra luz esquiva
> tantos Ícaros libres desbarata:
> después que a cuantos mira, a tantos mata,
> ¿queréis, que sólo con mirarme viva?[7]

---

[5] Although there is, as Batllori points out, a movement towards a poetic that lays greater stress on originality in the seventeenth century, the imitation of themes and images of classical and contemporary poets continues.

[6] Juan de la Cueva, *El infamador, Los siete infantes de Lara y El ejemplar poético*, ed. Francsico A. de Icaza (Madrid, 1924), pp. 218-19

[7] Pedro Soto de Rojas, *Obras*, ed. Gallego Morell (Madrid, 1950), p. 120.

As so often before, the beauty of the lady is considered a fatal attraction, of which the lover is warned to be wary by example. But this time, instead of appealing to a legendary example, the lover sees a whole series of examples closer at hand and all have met the fate of Icarus. The example of so many Icaruses persuades him to resist the lady's appeal for patience, and not to persist in an adventure that has brought downfall, not this time to one man, but to many.

Another, very different, sonnet by Soto seems to me also based on the image of Icarus, although there are some aspects of the poem that resist analysis.

> Barro naciste, Búcaro: Fortuna
> movió al actor, que os informase hermoso.
> Fénix os levantó con poderoso
> brazo al soberbio cerco de la luna.
>
> Vistes os (¡a si yo¡) do nunca alguna
> forma gentil; en tanto que lloroso
> pudiera ser sepulcro lastimoso
> de mi reciente amor, su primer cuna.
>
> Ya (¡miserable vos!) venís cayendo;
> sino feliz, pues libre de mi ingrata;
> ¡ay dudoso de mí que voy subiendo!
>
> Pues si al bajar en agua os desbarata,
> ¿qué hará si subo, que en su luz me enciendo,
> que cera soy, y un búcaro desata? [8]

This much seems clear: the poet addresses a clay vessel, perhaps a gift from him, which has been raised to the face of the woman (Fénix) he loves [9] ("soberbio cerco de la luna"), causing him to feel envious. When the *búcaro* falls (or is thrown down), its fate is ambiguous, for, though it falls, it is at least free of the ungrateful woman who held it. The destruction of the vessel makes the lover fearful for his own fate for, if she could destroy something made of clay, how much more will she endanger an object made of wax? [10] There is behind these events involving the clay vessel, I think, the image of Icarus, beginning with

[8]   Soto de Rojas, ed. cit., p. 111.
[9]   Cf. Soto's other sonnet, p. 164.
[10]   Cf. Garcilaso "si a vuestra voluntad yo soy de cera". *Obras completas*, ed. Elías L. Rivers (Madrid, 1964), p. 22.

the upward movement toward the celestial beauty of the woman, the uniqueness of the flight ("do nunca alguna / forma gentil") and ending with the fall into water and the feeling of the lover that he is as wax in her hands. The word "desbaratar" which we saw in the previous sonnet in the context of an allusion to Icarus also suggests that the same imagery is involved here. The main difficulties are two: the play on the recurrent baroque theme of the cradle and the grave and the phrase "al bajar en agua os desbarata." It is possible that the "sepulcro lastimoso / de mi reciente amor, su primer cuna" is the woman's mouth, which might have been the birthplace of their love (if she had spoken to him) and which becomes instead the grave of the *búcaro*. This implies that the fate of the vessel was to be eaten, a common practice in the Golden Age,[11] which would mean that "os desbarata en agua" must allude to the bodily functions of elimination, frequently expressed in the euphemism "hacer aguas" at the time. This possibility is perhaps also connected with the common vulgar use of the word *cera* for excrement. At all events we have another example of the lover identifying with Icarus, this time through the intermediate image of the clay vessel, an unflattering form for Icarus to assume.

The enormously fertile marriage between the lover's apostrophe to his thoughts and the image of the flight of Icarus inspires Soto in a more traditional poem. The sonnet begins with a characteristically baroque warning about the limitations of mortality. The personification of the lover's thoughts is reminded that it is only "de cera y polvo... porción ligera," and that excursions into foreign elements are likely to be resisted by the natural order of the cosmos.

> ¿Dónde vuelas, soberbio pensamiento?
> Ícaro mozo, mi consejo espera,
> mira que a polvo humilde y blanda cera,
> ni el sol perdona, ni respeta el viento.[12]
>
> Fénix es sol, y su divino aliento
> la procelosa de Aquilón esfera;
> de cera y polvo, tú, porción ligera,
> teme, vuelve a la tierra, que es tu asiento.[13]

---

[11] For information on the habit of eating *búcaro* see Lope de Vega's *Dorotea* (passim), Marie Catherine, comtesse d'Aulnoy, *Relation du voyage en Espagne*, ed. Foulché-Delbosc (Paris, 1926) and P. Bomli, *La Femme dans l'Espagne du Siècle d'Or* (La Haye, 1950).

[12] Cf. Villamediana, "nieguen, Amor, las plumas de tus alas / el ser de cera al sol, de nieve al viento" (see above, p. 151).

[13] Soto de Rojas, ed. cit., pp. 37-38.

The lover begs his thoughts to face the dangers boldly in the hope of reaching the goal of unity with the beloved and in the confidence that, even if the intention falls short, he will be immortalized in the attempt. The lover's stoic persistence will be commemorated in the poem which is the record of his tragic but noble experience.

A beautiful poem by Pedro de Quirós also continues, in melancholy vein, the tradition of the lover's complaint to his thoughts:

> Altivo pensamiento,
> no afectes ardimiento soberano,
> porque es atrevimiento
> seguir tanta deidad con vuelo humano.
> Mira que la ventura
> está, cuando mayor, menos segura.
>
> Pensamiento atrevido,
> para estar de ti mismo confiado
> eres tan desvalido
> como de nobles causas engendrado;
> teme, si al sol te igualas,
> que a tu calor se quemarán tus alas.
>
> No busques tanta gloria,
> pues te falta caudal para el empleo,
> imposible victoria
> es la que pretendió sólo el deseo,
> y a una luz tan divina
> el atreverse es la primer rüina.
>
> Incontrastable muro [14]
> mal combatir intenta tu cuidado;
> más rebelde, más duro
> le hallarás mientras fueres más osado;
> que está en un amor muerto
> dormido el gusto, y el rigor despierto.
>
> En la luz de su esfera
> rigor fatal conocerás de muerte,
> si con alas de cera

---

[14] "Muro" refers here, presumably, to the wall of the castle of the lady's resistance which must be stormed by the lover. Cf. "ni penetres las paredes" in Góngora (see above, p. 90).

de Ícaro sigues la ambiciosa suerte.
Mira que es desvarío
esperar que amor venza un mármol frío.[15]

The lover rebukes his thoughts for their futile hopes of softening the marmoreal heart of his lady. This love is hopeless ("un amor muerto"), yet she is still "luz tan divina." The contrast between such devotion and the apparent coldness of the woman in question leads to a sense of disillusion rare even in this tradition, leading to the gloomy conclusion that "la ventura / está, cuando mayor, menos segura." This line and also the thought that "a una luz tan divina / el atreverse es la primer rüina," express a conviction, in strong contrast to that of the earlier poets we have seen, that to aim so high is completely futile. The consolation of immortality is not even considered.

An unusual poem, in its contemplation of the flight of Icarus without any explicit analogy to the particular experience of the voice of the poem, is this sonnet by Martín de Saavedra y Guzmán:

Veloz camina con osado vuelo
joven alado, intrépido, arrogante;
menospreciando la Deidad brillante,
aspira a penetrar celeste velo.

¿Siete planetas no le dan recelo,
¡o juventud por hados inconstante!
qué presto muda el ser, muda semblante,
quien sin consejo se remonta al cielo?

¡O blanda cera, que al dorado Apolo,
y sus lucientes rayos, atrevida
intentaste llegar, sin temer males!

Este, pues, peregrino; este, pues, solo,
que se entregó a los riesgos de la vida,
cayó en el mar, dio nombre a sus cristales.[16]

The voice that reflects upon the flight and fall of the young man expresses impatience with his arrogance and recklessness and wonder at his colossal daring. Then the final three lines put all this into perspective as the attitude changes to one of grudging admiration for the uniqueness

---

[15] *BAE*, XLII, p. 422.
[16] Martín de Saavedra y Guzmán, *Ocios de Aganipe* (Trani, 1634), p. 205.

of the venture which comes to stand, in line 13, for a whole approach
to life. There is in these last lines respect for resolution in the face of
evident danger and the suggestion that such boldness in the face of
difficulty con grant immortality.

It is now time to look at some less traditional applications of the
myth of Icarus. The feathers of his wings have already suggested, to
Herrera and others, the image of the poet borne aloft on wings made
of the quill pen with which he writes. A much less prestigious association is made by Polo de Medina in his *Academias del jardín*. He is
describing an open-air function at which one of the attractions is a
display of fireworks. These have always suggested to the poetic mind
parallels with the heavenly bodies [17] but Polo goes one step further and,
looking from the multiplicity of artificial suns in the sky to the sea
of plumes worn by the elegant guests, he portrays these latter as so
many Icaruses.

> Con la confusión de plumas,
> sin que tantos soles teman,
> Ícaros no dando en luces
> veloces el aire peinan.
> Atrevidos los penachos,
> les da su altivez licencia
> que en blandos halagos sirvan
> de abanillo a las estrellas. [18]

The attempt to fly of these daring challengers of the skies in innocent
enough—they are really no threat ("no dando en luces") and thus need
not fear. The comparison with Icarus serves here only to point gently
to the vanity of all these plumes waving in the air.

Also from the *Academias* comes a description of a painting of "la
desgracia de Ícaro [que] experimenta su desobediencia en su incendio,
y derribándose por los aires se sepulta en el mar." Under the painting,
as if they were the explanatory verse under a woodcut in an emblem
book, are these words:

> Por mares de esplendor navegas luces
> con blandos remos, Ícaro atrevido,
> a perderte en el sol vas, mariposa;

---

[17] Cf. for example Leopoldo Lugones "Los fuegos artificiales". *Obras poéticas completas,* ed. Pedro Miguel Obligado (Madrid, 1948), pp. 255-62.
[18] Polo de Medina, *Obras completas* (Biblioteca de Autores Murcianos, Murcia,
1948), p. 80. Subsequent references are to the same edition.

mas una ola furiosa
te despeña, encendido
penacho, destrozado por las nubes,
y en veloz precipicio vuelves luego,
y con alas de fuego
pretendes en el húmedo elemento
los vientos de cristal volar sediento;
pero dan las espumas
blando sepulcro a tus flamantes plumas (p. 25).

Once again the reference to the burning of the wings, and again the parallel image of the butterfly, but the most interesting aspect of this short poem is the reversal of the imagery of sea and sky. The sky is "mares de esplendor" in which Icarus is shipwrecked by a furious wave, while the sea is "vientos de cristal sediento," an image worthy of Góngora. The background to this reversal of imagery, in which Icarus' wings become oars, is once again the euhemeristic explanation of the myth that Daedalus and his son escaped by sea. Usually the invention of sail-power is attributed to Daedalus, though, and the mention of the oars is slightly incongruous.

Icarus appears again in Polo, though in a minor and rather un-distinguished role. In a sonnet entitled "a una mariposa que se ahogó en un vidrio de agua," much of the imagery again derives from the contrast between two elements, this time fire and water. The poet considers that the butterfly, by virtue of its bright colours and its fatal attraction to fire, was destined to die by that element.

Avecilla infeliz, que tantas flores
en esas braves   alas extendiste,
¿cómo, si para fénix floreciste,
Ícaro se apagaron tus colores?

En tu achaque la luz, es tus rigores,
y en llama de cristales falleciste,
que si ha de ser estrago para un triste,
aun el cristal presumirá de ardores (p. 411).

The colourful insect deserved a noble death—that of the Phoenix with the promise of rebirth, and instead died by drowning, considered here an ignominious death. The only function of the figure of Icarus in these lines is as an example of death by drowning, a prosaic attitude

towards a myth which had previously expressed a yearning for immor-
rality. The grandiose fall of Icarus is miniaturized into this insignificant
incident.

A similarly disillusioned niew of the meaning of the flight of Icarus
this time in an amorous context, is expressed in a sonnet by Francisco
de Trillo y Figueroa, which is a distant echo of the *Beatus ille* topos:

> Dichoso aquel a quien la amarga muerte
> no tronca el tiempo de sus dulces años,
> y aquel que no alimenta desengaños
> con el cebo engañoso de la suerte.
>
> Dichoso (si hay alguno) aquel que advierte
> su riesgo al resplandor de los extraños,
> y aquel que, mariposa a los engaños,
> entre las llamas el ardor advierte.
>
> Dichoso el que con vuelo reposado
> a la cumbre se acerca fatigable
> de la alta ruina a que el honor aspira,
>
> y mucho más aquel que retirado
> vive de la fortuna incontrastable,
> limando con su paz su cruel ira.[19]

Happy is he who can avoid the dangers of worldly ambition, says the
poet. Happy is he who can learn from the failure of others ("que advierte / su riesgo al resplandor de los extraños"). He is like a butterfly
who is not blinded by the flame that threatens him and like an Icarus
who flies cautiously towards the attractions of fame and fortune, prepared to turn back ("a la cumbre se acerca fatigable") and avoid "la alta
ruina." [20] The feeling is very strong that, although there are few who
can do it, to refuse to engage in such worldly pursuits as endanger our
happiness is the only way to find peace.

A dim view of the kind of emotional involvement that the earlier
poets admired in Icarus is also expressed by Manoel da Faria e Sousa
in this Spanish sonnet:

> Volando por el diáfano elemento
> tímido viejo y mozo temerario,

[19] *BAE*, XLII, p. 47.
[20] The phrase seems reminiscent of Sannazaro (see p. 50).

hicieron ver, con vuelo extraordinario,
pájaros racionales por el viento.

Si racional ha sido el pensamiento
para poder huir, suceso vario
con un castigo le mostró, plenario,
que ha sido irracional el ardimiento.

Cuando alguno de vida se despoje,
quien tanto en excederse a sí se emplea,
es justo que padezca igual desaire.

Cada cual contra sí solo se enoje;
y jamás dichoso fin se crea
quien expusiere la razón al aire.[21]

The implication is quite clear here that man's reason is his safe guide and that giving in to the emotions is the great danger. It is reasonable to take to the air in order to escape but the different outcome of the two flights is an evident vindication of the prudence of the father and a warning against the irrational action of the son. We have only ourselves to blame if we cast reason to the winds.

We return to the lover's thoughts for two sonnets in which they are addressed as Icarus. The first, by Bernardino de Rebolledo, is quite original, at least after the first quatrain. The first lines offer little that is new.

Ícaro pensamiento que, atrevido,
a la región suprema levantado,
sacrificó a dos soles su cuidado
por la gloria de verse bien perdido.

An amorous thought, attracted by the lady's beauty, ignores the dangers and, for the sake of a glorious demise, meets death willingly in the suns of her eyes, expressed more elliptically than we have seen them before. Now, however, the lover's thoughts are attracted by a new goal:

De inferiores objectos atraído,
en humildes prisiones enlazado,
quedó de luz y de razón privado,
a subjección indigna reducido.

[21] Manoel da Faria e Sousa, *Fuente de Aganipe* (Madrid, 1646), f. 70r.

Submission to this new temptation, presumably the physical delights of the body, leads to enslavement, which is ended by the realization brought about by an undefined crisis:

> Produjo largo error grave escarmiento
> que a la dura prisión rompió los lazos,
> volviendo al curso de su antiguo vuelo,
>
> cual generoso halcón que, hallando el viento
> libre de los odiosos embarazos,
> con prestas alas se remonta al cielo.[22]

After their *escarmiento* the thoughts are free to resume their natural quest for the ideal, symbolized in the "región suprema" which attracted Icarus. The two poles of temptation here are reminiscent of the dual dangers that Icarus was counselled by his father to avoid.

In the other sonnet, by José Delitala y Castelví, the lover's thoughts, as they fly recklessly upward, are called Icarus.

> Si a la esfera del sol remonta el vuelo
> un pensamiento loco y atrevido,
> Ícaro es ya, pues mide condolido
> la distancia que halló del cielo al suelo.

This Icarus' flight is crowned by an achievement of sorts, that of dis-illusion.

> Incapaz de la luz logra el desvelo
> cuando de su ambición llora advertido,
> descendiendo a beber con pecho herido
> todo el cristal que fatigó su anhelo.

He falls short and, in his fall, he is said to drink in the "cristal que fatigó su anhelo," the air in which he flew. In the first tercet, the presumption of immortality proves fatal.

> Ya de inmortal el presuroso día
> presumir quiso, pero viose luego
> reducida en extremos su osadía.

---

[22] *Ocios del conde don Bernardino de Rebolledo* (Amberes, 1660), p. 52.

The last three lines express admiration for Icarus who dies, not from the heat of the sun precisely, but from his restless search for an unattainable ideal:

No le rindió la actividad del fuego,
cuando intrépida muere su profía
de un imposible, de un desasosiego.[23]

A sonnet by Miguel de Barrios, alias Daniel Leví de Barrios, provides us with one of the most striking allusions to the myth we are discussing. The epigraph to the poem, which seems to be necessary to its understanding, reads as follows: "a una fulana de la Fuento, que al subir a un andamio, salió un toro, a quien huyendo un tropel de gente, atropelló la escala, de donde cayó, y luego murió." This is the text of the poem, which is not without its difficulty.

Esta que fue de amor la dulce Fuente
que le daba a beber néctar süave,
cuando atrevido, mucho más que grave,
entraba caudaloso en su corriente:

ya en eclipse mortal de su occidente,
falta de luces, en las sombras cabe,
dejando sentimientos a quien sabe
que halló su ocaso en su florecido oriente.

Ícaro de esplendores, pretendiendo
con las alas de amor volar cegando
a cumbre artificial iba subiendo

hiriendo vidas y almas abrasando,
cuando asaltada de un veloz estruendo
cayó muriendo, por subir matando.[24]

The lady, who used to be a source (her name appears to be Fuente) of love for the lover who would dare give himself up to her attractions, is now dead *(falta de luces)* and leaves behind the regrets of those who knew her that she died so young. The poet portrays her as Icarus in her youthful beauty as she climbs onto some kind of platform, probably at a *fiesta de toros*. She who wounded the hearts of so many by being so

[23] José Delitala y Castelví, *Cima del monte Parnaso español* (Caller, 1672), p. 141.
[24] Miguel de Barrios, *Flor de Apolo* (Brussels, 1665), p. 206.

attractive and causing them to fall, falls herself to her death. This is
the first time since Góngora that we have seen Icarus as a woman.
Both the poet from Córdoba and Barrios use Icarus as the symbol for
the haughty, disdainful woman, instead of the more frequent image of
the victim of such a woman's beauty.

Similiar only to the extent that it represents a more critical attitude
to the myth than many we have seen, is this light-hearted version of
the fall of Icarus by Gabriel del Corral:

> Dédalo, en nuevo ejercicio
> de volar alicionaba [25]
> al hijo, a quien moderaba
> poco tan piadoso oficio.
>
> Y dejando de volar,
> Ícaro dijo al caer:
> padre, más he menester
> que me enseñes a nadar.[26]

A clever stylization of a brief reference to the story of Daedalus
in Virgil—"bis conatus erat casus effingere in auro, / bis patriae cecidere
manus" (*Aeneid* VI, 32-3)—is presented in the following sonnet by
Manoel da Faria e Sousa. This is the later of two published versions: [27]

---

[25] In the text line 2 reads "de volar no alicionaba", which makes no sense.
[26] Gabriel del Corral, *La Cintia de Aranjuez*, ed. Joaquín Entrambasaguas (Madrid, 1945), p. 45.
[27] The earlier version, which appeared in Faria e Sousa's *Divinas y humanas flores* (Madrid, 1624), f. 12 r., reads as follows:

> Obligada dos veces la escultura
> de Dédalo dejó la diestra mano,
> para haber de emular del hijo vano,
> el daño, la caída, y la locura.
>
> Dos veces el cincel mostrar procura
> como al aire volaba un cuerpo humano,
> el peligro del rayo soberano,
> 'a muerte en Sol, y en mar la sepultura.
>
> Pero dos veces de dolor vencidas
> las manos, desmayó sin duda alguna,
> porque a tal simulacro el fin no cuadre.
>
> Así que el joven tuvo tres caídas,
> desde la esfera de las llamas, una,
> y dos, desde la idea de su padre.

In line 5, the text appears to have "sincel" or "fincel".

En gentil elegancia de escultura
Dédalo pretendió, con diestra mano,
al mundo presentar del hijo vano,
el daño, la caída y la locura.

Dos veces el cincel mostrar procura
como al aire volaba un cuerpo humano,
el peligro del rayo soberano,
la muerte en sol, en mar la sepultura.

Pero dos veces quiso la Fortuna
que no acertase, con dolor interno,
de las ideas dos el fin de alguna.

Cayó tres veces, pues, el joven tierno;
desde la esfera de las llamas una,
y luego dos desde el cincel paterno.[28]

Twice Daedalus tries to portray the death of his son and twice his sadness overcomes him. By a clever conceit, the poet sees Icarus as falling three times. It is characteristic of the seventeenth century that the sympathies of the poet are with the father, while Icarus is reduced to "hijo vano" and his flight to "locura," something that is not present in Virgil, where there is no censure of Icarus.

Several other works from the later seventeenth century command our attention, though they are substantially different, for various reasons, from the poems we have been studying.

Sor Juana Inés de la Cruz's "Primero sueño"

This magnificent poem owes its language and imagery to the poetic tradition we have been discussing, particularly, in an apparent paradox, to the poetry of courtly love. In her attempt to express the passionate quest of the soul for an understanding of the central principle of the universe, she adopts the form of the erotic tradition, with its yearning for transcendence and longing for the ideal. In the soul's flight upwards toward the "causa primera" she identifies in a sense with the Petrarchan lover in his adventure and makes his symbols and myths her own.

---

[28] Manoel da Faria e Sousa, *Fuente de Aganipe* (Madrid, 1646), f. 70v. In lines 5 and 14, as in the other version, the text has "sincel" or "fincel".

At critical moments in the work the familiar images of Icarus and Phaethon, with all the associated imagery that the Spanish love tradition has grafted onto them, appear as symbols already charged with enormous emotional meaning.

When Sor Juana's soul, in its "alado atrevimiento" (1. 368), seeks to contemplate the "céntrico punto" (1. 409) of the universe and is blinded and repulsed by the nightmare brilliance and complexity it finds, this setback is expressed in two images, firstly in terms of the danger of trying to look directly at the sun, and then, in an image suggested by association with the sun, by allusion to the experience of Icarus:

> Tanto no, del osado presupuesto,
> revocó la intención, arrepentida,
> la vista que intentó descomedida
> en vano hacer alarde
> contra objeto que excede en excelencia
> las líneas visuales
> —contra el sol, digo, cuerpo luminoso,
> cuyos rayos castigo son fogoso,
> que fuerzas desiguales
> despreciando, castigan rayo a rayo
> al confiado, antes atrevido
> y ya llorado ensayo
> (necia experiencia que costosa tanto
> fue, que Ícaro ya, su propio llanto
> lo anegó enternecido)—
> como el entendimiento, aquí vencido
> no menos de la inmensa pesadumbre
> (de diversas especies conglobado
> esférico compuesto),
> que de las cualidades
> de cada cual, cedió...[29] (11 454-475)

As with the lover confronted with the brilliance of his beloved's beauty, it is not that the soul's resolve weakens but rather that the brightness of the object of its quest dazzles and overwhelms it.[30] The soul is punished for its effort to reach the center of the universe just as Icarus, for his "confiado, antes atrevido / ... ensayo," was drowned in a sea of his

[29] Sor Juana Inés de la Cruz, *Obras completas*, ed. Alfonso Méndez-Plancarte (México, 1951), I, p. 346-7.
[30] A particularly close parallel with the lover is offered by Delitala y Castelví's "no le rindió la actividad del fuego..." (see above, p. 135).

own tears, an image that Sor Juana could only have found in Petrarchan
love poetry. That the poet should refer to Icarus' adventure as a "necia
experiencia" at this moment is not so much a condemnation of his
flight as an expression of the soul's dejection at its failure.

As the soul reflects upon this failure to reach its desired goal, one
of the consolations, to which the courtly lover also had frequent recourse,
is that, although the exploit was not crowned by complete success,
it was none the less glorious and dignifying. A whole strophe is devoted
to the consideration of the catastrophic fall of Phaethon who, though
his flight ended in tragedy, earned immortality for his courage. Sor
Juana says, somewhit surprisingly, of his flight:

> Tipo es, antes, modelo:
> ejemplar pernicioso
> que alas engendra a repetido vuelo,
> del ánimo ambicioso
> que —del mismo terror haciendo halago
> que al valor lisonjea—,
> las glorias deletrea
> entre los caracteres del estrago. (11. 803-810)

It seems that Sor Juana is echoing the moralists who complain that the
imagery of love poetry is dangerous, but her complaint is a very personal one and from somcone who has already been seduced into an
adventure that leads her against convention. The example of Phaethon
is pernicious in that it encouranges those who, because of natural ambition, are tempted to reach for the impossible.[31] Sor Juana's apparent condemnation of Phaethon results, not from the conviction that his example
should be avoided, but directly from the particular situation of the soul
in its moment of disappointment.

An ode by Manoel da Veiga Tagarro

The longest poem in the period based on the story of Icarus is in
Portuguese. It appeared in Manoel da Veiga's Laura de Anfriso, and
is in many ways different from most of the poems we have seen.
Although much of the work is narrative, it qualifies rather as an ex-
tended lyric than as a fable. The author, or his editor, calls it an ode.

---

[31] Cf. Ovid (Metamorphoses II, 327) "Hic situs est Phaethon, currus auriga pater-
ni, / quem si non tenuit, magnis tamen excidit ausis".

This is the text which, to my knowledge, has not been reprinted since its first edition.

1. Das cadeias de Minos vai fugindo
   Um nôvo nadador, caminho abrindo
   Pelo reino das Aves:
   Como quem em seu peito tinha as chaves
   Da grã sabedoria,
   Donde nasceu tã súbita ousadia:

2. Que não intenta um triste? ou que não ousa?
   Se entre duros tormentos não repousa?
   O engenho da dor
   É entre outros engenhos o maior;
   Tudo vê, tudo entende,
   Tudo alcança, obra tudo, tudo emprende.

3. Está Dédalo as asas fabricando,
   O filho para os ares animando;
   Já de pena o vestia;
   Já entre esperança, e agonia
   Lágrimas derramava,
   Como quem sua morte adivinhava.

4. Filho meu pelo meio voareis
   Para que o raio ardente não proveis
   Da reluzente esfera;
   Que como vossas asas são de cera:
   Ficarão derretidas,
   E vossas esperanças já perdidas.

5. Isto dizendo, o abraça ùltimamente
   E já o ar suspenso prova, e sente
   Milagrosos extremos;
   Levando em vivas naus, de cera os remos,
   Que com nobre artifício
   Imitam das barquinhas o exercício:

6. Entretanto seguro o filho vai
   Enquanto segue o acautelado pai;
   Mas logo de atrevido
   Com o vôo desusado esvaecido
   Se alevantou nos ares,
   Dando penas ao sol, e nome aos mares.

7. As correntes do mar impetuosas
   Lágrimas receberão saudosas,
   Que os olhos destilarão
   Do pai choroso, quando contemplarão
   As penas sôbre as águas
   Ai que duros tormentos! ai que mágoas!

8. Assim Dédalo triste vai chorando,
   Ao sepultado filho exéquias dando;
   Até que enfim parou;
   E o remígio das asas pendurou
   Para eterno exemplo,
   Fazendo a Febo um suntuoso templo

9. Ali pinta de Andrógeo a fera morte; [32]
   Dos Cecrópidas pinta a dura sorte: [33]
   Tambén urna pequena
   Inocências catorze ali condena,
   Contra os Pais infiel,
   Duro estipêndio, téssera cruel.

10. Ali defronte Creta respondia,
    Que os açoites do mar tambén sofria,
    Ali o Amor do Touro,
    Que o corpo tem de leite, e os cornos de ouro,
    Por quem se viu perdida
    Pasifaé Rainha alta, e subida.

11. Ali pinta com mão maravilhosa
    A vaca de madeira mentirosa,
    Que nos campos pastava;
    E a rainha infeliz dissimulava;
    Ali o grão portento,
    De Venus torpe infando monumento.

12. O cego labirinto ali pintava,
    Que com engano sôbre si tornava,
    Assim mesmo ocorrendo,

[32] Androgeus was the son of Minos and Pasiphae. According to legend he earned the jealousy of Aegeus, king of Athens, by winning the Athenian Games. When Aegeus killed him, Minos took his revenge by laying siege to Athens and exacting yearly tribute of seven men and seven women to be sacrificed to the Minotaur.

[33] According to one legend the Athenians were supposed to be descended from Cecrops.

As voltas e caminhos retorçendo,
Enrêdos duvidosos,
De paredes sofismas flexuosos.

13. Mas de Ariadne as lágrimas atenta
Dédalo que com arte o fio inventa.
O qual enovelasse
Para que assim Teseu saída achasse;
Tambén te aqui pintara,
Ó Ícaro, se a dor não no estourara.

14. Três vêzes debuxar-te pretendia
Três vêzes o pincel da mâo caía
Ó menino imprudente!
Que serás dor do Pai perpètuamente!
Pois no ares pagaste
A glória juvenil com que voaste.

15. Aprendam em teu dano os voadores
A temer da Fortuna os resplandores;
Que enfim asas de cera
Mal podem sustentar ardente esfera;
Vai a Fortuna ardendo,
Ouro, quanto mais cera, desfazendo.

16. Ai de quem de ouro as verdes asas teve
Mas à vista de um sol voando em breve;
En tão alta excelência
Logo provou de sorte a inclemência:
Ícaro morre em águas;
Ai daquêle que morre, e vive em mágoas!

17. Dédalo, dividamos o exercício:
Eu tomo sôbre mim o triste ofício,
Que tus dor te impede;
Eu lavrarei, se a Musa mo concede,
Nos bronzes da memória
De teu amado filho a dura história.

18. Quando em seu próprio dano a alma se enleia
Milho sabe pintar a mágoa alheia;
Eu pintarei os teus
Tormentos desiguais, tu pinta os meus;
Que eu triste quando os pinto,
O pincel frouxo, e mão caída sinto.

19. Pinta quem morre em mar de pranto amaro
    Vendo eclipses a pares do sol claro;
    O teu filho acabou
    Porque do sol ardente provocou
    Os raios que o mataram;
    E eu morro porque os raios me faltaram.[34]

The first eight stanzas, with the exception of the second, narrate the outlines of the story as told by Ovid in *Metamorphoses*. Stanza 2 is a parenthetical expression of sympathy with the fate of Icarus and a commentary on the power of sadness which can lead men to great feats of ingenuity. In stanzas 1 and 5 the belief that dates back to the Greek mythographers, that Daedalus and his son really escaped by sea seems to be implied, for in the first stanza, the elements of sea and sky are reversed as we saw them in two sonnets by Polo de Medina and in stanza 5 the image of Icarus' wings as oars occurs once again. A curious omission is Daedalus' warning about flying too near the sea. The warning about going too high is the advice that becomes important, but most poets keep the idea of the warning of two hazards to be avoided by flying a middle path. Another departure from Ovid is the dedication of the temple which comes, as we also saw in two Spanish poems, from Virgil.[35]

In the next five stanzas Daedalus is seen at work on the decorations in this temple, re-creating the history of the labyrinth he built and the tragic events associated with it. At the end of stanza 13 we see again the story of Daedalus attempting to depict the death of his son and being overcome by grief, based on *Aeneid* VI.

Stanzas 15 and 16 draw a moral from the story of Icarus' flight—all those who fly (on the wings of ambition) should beware of the attractions of Fortune, for she can melt gold, let alone wax. As in *Soledades*, flight is used as the image of worldly ambition and Icarus is the example of the person whose downfall is caused by the inability to resist the temptations of fame and fortune.

The poem ends with a touching apostrophe to Daedalus the artist. The poet will take from Daedalus the grave responsibility of recording for posterity the death of his son if the legendary artist will only give immortality to the poet's great sadness for, if Icarus died because the rays of the sun were too bright, the poet suffers because the sun does

---

[34] Manoel de Veiga, *Laura de Anfriso* (Evora, 1627), ff. 42r-44r.
[35] See above, pp. 136 and 137.

not shine at all, that is, presumably, his lady has refused to look kindly on him.

The "Fábula de Ícaro" by Hierónimo Barrionuevo y Peralta

It is curious that such a popular myth should have inspired, in an era of many such compositions, only one lengthy narrative on the subject. Cossío considers Barrionuevo's the only one and he has published two stanzas of it (p. 628). It is not a particularly distinguished work but it merits our attention here as the only extant poem in the genre. This is the text, after the manuscript in the Biblioteca Nacional in Madrid:

1. Aves que de esos cielos los candores
   cortáis siempre ligeras con desaires,[36]
   enamorados tiernos ruiseñores
   que festejáis las selvas con donaires;
   jilguerillos pintados de colores,
   ramilletes curiosos de esos aires,
   a todos os convido en este canto
   a ver volar, y a levantarse tanto.

2. En Creta un laberinto fabricado
   al minotauro estaba, tan curioso
   que el que una vez entraba descuidado
   el quedarse allá dentro era forzoso,
   siendo para el sustento dedicado
   del minotauro horrendo y espantoso,
   que de la humana sangre siendo ingrato
   era a su gusto el ordinario plato.

3. Dejo aquí de contar quien éste fuese
   ni quien lo fabricó ni por qué modo;
   solo quiero decir, aunque me pese,
   que regado de sangre estaba todo,
   no hallándose quien solo se atreviese
   a entrar en él allí por ningún modo.
   Teseo solo du un ovillo armado
   entró y salió dejándolo burlado.

---

[36] Cossío (p. 628) transcribes "desgaires", which is the most probable reading. The text seems to have been altered at this point and the "g" is half obliterated. Lines 2 and 4 both seem to have been changed in an otherwise very clear manuscript. Both lines appear to have read "desgaires" originally.

4. A éste pues condenaban como a muerte
   furioso en quien el monstruo ejecutaba
   y aquel que le cabía triste suerte
   poco o nada la vida dilataba;
   sólo Dédalo fue, si bien se advierte,
   el que tanta clausura profanaba,
   pues siendo padre e hijo condenados
   fueron de aquesos aires invidiados;

5. porque estando en mitad deste retiro,
   teniendo varias plumas allegadas
   que juntas con el hilo, no me admiro
   que en cera fuesen alas bien pobladas,
   con las cuales en uno y otro giro
   dando en aquesas nubes aletadas,
   así buscando losas con desvelo,
   coronarse querían de ese cielo.

6. De la manera que el cerúleo campo
   el caballo naval corre ligero
   y entre la espuma cana vuela franco
   sin tropezar en nada muy severo,
   oyéndose del uno y otro banco
   crujir juntos el hierro y el madero,
   de esta suerte los dos en compañía,
   al padre el hijo alegre le seguía.

7. Pero como [?] en la grandeza,
   devanecióse aquel que siendo pobre
   al salir a volar con la riqueza
   en alas de ese lustre de oro o cobre
   así en vaivenes dando de cabeza
   Ícaro, porque nada allí le sobre,
   comenzó a hacer puntas levantadas
   en lucidas esferas estrelladas.

8. El padre como más esprimentado
   al hijo reprehende y amonesta,
   diciéndole que tema desbocado
   la caída del cielo allí funesta.
   El mediodía entrado, es acertado
   ni subir ni bajar la airosa cuesta.
   Pero él en escollos de arreboles
   hizo en el cielo varios caracoles.

9. Ya se remonta, ya se considera
    ser planetas del cielo levantado,
    hiciendo de las plumas escalera,
    inadvertido mozo malogrado;
    llegó a verse tan alto que pudiera
    desmentir a las nubes descollado,
    altivo, presumido, presuroso,
    que el oro apenas se miró en su bozo.

10. Eolo, padre antiguo de los vientos,
    levantando a mirarle la cabeza,
    hizo entonces notables sentimientos,
    envidioso de ver su ligereza,
    y haciéndole la salva en instrumentos
    las ninfas desas auras y belleza
    con amoroso canto pretendían
    gozar del bien que entonces poseían.

11. Cortés el mozo suspendió la gala
    en el volar y, reprimiendo el vuelo,
    no le parece la región tan mala
    al contemplar alegre tanto cielo
    hasta que allí invidioso le regala
    el compuesto de plumas ese Delo
    desatándolas todas poco a poco,
    volviéndose de pena el mozo loco.

12. De la manera que el neblí ligero
    la perdiz de su furia salteada
    desplumada en el aire lo primero
    deja la vida de ella deseada
    y puesta entre las uñas astillero
    al suelo llega muerta ensangrentada,
    Ícaro, desta suerte derribado,
    a los rayos del sol cayó turbado.

13. Hacia bajo llevaba la cabeza,
    manos y pies abiertos y estirados,
    perdida ya del todo la belleza,
    descompuestos los miembros delicados,
    mostrando en el bajar tan gran presteza [37]
    que al pasar esos aires dilatados

[37] Cossío has "tanta presteza", which is, in my opinion, a misreading.

cometa pareció precipitada
que se acaba muriendo de abrasada.

14. En el mar acabó tanta hermosura;
     en el mar se acabó el ardiente fuego;
     el mar le señaló la sepultura
     y sólo en él halló el fatal sosiego.
     El mar gozó en aquesta coyuntura
     del nombre dilatado de que luego
     por ser de Ícaro solo monumento
     le llamaron el ícaro elemento.[38]

This is by far the most fanciful version of the Icarus story we have seen and by no means the most successful artistically. The narrative has been reduced to its basic elements, referring only briefly to events such as Daedalus' admonition to his son, traditionally one of the focal points of the story, and elaborating on several elements that are new, at least to the tradition that we have been dealing with. The first stanza, an invitation to the birds to listen to the poet's tale, is new, as is the rather lurid description of the minotaur in its lair. The poet leans toward complex analogies, such as that with the boat (stanza 6) which we have seen before in simpler terms, or (stanza 12) the parallel made between Icarus' fall and the world of hawking, reminiscent of the passage at the end of Góngora's *Soledades* discussed in an earlier chapter. The critical moment of Icarus's fascination with his ability to fly obviously attracts the poet for he presents a delightful, rococo picture of Icarus serenaded by nymphs and admired by Aeolus.

The style of the poem is rather mannered and subject to sudden changes of tone, as when the lighthearted first stanza gives way to the frightful description of the monster in the following lines. Such expressions as "era a su gusto el ordinario plato", or, in another tone, "no le parece la región tan mala" seem almost prosaic, a word that occurred to Cossío also in his brief remarks on the poem (pp. 627-629). While some passages are comparable with the finest baroque poetry (notably octave 6) the total effect is somewhat confusing, as if the poet were not quite sure of himself.

---

[38] The manuscript is entitled *Comedias y poesías varias, por Juan Cantón de Salazar.* MS original. Año de 1700. A marginal note, however, ascribes the works to Barrionuevo. For Cossío's comments on the poem and some remarks on the biography of the poet, see Cossío, *Fábulas,* pp. 627-629.

CONCLUSION

The first lesson of the preceding pages is the great richness and diversity achieved over a considerable period of time by a large number of poets, all of whom believed strongly in the doctrine of *imitatio*. Though a great many of the poems have been seen to be derivative —and all probably are, since the artful reworking of traditional motifs was the poets' aim—the vast majority are skillfully original, even to the modern reader, and many quite brilliantly so. This study of one of the most popular myths of the period, as well as providing a chronicle of certain changes in attitude to the myth, has reinforced impressions of the particular genius of some of the poets we have looked at. Góngora's ingenious reworking of the elements of the myths into brilliant conceits stands out, for example. In contrast to it, Lope's use of pagan mythology seems less precise, sometimes even confused. The figure of Icarus as symbol of the aspiration of the artist holds such a fascination for poets like Herrera and Villamediana, that he seems to illuminate whole aspects of their work.

The focus of our study has been narrow in order to concentrate on one of the myths most alluded to in the period. Both the poets and their critics and detractors perceived Icarus to be particularly appropriate as a symbol of the Petrarchan lover/poet and the young flyer is at the very center of a whole complex of images central to the Petrarchan tradition, most of them also mythological—Prometheus, Phaethon, the Phoenix, the butterfly and even Cupid himself. But although the image of young Icarus remains a constant of the tradition, particularly in Spain, the context in which it is evoked and the connotations of the references undergo major changes. Stated very broadly, the earliest versions of the story, including all the Italian poems, portray Icarus as a symbol of heroic ambition, seeing his fall as conferring immortality, while later writers tend to present the young flyer as a source of *escarmiento,* an example to be avoided. In France Icarus' career is brief and parallels the period of ascendancy of the most flamboyant, overpetrarchising while his fall from grace coincides with the rise of classicism.

The first thing that stands out in Spain is the increasingly moralistic attitude toward mythology in general and to our myth in particular, that is evident in the translations of Ovid and the manuals of mythology. The earliest translations of the story appeared without commentary, content to retell the stories, while all later versions included moral or euhemeristic interpretations. In the manuals there is a trend toward a more analytic, pedantic treatment of myth and this scholarly activity reaches a peak in the decade 1580-1590. While earlier writers seem to be attracted by the sheer power of the myth, later translators and commentators feel the need to explain it in terms of Christian morality, reducing myth to allegory. This means increasing criticism for Icarus's disobedience, vanity, even profanity and a greater readiness to see his death as a result of silly pride or as punishment for a transgression of the natural law. Even his father, who has been since classical times a constant symbol of the artist, the old artificer, is constantly condemned in the seventeenth century for daring to leave his native element.

A similar trend is clear in poetic evocations of the myth. The early versions of the story, deriving directly from Sannazaro and Tansillo, are heroic or tragic, while the majority of later versions are comic or critical. In Garcilaso's Sonnet XII, the poet sees the danger exemplified in the story but, refusing to be deterred, looks rather at the glory that might be his posthumously. In this context Cossío speaks of the "aspiración meramente artística y ajena a toda preocupación moral" in the Italian Renaissance poets and their early Spanish imitators (p. 51). As we go on, moral questions seem to preoccupy even the lyric poets (with notable exceptions such as the "romantic" Villamediana) and Icarus is increasingly mocked, chided or condemned. He becomes more frequently a symbol of man's rashness or cupidity than an expression of his highest aspirations in love or art. In a sense this constitutes a return to the classics for, as we saw, most classical interpretations of the story of Icarus were critical.

This general change is paralleled by other developments in poetic practice. Not least of these is the growth, nurtured by Góngora, of the burlesque treatment of mythological subjects, confronting the hallowed figures of the classical pantheon with grotesque—often all too human— situations for comic effect. Such associations, of Icarus with the proverbial vanity of court life or with the effort to raise the river Tajo to the city of Toledo, for example, devalue the myth, in that they make it ever harder to evoke them in serious contexts. Some of the factors contributing to the development of this less idealistic view of the classical myths are undoubtedly the continual quest for originality within a finite area; the developing spirit of rationality as evidenced in the increasing scholarliness of the manuals; the general trend toward more complex imagery which reflects the taste for *agudeza* or wit of a rather erudite kind; and perhaps connected with all this, the atmosphere of the Counter Reformation and a consequent reduction in the willingness to treat classical mythology completely seriously.

The trend toward burlesque is also connected with the more general disfavor into which both the forms and the ideology of the Petrarchan tradition were coming. This may be seen very clearly in England in the sonnets of Sir Philip Sidney in which centuries of convention are examined quizzically. There are two other symptoms of what seems ultimately merely to be the exhaustion of the possibilities of a convention. The first of these is the tendency toward ever greater obliqueness of reference, partly due, again, to the constant search for originality and partly, also, to the developing taste for greater "erudición poética". These more oblique references, to feathers, wax or a fall, lead, in lesser poets, as often to obscurity as to insight. Second and related is the trend toward what might be called miniaturization. Icarus, who had once occupied center stage in a sonnet or a longer poem, becomes part of the decor, an image alluded to in passing. What had been the subject of a sonnet for Tansillo or Garcilaso, becomes a detail in a much more complex structure in the baroque poets.

Why this particular myth should have appealed so greatly to the poets of Spain seems to defy reasonable analysis. The most likely answer is fairly mundane. The Petrarchan tradition was imported from Italy at the time of the flourishing of a particular poet, Luigi Tansillo, who was a friend of Garcilaso, the man most responsible for bringing the tradition to Spain. It seems probable that the whole vogue of the myth of Icarus in Spain stems directly from the association between these two poets. This would explain the suddenness with which the fascination begins and the frequency with which certain aspects of the story are referred to. (That we can point so clearly to the few cases where inspiration comes from an entirely fresh source, the *Aeneid*, for example, suggests the homogeneity of the majority of versions.) This corroborates a belief about Renaissance poetry in general, that poets found their inspiration more often in contemporaries, in their own country or in Italy, than they did in the classics.

It is impossible not to see in the kind of changes referred to above a very poignant picture, though not an explanation, of the decline of the lyric genius at the end of Spain's Golden Age, but can we go further? I suggested at the outset that we may infer something about the values of his age by the artist's conception of the myths of our civilization. The image of Cupid on 42nd Street tells us something about contemporary views of love. In the same way it seems to me possible to suggest that the changing light in which Icarus is portrayed through the poetry of Spain's Golden Age has something to tell us about the values of that time. We have seen that it became increasingly harder for Spaniards, both scholars and poets, to see that "something of magnanimity" that Sir Francis Bacon saw in the perilous flight of Icarus. It is difficult not to see in this change an analogy for the change from the expansive, optimistic spirit of the early sixteenth century to the much more closed world of Counter Reformation Spain.

BIBLIOGRAPHY

Critical and Reference Works

Alemany y Selfa, Bernardo. *Vocabulario de las obras de don Luis de Góngora y Argote.* Madrid, 1930.

Allen, Don Cameron. *The Harmonious Vision; Studies in Milton's Poetry.* Baltimore, 1954.

— — *Image and Meaning.* Baltimore, 1960.

— — *The Legend of Noah; Renaissance Rationalism in Art, Science and Letters.* Urbana, 1949.

Alonso, Dámaso. *Cuatro poetas españoles.* Madrid, 1962.

— — *De los siglos oscuros al de oro.* Madrid, 1958.

— — *La lengua poética de Góngora.* Madrid, 1950.

Amos, Flora Ross. *Early Theories of Translation.* New York, 1920.

Andrews, J. Richard. *Juan del Encina; Prometheus in Search of Prestige.* Berkeley, 1959.

Ashton, J. W. "The Fall of Icarus". *Renaissance Studies in Honor of Hardin Craig.* Palo Alto, 1941, pp. 152-9.

Aulnoy, Marie Catherine, comtesse d'. *Relation du voyage en Espagne.* Ed. Foulché-Delbosc. Paris, 1926.

Ayrton, Michael. *The Testament of Daedalus.* London, 1962

Bachelard, Gaston. *L'Air et les songes.* Paris, 1943.

Batllori, Miguel. *Gracián y el barroco.* Roma, 1958.

Beardsley, Theodore. *Hispano-Classical Translations Printed between 1482 and 1699.* Pittsburgh, 1970.

Bomli, P. *La Femme dans l'Espagne du Siècle d'Or.* La Haye, 1950.

Born, L. K. "Ovid and Allegory". *Speculum,* 9 (1934), pp. 362-379.

Brockhaus, Ernst. *Góngoras Sonettendichtung.* Bochum, 1935.

Brower, Reuben Arthur (ed.). *On Translation.* Cambridge, Mass., 1959 (Harvard Studies in Comparative Literature, Vol. 23).

Bush, Douglas. *Mythology and the Renaissance Tradition.* Minneapolis, 1932.

Cabañas. Pablo. *El mito de Orfeo en la literatura española* Madrid, 1948.

— — "Ícaro o el atrevimiento". *Revista de Literatura,* 1 (1952), pp. 453-460.

Celaya, Gabriel. *Exploración de la poesía.* Barcelona, 1964.

Cioffari, Vincenzo. *Fortune and Fate, from Democritus to St. Thomas Aquinas.* New York, 1935.

Collard, Andrée, *Nueva poesía, conceptismo y culteranismo en la crítica española.* Madrid, 1968.

Cooke, J. D. "Euhemerism: a Medieval Interpretation of Classical Paganism". *Speculum,* 4 (1927), pp. 396-410.

Cossío, José María de. *Fábulas mitológicas en España.* Madrid, 1952.

Croce, Benedetto. "Per un famoso sonetto del Tansillo". *La critica,* 6 (1908), pp. 237-240.

Curtius, Ernst Robert. *European Literature and the Latin Middle Ages.* New York, 1953.

Deferrari, Roy Joseph, Barry, Sister M. Inviolata, and McGuire, Martin R. P. *A Concordance of Ovid.* Washington, 1939.

Demerson, Guy. *La Mythologie classique dans l'oeuvre de la Pléiade.* Geneva, 1972.

Durán, Manuel. "Manierismo en Quevedo". *Actas del Segundo Congreso Internacional de Hispanistas.* Nimega, 1967.

Eigeldinger, Marc. *La Mythologie solaire dans l'oeuvre de Racine.* Genève, 1969.

Fucilla, Joseph G. *Estudios sobre el petrarquismo en España*. Madrid, 1960.
— — "Etapas en el desarrollo del mito de Ícaro en el renacimiento y en el siglo de oro". *"Superbi colli" e altri saggi*. Rome, 1963, pp. 45-84.
— — "Fuentes italianas de Francisco de Figueroa". *Clavileño*, 16 (1952), pp. 5-10.
Gallego Morell, A. "El mito de Faetón en la literatura española". *Clavileño*, 37 (1956), pp. 13-26 and 38 (1956), pp. 31-43. Also published as a book by the Consejo Superior de Investigaciones Científicas. Madrid, 1961.
Gilman, Stephen. "An Introduction to the Ideology of the Baroque in Spain". *Symposium*, 1 (1946), pp. 82-107.
— — *The Art of "La Celestina"*. Madison, 1956.
— — "The Fall of Fortune, from Allegory to Fiction". *Filologia Romanza*, 16 (1957), pp. 337-354.
Green, Henry. *Shakespeare and the Emblem Writers*. London, 1870.
Haldane, J. B. S. *Daedalus; or Science and the Future*. New York, 1924.
Hardt, Manfred. *Das Bild in der Dichtung*. Munich, 1966.
Harlan, Frances. *The Sonnets of Villamediana*. Unpublished doctoral dissertation, New York University, 1949.
Hennebert, Frédéric. *Histoire des traductions françaises d'auteurs grecs et latins pendant le XVIᵉ et le XVIIᵉ siècles*. Gand, 1858.
Highet, Gilbert. *The Classical Tradition*. Oxford, 1949.
Huizinga, Johan. *The Waning of the Middle Ages*. London, 1927.
Jacobsen, Eric. *Translation, a Traditional Craft*. Copenhagen, 1958.
Jammes, Robert. *Études sur l'oeuvre poétique de Luis de Góngora*. Bordeaux, 1967.
Jung, Marc-René. *Hercule dans la littérature française du XVIᵉ siècle*, Genève, 1966.
Lapesa, Rafael. *La trayectoria poética de Garcilaso*. Madrid, 1968.
Larwill, Paul Herbert. *La Théorie de la traduction au début de la renaissance d'après les traductions imprimées en France entre 1477 et 1527*. Munich, 1934.
Levin, Harry. *The Overreacher; a Study of Christopher Marlowe*. Cambridge, Mass., 1952.
Lewis, C. S. *The Allegory of Love*. New York, 1958.
Lida, María Rosa. "Transmisión y recreación de temas grecolatinos en la poesía lírica española". *Revista de Filología Hispánica*, 1 (1939), pp. 20-63.
López-Rey, José. *Velázquez; a Catalogue Raisonné of his Oeuvre*. London, 1963.
Malkiel, María Rosa Lida de. "Perduración de la literatura antigua en Occidente" *Romance Philology*, 5 (1951), pp. 99-131.
— — "La tradición clásica en España". *Nueva Revista de Filología Hispánica*, 5 (1951), pp. 183-223.
Matthiesen, F. O. *Translation: an Elizabethan Art*. New York, 1965.
Maza, Francisco de la. *La mitología clásica en el arte colonial de México*. Mexico, 1968.
Mele, Eugenio and González Palencia, Ángel. "Notas sobre Francisco de Figueroa". *Revista de Filología Española*, 25 (1941), pp. 333-382.
Murray, Henry A. "American Icarus". *Clinical Studies of Personality*, Vol. II of *Case Histories in Clinical and Abnormal Psychology*. New York, 1955, pp. 615-641.
Nelson, John Charles. *Renaissance Theory of Love; the Context of Giordano Bruno's "Eroici furori"*. New York, 1958.
Ogilvie, Daniel M. *Psychodynamics of Fantasized Flight*, unpublished dissertation, Harvard University, 1967.
Orozco Díaz, Emilio. *El teatro y la teatralidad del Barroco*. Barcelona, 1969.
The Oxford Book of Italian Verse. 2nd. ed. Oxford, 1952.
Panofsky, Erwin. "Renaissance and Renascences". *Kenyon Review*, 6 (1944), pp. 201-236.
— — *Renaissance and Renascences in Western Art*. New York, and Evanston, 1969.
— — *Studies in Iconology*. New York, 1967.
Parker, Alexander A. "La agudeza en algunos sonetos de Quevedo". *Estudios dedicados a don Ramón Menéndez Pidal*, Vol. III, Madrid, 1952
Patch, H. R. *The Goddess Fortuna in Medieval Literature*. New York, 1967.
Penney, Clara Louise. *Printed Books in the Hispanic Society of America*. New York, 1965.
Porqueras May, Alberto. *El problema de la verdad poética en el Siglo de Oro*. Madrid, 1961.
— — *El prólogo como género literario*. Madrid, 1957.

Praz, Mario. *Mnemosyne: The Parallel between Literature and the Visual Arts*. Princeton, 1970.
— — *Studies in Seventeenth Century Imagery*, 2nd ed., expanded, Roma, 1964.
The Renaissance Philosophy of Man. Ed. Ernst Cassirer, Paul Oskar Kristeller, John Hermann Randall, Jr. Chicago and London, 1969.
Ricciardelli, Michele. "Il mito de Icaro e la correlazione". *Romance Notes*, 8 (1967), pp. 287-8.
Rojas, Fernando de. "El testamento de...". *Revista de Filología Española*, 16 (1921), pp. 366-388.
Rozas, Juan Manuel. "Dos notas sobre el mito de Faetón en el siglo de oro". *Bole·ín Cultural de la Embajada Argentina*, 2 (1963), pp. 81-2.
Russell, Bertrand. *Icarus; or the Future of Science*. London, 1926.
Sandys, John Edwin. *A history of Classical Scholarship*. Cambridge, 1906-08.
Savory, Theodore. *The Art of Translation*. London, 1957.
Schevill, Rudolph. *Ovid and the Renascence in Spain*. Berkeley, 1913.
Segal, Erich. "Hero and Leander, Góngora and Marlowe". *Comparative Literature*, XV (1963), pp. 338-356.
Seznec, Jean. *The Survival of the Pagan Gods*. New York, 1953.
Shroder, Maurice Z. *Icarus; the Image of the Artist in French Romanticism*. Cambridge, Mass., 1961.
Slochower, Harry. *Mythopoesis: Mythic Patterns in the Literary Classics*. Detroit, 1970.
Smith, Hallett. *Elizabethan Poetry*. Cambridge, Mass., 1952.
Solalinde, Antonio. "La fecha del *Ovide Moralisé*". *Revista de Filología Española*, 8 (1921), pp. 285-288.
Ticknor, George. *History of Spanish Literature*. Boston, 1863.
Valgimigli, M. "Comunicazioni ed appunti". *Giornale storico della letteratura italiana*, 53 (1909), pp. 176-178.
Vivier, Robert. *Frères du ciel, quelques aventures poétiques d'Icare et de Phaéton*. Brussels, 1962.
Wadsworth, James B. *Lyons, 1473-1503*. Cambridge, Mass., 1962.
Waith, Eugene M. *The Herculean Hero: Marlowe, Chapman, Shakespeare and Dryden*. New York, 1962.
Woodward, L. J. "Two Images in the Soledades of Góngora". *Modern Language Notes*, 76 (1961), pp. 773-785.

BIBLIOGRAPHY

Poetry Texts

Acuña, Hernando de. *Varias poesías*. Ed. Helena Catena de Vindel. Madrid, 1954.
Aldana, Francisco de. *Poesías*. Ed. Elias Rivers. Madrid, 1957.
Anguillara, Giovanni Andrea dell'. *Le metamorfosi di Ovidio, ridotte da... in ·ttava rima con l'annotationi di Guiseppe Horologgi*. Venice, 1571.
Anonymous. *Ovide moralisé*. Amsterdam, 1915-1938. Facsimile, Wiesbaden, 1966.
— — *The Romance of Flamenca*. Ed. Marion E. Porter. Princeton, 1962.
Arguijo, Juan de. *Obras completas*. Ed. R. Benítez Claros. Santa Cruz de Tenerife, 1968.
Avalos y Figueroa, Diego de. *La miscelánea austral*. Lima, 1603.
Barbezieux, Rigaud de. *Les Chansons du troubadour...* Ed Joseph Anglade. Montpellier, 1919.
Barrionuevo y Peralta, Hierónimo. Ms. in Biblioteca Nacional de Madrid, entitled *Comedias y poesías varias, por Juan Cantón de Salazar*.
Barrios, Miguel de. *Flor de Apolo*. Brussels, 1665.
Boccaccio, Giovanni. *Opere minori in volgare*. Milano, 1971.
Bruno, Giordano. *Opere italiane*. Ed. G. Gentile. Bari, 1908.
Cancionero antequerano: 1627-1628. Madrid, 1950.
Caro, Annibale. *Rime*. Venice, 1757.
Castellani, Tommaso. *Rime diverse*. Venice, 1549.
Cervantes, Miguel de. *La Galatea*. Ed. Juan Bautista Avalle-Arce. Madrid, 1961.

Cetina, Gutierre de. *Obras.* Ed. Hazañas and la Rúa. Sevilla, 1895.

Chaucer, Geoffrey. *Works.* Ed. F. N. Robinson, 2nd ed., Boston, 1957.

Corral, Gabriel del. *La Cintia de Aranjuez.* Ed. Joaquín Entrambasaguas. Madrid, 1945.

Cruz, San Juan de la. *Poesías completas.* Ed. Dámaso Alonso. Madrid, 1959.

Cruz, Sor Juana Inés de la. *Obras completas.* Ed. Alfonso Méndez-Plancarte. México, 1951.

Cueva, Juan de la. *El infamador, Los siete infantes de Lara y El ejemplar poético.* Ed. Francisco A. de Icaza. Madrid, 1924.

Delitala y Castelví, José. *Cima del monte Parnaso español.* Caller, 1672.

Desportes, Philippe. *Les Amours de Diane.* Ed. Victor E. Graham. Geneva, 1959.

— — *Les Amours d'Hippolyte.* Ed. Victor E. Graham. Geneva, 1960.

— — *Cléonice, Dernières amours.* Ed Victor E. Graham. Geneva, 1962.

— — *Élégies.* Ed. Victor E. Graham. Geneva, 1961.

Du Bellay, Joaquim. *Les Regrets et autres oeuvres poétiques.* Ed. M. A. Screech. Geneva, 1966.

Faria e Sousa, Manoel da. *Divinas y humanas flores.* Madrid, 1624.

— — *Fuente de Aganipe.* Madrid, 1646.

Figueroa, Francisco de. *Poesías.* Madrid, 1943.

Figueroa, Suárez de. *La constante Amarilis.* Madrid, 1781.

Foulché-Delbosc, Raymond. *Cancionero castellano del siglo XV.* Madrid, 1915.

Garcilaso de la Vega. *Obras completas.* Ed. Elías Rivers. Madrid, 1964.

Garcilaso de la Vega y sus comentaristas. Ed. Antonio Gallego Morell. 2nd ed., Madrid, 1972.

Góngora, Luis de. *Letrillas.* Ed. Robert Jammes. Paris, 1963.

— — *Obras completas* Ed. Millé. 6th ed. Madrid, 1967.

— — *Soledades.* Ed Dámaso Alonso. 3rd ed. Madrid, 1956.

— — *Sonetos completos.* Ed. Biruté Ciplijauskaité. Madrid, 1969.

Gower, John. *The English Works.* Ed. G. C. Macaulay. London, 1900.

Gracián, Baltasar. *Agudeza y arte de ingenio.* Ed. Evaristo Correa Calderón. Madrid, 1969.

Guarini, Giovanni Battista. *Rime.* Venice, 1598.

Herrera, Fernando de. *Poesías.* Ed. Vicente García de Diego. Madrid, 1962.

— — *Rimas inéditas.* Ed. José Manuel Blecua. Madrid, 1948.

Jodelle, Étienne. *Oeuvres complètes.* Ed. E. Balmas. Paris, 1965-68.

Leonardo de Argensola, Lupercio and Bartolomé. *Rimas de...* Ed. José Manuel Blecua. Zaragoza, 1950-51.

Lorris, Guillaume de and Jean de Meun. *Le Roman de la rose.* Ed. Félix Lecoy. Paris, 1968.

Lugo y Dávila, Diego de. *Teatro popular.* Madrid, 1622.

Manrique, Gómez. *Cancionero de...* Ed. Antonio Paz y Meliá. Madrid, 1885.

Medina, Polo de. *Obras completas.* Murcia, Biblioteca de autores murcianos, 1948.

Mena, Juan de. *Laberinto de Fortuna.* Ed. John G. Cummins. Salamanca, 1968.

Molière, Jean Baptiste. *Oeuvres complètes.* Ed. R. Jouanny. Paris, 1962.

Ovid, *The Metamorphoses.* Translated by A. E. Watts. Berkeley, 1954.

Ovidio. *Del metamorphoses.* Tr. Felipe Mey. Tarragona, 1586.

— — *Las heroidas.* Tr. Antonio Alatorre. México, 1950.

— — *Los metamorphoseos.* Tr. Antonio Pérez Sigler. Salamanca, 1580.

— — *Las metamorphoses, o Transformaciones repartidas en quince libros y traduzidas en castellano.* Anvers, en casa de J. Steelsio, 1551.

— — *Las transformaciones.* Tr. Pedro Sánchez de Viana. Valladolid, 1589.

— — *Transformaciones.* (Catalan translation.) Barcelona, 1494.

Petrarca, Francesco di. *Canzionere.* Ed. G. Contini. Torino, 1964.

Poetas líricos de los siglos XVI y XVII. Ed. Adolfo de Castro. Vols. 22 and 42 of *Biblioteca de Autores Españoles.*

Portugal, Manuel de. *Poesía española.* MS 756 of the Biblioteca Nacional de Madrid.

Quevedo, Francisco de. *Obras completas.* Ed. José Manuel Blecua. Barcelona, Planeta, 1963.

Rebolledo, Bernardino de. *Ocios del conde don...* Amberes, 1660.

Ronsard, Pierre de. *Les Amours.* Ed. Henri and Catherine Weber. Paris, 1963.

Saavedra y Guzmán, Martín de. *Ocios de Aganipe.* Trani, 1634.
Sannazaro, Iacopo. *Opere volgari.* Ed. A. Mauso. Bari, 1961.
Soto de Rojas, Pedro. *Obras. Ed.* A. Gallego Morell. Madrid, 1950.
Tansillo, Luigi. *Il canzoniere.* Naples, 1926.
Tasso, Torquato. *Rime.* Bologna, 1900.
Vega Carpio, Lope de. *La Dorotea.* Ed. Edwin S. Morby. Berkeley, 1958.
— — *Obras poéticas.* Ed. José Manuel Blecua. Barcelona, 1969.
Veiga, Manoel da. *Laura de Anfriso.* Évora, 1627.
Villamediana, Juan de Tassis, Conde de. *Obras.* Ed. Juan Manuel Rozas. Madrid, 1969.

BIBLIOGRAPHY

Prose Texts

Alciati, Andrea. *Emblemata.* Antwerp, 1692.
Alfonso X, el sabio. *General estoria.* Pt. I. Ed. Antonio Solalinde. Madrid, 1930.
Armenini, Giovanni Battista. *De veri precetti della Pittura.* Ravenna, 1587.
Bacon, Francis. *Works.* Ed. Spedding, Ellis and Heath. Boston, 1891.
Baudoin, Jean. *Recueil d'emblèmes divers.* Paris, 1638.
Boccaccio, Giovanni. *Genealogiae.* Venice, 1494.
Bode, Georg Heinrich (ed.). *Scriptorum rerum mythicarum latini tres...* Celle, 1834, facsimile edition Hildesheim, 1968.
Carrillo y Sotomayor, Luis de. *Libro de la erudición poética.* Ed. Manuel Cardenal Iracheta. Madrid, 1946.
Cartari, Vencenzo. *Le imagini colle sposizione degli dei degli antichi.* Venice, 1556.
Conti, Natale. *Mythologiae sive explicationis fabularum libri decem.* Venice, 1551.
Dolce, Lodovico. *Le Transformationi tratte da Ovidio.* Venice, 1553.
Dolet, Étienne. *La Manière de bien traduire.* Lyon, 1542. Reprinted in *Babel,* 1 (1955), pp. 17-20.
Du Bellay, Joaquim. *La Deffence et Illustration de la langue françoyse.* Ed. Henri Chamard. Paris, 1904.
Giraldi, Lilio Gregorio. *De deis gentium varia et multiplex historia in que simul de eorum imaginibus et cognominibus agitur.* Basel, 1548.
Horozco y Covarrubia, Juan de. *Emblemas morales.* Segovia, 1589.
Hygini fabulae. Ed. Mauricius Schmidt. Jena, 1872.
Machado de Assis, Joaquim Maria. *"The Psychiatrist" and Other Stories.* Berkeley, 1973.
Malón de Chaide, Fray Pedro. *La conversión de la Magdalena.* Ed. P. Félix García. Madrid, 1947-57.
Menéndez y Pelayo, Marcelino. *Biblioteca de traductores españoles,* Vols. 54-57 of *Obras completas.* Madrid, 1953.
Palaephatus. *Le premier livre des narrations fabuleuses.* Lyon, 1558.
Pérez de Moya, Juan. *Filosofía secreta.* Ed. Eduardo Gómez de Baquero. Madrid, 1928.
Quevedo, Francisco de. *El buscón.* Ed. Américo Castro. Madrid, 1960.
Rabelais, François. *Oeuvres complètes.* Ed. Pierre Jourda. París, 1962.
Rojas, Fernando de. *La Celestina.* Ed. M. Criado de Val and G. D. Trotter. Madrid, 1965.
Schottus, Andreas. *Adagia Graeca.* Antwerp, 1612.
Victoria, Baltasar de. *Teatro de los dioses de la gentilidad.* Salamanca, 1620.
Wallein, Thomas de. *La Bible des poetes de Ovide Metamorphose.* Paris, 1520.

"Once I began this book, I could not put it down, almost literally . . . I was so taken with the humanity of the characters."

 —Joel Williamson, author of *The Crucible of Race*

"When you first read *The Road from Chapel Hill*, you might think of *Cold Mountain*—a novel sprawled over the state of North Carolina with a backdrop of the Civil War, a genteel young woman reduced to poverty, a tale of hardship and deprivation and finally triumph—but Joanna Catherine Scott's novel is different in many ways, not the least of which is that one of her primary characters is an escaping slave. A narrative that captures the Civil War era admirably and brings a variety of characters alive."

 —Fred C. Hobson, co-editor of *The Literature of the American South* and Lineberger Professor of the Humanities, University of North Carolina

"A truly remarkable novel, *The Road from Chapel Hill* reveals the human costs and trials of war in ways nonfiction simply cannot. This masterful weaving of stories of heroism and courage amidst the hardships and cruelties of the bitterly divided Southern home front deepens and enriches our understanding of the two great tragedies of American history—human slavery and the Civil War needed to end it. Joanna Catherine Scott, drawing on broad and careful historical research, has created memorable characters who exemplify the ultimate triumph of love, hope, and compassion. This is a book that will be read—then read again—with appreciation and admiration."

 —Robert Anthony, Curator, North Carolina Collection, Wilson Library, University of North Carolina at Chapel Hill

THE ROAD FROM CHAPEL HILL

JOANNA CATHERINE SCOTT

BERKLEY BOOKS, NEW YORK

THE BERKLEY PUBLISHING GROUP
Published by the Penguin Group
Penguin Group (USA) Inc.
375 Hudson Street, New York, New York 10014, USA
Penguin Group (Canada), 90 Eglinton Avenue East, Suite 700, Toronto, Ontario M4P 2Y3, Canada
(a division of Pearson Penguin Canada Inc.)
Penguin Books Ltd., 80 Strand, London WC2R 0RL, England
Penguin Group Ireland, 25 St. Stephen's Green, Dublin 2, Ireland (a division of Penguin Books Ltd.)
Penguin Group (Australia), 250 Camberwell Road, Camberwell, Victoria 3124, Australia
(a division of Pearson Australia Group Pty. Ltd.)
Penguin Books India Pvt. Ltd., 11 Community Centre, Panchsheel Park, New Delhi—110 017, India
Penguin Group (NZ), Cnr. Airborne and Rosedale Roads, Albany, Auckland 1310, New Zealand
(a division of Pearson New Zealand Ltd.)
Penguin Books (South Africa) (Pty.) Ltd., 24 Sturdee Avenue, Rosebank, Johannesburg 2196,
South Africa

Penguin Books Ltd., Registered Offices: 80 Strand, London WC2R 0RL, England

This book is an original publication of The Berkley Publishing Group.

This is a work of fiction. Names, characters, places, and incidents either are the product of the author's imagination or are used fictitiously, and any resemblance to actual persons, living or dead, business establishments, events, or locales is entirely coincidental. The publisher does not have any control over and does not assume any responsibility for author or third-party websites or their content.

PRINTING HISTORY
Berkley trade paperback edition/November 2006

Library of Congress Cataloging-in-Publication Data
Scott, Joanna C., 1943–
    The road from Chapel Hill / Joanna Catherine Scott.—Berkley trade pbk. ed.
        p. cm.
    ISBN 0-425-21252-1
    1. United States—History—Civil War, 1861–1865—Fiction.   2. Slaves—North Carolina—Fiction.
    3. North Carolina—History—1775–1865—Fiction.   I. Title.

PS3569.C638R63   2006
813'.54—dc22
                                                                        2006048439

PRINTED IN THE UNITED STATES OF AMERICA

10   9   8   7   6   5   4   3   2

for Tom

THE ROAD FROM
CHAPEL HILL

CHAPTER ONE

THE sharp clang of the mine bell woke her. She lay a moment, prone, reluctant, half inside a vanished dream, then stirred and sniffed and wiped her eyes on the corner of her apron, wincing at the drag of rough cotton on her skin. She sniffed again, sharply this time, and with a little exclamation, slipped backwards off the bed. With an abrupt, almost dismissive, movement, she flung aside the strip of fabric separating her tiny bedroom from the main room of the cabin and flounced toward the smoking fireplace, the mud-caked bottoms of her petticoats patterning the ash-scrubbed floor a reddish brown.

Wadding up her apron, she wrapped it round the handle of a sizzling pan, and with a little grunt of effort, swung it two-handed off the fire and set it, still snapping and sizzling, on the hearth's uneven stones. Blue heat rose, threatening an explosion into flame. She jerked her hands away, smacking the apron up against her skirt. Would she never get it right, this cooking like a Negro woman on an open fire, she who had never cooked but on a stove? How could Papa do it to her? How could he bring her, Eugenia Mae Spotswood, down to this? And now dinner was burned again, and her thumb burned to the bargain.

She stuck the knuckle of her right thumb in her mouth and went to the doorway of the cabin, where she stood looking out into the shadowed lane, the smell of burned pork grease behind her in the room. Once, before Papa was forced to sell their farm near Wilmington, she had had a servant to help her cook and clean the house, a proper house, with a proper kitchen separated from it by a covered walk, and a boy to chop the wood and haul the water and do jobs about the place and drive the gig, a gardener too, and hands to work the fields, nineteen of them. Twenty-three slaves they had owned altogether, twenty-three. And she had aspired. All her dreams had centered on the luxury of owning more.

She had been pretty then, before her skin was ruined by the sun, her hands turned hard and calloused by hard work. Young men had courted her. Her favorite, she once had thought, was Ben, whose father owned a rice plantation on the Cape Fear River with a hundred slaves and more, and a house in Wilmington with a shady gallery out front where you could sit and sip iced tea and wave at people going by below as if you were a famous general or a queen.

Then Christopher had come along, with his blond curls and that way he had of smiling sideways at her when he came into a room, and her heart had melted after him. He was at university in Chapel Hill and one day would be a famous lawyer. His father owned a railroad company, or at least a part of one, and made investments in other people's businesses so that everybody touched their hats to him and asked for his advice.

There had been other young men too, with soft white hands

and pure white linen shirts and prospects. She had loved all of them. What fun it had been trying to decide which one she loved the best.

A sigh came out of her, a tremulous sound, and as though her strength had followed it, she leaned into the doorjamb, tilting her head against the wood.

Back in those lost, luxurious days she had expected to take at least one slave with her into marriage, a little piece of property. If she had married Ben or Christopher, or any one of them, she would right now be mistress of a stylish house, her silver card tray full and overflowing with cards left by everybody who was anyone in town. There would be dinner parties every week, the finest of fine gowns and bonnets, ribbons for her hair, and before long pretty children smiling at her from their nurses' knees. This was the life Papa had promised her, his treasured only child.

"Twenty-three slaves," she said aloud, "twenty-three," as though to persuade herself it really had been true.

And Papa would have bought more, he had been planning it, but blight had hit the crops and he was forced to use his savings to get them through the year. Next year, blight hit again, and then a hurricane. With each new disaster, he sank deeper into debt, until they were forced to start selling their possessions.

First to go were the silver spoons and platters, the silver egg stand with its tiny dainty legs that once had been Mama's, then the elegant buff china, the ornaments and crystal glasses, the Sunday dishes with the roses painted round the rims, the fancy quilts, Eugenia's rich, brocaded black silk dress with the lace sleeves and matching scalloped collar, her crystal perfume bottles and embroidered handkerchiefs.

The furniture went too, stick by reluctant clinging-to-its-owner stick, the slaves as well, the boy and gardener and house-maid first, all complaining loudly, and then the hands who worked the farm. With them gone, there was nothing for it but to start selling off the hogs and chickens, the cows, all the mules but one, a stubborn ugly thing with one ear torn and vicious lashing hooves. All Papa kept was one farm wagon for the mule to pull and one horse, not the best, to pull the carriage, also not the best.

As Papa's fortunes slipped, Eugenia's invitations, to a dance, a party, a visit to the beach, became fewer, and then fewer still, until no invitations came. Fashionable society abandoned them, and with that abandonment died all her hopes. She found herself beside her father in the fields, a fumbling and resentful worker with no idea of how things should be done.

Despite it, the crops that year grew strong and flourished, and Papa began to tap his fingers on his chair arm in the evenings in a planning way, until a violent hailstorm, in the space of half an hour, destroyed it all.

Once more the creditors closed in, demanding and demanding, and with them came complete humiliation—*not a penny left, oh, not a penny left*—she must run tick at Mr. Newton's store. To not afford a candle. It was insupportable.

Papa became more grimly silent every day. His eyes took on a cloudy, beaten quality, and his nature, which had been affable and steady, took on a snappish, unexpected cast. Unhappiness dragged at the corners of his mouth, and though Eugenia wanted to accuse, berate, to beat her fists against his chest and rail, she felt a hardness growing in him that she dared not go against.

And then one day he came to her with a letter in his hand. "I have accepted a position at a gold mine, in a supervisory capacity."

"A gold mine, Papa? Where is this gold mine?"

"Near Charlotte. South of Salisbury."

She stared at him. "You would leave Wilmington, you would

leave behind the ocean and everything we know, and travel half across the state to work for someone else?"

"I'll be a partner shortly. I have been promised it."

"With nothing to invest? Papa, I fear a fantasy has taken hold of you. No good can come of it."

"Eugenie, it's an opportunity. There's a fortune to be made in gold, everyone has heard of it, and in no time I'll have plenty to invest. I admit that to give up being my own master in the meantime will be hard, but for your sake I am prepared to undergo it." He hesitated, not quite looking at her face. "I expect you shall do the same for me."

And so the house and land were sold, the decision made with no regard for her. She wept alone, throwing accusations at the empty air, but when it was all done, and they drove off one early morning, unseen and unfarewelled, she found it almost a relief to leave. Across the creaking of the carriage, Papa talked in an excited, nervous voice about how they would start again with no one knowing who they were or how reduced they had become. She could not bear to hear that word *reduced*, or even think it. It made her mind fog up and cloud with disappointment and despair.

And for all this did Papa apologize? No, not at all. All he had to say was, "Thank God your poor mama is not alive to see this day."

"Why, sir, I am still alive," Eugenia said.

She had intended to reproach him, but he misunderstood, taking her words for an attempt to comfort. He dropped the reins and took her in his arms and wept, a grown man wept. Thinking of it now she shivered once more with the shame.

That she should be reduced to living on this wretched ugly goldfield side by side with crackers, slaves, and foreigners, in this horrid little cabin, with no view out the door but another row of cabins as horrid as her own, boiling in the summer and leaking bitter cold in winter no matter how she stuffed the gaps between the planks, with one room for the kitchen and the parlor, and just one other room, a tiny one, barely a room at all, for her to sleep in, while Papa had nothing but a loft he had fashioned with his own hands underneath the roof. No more to the place but a storeroom propped tipsily against the wall around the back, and an outhouse shared with half a dozen other families. No lawn to walk on, no garden filled with herbs and vegetables and flowers, just naked ground with here and there a patch of stringy weeds.

That she should be reduced to washing her own clothes, and Papa's too, and scrubbing her own floor, without a single slave to help her, that she should have to sit up half the night and stitch and mend to keep her gowns and Papa's shirts from falling into rags, that she must knit stockings till her fingers twisted and grew stiff from working with the needles, and ruin her hands further with tallow and beeswax, melting it and pouring the evil-smelling potion into candle molds and fixing in the wicks, which she must weave herself.

And the constant rumbling of this place, the tumbling and the grinding, the harsh, hypnotic hiss of steam escaping, slap and sluice of sulphurous-smelling water pumped out of the shafts, the beastlike cough-cough-coughing of the pumps, and the thudding dull explosions from below.

Men died in this place, women too, as though a bonus would be paid for it—from cholera, the bloody flux and yellow fever, bilious colic, pleurisy, the shaking ague, rupture of the heart. Others died when shafts caved in on their heads, or air turned bad, suffocating them below the ground. They died from a foot or hand ripped off in a spinning windlass, a leg mortified up to the knee, an arm up to the elbow, or else the rope that held a kibble frayed and split and sent them plummeting three hundred feet into the dark. Others vanished in some deep unheard explosion, or tumbled down a flooded shaft to drown.

And she, because she was a woman, must serve time as nurse at the makeshift hospital three nights a week from six to midnight, and every other Sunday afternoon, although there was little she could do but watch the injured miners die—an eye gouged out by flying rock, a head exploded by a loose plank falling, silent in the darkness of a shaft, a face boiled off by steam—adding their screams and moans and suppurating wounds and gray dead faces to her dreams. And the resigned plodding back and forth of the hearse.

All this was bad enough, but each day at dawn—*humiliation, oh, humiliation*—she must make her way down to the rocking cradles where the dross sluiced from the steam-powered rockers was rewashed. The first time she had seen the place she had to work, a mad idea had come into her head that she was going boating—the rockers looked like a row of blunt-ended wood canoes lined up for a race—but then she saw they were connected in sets of three or four by upright posts with rails across the top.

On one of these contraptions, she was required to balance with one foot on each side of a rocker, and leaning on the rail for balance, press down on one side, then the other, while water mixed with dross rolled across the quicksilver gliding in its bottom, trapping whatever gold came past. One person could rock a set of these canoes, but it was wet and slippery work and must be done barefooted to get a proper purchase on the wood. Eugenia had tried it once in shoes but the wet soles skidded out from under her.

Here, with grime-faced little girls who had never seen a hairbrush or a comb, and the occasional drunk Irish or indignant slave, she must step side to side all day until her face flushed red as brick and she felt her head might burst from all the noise, and her knees and hip joints creaked with pain. When the change of shift bell clanged, when she was aching and exhausted and dragged down in her soul, she must hoist herself over to the cookhouse, there to labor further over vast amounts of food with which to feed the single hands. And after that she must go home—*home? it was not home*—and cook and do for her papa.

Today Papa had gone off with two buttons missing from his shirt. Time was when she would have blushed to think of it, but she found a stranger sitting in her heart, a strangeness speaking in her head: *I do not care I do not care. It is his own fault his own fault. I cannot be responsible for buttons on his shirts or worry if his underdrawers have strings in them. I do not care.* She knew she would not sleep again tonight. She could feel the clangor of exhaustion starting in her head that would prevent it.

Turning back into the cabin, she went over to the hearth and looked down into the pan. The grease was blue still, volatile. She took a long fork from beside the fire and turned the piece of pork, the grease crackling under it. Fumes stung her eyes and caught sharply in her throat. She jerked her head aside and coughed. Perhaps if she cut off the outer part . . .

Once more she wadded up her apron, and leaning down, hoisted the pan onto a table made of planks across a pair of trestles, the planks so warped from scrubbing that the edges curled. She went to a side cupboard and jerked at its resistant door. It flew open with a rush and she lifted down a metal serving dish, which she set on the table by the pan, and taking up a carving knife, began cutting off the blackened outer meat, the burned grease shifting sluggishly from one corner to another with the shifting movement of the pan. With the salvaged meat sliced and set out on the platter, she took up the pan, which was now cool enough to hold barehanded, and carried it outside into the lane. A dog came slinking from around the corner of the cabin.

"Here," she said. "Here."

It was no one's dog, just one of those that hung about the mine scavenging, a long-legged thing, of a pale sand color, with a looping look about it as though it had been made of curves. Its ribs pushed at its almost hairless skin, and its long thin tail curled underneath its rump. It tilted up its head and sniffed, eyeing the pan.

"Come on."

She watched it eat, and when it scooted the pan against the step, snuffling in the corners to get at the last drops, she said, "There," and pushed it aside with her knee.

Back inside the cabin, she sank the pan into a scum-rimmed bowl of water, then set out on the table a pair of metal plates with knives and forks, filled two metal cups with water from a pitcher, and set them by the plates. One tilted on the warped edge of a plank and she moved it to a flatter spot, thinking of the beautiful buff china they had sold in Wilmington, the imported walnut dinner table polished to a mirror shine.

A strand of hair fell across her eyes and she pushed it away with the back of her wrist, but it fell again. She went into the cabin's other room, and with the corner of her apron wiped a swathe of dust from the looking glass hung on the wall. Her reflection, apron in hand, regarded her distastefully. Her face had coarsened, her skin completely lost its delicate pure whiteness. Indeed, it was not white at all, but a lightish shade of brown, as though the Negro labor she performed was turning her a Negro. Her hair, which once had bobbed and gleamed, its tight nut-colored curls tumbling in contrived confusion down her neck, had lost its luster and was pulled back from her face, secured inside her bonnet lest she catch it in some piece of machinery, or set light to it at the cooking fire.

Leaning in toward the glass, she examined red-rimmed eyes, a swollen nose. Could she not get through one single day without descending into tears? She had told herself she would get used to her new life. Papa had said it too. "With time," he said, not finishing the sentence, as though he understood he spoke a lie, that time inflames, it does not heal.

CHAPTER TWO

THE year was eighteen sixty, and farther to the east, the little town of Chapel Hill was in a stew. Word was out that Mr. Morgan's runaway had sneaked in from the woods last night and made off with a knife from Mr. Ruffin's store. Miss Caroline, who ran the ladies' clothing store, had been working late finishing an order, and had just blown out the lamp when she looked up and saw an awful threatening face pressed against the window. She felt terror, just pure terror, take her, she told everybody who would listen, and gave up a prayer of thanks she was in darkness in the back part of the shop. If that boy Tom had come a minute earlier before she blew the lamp, if he had seen her there, a woman all alone, it might have been her window that he smashed, and who knows what then?

She knew right well who he was the minute she looked up and saw him. Everybody knew Sam Morgan had a loose slave roaming in the woods, making not one effort to corral him. He is not worth my time, Sam always said when anybody asked. But that was not the point, and now the wanted notice had been pinned outside the church so long no one paid attention. It was a disgrace. The patrol had never found him, and some people said he had gone north, but now they knew he hadn't, because she had seen Tom there as large as life, and heard the window shatter in Doug Ruffin's hardware store and seen him run back past. She could swear he had been brandishing the missing knife.

Clyde Bricket, who lived on a poor dirt farm just south of town, had ridden into Chapel Hill that day to do some errands for his pa. As he urged the mule down Franklin Street, he found it seething with upset. All the storekeepers and businessmen were outside with their handguns and their shotguns and their rifles. Others were there too, farmers with their produce carts tangled in a mess of wheels and hooves and mule breath, the postman with his mail pouch and a whistle round his neck, the butcher in his black-and-white-striped apron, the old bald Baptist organist, the bank clerk in his eyeshade, people in black flapping gowns from the university across the way. Women were demanding safety for their children, the children running in and out and climbing in the chestnut trees as though it were a holiday, and dogs running after them and barking. Judge Graham, who was head of the patrol committee, had ridden down from Hillsborough and was shouting out for silence on the courthouse steps, while a cluster of free Negroes jostled, big-eyed, on the edges of the crowd.

Miss Caroline was putting up a tumult, red in the face and with her bonnet falling off. She had a shotgun and swore that she would join the men, she was outraged, how could Sam Morgan let that boy stay loose out in the woods so long, where was Sam anyway, why was he off gallivanting down in Wilmington, he should be flogged himself. And now his boy was not just running loose, but armed. Who knew what he'd get up to, we women are no longer safe, we must think about our daughters, and our businesses as well. If he'll steal from one, he'll surely steal from others and before too long we will have packs of runaways off in the woods, scheming plots to ruinate the town. Chapel Hill will get a reputation, men will fear to send their sons to university in such a place, the local businesses will fail, we'll all end up bankrupt in the Greensboro poorhouse, every one of us, how could Sam Morgan let things come to such a pass?

And so she went on and on, running from one group to another until the men grew tired of her and someone took away her shotgun and told her to sit down here, ma'am, right here on this bench and calm yourself, let us take care of things. A search party was to start out beating through the woods at dawn.

When Clyde heard this, he decided then and there he would not go home that night. Pa would give him every sort of whupping for it, but ever since ol' Sam Morgan put the wanted notice up with $5 Reward dark and big across the bottom, he had dreamed of catching Tom. He asked the hired slave Amos how come Tom had not been caught already. Amos laughed and said some niggers have magic invisibility, he had an uncle once who did, why he could walk up to a tree and purely vanish into it. Clyde said, You are lying to me, boy, there's no way a feller of that size could get hisself inside a tree, his shoulders would stick out. But Amos only shook his head and pulled his hat down low across his eyes and clicked his tongue to get the mule a-going down the field.

So then Clyde asked Pa, Why ain't the patrol done picked Tom up? and Pa said, They are too soft, they will not go into the woods at night on 'count they'd have to go afoot, why a man would think their backsides had been took 'n' glued onto their saddles. Anyways, he said, that Tom, he is a slippery one for sure, it will take a clever man to catch him. I got a mind to go out on my own account and round the good-for-nothing up and pick up the reward.

Clyde said, Go on then, do it, Pa, but Pa tipped back his hat and said, Now ain't that like a green-eared boy rushin' off half-cocked, a man got to figure out hisself a strategy in such a situation. He never did, though, just set Clyde to watching the stocks of food in the pantry and the smokehouse, and had him count the chickens and the blankets every day, and keep a close eye on the corn crib. Old Mary better not be passing anything of ourn to that there boy of hers, she is his mother after all, and mothers can be downright tricky. Pa had his eye on Ma when he said that. Clyde did not know what to make of it.

Old Mary watched Clyde checking everything and counting, saying nothing. It made him feel uncomfortable and angry. Old Mary better watch herself, Pa said, I got a mind to send her back to ol' Sam Morgan and get myself another hire. He didn't, though. Old Mary was too good with Ma, who had been Strangely Silent far back as Clyde remembered.

As one week followed on the next and Tom was still out loose, Clyde fell to thinking hard on that five dollars. He thought about it more and more until he thought about it all the time: when he was in the field with Amos, helping him cut down trees for a new tobacco patch, when he was jerking up and down the hard, resistant soil behind the hard, resistant mule, when he was lying on his cot at night. Someday, somehow, he was going to catch that Tom. Then he'd buy hisself a gun. He'd been saving up for one and already had a half a dollar. Once he had a gun, it'd be easier than spit to catch another runaway, and then another. Pretty soon he would be famous, and have a horse to ride like Uncle Benjamin, who was a preacher and went about the place saving people's souls.

Clyde's luck was in. When Judge Graham counted up the

men, and the patrol captain counted again, they allowed as how they needed more to make a party big enough to search the woods. Someone must ride farm to farm carrying a letter.

And here was Clyde, his face on fire with willingness. Yessir, yessir, he could do that right enough. He had a mule. He could do that.

But a mule was too slow for the job, and so after some discussion Clyde was loaned a horse and sent off to call recruits. He headed out of town away from home. He would not recruit his pa. Pa would only smack him upside the head and say, Boy, you are too young for such goings-on.

He was not too young, he was almost thirteen years, a recruiter on a handsome horse. It did not like him much, being a strange rider, and he had to pay attention to its tricks, but pretty soon he got the hang of it and spent all day riding dusty roads and trails to farmhouses, sitting proud and straight like a captain or a colonel of militia, saluting at the farmers when he came upon them in their fields. Several farmers' wives said, Come on in and eat, but he did not stop, just took a chicken leg to eat along the way, a hank of bread, a refill for his water pouch.

Yessir, Clyde thought, riding down the road, the big horse powerful between his legs, it was near as good as being a patroller, riding onto anybody's property and pounding on their door, and them all helpful and respectful when they saw the judge's letter, taking off their hats and speaking straight on to him like he was a man. Ever since word came farm to farm last fall about that John Brown feller's insurrection up to Harpers Ferry, everyone had been downright touchy about nigras, which made them anxious for the hunt.

When the sky began to lower and a breeze sprang up, he figured he had done a good day's work. He had recruited fifteen men, anybody would be proud of that. When he'd given his report, Judge Graham would pound him on the back and shake his hand, and maybe offer him a shot of whiskey. Clyde, he'd say, we need a man like you to search the woods with us tomorrow.

But Judge Graham wasn't at the courthouse, only the patrol captain waiting on the courthouse steps, and all he said was, Where you think you've been all day wearing out that horse, it's almost nightfall. Then he took away the horse and gave Clyde back the mule, and went off without one word of thanks.

Miss Caroline was kind, though. She let him sleep in the back room of her shop, and along with half a dozen others, fed him beef stew and biscuits and apple cider until he couldn't eat no more. In the morning, Clyde asked if she would kindly let him have a hank of rope for tying up, but while she was off looking for it in her storeroom, the search party set off down the road toward the woods. By the time Clyde set out after them, kicking the mule and muttering all the cusswords he could think of, the riders were clear out of sight, vanished around a curve in the road. By the time he caught up, he found their horses tethered to trees and the search party busy with hatchets, cutting branches for beating through the undergrowth.

Clyde slid down off the mule and tied it up beside the horses. He didn't have a hatchet to cut himself a beating branch, and at first the patrol captain said, You can stay here and make sure no one steals the horses. Clyde said, There ain't no one going to steal them, no one is about, I am coming with you, Judge Graham said as how I could—which was not exactly true, but almost. So the patrol captain tossed him a branch he'd cut that was too small for him. Come on along, he said, if you're so all-fired.

So Clyde came on, but the woods were dense and soon he fell behind. For a while he followed the rhythmic swish and thwack of leaves on undergrowth, the occasional low call of one man to the next. Then he followed the swish and thwack alone, and then a distant rhythmic rustling, and then there was nothing but the rustling of the woods themselves.

At first this did not bother him. It meant that when he tracked Tom down, no one would argue about him getting the reward. It was early still and chances were he'd find Tom snoring in his hideaway. He'd creep up on him and tie the rope around his legs. When Tom jumped up, he'd jerk the rope and send him sprawling, and before he had a chance to catch his wind, he'd get his hands tied up as well. It was a surefire plan, easier than spit, and Clyde swung through the woods, aglow with confidence.

But pretty soon he found himself in woods he did not know, and although he kept his eyes about him all the time, he did not see any sign of Tom or of a place where he might hide, nothing but a couple students from up the university who, from the looks of them, had spent the whole night out there getting liquored up. He saw a family of coons sleeping in a tree, three of them, each one sprawled along a branch with its chin stretched out and its four paws hanging down. He lifted an imaginary gun. *Boom-boom!*

Pine pollen tickled in his nose and when he sneezed it seemed as though a giant hand had clapped upside his head. He began to feel as though the trees were watching him, and if he weren't careful they would do him harm. He told himself he was too old to be thinking such tomfoolery, but his heart was going like a kettledrum and he felt hot and flushed about the face. All around, insects worked themselves into a frenzy, rattling, buzzing, the sound of darting and attack, as though a bunch of enemy was getting theirselves ready to take him by surprise. The whizzing sound of what he figured must be Morgan's Creek seemed like someone whispering a plot, a woodpecker rattling on a tree was someone shooting after him, some old crow barking was one of them mad dogs. If they bit you, you'd set to foaming at the mouth and your arms and legs ajerking, and then your eyes would roll up in your head and that was it for you, they'd dig a hole and plant you in the ground. To make him brave and keep himself from turning back, he sang under his breath, *Run, nigger, run, patty-roller will catch you, Run, nigger, run, I'll shoot you with my flintlock gun.*

He came across a rise, and there, squatting on the rocks beside the creek, a mess of nigras, six or eight of them. Clyde stopped and stared, his heart shrunk to a tiny fist. The nigras all jumped up and he felt his chin shake and a taste like burning come into his throat. He tried to turn and couldn't move. The nigras stood there staring back at him. And then they vanished, they entirely vanished, every one. It happened right before his eyes. He thought about how Amos said some niggers have magic invisibility and his privates tightened till they hurt.

He ran then, his beating branch gone, hat half off his head, tearing at the bushes with his hands, a sobbing starting in his throat. When he could run no more, he stopped—no sound but the wind rattling the treetops, the high whoop of a single bird—then floundered on again, down into a gully and across another creek, or maybe the same creek but another bend. He knew he was lost, and somewhere out here was a big black nigra with a knife. He felt a trickle going down his leg and stopped to fumble with his pants. It comforted him to hold his organ in his hand, and feel the warm pee coming out and see it patter, steaming, up against a tree. His breath slowed and his heartbeat slowed. And then he felt it. Someone watching him. Clyde watched his pee, as if by concentrating on the yellow arc of it, whoever watched would not be there.

He did not seem to lift his eyes. It was as though they lifted of their own accord. He looked into Tom's face. He looked down at the skinless, headless squirrel Tom held in one hand, at the winking knife held in the other. And jerked himself inside his pants and fled, a high shrill caroling breaking from his throat.

THEY said he was a hero, laughing, and Clyde hoped they wouldn't notice how his pants were wet. They'd shot Tom from behind, below the knees, and hauled him out with his feet snagging on the undergrowth, and tied him up real good, and slung him on the mule. At first his feet dragged on the ground, so they thought awhile, and then they tied a rope between his knees and jerked them up. But then he was unbalanced and kept tilting back, threatening to tumble off the mule's rump, so they untied the rope that held his hands behind and tied them at the front, and looped the rope around the one between his knees, and that worked fine.

Tight as an Indian pony, someone said, and the patrol captain said to Clyde, You found him, hero, so you take him in, and Clyde swaggered down the road to Chapel Hill, sometimes leading the reluctant mule, sometimes whacking from behind, half dazed with the adventure of it all, half terrified of the whupping he was going to get from Pa for being out all night, the men riding on and falling back, joking with each other, talking about what they'd have for breakfast, tossing tobacco pouches back and forth. Someone had a flask of whiskey and made Tom have a swallow to stop him moaning so. And the blood all running down, dripping off his naked heels.

They hauled him up before Judge Graham on the courthouse steps, and the judge gave the patrol captain a receipt and said they had to have a doctor see about those legs, and then they took him off to lock him up until Sam Morgan got back into town. No one said a thing about five dollars, so Clyde set himself before the judge, who did not smile, but looked down at him with a solemn face and seemed sad, and when Clyde said he was the one found Mr. Morgan's Tom and asked for his five dollars, the judge just sighed.

I am entitled, Clyde said, since I found him.

Judge Graham sighed again, and said he might have found him but he didn't catch him, so he could have two dollars, nothing more, and you get on out of here, young man, you're not old enough to be involved in doings of this sort, just go on home. So Clyde went home, and when his father saw the two dollars, he didn't whup him, but snatched it from his hand and said, Let that be a lesson.

Clyde went out back and kicked the hog trough as he crossed the yard, and limped on through the grass, whacking at it with a stick, and limped and stamped across the rattling wooden bridge over the creek, and smacked the stick so hard against the rail it snapped, and flung it in the creek, and cursed aloud and went on down the beaten path until he came to Old Mary's swept yard. He kicked the fence. It was a rickety affair, made of twigs stuck in the ground and bound with twine. A section swayed and fell and he stepped over it and went across the yard. In front of Old Mary's door, he raised his hand. And let it drop. And tensed to turn and creep away. But as he did, the door swung back and Old Mary stood before him.

We done catched your Tom today, Clyde said.

Old Mary bent toward him, half smiling, as though she had not heard.

We catched him good. Chased that nigra through the woods and shot him in the legs and hauled him off to jail.

Old Mary looked into his eyes, and lifting up one hand, took hold of the upright of the door.

Clyde felt heat rushing in his head. He said, They give me a reward.

• • •

THAT night he dreamed about Old Mary's Tom, the way he hadn't said a word, just moaned, big tears rolling down his face, and his pants ripped open by the buckshot, blood drip-dripping all along the road behind the mule, each drop kicking up a little spurt of dust.

It was that little spurt of dust that woke him. He saw the red drop gather at the bottom of the nigra's heel, and then fall slow, slow, slowly down, and then the little spurt, and he woke up, his heart knock-knocking at his chest, the wetness coming in his pants. He pushed the blanket back and got up out of bed and went outside and peed, looking at the high tops of the pine trees lined against the sky. He came back in and lay awake, listening to Pa grunting in his sleep, and then, although he did not seem to sleep again, he saw the red drop slowly gathering, slowly falling down toward the dust.

CHAPTER THREE

A T Mr. Morgan's place, Tom's legs began to heal. First the bleeding stopped, then scabs began to form, their bright red clotted surfaces becoming crimson brown, an unkempt patterning, like deformed creatures hatching from his flesh. And then the slow work of the tissues underneath, the reaching out and clinging, the meshing and the weaving, and the knitting of the bone.

His healing was still incomplete when, like a pair of turkey vultures scenting out a carcass, here came a pair of traders down from Maryland, hunting after slaves to sell into the gold mines out Charlotte way. Mr. Morgan met them in the yard, turning up a pair of empty hands. He had only one slave he wanted to get rid of, but he was no good for anything since he could barely walk.

One of the traders was a tall, lank man with a cruel, smiling face. The other was short, but broad and strong, with a round, plump face, which from a distance gave the impression of good-will, but up close his eyes were sharp. The tall one jerked his chin and asked if Mr. Morgan wouldn't kindly get this no-good fellow out so they could take a look at him, and Tom came limping on a pair of stripped-down branches propped beneath his arms.

The tall trader jerked his chin. "Let's take a look at them there legs."

The short trader came and squatted beside Tom. Rolling up his overalls, he prodded at the sculpture of his gnarled and palely gleaming reinvented flesh, while the tall one stood and nodded, grunting, at the murmured comments of the other, and Mr. Morgan watched them narrow-eyed behind.

When they had finished their inspection, the traders went off and leaned against the kitchen garden fence with their arms on the top rail, their heads close and their voices low. After a while, the tall one spat and punched his fist into his palm. The short one pulled a tobacco pouch out of one pocket of his shirt and a pipe out of the other. He stuffed the pipe, struck a match against his thumbnail, and held it above the bowl, sucking sharply to draw down the flame. His chest jerked and he shifted the pipe to the corner of his mouth, blowing a sideways spurt of smoke. The two men exchanged a glance, a laconic nod, and came strolling back across the yard.

The tall trader cleared his throat with a wet rushing sound and spat. He offered Mr. Morgan what he called a decent price to take Tom off his hands. Mr. Morgan looked down at the gob of greenish yellow phlegm congealing in the dust and observed that Tom had always been a good boy, never any trouble, and he had a mind to keep him after all. And so the dickering began.

NOW, slung crosswise at the back end of the traders' wagon, Tom lay staring at the blue unchanging sky, listening to the

rattling of wheels against the road, the slow and dreamlike shuffling of the mules' unwilling feet. His head knocked erratically
against the wooden side, the reverberation coming through his
jaw. From time to time, he squirmed away, was inch by inch
jerked back, and squirmed away again, carefully, because with
every movement a dull worm of pain crawled in his legs. He
could not tell how long he had been traveling, how many times
the wagon had swung about to clatter up the trail onto another
farm for the traders to negotiate another buy, how many detours
and backtracks they had made pursuing leads, how many times
they had camped beside the road while one trader went off with
the cart, coming back the next day or the next, or the day after
that, with another pair of black feet trailing on behind, or else
with a chagrined face and nothing following but low dust on an
empty road.

Half a dozen or so children rode between Tom and the
traders, the ones who were too young to walk. They sat on bundles, or wedged between them, and seemed to understand they
must not make a noise. If one began to cry, the others would
rock it in their arms and hush and comfort it. One, a little boy
with the blue eyes of the father who had bred him for the trade,
took pity on the dismal figure sprawled behind him. He pushed
a bundle back, indicating that Tom use it as a pillow, which he
did, propping himself against it with a new wound now, one in
his heart, the wound of unexpected kindness.

He did not thank the boy, or even look at him. Instead, he
watched the clanking coffle coming in red dust behind. A double
row of men came first. Theirs was the clanking of the chains that
held them wrist by wrist, ankle by ankle. The women came behind, loosely roped, the older children with them, some clinging
to their mothers, others, as if they had no comprehension of what
was happening to them, darting in and out and laughing, play-

ing chasing games, kicking up dust into the glinting light so that
it seemed a procession of the damned, already half-consumed,
floated in a cloud of golden fire along the road.

A cloud that sang, morning to night. The traders, fancying
themselves a pair of jolly dogs, sang along from time to time.
They knew the slave songs well and roared the words, smacking
their feet in rhythm against the wagon's floor, sometimes passing
whiskey back and forth. If the singing faltered, a sharp whipcrack
overhead brought music back into resistant throats. It was a
trader's trick. If their wares were singing, they could not be plot-
ting an uprising as they went.

And so the coffle sang, the old rebellious slave songs dropping heavily behind them on the road, hymns reaching up
toward heaven, falling back, as though whatever plea they bore
had been denied.

Sometimes it seemed to Tom the voices of the coffle singing
all together were a single voice. It was his father calling out
goodbye as he ran off in chains behind the cart when he was
sold. It had been when Tom was very young. The overseer, a big
man with a heavy red mustache and eyes that never seemed to
fix on anything, had said that he was going to whip Tom good,
the way he needed to be whipped to get his lazy bones a-going.
But when he raised his arm Tom's father leaped on him and
wrapped his hard black hands around his throat and almost
strangled him. So they hung a chain around his neck and fixed
him to a peach tree in the yard, where he jumped about all night,
shouting out, "Perdition on your heads!" like a preacher making
a revival. Next day, a stranger came riding in a cart and they un-
chained Tom's father from the tree and chained him to the axle
of the cart. The cart jerked and he went running off with mud
flying up behind his feet like wings.

Sometimes, half asleep, Tom fancied he was riding in that

cart, going with his father. Then he would flinch awake, and raising his head above the wagon's tailboard, search the faces of the men who might have been his father and were not. Sometimes, as he watched the turkey vultures circling overhead, he wondered what it would be like to be so high and looking down. He thought about the roosting tree near Morgan's Creek. He had lived in a den beside that creek when he was in the woods. It was underneath some overhanging rocks where somebody had leaned rough boards to make a shelter. Outside, the den was tangled all across with creepers so it was barely visible, and the turkey vultures' roosting tree was on the hill above. Their heavy black shapes sat along its branches late into the morning when all the other birds had done with shouting at each other and flown off for the day. It was an enormous hickory that had been girdled and was dead, not one leaf remaining. Not until the sun was well up in the sky and the day was humming warm would the turkey vultures lean out on their wings and leave their tree behind. Tom wondered what it would be like if he could lean out on the air and glide, climbing up the sky to join them with his red head flashing in the sun. Up that high, he would see his mother's cabin back at Bricket's place and all the way to Down-the-River where his father was.

He had not meant to take the knife. He had not planned it. He had broken from the woods at dusk one day to find himself beside a road he did not recognize. He followed it, looking about at the neat white houses that were not farmhouses, at the high red buildings stretching off at one side of the road. There were paths between the buildings, and young white men walking back and forth, some of them with books, and he understood that these were students at the university, that he was in the place called Chapel Hill where his mother had been brought to be hired out.

He turned, intending to go back into the woods, but curiosity took him by the arm and turned him round. One shadow to the next, he made his way past buildings that he had no name for with glass windows at the front, and behind the glass, so many things that he would like to touch and carry in his hand. Here were bolts of lace and fine print floral fabrics, rows of lustrous buttons, here a black machine on tall black legs with a single eye that looked at him, here pillows and bolsters piled up on a bed with gleaming golden knobs on top of gleaming golden posts. A longing rose in him to climb up on that bed and go to sleep. He had never in his life slept in a bed. He pressed his hand against the pane as though to touch it through the glass, then pushed himself away and went to the next window. Here were lamps and lanterns, pans and kettles, a row of kitchen bells, serving ladles, heavy cooking spoons. And here were knives of every sort, arranged in rows. Tom's breath stopped. If he could have a knife. If he could have just one. That one right there. He could skin a squirrel with that knife.

A lamppost stood behind him on the street. Its flickering lantern shone onto the knife. For a while he just stood before the window, looking in. He had stolen from farms before, chickens snatched from coops, corn raids in the night, but he had never stolen from a place like this. He looked about for someone who would grab him by the scruff and call out for a pattie-roller, but everything was silent, not a soul about.

He pushed against the glass with his flat hand, and hit it with his fist. It made a thick, dull sound. Then he went off, searching for a rock, and came back with half a brick that had been propping up one side of a rainwater barrel. He banged it against the window and it made a loud, reverberating sound, so he pulled his shirt across his head and wrapped the brick in it, and standing back, flung it at the glass. He had not meant to do it. He had not meant to steal. And now they said he was a thief, that he was bound for hell.

He lay very still and listened to the moaning of his legs, the humming of investigative flies. They had gentle voices, like his mother. One landed on his face and he felt its tiny running feet, like the stroking of a hand. He thought about the kindness of his mother's old hands touching him. He thought how, when he was living in the woods, he would go creeping to her cabin after dark. He would drag a leafy branch behind him so as not to leave a track, and watch the cabin first to make sure no one was about, and then sneak in and let her cry a little on his neck. Then she would mix salt and pork fat in a basin with some Indian meal and shape it in a ball, flattening the top and bottom so it would not tumble in the fire while it was being cooked. She would take a hoe and set it with the wooden handle on the floor and the slanting iron in the fire, and set the hoecake on the hoe and bake it.

One night the pattie-rollers had come riding. His mother had said, "Quick, son, quick," and lifted up a floorboard. Tom slid down into the musty smell of sweet potatoes and tucked himself way back against the bottom of the wall. He lay there listening to the pattie-rollers' voices up above, their footsteps rattling on the floor, and his mother's loud voice saying, no, she had not seen him, no, she had not seen him. There was a scuffling sound, the sound of something heavy dropping to the floor, and then the scraping of the floorboard lifting. Light flashed against the sweet potatoes and Tom squeezed his eyes tight shut and barely breathed until the pattie-rollers left. When he crawled out, his mother's face was swollen up and bruised. "I'm sorry, sorry," he had said, and she had held him in her arms and kissed him hard and said in a fierce voice, "Don't never say you're sorry when it ain't your fault."

Tears came to Tom's eyes; he brushed them off. Behind him, he could feel the little blue-eyed boy watching him, but when he turned, the little boy was looking somewhere else.

• • •

THE road cut south and west between patchy fields punctuated by the bend and bow of shabby-hatted workers wielding hoes. Now it crept a stealthy narrow course through woods, the trees close overhead, making shifting patterns on the bright blue sky. Here was a clanking waterwheel, here a farmhouse chimney curled out smoke, its pungent smell mixing with the mustiness of new-turned soil.

From time to time a stage or carriage passed, the passengers turning fastidious eyes away. Not so the turkey vultures. They were faithful and observant as devoted friends, circling and circling above the doleful singers, watching with sharp, unblinking eyes for one of them to drop, which one did at last, as though obligingly. It was a woman. Belinda was her name. Tom knew it from the impatient conversation of the traders when they climbed back into the wagon after swinging her off into the high grass of the ditch. What a bargain they had made, a slave who could not even make the journey to be sold. It disgruntled and annoyed them, and they blamed each other. The sky was clear of turkey vultures all that afternoon, but by morning they were back, patient in the blue relentless sky.

The coffle lagged that day, and although from time to time one of the traders shouted out to Virgil or Joel or Nicodemus or Joanna, "Look lively, there," their voices were not angry, simply businesslike, and for that day they did not push the pace. As traders go, these two were not unkind. Their wares were fed and rested regularly to keep them from deteriorating on the road. Tom they cared for with a sort of calculating tenderness. First thing in the morning, and again when they pitched camp at night, they took away his makeshift crutches and stood together watching, the short one with his pipe held meditatively between one finger and a thumb, sucking at it with a bilious, gurgling

sound, smoke trickling out around it as though from a conflagration in his head. And Tom would take a step, and take another
step, and when he fell, the tall trader laughed his cruel laugh,
and hauled him up and had him try again.

Even though his bones still hurt inside his legs, Tom pushed
himself each day to walk a little farther and a little farther on his
own. He could feel the muscles coming back to life. He could
feel them starting to grow strong. After a while he could hoist
himself into the wagon unassisted. That was the day he tossed
his crutches in the ditch and told the traders he would walk.

And walk he did, awkward but unshackled, and felt his legs
grow stronger all the time. Soon they would be strong enough to
run. He would go by night, he had decided it. He would wait until the traders were asleep and slip off into the blackness of the
woods. Chained by his injury, he slept apart, preferring the company of the mules to that of his unhappy kind. The other men
slept hobbled, the women roped, clustered on each other with
their children like a wasp's nest in a tree. Tom slept little, but lay
bending up his legs and stretching them, watching the closed sky
and the wide open moon, listening to the noises of the night, the
struggling and groaning of the women taken up into the wagon
with the traders, the wagon's creaking protests, the human
protests cut short by a hand across the mouth or clamped tight
on the throat, the chained-up men ignoring them, or seeming
to, as though if they acknowledged what was happening they
would be complicit, the women shifting uneasily in their not-
sleep.

The mules slept mute, rooted to the ground, their heads sunk
down like old men waiting patiently to die. But then one moved,
the merest twitching of a hock. The other coughed, the barest
sound. It floated Tom up out of sleep, unaware of what had
wakened him. He lay listening into the dark and before long be-

came aware that he was not alone. The little blue-eyed boy was sleeping curled up on the ground nearby, close, but not quite close enough to touch.

Each night after that, he crept closer until he was sleeping at Tom's side. They never touched or spoke, by day ignoring one another, but at night Tom lay and listened to the child's breathing, even fancied he could hear the thudding of his heart. This determination to draw close baffled and discomforted him at the same time as it comforted. It was as though the child were asking something of him, he did not know what. He had never had a friend, his mind did not encompass such a thought, but these days when he thought of running off, the little blue-eyed boy was running at his side.

BUT now a dreadful thing had happened. There were no woods. The fields were all torn up. The hills were torn up too, their insides heaped in the full light of the sun. Ahead, between the mules' jackrabbit ears, Tom saw porch-fronted houses and a church spire quivering in a haze of pale gold dust. Across from them, on a raised weed-ragged track, a morose train squatted silently.

The short trader made a convulsion in his throat and spat an arc of tobacco juice onto the road. "Gold Hill, by God, at last!"

The tall trader pulled back on the reins and the mules stopped. Calling to the children to get themselves down off the wagon, he lifted almost tenderly the ones who were too small to scramble down alone, smiling at them with his cruel smile. The short trader unharnessed the mules and led them to a creek a little off the road, while the tall one pulled out the long chain that kept each pair of men behind the one in front, and then unlocked their wrist and ankle shackles, all the while telling in a violent joking voice as he went one pair to the next what would happen to anyone who took it in his head to run. Then he herded everyone toward the creek, where he made them, men and women separate, strip off their clothes and bathe, he watching with a rifle in his hands.

As Tom waded out into the creek, he saw the naked little blue-eyed boy turn toward him with a look like disappointment. Heat came inside Tom's head, and a thumping started in his chest. He swung around as if to make a dash for it, but the tall trader jerked his gun and said, "Get back, you!" By the time he jerked his gun again and shouted, "Everybody out!" the cold had calmed Tom down.

Meantime, the short trader had tossed down the bundles from the wagon. Now he came with scissors and a razor in his hands, and as the dripping bodies came up from the creek, he made them kneel one by one in front of him, and cut their hair off close against the skull, and shaved the men.

From the bundles on the road, the traders now produced calico shirts and dresses, coarse-woven trousers, stiff-soled shoes, colored head rags for the women, wide-brimmed clean straw hats, not too crumpled, for the men. When these were sorted out and everyone was pinned, tied, buttoned, and lined up back-to-back, the tall trader unscrewed the lid from a glass pot, scooping out of it a handful of a glutinous white substance. He passed the pot to the short trader, who scooped a handful too, and the pair of them moved along the double row, greasing the cold washed faces till they shone. Then they tossed the bundles of old clothes back into the wagon, tossed the children in on top of them, and everyone went on toward Gold Hill.

SOMEHOW word had gone ahead that they were coming and the superintendent met them at the entrance to the mine. A clangor hung behind him in the atmosphere, like a wake behind a boat.

He was a large man, with a purse-mouthed Cornish accent and a heavy-jowled red face.

"What's all this lot, then?" he said, squinting up his eyes.

He clasped his hands behind his back and looked the spruced-up men and women over with suspicion, muttering about the trouble foreign niggers brought with them. A man could not sleep easy in his bed with the likes of them about, he said. They were trouble through and through, with no thought in their heads but to steal gold, plot rebellion, run away. He turned the whole lot down.

With offended looks, as though their virtue had been questioned, the traders assured him of their wares. They swore that not one was a troublemaker, all were strong and healthy, all willing to work. It was simply the misfortune of their owners that had caused them to be sold.

The superintendent shrugged. For all he knew, the whole lot had been stirred up by a pack of abolitionists and were scheming to import some deep-laid frightful plan. No sir, he preferred to get his workers from the local farms so he could know with some assurance they could be relied on, and if not, he could send them back.

Pressed hard, he dickered about prices for a couple of the women, at last buying one with a little girl to be a cook, another for a general help. The tall trader assured him that his choice was sound, but since both were guaranteed with child, there would be an extra charge. The superintendent set his hands against the women's bellies and declared he did not pay for unseen pregnancies. With a knowing snigger, the tall trader assured him that, although unseen, the pregnancies were real, and he could guarantee it. And so the arguing went back and forth until a price was reached, the two women listening with blank, exhausted faces.

By the time it was all done, the tall trader had stuck his

thumbs into the armholes of his waistcoat and offered to throw in Tom at a good price. The superintendent hesitated, the tall trader looking at him slantwise, as if he read the thought: *too cheap to turn down.*

"He can work," the trader said, stretching his thin lips. "He can surely lift a load. Here, feel these fine muscles," hissing in Tom's ear, "No limping, d'ya hear me, boy?"

The superintendent felt, and then demanded all Tom's clothes come off while he looked him over carefully. When he saw his legs, he screwed his face up. "What's this here about?" addressing his question not to the tall trader but to Tom himself.

The tall trader half-stepped forward, as though to take the words from Tom and shape them to his patter, but Tom, naked, answered nakedly, "It were because I run." Which would have queered the deal except that Tom, looking up, saw whipping in the tall trader's face. "I cain't run now with these here legs," he said, and sold himself.

As Tom watched the polished faces turn away, the little blue-eyed boy looked back at him with an expression on his face like longing, as though he—how could he?—loved him. Then the calico shirts and dresses shuffled off along the road, toward another mine, another superintendent, another round of bargaining. Tom stood staring after them, still naked with his clothes piled at his feet, but the little blue-eyed boy did not look back again. Shortly, he heard singing going down the road.

The superintendent, twenty paces off, called to him impatiently. Tom bent and pulled on shirt and trousers, shoes and hat, and followed him.

CHAPTER FOUR

So this was hell. This was where a thief was doomed to burn and burn again. Tom had often heard the preacher tell of it. Bible underneath his fist, he would raise his eyes and fix them on the Negroes jostling gape-mouthed in the church's gallery, and pause, and draw in a deep breath, and wait until the jostling stopped and every face turned fearfully on his. "Obey." The word would be a whisper. "Obey." A little louder. Then, in a measured roar, "Obey them that have the rule over you, submit yourselves." And if you do not, you will be sent down deep inside the earth where there is everlasting fire, where your flesh will never be consumed, where your soul will forever be in torment. Sometimes the preacher would describe the way their flesh would burn, sizzling up and bubbling, falling off the bone, only to be instantly restored to burn again. *Thou shalt not steal. Thou shalt not. Thou shalt not.* He was a thief.

Now he was being led down deep into the earth. He clung in

panic to the uprights of the narrow ladder, his leg bones shriek-
ing out in pain each time he turned, precarious on a narrow platform slick and slippery with liquid mud, to start down the next
sheer set of steps.

Before they sent him down the shaft, they had given him a
pair of jackboots and a wide-brimmed hat, thick and lined with
felt, heavy on his head. Onto the hat they had secured with clay
a lighted candle. Its tiny light revealed plank timbering, and in
places where the timbering had fallen or been torn away, blank
dripping rock. An enormous pipe thumped, thunderous in the
narrow space, like a giant finger pointing downward to his doom,
and from the depths rose the ghastly incoherent sorrow of the
damned.

As he came to the bottom of another set of steps, turning
painfully to set his foot upon the top rung of the next, Tom lost
sight of the tiny firefly below him in his companion's hat, and
leaning out, saw, far down at the bottom, the pinprick lights of
hell flickering back and forth.

Beside him, a heavy trembling rope strained toward the surface, hauling a great metallic barrel humped with evil-smelling
rock. As it passed, Tom's stomach shifted, rose, and fell into the
outer dark. An agitation of the ladder and the man below him
swore, his strange, foreign-sounding voice echoing and echoing.
Tom felt a jumping in his throat and heard himself begin to cry.
Demons would be there to meet him at the bottom, to jeer and
prod him with their forks, and to lash their tails and shove him
in the flames.

But demons were not at the bottom of the shaft, nor hellfire
either, just men, wild looking, black and white, with mud-
streaked faces and candles in their hats, and he realized this was
where he was to work. His companion from the ladder was still
swearing, softly now, shaking vomit off his sleeve.

"First time?" one of the Negroes said, and laughed. And then more bitterly, "First time or last, a man don't never get accustomed."

He struck a match against the black rock wall and lit a new candle in Tom's hat. Then he slung around his neck a pair of extra candles linked by one continuous long wick. A white man handed him a pickaxe.

His companion from the ladder jerked his head. "Come on, if yer comin'," and, shouldering a sledgehammer and a heavy metal auger, set off into the mine.

The other men went about their own concerns, taking their swaying shadows with them. Tom, after a moment's shivering hesitation, scrambled after his companion, stumbling over rock piles, skidding across slippery surfaces, flinging out a sudden hand against the wall, along a tunnel where the air smelled rank and swirled with smoke, and water slopped about his feet. Other tunnels went off at either side. In them he could hear men calling to each other, their voices coming back and coming back again so that there seemed to be a thousand unseen callers, one man coughing, coughing, the sound of it like someone beating on a can, and the traveling click-click-click of metal against rock. At intervals, a candle trembled on an iron spike secured into the wall, clinging to its own pale light as though it feared the blackness, like a soldier, recruited to subdue an enemy, who cannot bring himself to leap out of the ditch.

Toward them came a pair of wide-brimmed hats with candles like his own, a pair of low-bent straining bodies hitched by straps and chains to a high-sided metal cart which, piled with rock, ground behind them on twin rails, the men's twin breaths groaning through the darkness, throwing huge distorted shadows onto blackly glistening walls. They passed with no acknowledgment.

Gradually the tunnel lowered, forcing Tom to bend and then bend lower still, to crawl. The man who led him stopped.

"Thar, we 'ave to dig in thar. You go on in first and I'll be comin' after. Go in on yar back and chip the rock above. Careful it don't fall down on yar hat and put yar light out."

Then Tom was on his back, the man was pushing at his feet, saying, "Thar, in thar, go deeper now," and water was creeping up his back and in his ears, the rock so low above his face he could barely raise the pick to chip at it. He understood what he was meant to do, but could not do it. The musty smell of sweet potatoes came to him and he was shivering underneath his mother's cabin floor, the boots of the patrollers loud above his head. Shifting, dust-filled light slanted through the floorboards and he heard men's voices, and the thump and whimper of their fists, and then his mother's fall.

"So let's be gettin' on with it," said his companion's voice.

Tom lay there with the pick against the rock above his face, pushing hard, as though to keep the weight of it from falling down to crush him where he lay. He heard voices echoing and circling, and then a shout, and shortly after it, a dreadful roar, another, and another, as though of Lucifer himself. A surge of sulphurous wind engulfed him, catching like a pointed object in his throat. The tiny radiance of the candle in his hat flickered and went out.

Tom's breath gathered itself like a cornered animal inside his chest and would not budge. His rib cage heaved and froze and heaved again. A great gasp came out of him, another, and another, and yet he could not breathe. He held the roof up with his pick and struggled with his breath, feeling his eyes grow wide and wider, as though, if they opened wide enough, they would show things to him in the dark.

"What you up to in thar, lad?" his companion's rough voice called beyond his feet. And then, "Goddam! Why do they have to send me down another green one? All the time, I tell them all the time, don't be sendin' green ones down the mine. But do they listen? They do not." A hawking sound, the sibilant wet sound of spitting. "Come now," he said in a resigned, cajoling voice, "it be'int yar fault. Yar sartin' not the first to panic in the dark. Happens to the best of um."

Something gave inside Tom's chest. He opened up his mouth and howled.

"Shurrup, you daft black nutter," his companion called, but he could not. He held the roof up with his pick and howled and could not stop.

Now other voices came from in between his feet. Someone shouted. Someone swore. "Goddam the nigger for a funker!" Something scrabbled at his boot, a fierce grip around his ankles, and he was hauled out along the tunnel howling still.

CHAPTER FIVE

⁓⊙⁓⊙

ABOVE Tom, on the surface, Eugenia Mae stood at the front door of the cabin, looking down the lane toward the mine with the half-impatient manner of a woman expecting someone to arrive. She was angry with herself. She had wept again when she got home from work, and fallen off to sleep exhausted. It happened every day. She could not seem to help herself. All day she would control the creatures chewing at her heart, but then, alone back at the cabin, would come a great welling up of emptiness, and behind it tears.

Late sun glinted on a string of puddles down the center of the lane. Soon it would be dark. The men from down below were right now crawling up, like blind creatures hatched out of the earth, another brood milling on the surface, one by one vanishing below to be spat back up at midnight, then another lot at dawn.

A young woman came stepping up the lane, her skirts bundled in her hands to keep them off the ground. Didema Ware.

Eugenia did not like her. She was the sort who relished other people's trouble, telling everything she knew to anyone who would stay still long enough to hear it, and when she had nothing left to tell, or nothing worth the telling, she would tell it anyway.

"Hello, Eugenia Mae."

"Hello, Didema." Eugenia spoke reluctantly, with the air of someone forced to acknowledge an inferior. She looked down the lane toward the mine.

Didema stepped into the door across the way, vanished for a moment, and then reappeared to prop herself against the doorjamb, intent on conversation.

Eugenia ignored her.

"Something's been going on down there," Didema called, jerking her head toward the mine.

Eugenia looked at her.

"They hauled someone up the north shaft an hour back or so. One of the miners hurt. Another goner, likely."

"Who?"

Didema shrugged. "He was bawling loud enough to split the sky."

"You did not go to see?"

"I've already done my shift down at the hospital today, no call to go seeking out more work." She took hold of both sides of her apron and jerked her head toward the room behind her. "Anyway, it's not my man. I got him right here sleeping safe and sound, that's all I care about." She stopped, sucking in her breath. "Your father not home yet?"

Eugenia did not answer. She stepped into the lane, looking toward the mine.

"You been in town today?" Didema asked. "I heard at the post office they nominated that Abe Lincoln. Miz Hedra says if he's elected . . ."

Eugenia cut her off with a sweep of the hand and set off

down the lane to where it opened on a vast expanse of muddy ground, rutted, dotted with abandoned holes half filled with water from the recent rains, a world that thumped and rattled, hissing with the pumping stroke of steam, the creak of rods, the snappish leap of pistons up and down. Voices shouted, slave-pushed wooden barrows, mule-hauled wooden carts, clattered back and forth, hauling the day's last loads of ore to the great stones of the crushers, like offerings to some god primitive and pagan; and back behind the cabins, water spat out of a pipe into a noxious-smelling muck left bloodied by a sun that now slipped furtively away behind the hill where, on the mustering ground, the steady left-left of militia drilling could be heard.

She went toward the hospital, walking faster now Didema could not see her, tension starting in her stomach. If Papa should die on her . . . But no, the hospital was quiet, just three miners sleeping on their cots, one breathing with a rasping sound.

On toward the cookhouse, past the slave quarters where the Negroes were eating their evening meal, sitting on their doorsills or on the ground, hunkered down in the stink of their own bodies, digging with their fingers into little cedar tubs or iron pots, a few with bent or snapped-off iron spoons, some with bits of wood, the children scooping with their hands. They watched her pass, heads turning, but with no greeting, barely even recognition in their eyes. Behind them, the open doorways of their huts were filled with filthy dark confusion. Somewhere in there were three with bleeding backs, the three who had run off last night, and been brought back, soundly whipped by the patrollers. It had been six months, almost seven, since the news of John Brown's raid on Harpers Ferry swept through the Negro quarters, stirring them into a frenzy of excitement. They had calmed since then, but almost every night a simmering agitation propelled one or more of them toward the western mountains, trading the search for gold for the golden search for freedom. *They want to be here in this place no more than I.*

Eugenia sniffed. At least when they set out from Wilmington for Gold Hill, she had something to console her: the thought that Papa was to be a partner in the company. Little did she think that when they got here they would find the company he came to work for had been bought up, swallowed whole by the Gold Hill Mining Company, its partners now not partners but ordinary earners of a wage. Still optimistic, Papa had gone up and down the goldfields, interviewing other small concerns in hopes of wrangling a partnership out of one of them. But the Gold Hill Mining Company came behind and sat insistently before each of the small owners, smiling its wealthy golden smile, until all had been swallowed in its maw.

After several weeks of earning nothing, Papa had come back one night to the boardinghouse where they were staying to find Eugenia sitting on the step outside, their bags around her. "What will we do now?" she said, and he, with an enormous sigh, said, "We'll have to sell the horse and carriage."

Next day he sold them both, and bought himself a miner's shirt and hat and a pair of knee-high miner's jackboots, and went to sit, humbly resentful, before the hiring agent of the Gold Hill Mining Company.

And so he went to work, a wage earner, he who had never worked for another man in all his life. "I must do it, though, Eugenie. I must do it," he told her, smiling a bleak smile. "If I work hard enough, I will advance, I have no doubt of it."

"It has been promised?"

"It has been"—casting about him for a word—"it has been indicated."

Thinking of it now, Eugenia made a low, impatient hissing through her teeth. So they had nominated Mr. Lincoln, had they? She did not doubt it. Didema had not wit enough to invent a thing like that. She could not imagine what might come of it, whether it would be more rumormongering of civil war, or of a slave uprising. Every week some tale came running breathless down the road, warning of a band of Negroes, armed and out for blood, heading for the gold mines. Eugenia glanced behind her at the Negroes at their meal. She rolled her neck, feeling its small bones click.

THE cookhouse stood before her, a sprawling wooden structure with a push-off chimney at one end and the smell of grease infused into its walls. She stepped across the sill and looked about. To her right, plank tables set with knives and spoons and metal plates, long bench seats on each side. To her left, the kitchen area, hot and redolent of boiled pork and beans. In the center of the room, three Negro girls stood behind a row of kettles on a serving trestle. They were singing quietly together, waiting for the hungry miners to arrive. One had lifted off a lid and was stirring at the contents with a ladle. When Eugenia came in, she clicked the lid back down. They all stopped singing.

"Have you girls seen Mr. Spotswood?"

They made big eyes, shaking their heads no.

Beyond them, the door to the supply room stood half open. Eugenia went toward it, stepping around the girls, who kept their eyes turned down, although Eugenia knew they watched her.

Inside the supply room, pencil and paper in her hands, was Miz Hedra Perrin, her back toward the door. She walked up and down before the shelves, tapping at them with her pencil, her hips jerking underneath her skirt like a couple of wild creatures struggling to get out. She wrote something on her paper, pushed a jar of pickles to one side, and counted aloud the jars behind.

Miz Hedra Perrin was the superintendent's wife. She lived on the main street of Gold Hill, in a house with four rooms down, where she lived with her husband, and another four rooms up, which she rented out to single Cornish miners. The house had a wide porch at the front where every day Miz Hedra could be seen sitting fatly in a sagging-bottomed chair, waiting for her driver to come by with her high-wheeled, spring-bottomed gig, or her husband to come home for supper. She had no children, or none that had come with her from Cornwall, and she supervised the hospital and cookshop. She did not cook, but kept the key to the supply room, every evening counting and assessing everything. Then she drew up lists and next morning went bouncing on her springs to argue in her terse voice with Mr. Martin at the general store, or with the farmers come in from the countryside, their carts and wagons loaded with supplies of fruit and eggs and vegetables and smoke-cured ham.

Miz Hedra's other function was to organize the ladies' prayer meeting, which took place every Wednesday evening at her house. An ardent Methodist, she disapproved of Presbyterians, Episcopalians, Baptists, Papists, especially Papists, and all benighted foreigners, by which she meant Chinese. However, all the ladies of the town were welcome at her Wednesday meeting and they arrived at her door armed with plates of food and knitting bags and gossip, Miz Hedra welcoming them in with open arms and a proselytizing heart. On these evenings, her upstairs boarders were required to make themselves scarce, and so those who were not on shift went off to the grog shop where they spent the evening gambling and drinking gin, while at home Miz Hedra pleaded with the Lord to rid the mine of vice and ardent spirits, and passed out copies of the temperance pledge for the ladies to take home to their husbands.

Eugenia coughed. "Miz Hedra?"

Miz Hedra turned, a swift, impatient movement. She was short, not above five feet, with dainty wrists and ankles, the rest of her so fat that even her eyelids were fat, her earlobes too, hanging off her tiny ears like a pair of flesh-pink earrings. Eugenia she treated with a sort of condescending pity that was not quite viciousness, as though she knew everything about her and saw no hope at all. Sometimes she would touch her with her chubby baby's hands, pat her on the arm, or briefly grasp her wrist, or stroke the middle of her back the way she might have stroked a cat, a gentle threatening motion.

Eugenia knew Miz Hedra was crucial to her father's rise, if rise he could in this thunderous offensive place, and so she let her, but afterwards she would feel that softly vicious touch and a sensation like suffocation would come over her.

"Miz Hedra, have you seen Mr. Spotswood?"

For a moment Miz Hedra seemed not to recognize her. Then she said, "Oh, Miss Spotswood."

Eugenia saw the baby hand reach out and braced herself to feel the soft-fleshed fingers touching her, but it drew back as though offended, and tucked itself behind the shopping list. No, Miz Hedra had not seen Mr. Spotswood.

BACK at the cabin, Eugenia found the lamp lit and an enormous Negro squatting on the floor. He turned, one arm half raised as though he feared she might strike him. His head was shaven clean and his face shone blackly in the quavering light.

Eugenia smacked her hand against her heart. "Who are you? What do you want here?"

He rose, awkward and half stumbling, speaking to her feet. "Your papa done bought me, missie. He say I belong to you."

Eugenia looked behind her. A pair of miner's jackboots stood scuff-toed beside the door. "Papa?" she said, looking up at a square hole in the corner of the ceiling.

A pair of large crimson slippers, badly worn, reached one after the other down a narrow ladder. After them came Mr. Spotswood's blunt thick legs and thighs, the blunt thick body of the man, the blunt square head, the heavy-lidded eyes, where, behind a screen of pale blue confidence, there lurked the calculating panic of a gray fox treed by hounds.

"Papa?" Eugenia's eyes were on the Negro.

"A gift," he said. "I bought him from Mr. Perrin." And he leaned to kiss her.

She pulled away, looking the Negro up and down while she brushed her hands across her apron, a fastidious motion. He backed away from her, one knee giving under him, reaching behind himself to find the wall.

Eugenia turned back to her father.

"Eugenie, it's a start," he said. Not saying *one step back toward respectability*. Not telling how Tom had howled like a panicked dog while they hauled him up the shaft, clinging to the kibble's rope and bucking, throwing the thing off balance, making it clang back and forth against the pipe, the noise of his ascent magnified and hollowed and distorted. He did not tell how Mr. Perrin had raged against the vanished traders for selling him a funker, or how he, Spotswood, had turned his pockets inside out to find the dirt cheap price to take the fellow off his hands.

"But, Papa, this boy can barely walk. He can barely walk."

"Oh, he can walk. He may limp somewhat, but he can walk. He may be no good for working underground, but he can help about the house." Mr. Spotswood made a waving motion. "All sorts of tasks are available to him here, and by day I will rent him to the rockers." ·

Eugenia looked at the Negro who now stood backed against the wall, his hands flat up against it on each side, as though he would push a hole through which to run away.

"How, pray, will he do that?" she said. "I wear my poor legs out on the rockers every day, and he can barely walk."

Mr. Spotswood made a gesture of impatience. "Will you not be satisfied? You complain because you no longer have a slave to help you, and when I produce one, what do you do then? You whine. Eugenie, it's a *start*."

CHAPTER SIX

❧

HIS name was Tom and he was set to sleep in the lean-to storeroom back behind the cabin, directly behind the tiny room Eugenia Mae had taken as her own. Her bed was set against the wall and before she lay down that night, she took a candle and climbed up on the ticking mattress, examining the hardened mortar of dried mud between the planks in case there might be a gap through which Tom could spy on her. But the gaps were well stuffed here, with rags and bits of rope and corn husks, so she climbed back down and prepared herself for sleep.

Sleep did not come, however. No matter how her body tried, her head would not relax. She could feel the Negro through the wall, his presence, and even fancied that she heard his breathing. Tears came to her eyes. If she could hear his breathing, then he could hear hers too. It was too much, too intimate. Papa, no doubt, meant well, but for all the good this wall did, the fellow may as well be right beside her in the bed.

As that thought came to her, she waited for her senses to rise up and jangle in alarm, but the words lay flat inside her head. She had been frightened more than once by Negroes in her life, the towering blackness of them, the seductive pinkness of their palms, their musky smell, their false humility—even as a child she had known, without knowing how she knew it, that their humility was false—the way she could control them with a word, a movement of her hand, it was unnatural, even an animal, a horse or dog, took more controlling, and each time she read a newspaper report, the small hairs electric on her neck, of some black beast who had accosted, waylaid, ravished, or at least had been accused of it, she sensed, with the prurient awareness of a virgin with grown men at her beck and call, that there was menace underneath their deference.

Tom. She mouthed the word in case he heard her through the wall. *Tom.* It was a slave's name, an ordinary name. And yet something about this Negro was not ordinary. She turned her head in the darkness, staring at the wall, and fancied she could see him on the other side, glowing with the beauty young men sometimes have before they are completely men, black as a moonless night and with a gentleness about him that touched some deep-down memory in Eugenia's heart, the same black gentleness that sometimes came to her in dreams, faceless but comforting, a memory so indefinable she never found the words to ask Papa what it might mean. She felt it drifting down around her, buoying up her limbs so that she seemed to float.

When she woke she realized she was smiling. It was still dark, although what time it was she could not tell. She had not heard the bell, but it might have rung and she had slept through it, as she did from time to time, as though she were becoming so much a part of the mine that its racket was part of her as well. She listened for the Negro, then shifted on the bed and pressed her ear against the wall. Nothing. No sense of his presence. Was he sleeping? No, he was not sleeping. Was he gone, then? Run away? She thought he had not run away.

When she went out to start the fire, Tom was crouched in front of it, feeding it with sticks. He rose, steadying himself against the wall. "Miss Eugenia," he said.

That day he started on the rockers. Eugenia watched him leaning with both hands on the rail as he brought first this side of the cradle down beneath his naked foot, and then the other, the motion powerful and deliberate, making the movements of the little girls with whom he worked seem light and dainty, like a giant among elves.

The elves watched him as well. Eugenia could hear their whispered comments. "Oh, my, ain't that a fine big one?" "For shame, you brazen hussy, you."

Tom, eyes fixed between his feet, watched the slide and slide of quicksilver in the rocking cradle's grooves.

The foreman, chewing tobacco while he lolled against a post, watched his bearlike new recruit with a bemused expression on his face that did not rise to interest. After a while, he spat a jet of black tobacco juice onto the ground, pushed himself upright with one shoulder on the post, and went up and down about his business, adjusting the flow of water down the rockers, checking the grooves inside to make sure they had sufficient quicksilver to catch the gold, speaking a word here or giving an instruction there, shouting rather, or gesticulating, since the noise of the place made the very sky reverberate.

Across from Tom, Eugenia contemplated the thought that she worked as he worked, like a slave. Worse than a slave, she found, when payday came and Tom's chips of pounded gold were put directly in his hand. Papa took his cut, which turned out to be most of it, but first the gold was put into Tom's hand. Not so with her. Her pay, the full amount, was put into her father's hand. If she needed money she must beg. And so in one sense she resented Tom, but in another sense he fascinated her. *He is mine, belongs to me. I can do with him as I want, make him do anything.*

She began to notice how, from time to time, he winced or ground his teeth, and from this she came to understand he was in pain. It was worst, she thought, when he kept his face completely blank, his eyes inward-looking and yet focused, concentrated, as though he faced down something wild inside himself. He would not tell one word of where he came from, or why he had been sold, just looked at her with dark, bewildered eyes anytime she questioned him.

As for Tom, although he could now sometimes walk without a limp, the pain inside his legs had sunk down deep inside the bone, the right leg not so much, the left one just below the knee, a grinding point of pain, not constant, worsening as the day went by. In case Miss Eugenia should hear him moaning in his sleep, he slipped off with his blanket every night to stretch out on the ground amongst the shuffling, groaning mules and the sad blind horses used to power the windlasses, and if it rained, he crawled under a cart. When his leg woke him in the night, he would stretch it out, then, turning on his back, bend it at the knee and drop it to one side. Sometimes he would reach down and hold it in his arms, which seemed to help.

He treasured like a gift those nights when, exhausted, he sank into a painless void from which he would wake to the raucous clanging of the bell, feeling fine and clean and weightless. By midmorning, though, the grinding in his leg bone would begin again, softly at first, like the tuning of a fiddle, gradually working up to a relentless scraping across strings.

One day Eugenia said, "Tom, how did you hurt your legs?"

He was chopping wood and had the axe raised in the air. He brought it gently down and looked at her.

"It's nowt."

"How did they get hurt?"

He lifted up the axe. "It's nowt." And brought it down with a tremendous crash. The balanced log split neatly down the middle and the axe went on beyond, its head embedding in the chopping block.

"Show me your legs, Tom."

He set one foot on the block and wrestled with the axe.

"Show me your legs."

The axe head came out with a jerk and he stumbled backwards, almost fell.

"Show me."

When at last he did, turning up his overalls, she made a sound like sorrow in her throat. "Why did they shoot you, Tom?"

He set a new log on the chopping block. "It were because I run." And brought the axe down hard.

Later, when he came into the kitchen with his arms full of stovewood, she, not looking at him, stirring at a pan, said, "They hurt badly when you're working on the rockers, don't they?"

He clattered the wood onto the hearth at one side of the fireplace—there was no box to put it in—and when he turned it seemed to her there was fear in his eyes. *So,* she told herself, *he is afraid that I will think him useless. He is afraid that I will sell him.* A sensation came into her throat like triumph, or like power. *He is afraid of me.*

"Tom, would you like to quit the rockers?" *I am cruel, teasing him.*

But he would not admit to anything, to wanting or not wanting, and so she said, "Well, then, if you have no opinion on the matter, I will do with you as I want. You will drive a mule cart. I will arrange it with Papa."

"Yes'm," he said, and crouched—she knew that he crouched

painfully—setting one log and then another on the fire. He rose. "Yes'm," he said again, and went outside.

She did not turn her head, but stirred the pan, metal scraping against metal, the sharp edges of the spoon blurred by strange, unwelcome tears. He had not thanked her. She had wanted him to thank her.

"PANDERING, that's what it is," Mr. Spotswood told Eugenia. She had met him at the end of shift and they were walking home in the dim light, she wrapped in a shawl against the evening chill, he holding to her arm above the elbow, steering her around the piles of rock and stacks of wood hauled in for making shorings, interrupting himself to caution her to watch her step or mind this hole, or to shoo away the hopeful, skinny dog that trailed behind, or cast a baleful eye at some young miner pulling off his hat to her.

"Once you start pandering to Negroes there is no knowing how it all might end. This Tom must earn his living."

"But his legs are very painful, I can tell it from the way he moves. The bone in his left leg is damaged, I am sure of it. It needs more time to heal, which it will not treading all day on the rockers. What point in buying me a slave if we then work him into uselessness?"

In front of them loomed the bridgework of the aqueduct that carried water from the creek into the mine. They dipped their heads and passed beneath it, water rustling overhead.

Mr. Spotswood began to speak, but stopped because now they were coming to the millhouse, a rough-built wooden building on their right that throbbed and clanked and hooted steam and groaned, shaking all over with the effort of its enterprise.

When they had put it far enough behind them he went on. "A

slave learns early how to take advantage in whatever way he can, and this fellow must not be allowed to take advantage of your tenderness of heart. You let him for one minute get it in his head that you are pliable, that he can appeal to you for pity, and the next thing you will find him sleeping flat out on his back for the entire day, or worse, he will become presumptuous and steal from us, or, worse still, he will turn violent and the next thing you will find him creeping in the night to slit your throat."

"What rubbish! You've been listening to panicmongers. And anyway, I'm not suggesting we send him on a holiday, but simply set him to earn his keep another way. He can earn as much by driving mules as he can by rocking cradles. Just you wait and see, Papa. Kindness and the whip have much in common. They can both incite a man to work."

"And where did you discover *that* grand piece of wisdom?"

"In the hospital. From working there."

"The hospital? How so?"

"The men who are brought in there, whether black or white, are usually dying, you know that. There is little I can do for them except to dress their wounds and feed them whiskey and laudanum for their pain and give them kindness. It is the kindness, most of all, that eases their hard journey into heaven. The simplest things. To bring them water when their throats are parched, to sit beside them listening to their maunderings, to hold their hands, to let them think I am their mother at the end." *To kiss them too, on forehead or on cheek, and even on the lips if they request it. Oh, what a healing thing a kiss is.*

"I do not see what connection working in the hospital has with whipping or not whipping. It would be a monster who would whip a dying man. A working Negro is another matter."

"I think all men need kindness."

Eugenia felt her father's grip on her arm tense, pressing it against his side. They walked in silence, the wind catching at Eugenia's shawl. "I must concede that, child," he said at last, his words so low she barely caught them.

She thought about the time he wept when they were coming here from Wilmington, how she had repulsed him, and on an impulse reached up to kiss him on the cheek. If he would just turn to her, if he would confide . . . but no, whatever momentary weakness he had felt, whatever instinct to rail against the gods of fate, he sucked back down inside himself and stiffened up his spine. He shrugged and raised his eyebrows in a mimicry of resignation.

"If Mr. Lincoln ends up as our president, there will, no doubt, be so much pandering to Negroes that a little of our own will do no harm."

"I'm sure Mr. Lincoln would be proud of you."

Mr. Spotswood's voice turned snappish. "I don't want that black Republican being proud of me."

"I'm sorry. I was joking. You do agree, though? You will speak to Mr. Perrin?"

"I will. But if I see this fellow start to take advantage . . ."

SO Tom was set to driving a mule cart from shaft entrance to crushing mill and back. At the shaft, where patient circling horses turned and turned the windlasses, hauling the ore out of the earth, a pair of boys loaded up the cart, then trotted on behind while Tom urged the straining mules toward the crushing mill, where the three of them heaved the rocks into a pile for the mill workers to feed beneath the millstone. And it turned out he had a way with mules. He could make the most reluctant beast apply his strength to hauling with no more than a murmur or a clicking of his tongue. While other drivers lashed and swore, he never used a whip, never even flicked the reins, just talked low and confiding to the animal. He worked the windlass horses too, from time to time, leading the sightless beasts around their endless track, or talking them around, calming them with his gentle rumbling voice when some stupendous crash came up the shaft from down below.

Eugenia watched him, and it seemed to her that Tom could sense the way the poor blind creatures felt, the laboring mules as well. *How does it feel to be a mule? Like Tom himself? Like me?*

It seemed to her Tom had a vast reserve of strength. While other slaves lay flat out exhausted when their work was done, spending their free time staring at the walls inside a hut or at the sky, Tom followed her about, hoisting pots for her in the cookhouse, peeling potatoes, stirring beans and grits, or hauling corn pone from the ashes so she would not burn herself. He turned injured miners for her in the makeshift hospital, helped her change bandages and tend to wounds, hauled out stinking buckets of the patients' slops. He was especially good with newly injured men, talking to them the way he talked to frightened mules or horses, not saying anything particular, just talking gently, murmuring until they calmed. When she took a brush and knelt to scrub the cabin floor, he took the brush out of her hands and scrubbed it better than a housemaid, cleaned Papa's boots before she had a chance to take them up, stood patient in the washhouse poking boiling clothes down in the kettle with a charended stick, or heaved them out, slinging them across the line while Eugenia came behind him pegging them on tight, hot steam rising up to turn the pair of them to ghosts.

On Sunday, he carried her to church and back—Papa walked, he was too proud to be seen rattling in a mule cart—and then went off to hunt for gold in the abandoned shafts. It was allowed. He stole it on the job as well, as others did, Eugenia knew it, tucking a little nugget in the rolled-up bottoms of his pants, pressing gold dust in his hair. She had seen him when he thought he was alone spread a rag out on the floor and shake and scratch his head above it, catching in it his day's takings. Then he folded it up carefully and tucked it in the space behind a loose board in the wall. Sometimes, when he was not there, she would take it out and weigh it in her hand, and every time she tucked it back she knew it weighed a little more.

Sometimes when he reached to take the broom or brush out of her hand, her grip would shift at the last second—*inadvertent, it was inadvertent*—so his hand brushed against her own. When they stood together at some task, she would be surprised to find that she was close enough to feel the heat rise off his body and smell his spicy smell, and when he moved away, it seemed to her he had acknowledged something.

Anything she wanted him to do was done almost before she asked it, sometimes before she even thought of it. He worked harder than she had ever seen a person work, humming and singing to himself, and when she thanked him, he would glow.

And so Papa, with all his glum predictions, had been wrong, completely wrong, about Tom turning lazy. Which meant that she, Eugenia, had been right. She said nothing to her father, though, and if he kept an eye on Tom as he had promised, he said nothing either. She wanted him to speak, to praise Tom, and to praise her too, but he just went on pulling on his jackboots and going off to work each morning, each evening coming home and sitting down to supper in his worn crimson felt slippers, and afterwards, with a slug of whiskey at his elbow, spreading out the *Carolina Watchman* to click his tongue above the news.

Today was Friday, payday. Eugenia clutched the rocking cradle bar, her body swaying with the rhythm of its movement, her eyes unfocused, thinking of how, when Papa got home from work, he would spread out his account book and sit late into the night, huffing and sighing and making figurings and jottings. Every Friday was the same. She would go to bed and like as not come out in the morning to find him still sitting at the table, sound asleep with his face on his arms, and his arms crossed on his account book. Something was not going right, she knew it.

She wondered if, as he had been wrong about the handling of one slave, he might not have been wrong about the handling of their farm. He had blamed the blight, attacks of weather, the shortsightedness of bankers, but what if it had been his own mistakes that brought them down? And what about Mama? Eugenia had been barely five years old when she had died and time had wiped away the memories. Papa had always said he lost her from an illness of the brain, but from friends and neighbors Eugenia had gathered there was something else, not from what they said, but from what they did not say. Had Papa mismanaged Mama's fortune? Was that why she declined? Had she died of disappointment in her husband?

Eugenia shivered, thinking of the slough of disappointment she herself had traveled through coming here from Wilmington, how she had steeled herself, clinging hard to Papa's promise that it would be only for a short time, only until he built his fortune back. But what if he had misjudged how long that would take him? What if it were impossible? He had not yet been promoted. In the early days he used to talk about it constantly. These days he did not speak of it at all, and when she questioned him he fended off her questions. Were they doomed, then? Must they labor in this gold mine their entire lives? Who would she ever find to marry her? Some foreigner or cracker crawled up from the belly of the earth with whiskey breath and permanently blackened fingernails? Was Papa, when all was said and done, to be a failure?

CHAPTER SEVEN

ON the Bricket farm, Clyde turned thirteen and Pa gave him the afternoon off work. Clyde was surprised. He lit off down the road for Chapel Hill as fast as he could go before Pa changed his mind.

Old Mary had baked a cake for him today, they had eaten it at noon. It was the first cake anybody ever made for him. She made sweet sticky stuff called frosting that she'd learned to make when she was working for the Missus back on Mr. Morgan's place. She took some blueberries and forced them through a flour sieve and mixed the juice into the frosting so it turned pale blue. She let Clyde stick his finger in the bowl and have a taste. It tasted sweet and sour, the best thing he had ever ate.

Pa snorted when he saw it and said, If that ain't frippery, but Old Mary put a knife into Clyde's hand and said to close his eyes and make a wish, then he could cut the cake. Clyde thought a bit and then he closed his eyes and started out to wish to be a slave patroller like his pa, but then he felt Old Mary watching him and squinted up at her, and there she was, looking straight on at him like a nigra never does. So then he closed his eyes and wished she wouldn't look at him like that, the way she'd looked at him the day he told her Tom was catched.

Don't take all day at it, Pa said, so then Clyde cut the cake, and Pa ate twice as much as anyone, and Old Mary fed a piece to Ma.

Goddam Old Mary, Clyde thought walking down the road, and then said it out loud. Goddam. It weren't a crime to be a slave patroller. These nigras were a pestilence, they needed to be shown who in the world was boss, that's what Pa said. Clyde asked him once, What is a pestilence? but Pa just said, Go on, get out of here, so he asked his uncle Benjamin, and his uncle said it was a plague of locusts. When Clyde asked what a plague was, his uncle thought awhile and then he said it was a lot of them all over the place. He said the way the Chosen People rid themselves of pestilence was by going after them with torn-up sacks or branches and whupping them.

Thinking on it now, Clyde looked about him for a whupping branch, but there were only fields on both sides.

Patrollers whupped the pestilence. That's what they swore to do when they stood up before the judge. Repeat after me, Judge Graham always said. He'd heard Pa take the oath three times and knew it by heart. When he turned eighteen and it was time for him to swear, he would not have to repeat it after any judge. He'd stand up with his hand raised and say it by hisself.

He held his right hand in the air. I, Clyde Bricket, do swear, that I will as searcher for guns, swords, and other weapons among the slaves in my district, faithfully, and as privately as I can, discharge the trust reposed in me as the law directs, to the best of my power, so help me God.

Then the judge would give him a warrant to carry in his pocket and he'd ride out on a beat at night and be the captain.

Pa had never been patrol captain. When Clyde asked him why not, Pa clapped him upside the head and made his brain hurt and feel strange all day, so he didn't ask again, but when he grew up and went out on patrol he'd make sure he was captain and that everybody knew it. He'd get him a fine hat and one of them cigars and the other men would do exactly what he said, even those who thought they were his betters. He would not put up with any of them drinking on the job or playing whoop-and-hide. No sir, he'd not put up with anything like that.

Nigras got to be kept in control, you let them take an inch they'll take a mile, that's what Pa said. Clyde wasn't sure what the inch and mile meant, and he didn't want his ear clapped again so he didn't ask, but he thought it had something to do with how those nigras sure could run when they took off. Some were fast enough to stay ahead of a horse a good long ways before they tired.

He was going past some woods now so he took his clasp knife and cut himself a whupping branch, a long one with a lot of spring. He trimmed the leaves and snapped it up against a trunk. It made a hissing sound and then a crack, and bark jumped off the trunk. He folded up his knife and put it in his pocket and set off down the road again, slashing at the grass along the edge.

He was coming into Chapel Hill. The big house on the corner had sunflowers growing in a row behind the fence. Clyde stopped and glanced about and nobody was watching, so he went slashing down the row, the yellow heads falling off behind. With his breath thrilling in his throat, he hightailed it around the corner and headed for Uncle Benjamin's house, which was in a back lane a few blocks north of Franklin Street, not a fancy house with flowers, just a clapboard place with a rocker on the porch and a barn out back to keep the horse he rode about to visit the Lord's People. When first he went to live there, it was called Dead End Lane, but he said, I am a preacher not an undertaker, and renamed it Preacher Lane. He painted up a sign with strong black lettering and fixed it in the ground and said, Now that is a name befitting of a man of God. No one argued, since his house was the only one on the lane.

Uncle Benjamin was sitting in the rocker with his Bible on his knee. Hey there, son, he said when he saw Clyde, and stuck his finger in the page and closed the Bible over it. Clyde liked his uncle Benjamin, he called him son, which Pa did not, he called him boy just like he was a nigra.

Clyde asked, You making up another sermon? and Uncle Benjamin looked holy in that way he had. It will be a thunder of redemption, praise the Lord, he said. You want cold tea? It is— excuse me, Lord—goddam hot today.

So Clyde sat on the stoop and whittled at his whupping stick and sipped cold tea out of a jar, listening to Uncle Benjamin practice up his sermon. He thought about Old Mary, how he had gone with Pa when they hired her from Sam Morgan at the crossroads auction on the other side of Chapel Hill. She was the second slave Pa hired from the money he got paid patrolling. Pa tried to get Tom thrown in too, for cheap, since everybody said he were not good for much, but Mr. Morgan said, That boy may have a weak brain in his head, but I have got my pride.

Old Mary was pretty much used up, but kind, and Ma wasn't quite so queer after she came. She'd let Old Mary comb her hair and wash her good, and dress her up in day clothes, and lead her out to the front porch, where she'd sit in the slat chair with her arms set along its wooden arms, staring out into the yard morning until night, not saying boo to anyone.

Mealtimes, Old Mary would lead her to the table and set a plate in front of her, and as long as Old Mary stayed beside her, making clucking noises like a hen makes to its chicks, she'd eat. Pa would talk to her about the farm, or how the crops were light this year, or how the bowel complaint was going round and he hoped it wouldn't come to them, or how those students up to the university had got theirselves in trouble one more time for going out and gambling on some horse race. Ma never said a word through all of it, just sat there chewing on her food and staring straight ahead. When she'd done, she'd push her plate aside and go back to sit on the front porch.

Sometimes Clyde would go and sit with her. Sometimes he talked to her and told her things the way Pa did, but mostly he just sat. Sometimes Old Mary sat with them as well, snapping beans into her skirt, singing hymns and nigra songs. She had a deep full voice and Clyde was always surprised when he heard it because it wasn't like her speaking voice. It seemed too big for her, she being a small woman with not one ounce of fat.

Pa said that Ma fell Strangely Silent after Baby Sister died. Clyde could not remember he ever had a baby sister, but he remembered there used to be a cradle in the corner of the kitchen, and then the cradle wasn't there. It was out front in the yard collecting rain. When Old Mary came she tipped the water out and filled it full of dirt and planted it with flowers. It was the flowers in the cradle Ma stared at when she sat on the front porch listening to Old Mary sing. Pa said Old Mary had worked miracles with her, she had the touch, and up till now Clyde liked her pretty well. When Uncle Benjamin's sermon was all done, he just might tell him about that goddam way she looked at him these days, but then he thought how, when Uncle Benjamin heard Clyde had been the one catched Tom, he had said, Well now. Just like that.

So maybe when the sermon was all done he'd ask Uncle Benjamin to tell some more about what it was like when he used to be a constable in Norfolk. Clyde liked to hear him tell about that place of sin. You would not believe, Uncle Benjamin would say, you're too young to understand what wickedness goes on. Why, those nigras up at Norfolk live just like any white folk, in houses of their own, no supervision from their owners, and get up to any sort of mischief.

Being a constable meant he went about the place arresting slaves who didn't have a pass or had a forged one, or he broke up packs of them that got together in the night. He locked them up to keep them from fomenting trouble. Next morning, he'd take them up before the mayor and when they'd been sentenced he'd flog them, fifteen lashes, that was all, so he could go through a good many in a day, men and women too. As well as his regular pay he got fifty cents for every one he put in jail, and fifty cents for every one he flogged. He had flogged hundreds, and he hunted slaves who ran away and got paid by their owners. But then he went to a revival and got saved and turned into a preacher. Now he didn't do that flogging anymore, but said as how we should be as kind to these poor folks as it is reasonable to be. Pa said it were a family disgrace that Uncle Benjamin did not patrol. You ask me, it's a preacher's duty to help keep the peace, he said, your Uncle Benjamin may be my brother, but that getting saved has softened up his head.

After a while, Uncle Benjamin creaked back on his rocker and said, Amen, hallelujah, praise the Lord, you want more tea before I go out on my rounds? So Clyde knew there wasn't going to be a story about Norfolk after all. He watched his uncle saddle up his horse and start off down the road with his Bible in a satchel on his back and his black hat with the wide brim on his head. He said it were his preacher's hat, it made the wicked tremble. You keep out of trouble, son, Uncle Benjamin called out. He had forgot about his birthday.

Clyde stood with his whupping stick trailing from his hand until the horse and Uncle Benjamin were out of sight, then he thought about the schoolhouse where he sometimes went when Pa sent him on an errand into Chapel Hill. Get on with it, he'd say, and don't be loitering about, but Clyde would loiter anyway, then make up an excuse.

The schoolhouse was his favorite place to loiter and he headed for it now. It was on the other side of town, not too far out. For a while he crouched beneath the window, his head against the second log down from the sill, and listened to the chanted lessons and the precise voice of the schoolmaster explaining things he didn't understand. Then he climbed the chestnut tree in the side yard and hid amongst the leaves, peering at the boys lined up in rows. When classes ended and the boys came shouting and shoving at each other out the door, he froze above them, and when the yard had cleared, slipped down from the tree and went out to the street, where he pretended he was one of them, walking with his friends.

That night at suppertime he plucked his courage up. Pa, he said, I been thinking about that there boys' school down by Chapel Hill.

His father turned and looked at him with an expression like amazement on his face. Them boys getting ready for the university, he said. They goin' be lawyers and politicians and the like. You ain't their type. He reached across and took another chicken leg.

Uncle Benjamin ain't their type, and he can read near anything. Why, he told me he's read clear through the Bible start to end.

Your uncle Benjamin's a goddam preacher. I already taught you how to read and figure well enough to run a farm.

Clyde did not intend to be a farmer, though. When he turned eighteen he was going to go across to Raleigh, where he could get a full-time job as a patroller, or maybe he'd go be a constable up there in Norfolk. He did not say one word of this to Pa. If Pa knew he was thinking thoughts like that, about leaving the farm he'd broke his back on all these years so his boy could have a good inheritance, he'd surely take and clap him upside the head again. So he kept it to hisself.

CHAPTER EIGHT

"PROFITS are down," Didema Ware announced one evening at the hospital. She was coming down the double row of beds, zigzagging back and forth to lay her hand against each patient's forehead. "This one's afire. Dead by morning, I should think."

Eugenia ignored her as she always did. Didema was so full of dark gossip and opinion that if you believed everything she said you would just go out and hang yourself. Even the injured miners knew better than to pay attention. They watched her without comment, or stared up at the ceiling, concentrating on recovery.

"The mine machinery is out of date," Didema said. "The company cannot find investors. Pay is going to be reduced."

Eugenia stopped winding a bloodied bandage off a miner's leg. "What was that you said?"

Didema came across, eyes gleaming. "If they reduce the pay,

the foreigners are going to go on strike—if they don't go back to Cornwall."

A bumping sound and Miz Hedra's backside, wide and pinkly floral, bustled through the door, followed by Miz Hedra huffing with a pile of linens in her arms.

"Bed changing day," she said, and came down the rows of beds dropping two sheets—"one, two"—onto each one's foot.

"Miz Hedra," Eugenia said when she came near, "may I ask you something?"

Miz Hedra stopped, looking at her above the pile of sheets. "Well? What is it?"

"Is pay to be reduced?"

Miz Hedra looked her up and down. "What is it to you, Miss Hoity-Toity?" And went on down the row.

Later, helping Eugenia change a bedsheet, Didema whispered, "Don't you be paying attention to Miz Hedra, now. She's nothing but a foreigner."

But Eugenia had been cut by the remark. "I think it is not that. I think Miz Hedra does not approve of me, I do not know why. I have tried to be her friend, but she's grown so sharp with me of late. And now she's calling me Miss Hoity-Toity."

Didema ran her tongue around her lips. "It's what she always calls you these days when you're not around."

"I do not understand."

"It's because you're pretty, and because you have a house slave of your own. It lifts you up above her."

"She could have a dozen house slaves if she wanted."

"She does not approve of slavery. I've heard her say so."

Eugenia straightened, balling the soiled bedsheet in her arms. "Does not *approve*? She whose husband makes his fortune off the backs of slaves? She who orders them about as easily as—"

"Hush, she's coming back."

When Eugenia turned and saw the fawning look Didema gave Miz Hedra, she wished she had not spoken.

THE next Sunday, Tom appeared after church with a bucket of whitewash and a brush, saying he would cheer her up by painting the inside of the cabin. Eugenia clapped her hands when it was done. If only she had some pretty fabric to make curtains. She begged her father until he put a little money in her hand, and next day after work set off walking to the general store to buy some chintz. But on the way, Tom appeared beside her with the mule cart and drove her down the main street to the store as if she were a lady.

The storekeeper, Mr. Martin, listened to her shining-eyed request with his scrawny neck stuck forward. "Painted what?" he said. "The inside of yer cabin?" He flicked a pair of watery eyes toward the window, outside which Tom waited in the mule cart, his back bent, forearms on his knees. "To cheer you up?" said Mr. Martin. "Well, now."

From the shelf behind, he pulled out a bolt of dark brown cloth, and with one hand underneath and a slapping of the bolt against the counter, jerked the fabric out in waves. Eugenia shook her head.

"Well, now," he said again, and bundling it to one side, produced dark red, then green, then gray, but Eugenia, pushing out her lips, shook her head at all of them.

"That's all, then," Mr. Martin said at last. He set both hands on the counter and leaned into his arms. "You want something fancy, you better go on up to Salisbury," and nodded without smiling when she thanked him. "Most folks don't need no Negro to tell them how they should be cheerful," he said, but the door had slapped behind her and she did not hear.

• • •

EUGENIA had never been to Salisbury before, had never had occasion. It would be a grand adventure, like a holiday. Papa, cajoled and pleaded with, arranged a day off work for her, and for Tom too, so he could drive her. Eugenia was so excited she was out of bed before the morning bell. She combed her hair by candlelight, put on her best gown and bonnet, and coaxed a little extra money from Papa before he went off for the day.

The bell rang and had not stopped ringing when Tom came rattling in the cart and helped her up onto the bench beside him. She shivered in the early morning air, so he went inside the cabin and came back with a blanket, secured the string latch behind him, and tucked the blanket round her knees. Eugenia laughed, directing him. She ignored Didema Ware, who had cracked her door and stood watching from the shadows.

Tom clicked his tongue and off they went in the dim light along the narrow dusty lane, out onto the dusty road leading north to Salisbury. Past the mining office and the blacksmith, past the crouched row of miners smoking and talking sideways to each other on the porch outside the general store, past the post office and the saddler and the grog shop, the attorney's office, the Presbyterian church, its manse and graveyard, past Miz Hedra drinking early morning coffee on her porch, sagging in her heavy-bottomed chair, her speculative, almost vicious eyes, unwaving hand, on up the clattering road beside the train line, dust trailing in a low red cloud.

As the din of Gold Hill fell away behind them, the ruined hills gave way to woods and then to farms, and woods again, and farms. The mule trotted smartly, as mules never do, and the air was clear and silent, only Tom's voice, deep and gentle and assuring, calling out encouragement from time to time. The day turned warm, the sky bright blue. Eugenia pulled the blanket off her knees and tossed it behind her in the cart. She felt light, as though she would float off with happiness, Tom's voice circling and circling round her head like some large kindly bird.

She glanced at him from time to time, wanting to reach out and touch him, to feel the warmth of his body, the sensation of his skin on hers. Several times, when the cart rocked, she contrived to fall against him and was obliged to hold his arm, or press her hand against his knee to push herself back up. Tom let her touch him, saying nothing, looking straight ahead, but she fancied she could feel him feeling her against him, and fancied too, that he was holding himself from reaching out to her.

And then, as though the journey had taken only minutes, they were suddenly in Salisbury. Eugenia felt her heart surge. "Oh, look, Tom, look. It's just like Wilmington."

She could not look enough, at the gracious tree-lined streets, the grand houses with their sparkling white paint, their wide verandas and second-story galleries. The flower gardens too. They took her breath away. It had been so long since she had seen a flower, much less a flower garden. The smell of blossom made her giddy and excited and she could hardly stay still on her seat.

She had with her a clipping from the *Carolina Watchman* with the address of what claimed to be Salisbury's best dry goods store. *A. Myers, Number 4, Granite Building*, said the advertisement. *British, French, and American Dry Goods. Laces, Bonnets, Hats, Caps, Gent's Clothing, Boots & Shoes, Trunks, Cloaks, Mantles, Shawls, etc. Choice, Fancy, and Imported Fabrics. Nothing But the Best.* Tom asked directions from a Negro, who swung himself onto the cart, rode with them to a main street lined with shady spreading elms, and then swung down again.

Here Eugenia was delighted to see a parade of girls about her age. In frilled skirts and parasols they strolled up and down the wooden sidewalks, arm in arm and laughing with each other, chattering, turning to gaze into store windows, glancing prettily back across their shoulders. Like butterflies, they fluttered in and out of stores, carrying small packages, exclaiming and comparing. Oh, she would love to be among them, she would love to have them for her friends. She was so busy admiring them that it was a moment before she realized there were men here too, young men, hats tilted rakish on their heads, and the girls were staring at them, eyeing them, showing off for them, turning away and blushing, making comments in their hands. Oh, what fun! If only she could join them!

Number 4, Granite Building, turned out to be as granite as it sounded, an imposing edifice three stories high, with *A. Myers* carved above the entrance and an elegant brass lamp on either side. The clerk was unctuous and Eugenia soon discovered the advertisement was right. Here she had a thousand things to choose from, and she wanted everything, spending half an hour and more deciding on a pale blue chintz with sprigs of yellow flowers. She bought some ribbons for her hair as well, although she had no idea when she might have occasion to wear them, perhaps to church or prayer meeting, and because she felt guilty about spending extra, bought a new pair of size large crimson slippers for Papa.

Outside, she dawdled on the sidewalk watching the young people going back and forth. She wanted to belong here with them, had been born to live right here in a town like this, a town with shady trees and street lamps and stores with carpets where you could come with your friends and buy anything you wanted.

A group of girls came laughing up the sidewalk. Eugenia smiled and raised her hand, but they looked straight through her. No, not quite: their eyes rested on her as if she were no more important than a post or—*do not think it, do not think it*—no more important than a slave. Their looks swirled in her head and for a moment she fancied she was one of them, looking out of their eyes and seeing herself in her unfashionable threadbare gown, her limp-brimmed bonnet. *White trash,* their faces said, *white trash.*

And now here came Tom, in his straw hat and overalls, pulling up behind her in the dilapidated cart, the mule eyeing the pretty girls out of its stupid, mulelike face. It bared long yellow teeth and made a noise like snickering.

"Well, I declare!" one of the girls said.

The mule turned its head and looked at her. Its back legs stiffened and its haunches lowered almost imperceptibly. A splashing sound.

"Well, I declare!" the girl said again, and snatching her skirts around her, went flouncing off, followed by her friends.

Tom grinned down at Eugenia. "Time to go, Miss Genie."

As they pulled away, he said, "Guess dis ol' mule don' much fancy pretty ladies."

Eugenia began to laugh. She laughed all the way through Salisbury and out onto the open road before she calmed. But then she caught Tom looking at her sideways. "Well, I declare!" she said. Tom slapped his knee and they both caught the infection, making jokes and singing and breaking out in laughter all the way back home. As they drove past Mr. Martin's general store, Miz Hedra burst out of the door and stood on the veranda looking after them, a sour look on her face.

CHAPTER NINE

Eugenia and Tom were at the cookhouse peeling potatoes into a bucket, the dark skins looping off, the solid white shapes underneath falling with little bright plops and splashes into the water. Eugenia looked at the dark skins and the whiteness underneath. She looked at her hands, and then at Tom's. She had thought her hands had lost their whiteness, but beside Tom's they were almost shocking, like potatoes that had lost their skin.

"Tom, what does it feel like to be black?"

He looked up from his work. "Don't rightly know, Miss Genie. Maybe 'bout the same as feelin' white."

"And what do you think *that* feels like?"

Tom said nothing.

"Well then, what do you think it feels like to be *me*, Eugenia Mae?"

"Don't rightly know, Miss Genie. Angry, mebbe."

"Angry? Why would you think that?"

He shifted uncomfortably. "Don't know, Miss Genie."

"Do you think I'm angry with you, Tom?"

"No, Miss Genie."

"Who with, then?"

He half glanced at her. "Your daddy, mebbe."

She said nothing, just watched him pick up another potato from the pile beside him on the floor and start to peel. How did he know? She had never said a word to him, never quarreled with Papa, but always smiled and kissed him, calling him "dear Papa" and "sweet Papa" and other such endearments. But in the same way Tom could tell the mules were miserable and would best respond to kindness, he knew that she was angry with Papa. Was that why he treated her so kindly?

On an impulse, she reached out and touched his hand. He had just dropped a peeled potato into the bucket and as her fingers touched him he became completely still, his hand held out above the water. Eugenia set her knife down and took his hand in both of hers, rubbing a thumb across it as though the color would come off, then turned it, examining the pale skin of the palm, her head and his bent close together as though intent on some discovery.

"Have you never been angry with *your* father, Tom?"

He did not answer her at once, then in a low voice, "No'm. Never."

"Where is he, your father?"

"Gone off, Miss Genie. Sold."

"When?"

"When I were young."

"Where is he now?"

"I dunno where he is. Someplace called Down-the-River. Mr.

Morgan took and sold him to a trader come through Chapel Hill."

"Is that where you are from?"

"Nearby. The Morgan farm."

"And your mother?"

"Rented out across the hill."

"What is her name?"

"Mary."

"Do you love her very much?"

He nodded.

"My mother's name was Hester. She is dead."

Tom made a sound Eugenia could not interpret. She looked up at his bent head. She wanted him to look at her, to ask about her mother, but he kept his eyes on their joined hands. Evening light slanted through the window and glittered on his hair. No, it glittered on the gold dust in his hair.

"Tom," she said, "what are you planning to do with that gold you've been collecting?"

He drew a breath, but did not speak.

"No, no, I'm not accusing you of stealing. Everybody does it."

"I ain't a thief. It's just . . ."

"Are you saving up to buy yourself? Is that why you don't run? You could, you know, your legs are better now. You hardly even limp."

Tom looked sideways at the floor. "It's not just me."

"Your mother, then? You're saving up to buy your mother too? Come, you can trust me."

And then a footstep—Tom jerked his hand away—and Miz Hedra's voice. "Trust you with what? What is going on here?"

Eugenia scrambled to her feet. *Please God she did not see.* "Miz Hedra! You gave me such a fright!" Her face was burning and she forced a laugh, clapping her hands against her cheeks. They were wet with potato water and the sudden coolness startled her.

Miz Hedra looked from Eugenia to Tom and back again. "What is going on here?"

"Going on, Miz Hedra? Why nothing, just potato peeling." She swung around. "I think we're done now, Tom."

Miz Hedra watched Tom leave, then went to the door, and pushing it open, watched him walk away. She turned back into the room, her hand still on the latch, and made an important clearing of her throat.

But Eugenia had become a bustle of activity. Seizing up a kettle, she dropped back to her knees before the bucket, and with loud thuds and splashings, hastily separated the potatoes from the peelings and dropped them into the kettle. She rose, feeling Miz Hedra's eyes like spiders on her neck, and carried the kettle to the fire, where she slung it on a pothook, filled it with water from a pitcher, and swiveled it above the flame.

Behind her, she heard a soft wet sound—Miz Hedra snapping shut her mouth—then the sound of the latch clicking, the door closing, Miz Hedra's footsteps crunching off. She breathed a long sigh of relief.

MR. Spotswood came home late that night. Tom had gone off and Eugenia was sitting at the table stitching a loose hem. A pot of chicken stew from which she and Tom had already eaten made plopping noises on the fire, its smell rising up to fill the room.

From time to time Eugenia glanced toward the door, beside which Papa's new crimson slippers waited. She resented that he had never thanked her for them, just asked how much they cost, holding out his hand for the remainder of the money he had given her.

The latch clicked and Mr. Spotswood grunted as he came across the sill, glancing round the room. He pulled his boots off, set them side by side against the wall, and pulled the slippers on.

"Hello, Papa. You're late," Eugenia said accusingly.

His slippers sighed across the floor. With one foot he slid a stool from underneath the table, planted himself on it opposite Eugenia, and set his forearms on the table's buckled surface, hands clenched as though in prayer.

"Eugenie, I must speak with you."

She set her sewing down, tightness curling in her stomach. "Papa?"

"Here, give me your hand." He reached across and folded it in both of his, looking at her face.

Eugenia stirred uncomfortably. "Is something wrong? You are ill, perhaps? Some trouble at the mine?"

He let his breath out in a heavy sigh. "I did not want to speak of it to you."

"Of what? Papa, you frighten me."

"Of Tom. Of your . . . relations with him."

A tapping started in Eugenia's left temple. "Relations?"

"It is Miz Hedra, child. She has objected to what she calls your 'behavior.'"

The tapping in Eugenia's temple increased almost to painfulness.

"She has . . . she has taken me aside. She has *advised* me." He hesitated. "My dear, I know you're lonely here, but these British do not understand. They are not accustomed to our ways. They assume that slavery is cruel, that there is never any kindness, affection even, between slave and mistress. They have never known the devotion of a Negro who, having been kindly treated, responds with the devoted faithfulness peculiar to his race."

"And so you defended my . . . 'behavior'?"

Mr. Spotswood's backside shifted on the stool, his gaze to a knothole between them on the table. "I assured her it was nothing more than the kindness of a mistress to a slave. Indeed, I quoted your own words. 'Miz Hedra,' I said, 'kindness and the whip have much in common. They can both incite a man to work.'" He laughed uneasily, fixing his pale eyes briefly on Eugenia's face.

"And that solved the problem?"

"The problem is that Miz Hedra looks at the other slaves who work the mine. They are the only Negroes she has ever come in contact with. I think she fears them. She looks at their conditions, how they live here, she sees them flogged and paddled for stealing gold, for insolence, for lollygagging on the job, she sees them hunted down when they run off, and concludes that is the way of it in this part of the world, that any other way is some sort of . . . some sort of *perversion*."

Eugenia pulled her hand away with an offended motion. "You disillusioned her, I hope?"

"I tried, I did try, but she clings to her opinion." He stiffened his face and pursed his lips in imitation of Miz Hedra. "'It is *inappropriate*, Mr. Spotswood.'"

"That is what she said?"

He nodded.

Eugenia made a low sound of disgust. "Our entire *lives* here are inappropriate."

"She said it was unseemly in the daughter of a gentleman who wanted to advance."

"She *threatened* you?"

"If I do not succeed here . . ."

"But why should you not succeed? Why do you not advance? Have you not worked harder than anyone in this entire place? Have not the workers on your shifts brought up more ore? Have they not fallen less often down the shafts, less often blown off their hands with gunpowder? In all the time we've been here, your gang has never gone on strike. Does all this count for nothing?"

"If Miz Hedra continues her objections . . ."

Eugenia set her hand against her temple. It felt as though a nail were being forced into her head. "Miz Hedra has no right. She is a meddlesome woman. Who is she to say a little kindness to a slave is inappropriate? She who preaches every Wednesday night that God is love? She is a hypocrite."

"Don't say such things." Half glancing behind him as though Miz Hedra might be listening at the door.

"It is the truth. She's always watching, watching, always with her mouth turned down. I'll not give in to her. I will not."

Mr. Spotswood bowed his head, and raised it. His eyes shone damply and he sniffed. "Eugenie, I have no place else to go."

It was as though he hit her. Suddenly she saw him sitting there, not as the father who had disappointed her, but as a man disappointed in himself. She saw the way his hair had thinned, his eyelids twitched, his jowl sagged above the collar of his shirt. Why could she not pity him? She wanted to, but pity would not come.

She seized his hand and kissed it fiercely. "You must swear to me that you will not sell Tom."

"If you could be a little more discreet . . ."

"I will, I swear it. But you must swear to me that you will not sell Tom."

Mr. Spotswood pushed his stool back with a squeal of wood on wood and went to the fireplace, looking down into the pot of stew. "The fire is almost out. I must eat before my supper is completely cold."

"Papa, will you swear it?"

He took up the tongs and poked the fire ferociously. The glowing embers shifted, shooting sparks into the room.

CHAPTER TEN

THE weather cooled and froze. The main pump froze and broke. Work below ground stopped. The slaves hired from local farms went back to their owners and the miners sat about and smoked or went down to the grog shops where they caroused and fought out in the street, scuffling with each other in the snow until they got too cold to bother with the argument and went back inside to warm themselves with pannikins of gin and whiskey. Some, the more unsettled, sold everything they owned and lit out for the California goldfields.

Cold winds cut across the barren ground and cried in the night like tortured souls. The mules and horses, herded into the barn with old rugs and sacking flung across their backs, jostled together, growing overheated and disgruntled from the closeness of so many breathing bodies. Tom slept above them in the loft, wrapped in his blanket amongst piled-up hay that underneath smelled old and mildewy and ratlike, the hot smells of the shifting animals rising through the gaps between the planking, sweet and rank and comforting. When the snow began to thaw, he followed them outside again to sleep wrapped in his blanket on the ground.

By the time the last of the snow thawed, the new part for the pump was installed, the hired slaves reappeared, and the mine went back to work, Gold Hill's mood was gloomy from months of chewing on the awful possibility of civil war. Between Mr. Lincoln's election and his swearing in, not only had South Carolina seceded, but six more Southern states as well, and Mr. Jefferson Davis had been made into a Southern president. Gold Hill buzzed with gossip and opinion. Telegraphs whirred back and forth, and the *Carolina Watchman* gave itself to anguished speculation: Would North Carolina, in the end, secede?

Mining started at a frantic pace, as though every ounce of gold must be drawn up and taken firmly hold of before whatever might be coming came. The Gold Hill militia, which already drilled each morning, drilled each evening too, patrols were doubled, the miners slept with guns beside their beds, one ear cocked for trouble, and any slave found wandering was made to wish he never had been born. All must be inside their cabins before dark and not appear till dawn, when they must assemble for a head count before being marched like prisoners to machine or shaft. Night shifts were entirely canceled since it was too easy for a black skin to slip off in the dark.

Yet more and more slaves vanished and the lash cracked more. Slaves from other mines and from surrounding farms appeared inside abandoned shafts, then disappeared again, heading west toward the mountains, leaving in their wake a growing restlessness amongst the Gold Hill slaves. For every runaway chased down by the patrol and brought back bruised and rancorous, another one escaped.

Now a new rumor was spreading in the mine that a conspiracy

was under way inside the slave huts, that as one slipped off, and then another, and another, a marauding band was growing somewhere in the woods, which, when it was large enough, would swoop down on the town, murdering and stealing gold. No evidence had been amassed for this proposition, but the notion grew with every slave who vanished in the night. And so the curfew, and the head count, the militia drilling every morning in the bleak gray dawn, and again in the red mistrustful evening, not quite sure if it prepared for war or to put down a slave uprising.

To add to all the tension and confusion, a driver had been killed, a mule cart lost. Everyone had seen it happen. The soft mud bordering a disused pit had slipped, sending mule and driver tumbling, both giving such a shriek that everyone came running. At first they thought to haul them out, and so tossed down a rope, but the weight of the rescuers at the pit's edge caused another slide and the driver vanished under it, his hands still clutching for the rope.

Weighed down by its freight of ore, the cart went after him, and then the mule, pulled down backwards into the sucking mud, its eyes bulged out in panic and its front legs stuck up as though in surrender. The last thing to vanish was its head, sinking slowly, and everybody heard the way it snorted mud in through its nose, and at the last let out a bleakly human wail.

The watchers at the pit's edge took off their hats and held them to their hearts and shook their heads, crowding up together, touching each other and telling what every one of them had seen, nodding and confirming, as though they needed to be sure that it was so, as though they were afraid to leave each other's company. At last one and then another put his hat back on and the mourners drifted back to work.

Eugenia, hearing the commotion, had run to join the crowd

around the pit, and when the mule let out its awful wail, tears sprang to her eyes. She backed away, her stomach turning: this poor dumb creature with its brief unpleasant life. She did not go back to work, but went directly to her cabin, where she sat on the stoop, staring about her at the bleak desolation of this place in which she was doomed to spend her days at labor that might kill her in the end.

She thought about her mother lying in her grave. Before she left to come here to Gold Hill, she had thrown away the wooden cross Papa had planted at its head, and replaced it with a large flat rock, digging it in securely upright, and with an old blunt knife chipped into it "Hester." Other mothers, when they died, were laid to rest beside the graves of their dead children, but Mama had no child to keep her company in death. Once Eugenia had asked her father, "Were there none beside me? None?" but he looked pained and turned his head away and she did not ask again.

She tried to call up a memory of her mother's face, but no face came, no face ever came, nothing but her voice, one sentence only, like a legacy. The sensation of a hairbrush tugging at her hair, and then the voice, "Such curl, it is unnatural," and the hard downward stroke, bringing tears into Eugenia's eyes.

The bell rang for the end of shift and Tom appeared before her. "Miss Genie, you all right?"

She looked at him standing with his big hands hanging down and shook her head.

He squatted on the ground in front of her. "Miss Genie, don't be sad. That nigger, he—"

She cut him off with a fierce little laugh. "Don't you dare tell me he's better off in heaven."

"No, ma'am. I was goin' tell you don't be sad. Ain't no gain in bein' sad." And he looked up at her and smiled.

It was the first time he had looked directly in her eyes. It took her by the heart and made her shake, with fear, and with some emotion she had never felt before.

Tom saw her pupils darken and expand. He saw himself inside them. Impulsively, he reached to touch her, but as he did, her gaze shifted back behind him and she flinched away. It startled him. "Miss Genie . . . ?"

THAT evening, Eugenia was kneading dough when Didema Ware appeared in the cabin doorway, outlined against the dimming sky. "That boy of yours? That Tom? Don't he know what's good for him?"

Eugenia went on kneading, her hands white to the wrists with flour. She did not turn her head. "Beg pardon, Didema? I didn't hear you knock."

Didema rapped her knuckle on the door frame. "Eugenia Mae," she said, "everybody knows that boy is breaking curfew. They've turned a blind eye to it up till now, since they know he's yours and not too smart into the bargain, but it can't go on, it simply can't go on." She wagged a finger. "Sunset, Eugenia Mae, you know the rule. You got to get that boy corralled by sunset."

Eugenia turned her head with a deliberate motion. "Corralled? He's not a mule."

Didema's voice turned shrill. "One of these night's that lackwit boy is going to run. It is your duty to corral him."

"He will not run. And he is not a lackwit."

"Miz Hedra says he is a lackwit."

Eugenia smacked the ball of dough down on the table and took a stamping step toward her. "Have you been tittle-tattling with Miz Hedra again? What does she know of slaves, a foreigner?"

"She is the supervisor's wife. If she says that boy's a lackwit, then he is a lackwit."

"Pah! It's just the way of slaves. He's smart as you, Didema. Smarter."

Didema seemed to swell up all over, like an upset chicken. "You better watch yourself, Eugenia Mae. I've seen you with that boy. Miz Hedra says—"

Eugenia made a shooing motion, spraying flour and bits of dough into the air. "Go on, get out of here. Get out."

LATER that night, sprawled out on his blanket on the ground, Tom watched the night mist glistening around the mules' fetlocks, and then around their shoulders, rising light and wispy toward the moon. He had known this was Miss Genie's evening to bake bread and had come with an armload of stovewood for the fire. He was not yet at the door when he saw a figure standing there, backlit against the lamplight. Miss Didema. He stopped, stepped forward, stopped again. She and Miss Genie were talking about him, they were arguing. Fascinated, he stood listening, and not until he heard Miss Genie say, "Get out of here, get out," did he sidle round the corner of the cabin, where he set the stovewood down and went away.

Now he puzzled on Miss Genie. Other people, miners, said he was a lackwit, which he knew meant simpleton, speaking loud and slowly when they gave him orders, but Miss Genie always talked to him the way she talked to anybody else. He thought about how she had watched him on the rockers and decided that he hurt. Aside from his mother, and his father when he had him, and perhaps, the little blue-eyed boy who had traveled with him in the coffle, Miss Genie was the only person in the world who had ever cared whether he hurt or not. Lately she had changed, though. She was still kind, but not the way she used to be. And today, when he had tried to comfort her, she seemed afraid. He racked his brains, trying to remember what he might have done. Had he been too bold with her? Too free? He thought about the time they went to Salisbury, the way she laughed and leaned against him when the cart swayed on a rough part of the road, how she pretended it was accidental, how happy she had been that day. He thought about the time she took his hand when they were peeling potatoes at the cook-house, how she had asked him what it felt like to be black, and how Miz Hedra . . .

And then it came to him. Miz Hedra. She was frightened of Miz Hedra.

No sooner was the thought inside his head than he was wide awake. He sat straight up. Had Miz Hedra seen Miss Genie touching him? Things like that could get you into trouble. He had seen it happen to a man before.

So should he run? He knew where there were woods now. He had seen them when he drove the mule team to haul trees felled to repair the bridgework of the aqueduct. They were thin woods where he went, so spindly from the logging they were hardly woods at all, but as he came over the ridge above them, he had seen the way they went off into the distance, growing thick and heavy, bright green with new leaves.

He tested his leg, pulling it against him. No pain. Stretched it out in front. No pain still. Twisted it sideways, then the other way. It was late now. Miss Genie and her father would be sound asleep. He could creep in and get his gold . . .

Somewhere a girl's voice giggled and then stopped. Tom froze. He strained toward the sound. A man's voice murmured.

So those ladies called the "hoes" had come creeping in the night again. Miz Hedra would be furious if she discovered it. She would send out the patrollers. Tonight was not the night to run away. He glanced around. A cart stood not far off. He gathered up his blanket and crawled beneath it.

The hoes were nice enough, he thought. They sang and talked in loud voices and laughed a great deal with the men. They laughed with the slaves as well, they did not seem to care. They would stroke the slaves' black faces with their pure white hands, and wrap their pure white arms around their necks and whisper in their ears. They liked the slaves who carried chips of gold inside their pockets.

A mule coughed, shuffling its feet. And then a swishing sound, like fabric rubbing against fabric. He gathered in his breath and held it.

"Can I come in?" It was a whisper.

Tom breathed slowly out and turned his head, opening his eyes. He could not see her face, just a shape against the moonlight.

And then her breath against his cheek, the tickle of her hair, the smell of lavender.

"I'm Iris," she said into his ear. "Saw you getting under here and figured I'd just come across and offer you a kindness. I can be right kind." Her hand moved on his body. "That feel nice?"

For a moment he lay there, giving in to the sensation, but then he saw again Miss Genie's eyes darken and grow huge, saw himself inside them.

"Hey, boy," Iris said, "who you think you're shovin'?"

NOW he could not sleep. Mosquitoes sang their wicked songs about his head. He shuffled out from underneath the cart, and with his arms behind his head, lay looking at the stars. He had heard there was a star that led to freedom. Which one could it be? That big one there? That little one that seemed so far away? Did God live on the freedom star? At Sunday service, they had told him God was good, that Jesus loved him, and that they had a holy ghost that loved him too. He had never paid much heed to it until, when he was living in the woods, an owl had come to sit outside his den.

When first he heard its gloomy voice say, "Ho!" he jumped up with a panic in his chest because he thought it was a ghost, but when he crept out of his den, looking cautiously about, he saw, up on a branch, the ghost's head turn toward him in the moonlight, and its eyes turn, for a moment, gold. Then he knew it was an owl come to protect him and crept back inside his den. After that he figured what they said at church was true, because the holy ghost owl sat up on the branch outside his den each night, saying, "Ho," to tell him he was safe, and "Ho, ha," to tell him when he must take care.

Clang! The sound of metal falling somewhere back behind, and over everything the steady churr of insects, rising sometimes in a clacking sound, like celebration. A star came from the far-off dark and streaked across the sky. He knew it was the freedom star because it flew. If he could fly like that, he would be free.

CHAPTER ELEVEN

$\infty\infty$

I<small>N</small> April, when the news came, whistling and omen-filled along the wire, that Fort Sumter had fallen, all work at the mine abruptly stopped and the entire population of Gold Hill, black and white, seethed into the main street, filling up the tiny post office and jostling on its steps.

For a month confusion reigned, and then the wire sang again: North Carolina had joined the Southern Nation. Gold Hill, like it or not, was now at war.

The street rang out with ayes and cheers and the sound of guns shot in the air. The church bells rang, women laughed and wept, men who yesterday despised each other flung their arms around each other's necks and danced, the Negroes crowded round and stared and laughed, torn between curiosity and fear and the urge to head out for the mountains, and anyone who would rather have shouted boo at the decision kept his mouth tight shut.

In no time the place was inundated with recruiting parties, sweeping in like tidal waves, carrying off the miners in their wake. The foreigners, having no desire to give their lives for someone else's country, refused to volunteer, and being much resented for it, were followed everywhere with oaths and cries of "You damned Britishers!" and "You confounded Cousin Jacks!"

Mr. Spotswood tried to have it both ways, doing his duty in the militia, but staying close to Mr. Perrin and the other Cornish miners for the sake of whatever profits might be recouped from the failing mine. Evening after evening, he went off to meetings with them, and came back, sometimes after midnight, with a furrow down the center of his forehead and his breath smelling of gin, demanding to be fed.

One night Eugenia was astonished to see him burst in through the cabin door, his shirt torn and his hair awry, to report, panting and dripping water on the floor, that he had been attacked. Eugenia had heard some distant shots and shouting, but had paid no attention since such things were common in the mine these days. She wrapped her father up in towels and stood him by the fire, then scuttled up the ladder for dry clothes, scolding underneath her breath that he would catch his death, he would just catch his death, and when he was comfortable in nightshirt and crimson slippers, his hair still sticking damply to his head, she sat him at the table with a mug of soup.

"What happened? Tell me everything."

He slurped at his soup, holding the steaming mug two-handed. It knocked against his teeth and he set it down and waited till the trembling passed.

He had, he told her, been attending a meeting of the Cornish miners at Mr. Perrin's house, when thirty or forty men swept down on them, shouting, "Come out of there, you Britishers, and we'll teach you how to fight."

Miz Hedra, who had been serving cake, fell on her knees in

the middle of the room, the cake exploding in a mess of crumbs beside her, and gave herself up to loud importunings of the Lord. Mr. Perrin went boldly out to the front porch, intending to reason with the men, but they fired their guns in the air, and leaping off their horses, went for him, so he retreated back into the house and locked the door. Which did no good at all, since the attackers shot up the front windows and proceeded to force their way inside while the Cornishmen climbed out the windows at the back and bolted off into the night.

Mr. Spotswood stayed to help Miz Hedra. She had been knocked flat in the stampede, and since she wore no hoop, was now entangled in her skirts. He was attempting to rescue her from where she lay floundering amongst the cake crumbs, when he was leaped on from behind. He managed to escape by leaving his coat in the hands of his attacker and following the Cornishmen posthaste out the window. He knew he could not outrun men younger than himself so at the first opportunity climbed up the bridgework of the aqueduct and over the side of the wooden channel, where he flattened himself in the water. Moments later, a party of eight or ten rushed by beneath him.

"Good heavens," Eugenia cried when she had heard his story. "What shall we do? Whatever shall we do?"

"We must leave here. We cannot stay. Mr. Perrin has just this evening told me that the Gold Hill Mining Company is about to go into receivership."

"So suddenly?"

"It is not sudden, you know that. We have long been in a slide. Now, with everybody's mind on war, even our most diehard investors are turning their minds to how to make a profit out of it."

"Is there no hope at all? Some small enterprise, enough to get us by?"

"We would need capital. And where would we get miners?

Within the month, Gold Hill's militia is to be sent off to the front. The few men left will be needed for patrolling. The mine slaves, of course, will be sold off, but every day brings word of escapees banded together in the woods with who knows what nefarious activity in mind."

Mr. Spotswood clapped his mug down on the table with such force that soup bulged up and sprang over the rim. He jerked back, startled, then ran his tongue along the outside of his thumb, and with both hands seized hold of his head and held on tight, as if afraid his brains might follow the example of his soup.

"Calm yourself, Papa."

He breathed out heavily, looking up at her, his head still in his hands. "I do not understand why the slightest threat of trouble brings out the worst in every man."

"Come, come, your poor head. Are you trying to tear it off? That's better, yes. Now, tell me, what of the Cornishmen? What do they have in mind?"

"The Cornishmen are in a panic. Mr. Perrin and the others are heading out to California in search of a new venture."

"So you will join them? We will go to California?"

"I am not invited."

"Oh?"

There was silence for the space of half a minute, neither of them looking at the other. At last Eugenia said, "The army, then? You will go to war? But what is to become of me?"

"I do not plan to go to war."

"What then?"

He hesitated. "We are going to Australia."

"Australia? What, have you gone mad?"

"Mr. Perrin has a brother there. He writes that he is doing very well at copper mining in a place called . . ." He went across to where his steaming shirt hung by the fire and patted at its pockets. "I wrote it down . . . what did I do with it . . . ah, yes, here it is, no, the paper has dissolved. But I'll remember in a moment." He held a finger in the air. "Yes, that's it, Cappie-Oonda. An odd name, don't you think? It's what the local tribesmen call the place."

"Tribesmen? What sort of tribesmen?"

"Indians of some sort."

"Are they wild?"

"I understand they have been tamed."

"And you would have me go live in a place called . . . what was it?"

"Cappie-Oonda. But don't look so alarmed. The white men have renamed it Kapunda, which is more civilized."

He stopped, his eyelids twitching nervously. "I do not mean to say the place is uncivilized. There is quite a large town to the south called Adelaide. Mr. Perrin's brother says it is quite British. When we've made a little profit at the enterprise, we'll buy a townhouse there and you can enjoy all the refinements of society."

"Australia," Eugenia said. "It is hardly on the planet."

Her father made a strained sound, not quite mirth. "Once you have been there for a while, you will think back on Gold Hill and say the same of it. Mr. Perrin's brother says the weather in Australia is always warm. Think of it, Eugenie, never to be cold again."

"And what of Tom? Will he come with us? Or will we free him?"

"Free him? Don't be foolish. We will sell him for our passage."

"No. You promised me you would not sell him."

Mr. Spotswood stirred his foot against the floor. "I believe I did not promise."

"You as good as promised. You implied. You did, Papa, you did."

"Come, come, there is no need for tears."

"It is not right. Tom has done nothing to deserve it. If he is not to come with us to Australia, we should set him free."

"Believe me, for your sake I would like to, but I cannot afford it."

"Papa, but—"

"You make too much of it. This is not a time for sentiment about a slave. Tom has been sold before. He will be sold again. He is accustomed to it. It is his nature to be sold."

Eugenia screeched her stool back from the table and rose above him, red-faced and trembling. Mr. Spotswood's face darkened. "I have made up my mind to it, Eugenie. It's that or go to war."

Eugenia spun about, her skirts catching the stool, which fell over with a crash. The door crashed after her.

IT was almost dawn and still Eugenia had not slept. Her head ached and her skin itched and she struggled with the covers, making up a speech that would persuade Papa, knowing he would not be persuaded.

She had known, without acceding to the notion, that something of this sort might one day happen. It was a choice: Papa or Tom, a white man or a black, hardly a choice at all, yet she had wrestled with it all night long, knowing what her decision must come down to, knowing she was wrestling with straw, that there was only one thing to be done, that it was nothing, something that had been done by people just like her a million times, the way things were, the way they had been for the entire history of mankind, the way God himself intended it, and would punish her if she went against Papa.

But is not Tom God's creature too? Or is God cruel? She had no evidence that he was not.

Gradually, she slipped down into that half sleep where everything that happened back before the mind remembers is remembered. Once more the familiar gentle blackness took her in its arms. "Mama?" she said, startling herself awake.

She lay staring at the darkness with a lost thought sitting in her head, a dream and not a dream. And then a sound disturbed her. Someone sobbing? She stirred, turning her head to listen. No, she was dreaming still.

But there it was again, a low, wrenched sobbing coming from above, as if a disembodied spirit wept into the dark. And then she understood. It was Papa, weeping in his loft below the roof. Pity took Eugenia. He was her own papa. She would go to him and comfort him. They would be reconciled.

In her nightgown and barefooted, she climbed up to him, the dim light of the kitchen turning to pitch darkness as her head and shoulders rose into the loft.

"May I come up?"

A groaning came out of the darkness and he had her by the shoulders, pulling her toward him, his voice against her ear, "Tilda, oh, Tilda." Then he was kissing her, his hands were moving on her body. "Tilda, oh, my love."

Afterwards she did not remember coming down the ladder, but she must have, since she was sitting on her bed and crying, shaking, crying. Tilda—it could only be a slave name.

Eventually the shaking ceased and thoughtfulness took hold. She wiped her eyes, blew her nose on the corner of the bedsheet, and padded back into the kitchen where she stood with one hand on the ladder to the loft.

"Papa? Are you awake?" No answer. She went back to her room and sat down on the bed, leaning slightly forward, her hands against her knees. Was this, she asked herself, the reason why Mama declined and died, not from disappointment in her husband's failure as a businessman, but in his failure as a husband? Perhaps she could not bear the sense of how his juices rose when this Tilda was about, how his eyes clung to her breasts and to her buttocks when she walked away, the sense of how, when he made love to her, his wife, his mind was elsewhere.

So how to remedy the situation? *Sell her!* Mama had forced Papa to sell her. It was too late, though. The tumor of resentment growing in her brain had taken hold and in the end she died of it. She died of jealousy.

As this tale took shape in her imagination, Eugenia told herself it was not true, she must shake it off, it was too shocking: her father with a slave. And yet she was not shocked. It was a common thing, she knew, although no refined white lady ever spoke of it, or thought about it even, preferring to take refuge in a convenient cloying innocence, as though the light-skinned Negro children running on their properties did not wear their husband's faces or the faces of their sons. Well, she was no refined white lady now, and she could think of it.

She thought about Tom out there sleeping with the mules and nothing but the sky above, and it was as though he called her. She rose, and pulling on her gown, crept silently outside and went to where he slept, one arm flung out, the early light reflecting off his face. While she stood there looking down at him, shivering and shaking dew out of her hair, the sun came swimming up across the rim of the horizon. Eugenia felt a softening in her bones, as though her body wanted to lie down with him, to take him in her arms, to wrap herself in him, as though she wanted to become him.

"He is my friend," she said aloud, thinking, *No,* thinking, *I love him, no, it cannot be,* not believing such a thing could happen, not to her, knowing that it had.

"Tom?"

He opened his eyes and lay looking up at her, the panic of foreknowledge on his face.

A bugle sounded behind the low rise of the hill. Someone shouted an instruction. Eugenia glanced across her shoulder at the waking row of miners' cabins.

"Quick, Tom, you must run. Papa is going to sell you."

He scrambled up. "Miss Genie, why?"

"He is going to Australia, to some godforsaken copper mine he says is called Kapunda. He plans to take me with him. He plans to sell you for the passage money. You must get out of here at once."

"But, Miss Genie, I don't have no place to go. Less'n I go back to Mr. Morgan, but he done already sold me. He take one look at me, he sell me off again."

"No, no, you cannot go back there, you must not."

"I got no place but here with you."

"Even if we wanted to, Papa and I could not stay here. The mine is failing. The mint in Charlotte has been taken over by the government. Papa is deep in debt and frightened of the future. He will not hesitate to sell you, he will think nothing of it. And even if we stayed, everyone is in a panic that if the North comes marching down, the slaves will rise to join them and attack us from inside. Who knows what the men here at the mine might do to prevent *that* from happening? Some are already saying we should slaughter all the slaves, the men at least, before they rise and slaughter us. Before long, no doubt, they will be looking for excuses, and I fear Miss Hedra will provide one against you, Tom. She is not pleased to see us so easy in each other's company—I know it for a fact. If she should whisper it about the mine, I tremble to think what dreadful thing might happen to you. Papa might take it in his head to shoot you, or the men might come looking for you with a hanging rope. Do you understand what I am telling you? Of course you do. Don't put on your simple face, you are no simpleton. We are at war, Tom, and if the Southern Nation wins, you will likely always be a slave. You must go now, today, before it is too late."

"But my mother, what about my mother?"

Again the bugle sounded, the rat-tat of a drum. A shouted order floated on the air.

"I must go back before Papa discovers I am gone. When you see him going off to work, come directly to me. I will tell you what to do."

WHEN he came into the cabin, stepping soft and nervous, Eugenia was standing at the table, bundling things into a knapsack.

"Tom, there you are. Come here, come quick." She hesitated, looking at his face, then with a quick, decisive motion, drew a folded paper from the pocket of her apron. "Here, take this. It's your freedom paper. Put it somewhere safe. That's right, inside your shirt. Keep it with you all the time, show it when you need to, but do not pass it into anybody else's hand." She glanced behind him at the door. "You must get out of here before Papa finds out what I have done."

Tom stood before her helplessly. "Miss Genie, I don't know what to do."

"I'm going to tell you. Pay attention, now. I have a plan. You must go north, to Canada, where they will not send you back." She looked him up and down. "But first, take off those old boots, they're paper thin. Take these. By the time Papa misses them you will be well away. And here, an extra shirt." She stuffed it in the knapsack. "And this jacket of Papa's. The sleeves will be a little short but it will do. And this parcel of food should last you several days. Oh, and matches, and a fishing line and hook, Papa's folding knife."

Tears were in her eyes. Tom turned his head down, pulling on the boots. When Eugenia spoke again, her voice was light and tremulous. "I have left a note telling Papa that I must go to Salisbury for a few female provisions to carry with me on our expedition to Australia. He will not question it. Female matters are beyond him. You will drive the cart, of course, but when we are well away I will mysteriously lose you in the woods."

She secured the knapsack flap, and going to the fireplace shelf, took down the canister of tea leaves, stirred in it with her fingers, and drew out a roll of notes from which she peeled several. "Here," she said, holding them out, "it's not much, but it will get you somewhere, and you have your gold."

Tom put his hands behind his back.

"Don't be foolish. Take it." She tucked it in the pocket of his shirt.

"Oh, Tom." She turned away and then turned back, tears welling once more in her eyes. "Tom, I am your friend, I love you. There, I've said it now. I want you to be free."

She became bustling and businesslike. "You must take Papa's old cloak. He never wears it anymore and it's still in good condition. Yes, take it. Tom, don't look at me like that, you break my heart. I cannot bear to sell you and I cannot bear to send you off. Remember, when you've crossed the mountains, head toward the north. Do you know which way is north? Here, give me your hands. Keep the morning sun on this hand, and the evening sun on this. Keep going till you get to Canada. People along the way will help you, people who want the slaves to be made free."

"But my mother, what about my mother?"

Heaving the knapsack off the table, she held it out to him. "Here, hide this underneath a blanket so no one sees it in the wagon as we drive through town." She fumbled with her bonnet strings and tied them firmly, then took her cloak down from its peg and slung it around her shoulders. "Papa will not expect me back until this evening. That means we have all day, so when you run, run fast, and you will be well away before he can discover you are gone. Get whatever else you want to take—your gold—then fetch the cart. Do not be long."

CHAPTER TWELVE

H<small>E</small> did not use the roads, but paralleled them in the woods, going back along the route he had traveled with the slavers fifteen months before, not at any minute sure of where he was, but with increasing certainty heading toward Chapel Hill. He had his knapsack on his back and his gold was hidden in a tight flat package tucked into the waistband of his pants inside his shirt. In the pocket of his shirt he had his freedom paper, and from time to time he set his hand against it, smiling.

His smile was nervous, though. He had hankered after freedom all his life, but now he had it he did not know what to do with it except to walk toward his mother. He told himself he could be bold and open now, could greet anyone he liked, could pass the time of day with anyone he took a fancy to. But old habits clung on hard and it was a long time before he felt reassurance creeping up on him. Eventually it straightened up his back and he stepped onto the road, which stretched out flat before him, not a soul in sight. His stride grew long, and longer, and more certain. He whistled underneath his breath.

He was happy, was he not? He told himself he was. Had he not stored up every fleck and speck of gold he could lay his hands on, saving for his mother's price? Had he not lain awake night after night, thinking of the day when it would be enough? Was it enough? He thought it was enough. He thought about how Mr. Spotswood paid a dirt cheap price for him because he wasn't good for much, and figured that his mother, who was old and good for almost nothing now, would likely go dirt cheap as well.

But then he thought about the way his mother's cheeks had hollowed out, the way the skin around her eyes hung down, the way she stooped, and how he had no cart to carry her, nor any horse or mule. He thought about her leaning on a stick and shuffling down the road. How far to the north? How many days? Miss Genie had said people in the north would help him. But how was he to find them? How was he to find his way? Perhaps his mother knew.

To comfort himself, he made up a story with pictures in his head. In it he saw himself coming into Chapel Hill, walking tall and confident and free, past the little wooden houses, the white-steepled church, the storefronts with their fine displays. Soon he would be walking past the deep green shaded gardens of the university, and past the fine white houses where important people lived, and then on through the woods to Mr. Morgan's place, where he would stop before he went up to the door and take his freedom paper out, his mother's price as well. Then he would knock. "I come to buy my mother," he would say. And Mr. Morgan would read his freedom paper with a hard and serious face and come out to the veranda, where the two of them would sit down on the step like men together, and Mr. Morgan would say,

"This much," and Tom, "No, this much is enough, since she is old and useless now," and after a while Mr. Morgan would make a coughing in his throat and a humming sound like thinking, and then a sharp grunt of agreement. "Done," he'd say, and hold his hand out for the gold. Then Tom would go on to the Bricket farm across the hill and come out of the woods behind his mother's cabin and carry her off north. Somehow he would do it.

HE had been traveling all morning and not a soul in sight. Now he came around a bend and slowed, all his instincts telling him to turn and run. Ahead, a crossroads with a church and grave-yard on one corner, a store across from it with figures sitting on the porch. He stopped, then started up again. He was a free man now, a free man with his paper in his pocket. He could walk along the road.

Two men were on the porch, talking to each other. One wore a hat pulled low across his eyes, the other, hatless, wore a beard. A mule cart with a mule was tethered to the rail. It wore a feed bag and eyed Tom over it, munching in a melancholy way. In the cart, a bulging sack of something, maybe flour, and some broken-looking tools.

As he approached, the men stopped talking to each other and turned to look at him with that straight-on, suspicious stare he knew so well. Walk loose, he told himself. You is a free man now. You is entitled to walk along the road.

Now he was upon them, walking slowly with his eyes turned down, not sure if he should offer them a greeting, or if he did, what he should say. He tugged his hat brim, glancing sideways.

"Mornin'." Blood rushed in his neck.

Neither man replied, but he could see out of the corner of his eye the way they turned their heads to follow him. The hatted one made a hawking in his throat and spat across the rail into the dust. Blood pounded in Tom's head.

He kept on walking, one foot before the other, until he was well past. Then he turned his head across his shoulder, looking at the distance he had come, at the smallness of the store, the tiny figures of the men. He smiled and thumped his fist into his palm.

"You done it, boy, you done it."

His head came up again, his shoulders squared, and he resumed his easy stride. To be a free man walking down a road— he had never felt so proud in all his life.

He walked another hour or so and saw no living thing except flocks of hunchbacked crows feeding in the slashed-off corn, their heads moving up and down as though to dig themselves inside the earth.

Then something made him turn. Behind, a dust cloud was approaching, pale red, glinting in the sun. He saw the sold discarded people rising from the dust, dead faces and the clank of shuffling feet, the false bright voices raised in song. And in the cart, sprawled out behind the little blue-eyed boy, was he himself, his legs still raw with gunshot wounds and a fierce confined terror in his heart.

He looked about for cover, but there was none. Fields stretched on either side, low with stubbled corn. He looked back at the dust cloud. It was closer now. A mule, a cart, its driver a hatted shape against the sky. One of the men from back there on the porch. He pressed his hand against his shirt and felt the hard thump of his heart. He turned back to the road.

THE rattle of the cart was loud behind him now. The mule slowed. "Hot day," a man's voice said, and Tom looked up to see the hatted man regarding him, his face a shadow underneath the brim.

"A hot day, yessir."

"Offer you a ride?"

Tom hesitated, glancing side to side.

"C'mon now, I ain't about to eat you. Climb on up. I'll carry you along a ways."

And here he was, sitting by a white man, sitting next to him as if he had a right. Tom's head felt full and dizzy. His heart was skidding underneath his shirt. He felt inclined to cry, to laugh, to shout out loud.

"What's your name, boy? Where you headin' off to?"

"Tom. I'se goin' to Chapel Hill. I is a free man now."

The man tipped back his hat and turned to look at him, and he was not a white man after all. He had a scar across his forehead like a channel running slantwise down his head.

"You is a free man, is you? Well now, ain't that grand?" He pulled his hat back down and went on driving.

After a while, he reached beneath the seat and produced a brownish bottle. "Hot work," he said, and, handing Tom the reins, twisted out the cork and tilted the bottle to his lips. Then he drew the back of his hand across his mouth and took the reins, holding the bottle out to Tom.

"Go on. It's all I got. I got no water."

It was the first time since Tom was shot that he had tasted whiskey. It was fire in his throat and when it came down to his belly he could feel it spread.

The man reached for the bottle and took another suck. He handed it to Tom.

THE whiskey bottle rolled against Tom's foot. He looked at it between his knees and saw that it was empty. When had they drunk it all? How long had they been traveling? They were winding through thick woods now, the trees close overhead. He remembered talking to the hatted man, remembered words, words, flowing out of him. What had he told? He did not even know his name.

"What's your name?" Tom said, but his tongue got in the way and the words came out distorted.

The hatted man laughed. He leaned against Tom's shoulder, cheerful, confidential, breathing fumes into his face. "You pay 'tention to me, boy," he said, his words as thick and strange as Tom's had been. "You try to buy your mother, they goin' call the sheriff and clap you in the jail. You a nigger, boy, you ain't allowed to go about the country buyin' folks. They done made a law."

"You jokin' me. I never heard about no law."

The man spat onto the road. "They made a lot o' laws. They made a law that I could turn you in and pick up a reward."

Tom laughed. He shoved his shoulder up against the man and struggled with his tongue. "But you a nigger too."

"I knows a man what knows a man. He calls hisself a Baptist preacher, but he ain't."

Tom laughed again. "You jokin' at me, boy."

"I ain't. He's called the Reverend Mr. Baring. Some folks call him Mr. Angel. They say he pays a good price for a runaway."

"I ain't no runaway."

The man shrugged. He set his hand against the seat, pushing himself upright. "You anything Mr. Angel say you are."

Alarm penetrated the whiskey in Tom's head. He rose, unsteady in the cart. "This here is where you let me off."

"Hey, it were a joke. Sit down. You throwin' us off balance."

"You let me off."

"Sit down. It were a joke." The man tilted up his face and grinned under his hat. "I'll take good care of you, you'll see. This nigger ain't about to turn you in."

Tom turned as though to jump, but as he did, the man swept out his arm. "I said sit down."

Tom stumbled, tripped, sprawled backwards in the cart. In a second he was up, yanking the man's shoulders from behind. The man surged backwards, legs galloping in air, then the sharp smack of his skull against the pile of tools, a brief agitation of his limbs, and he was still, his legs still draped across the seat.

Tom, on hands and knees, looked down at him, surprised. He lifted up his hat. The man's eyes stared at him, unblinking. Blood oozed, black and sluggish, underneath his head.

NOW he was running through the woods, running and running, propelled by fright and whiskey into an exhausting pace. He ran until his legs would not run any more, then stumbled on until he found a creek. He scooped water in his hands and drank, then propped himself against a tree, panting, his heart curling and uncurling on itself. *You a nigger, boy, you ain't allowed to go about the country buyin' folks. They done made a law.* So was it true? Or was the hatted man a liar? Had he really killed him, or was he just knocked out? The last he had seen of him was a pair of angled knees above the cart, the mule proceeding stolidly along the road to Chapel Hill.

The sun was hot and low down in the sky, flicking arrows in between the trees. The shade steamed and the air hung still and breathless, as if every living thing had stupefied. Tom felt the whiskey catching up with him, his eyes half open now, and now half closed, his body growing heavy.

IT was early in the morning in the woods by Morgan's Creek. He had gone out hunting before the birds were up and every sound

was like a whiplash on the trembling air. He had killed a squirrel with a stone and was squatted in his den, skinning it with his
new knife. It was a grand knife, gleaming, sharp, and he was
smiling to himself, listening to the holy ghost owl saying "Ho"
to tell him he was safe.

Suddenly his head snapped up. They were coming, they were
coming after him. He could hear them on the far side of the hill.
Completely still, he listened. They were coming from above, on
foot, beating through the woods. He heard the thwack and rus-
tle and the thwack, the scuttling of animals disturbed, the hard
downbeat of wings as birds rose from their path. There was no
baying. They had not brought dogs.

For a moment hesitation took him, but then he heard their
voices, hard and organized against him. With his squirrel and
his knife still in his hands, he slipped back against the far wall of
his den, curled into a ball, and closed his eyes. His heart was
beating small and far back in his breast, as though it would
break through behind itself and find a space to squeeze into and
hide.

They were so close now he could smell them, the sweat and
the tobacco, their determination. He smelled no hate for him,
or anger. These men smelled impatient, as though they had a
job that must be got out of the way before they could go home
and eat.

The rustling and thumping broke and swept along each side
of his den. He did not breathe at all. They passed. He breathed,
but did not move until the sound of them had faded off and
gone. And then his legs uncurled. He stood, triumph sobbing in
his throat, went forward cautiously, and stepped into the dawn.

A boy was there in front of him. His hat was tilted back and
he wore a mask of concentration, peeing up against a tree, his
organ pale pink and small inside his hand. Tom dropped the

knife and squirrel as though they burned his hands and fled into the woods, up the hill and down the other side, into the gully at the bottom, out again, heedless of the spiderwebs that wrapped themselves about his head, slip-sliding across fallen branches soft and treacherous with rot. He fell, and scrambled up again, and ran, breath whistling in his throat. A shout, "Hey, you there, boy!" and then another, "Stop!" Tom felt his heart thump, a single drumbeat in his chest, and did not, could not, stop. Somewhere the holy ghost owl called out, "Ho," and then, too late, "Ho, ha."

And now he was roped onto the mule again, gunfire echoing inside his bones, and the Bricket boy was leading him along the road to Chapel Hill, where people milled about, the men with guns, a lady with her cap askew pointing at him, shouting, "Thief!" And now here came the mule hauling its load, the hatted man rising from the cart to point at him as well. "Murderer!" he cried, and all the people turned to look at him. Blood oozed from underneath his hat.

Above Tom's head, a blackbird shouted raucously and he jerked upright, trembling in the early morning gloom. His head thumped and the whiskey was sour and heavy in his belly. If he went back to Chapel Hill they would take away his gold and lock him in the jail, and then he would be sold again and go off clanking down the road in chains.

Then it occurred to him: if the hatted man was dead, they would not sell him, they'd take him to the hanging tree outside of town and hang him.

That thought brought him to his feet, swaying, struggling with the inside of his head. He could not buy his mother, he had to run away, he had to find the north. But when Miss Genie sent him off, she had talked so fast and so excitedly that now he felt confused. *This hand and this hand*, she had said. The morning sun on *this*, and the evening sun on *this*. Or had it been this hand and this?

And then a fat pink sun came swimming upward through the mist, shimmering and glowing, as though it beckoned him or called him, and his entire body turned toward it. After that, he forgot about the left hand and the right. Each morning when he woke his face turned like a flower toward the rising sun, and he followed it, keeping the evening sun behind his back, and it seemed to him he traveled toward the north where there were people who would help him.

He spoke to no one, trusted no one, moving silent as a bear, eating off the land, roots and nuts and whortleberries and wild currants, corn from farmers' cribs, raw fish scooped out of streams, honeycomb scooped with a stick out of a farmer's beehive. Sometimes he followed trails, sometimes the winding course of creeks, the straight run of a train line, once clattering across a plank road, another time crossing a river on a precarious, swaying railway bridge, taking to the roads only when the woods were too dense or the swamps too treacherous.

Once, between the trees, he saw a group of soldiers, half-armed and motley-uniformed, marching confidently down the road, young men full of vigor, the tap of drums and shrill of pipes advancing on ahead to warn him they were coming, trailing back behind to let him know that he had not been seen.

Once he saw a group of cavalry drilling in a field, the horses lining in a row, their riders lining up their bayonets, one with a flag fixed to a stick. A shout, and with the flag rushing in the lead, a furious gallop to the field's far end. Here they turned, lined up, and repeated the maneuver, then repeated it again, as though chasing down a magic enemy that appeared at one end of the field, and as the line of cavalry descended, vanished, only to reappear behind them at the field's other end.

A bugle sounded and the line broke, the horses milled, their riders dismounting to slap each other on the shoulder. Two men seemed to get into an argument and some others held them back, and then they all lined up with tin plates in their hands and filed before a steaming kettle. Tom's stomach twisted and water came into his mouth. He turned away and headed on.

CHAPTER THIRTEEN

THE countryside was changing, growing flatter and more vast, undulating greenness replaced by sandy ridges, and from time to time, low-lying soggy patches humming with mosquitoes. The woods were changing too, nothing now but pine, the dark trunks rising up so tall Tom had to tilt his head far back to see the harsh dark branches scribbled up against the sky. Beneath them, scrub no taller than his knee, so he could see between the trunks to more trunks, and then more, until they swam together in a blur.

Roots reared from the trail, forcing him to walk head down in case he tripped. Between the roots, the sand was pale and soft, scattered with the longest needles he had ever seen. Birds whooped and whistled, insects clicked and chimed. Flash of bright blue dragonflies, steady humming of green flies about his feet.

The insides of his eyelids dried and roughened and he walked, not weeping, but half blind with tears. He had not eaten for two days now, and the last stream he had stopped at had been yesterday at noon. His belly hurt from thirst and his head was dizzy from the sun beating down between the trees to burn his head and neck. He took his shirt off and slung it across his head with the two arms dangling, but it only made him hotter so he took it off and went along flipping it about his chest and back for the coolness of sweat drying.

Midafternoon, he came out of the woods and passed through a field of goldenrod. A lake stretched before him, wide, irregularly shaped. Daisies glittered on its banks, rising out of short grass stiff as wire. Waterweeds and lilies clustered round its banks and little sandy beaches edged out into it, like fingers pointing at the turkey vulture dipping and lifting in the blue sky of its depths.

He set his knapsack down, pulled off his boots, and waded out into the water, the relief of coolness climbing up his legs. When it was above his knees, he leaned and cupped his hands and drank, then stood watching the ripples spreading out from him across the surface, thinking of Miss Genie. He missed her so, it hurt his heart.

For a moment, anger rose. How could she have sent him off like this? But then he saw her standing in the kitchen with his freedom paper in her hand, saying, "Tom, I am your friend, I love you. There, I've said it now."

That she loved him, Tom had no doubt. And he loved her, it did not occur to him to question it. But the pair of notions were static in his head, nothing to be made of them, no actions taken, no consequences to unfold. In giving him his freedom paper, she had broken any right he might have had to be with her. And yet it hurt his heart to be alone. He wondered if Miss Genie missed him so, her heart hurt too.

When he thought about his mother loving him, the sensation in his heart was altogether different. It made him want to put his arms around her neck and cling on tight, to smell the warm, safe smell of her, and have her sing to him the way she did when he was small. Once he had been part of her and he wanted to be part of her again, to live beside her every day, to hear the clatter of her cooking pans, to chop wood for her fire, haul water for her wash trough, help her dig her garden patch, and sit with her on the front stoop in the evenings, the smell of cornbread fresh and warm behind them in the cabin, and outside, the sweetness of wild honeysuckle vines, the dusty smell of her swept yard. They would talk of nothing in particular, just daily conversation, ordinary remarks, about how the door hinge needed fixing, how the sunflowers were very tall this year.

A cloud passed across the sun and he set the back of his hand against his forehead and looked up, then turned and waded to the bank, dragging a wake of rising mud.

He caught a terrapin that night, and lit a fire and cooked it in its shell, the creature bubbling and grizzling till it died. When he figured it was done, he dug it from the ashes with a stick and broke it with a rock and ate. Then he kicked sand onto the fire and stretched out with his head propped on his knapsack, watching the water glowing luminously green until he fell asleep. In the morning, he scraped the terrapin's shell out clean with a flat stone and ate again, and drank, and heaving up his knapsack, continued on.

Toward evening, he began to notice gashes in the pines, and underneath the gashes, pouches carved out of the trunks, straight along the lower lip, the upper lip arched, two or three around each trunk, and down into the pouches slowly weeping gum, some the clear bright color of a sunset, others cluttered with spiderwebs and bark, leaves, insects. He understood these pouches were the work of people, so he trod carefully with his ears about him, but heard no one, just the keening of a high and distant wind. A dry storm crackled overhead.

But now the wind had fallen down into the trees and the air

was getting hotter, the heat coming from in front, coming with the wind. He topped a rise and fright jumped in his throat because he thought that he was seeing spirits. The undergrowth below him in the gully sparked with orange lights, but then he realized it was budding out in flame. Smoke rose like a ghostly presence in between the rigid, upward-thrusting trunks, fire blossoming and flaring underneath, dark black shadowy wreaths curling from the tips of flame.

As though it had seen him standing there, the wind raced up the ridge, herding the fire before it, the flames snapping at the grass and bushes, crackling and snarling. A long red-banded snake fled past him, like a tongue of fire scouting on ahead.

He ran then, snorting and tripping, flinging out his arms to save himself. But the fire was all around him, bark popping off the trees, his boot soles burning hot, but not yet burning since he ran so fast. Smoke in his throat, his lungs, his eyes, the sound of fire like gunshots coming after him. He couldn't see, he couldn't breathe, and he was going to die. "Oh, Miss Genie! Oh, Miss Genie!"

And then, as though his prayer had turned the wind, it gusted, swooped, and with a loud whooping like a train rushing through a station, chased the fire back down the hill.

Above him, a thunderhead, a lightning crack, and he was sprawled out on his back, mouth wide, drinking in the rain. When it stopped, the treetops overhead were clear dark green against a deep blue sky.

A woodpecker announced the dawn with a hard, determined rapping on the trunk above his head. He tilted back and lay watching its bright red crest jerk back and forth, the bark flipping away like chips from a woodsman's axe, the soft wood underneath loosening and falling in a patter to the ground, the busy feathered body flat against the trunk, clinging on as though it had been nailed there, the head now deep inside, now out again, now in, as if it played a game of hide-go-seek.

Reaching up, Tom touched the blackened bark. It peeled off beneath his fingers, layered paper thin, like a scab peeling off a wound. He wiped his fingers off in five black trails across his shirt, looking about him at a bright black forest floor littered with burned needles, fallen blackened limbs, enormous blackened pinecones. The whole world smelled of ash.

And now men's voices talking to each other, calling out. Tom rolled over and came up into a crouch, his head tilted at a listening angle. Someone was giving someone else instructions. These must be the men who carved the trees. They were just beyond the ridge. On hands and knees, slipping in the still-warm sand, he scrambled up and peered across the top.

Two men were there, one black and one high yellow. The black one wore a makeshift satchel from which a pair of metal pannikins bobbed, secured by their handles with a loop of string. In one hand he carried a wooden bucket, which he now swung down onto the ground beside a pine tree and stood watching while the high yellow plunged a long-handled ladle into the tree's pouch, scooping out what Tom knew must be a sticky mess of orange gum. After a while, the pair went on to the next tree, then the next, sometimes speaking to each other, sometimes working silently. Tom followed, watching them across the ridge.

From time to time, they came to a stand of barrels, three or four together, each with a square hole in the top into which they emptied their bucket. Once a boy came driving in a mule cart after them. He was barefoot and wore a straw hat with a turned-up brim. He hammered bungs into a pair of barrels, then he and the two men heaved the barrels up onto the cart and he went rattling on.

As they went, the understory changed. Grass and ferns

sprouted from the forest floor, shot through with miniature oaks and maples, holly, rhododendrons, tiny reproductions of the giant long-leaf pines. Low shrubs and bushes pushed out perfect leaves and the air smelled spicy sharp.

By the time Tom had followed the two men half the morning, he knew the black one's name was Peter, the high yellow's Ben. When the sun was overhead, the one called Peter squinted upward through the trees and threw his bucket down, and the one called Ben dropped his ladle in the bucket. Peter swung the satchel off his back, unhooked the metal pannikins, and handed them to Ben, who went off with them toward the trickling sound of water.

Peter drew a rag-wrapped parcel from his satchel, and when he had sat down with his legs crossed, he opened it, and spread food out on the rag. In a moment, Ben came back carrying the pannikins one in each hand carefully. He handed both to Peter, who held them out in front of him while Ben sat down with his legs crossed too. Then Peter handed Ben his pannikin and both men drank.

When they had finished drinking, Tom went down to them. "Scusee, is this here the north?"

They turned to look at him, and Peter said to Ben, sideways from the corner of his mouth, "Here's another one run off."

"No, sir. I ain't run off. I got my freedom paper here."

He reached to pull it from his shirt but Peter made a waving motion and smiled at him with big white teeth. "If you lookin' for work, you come to the right ol' turpentine plantation. That crew boss, Hiram, he always lookin' for another hand."

"No, sir, I'se not lookin' for work. I'se lookin' for the north."

"What's your name, boy?"

"Tom."

"Well then, Tom, since you lookin' for the North, you may's well set right on down here, since I dessay the North about to come to you. What you stare at me like that for, boy? Don't you know them Yankees comin' down the coast? Done took Fort Hatteras, Fort Clark, and comin' thisaway. Don't you know nothin' a-tall?"

"Been walking in the forest. Don't know nothin' 'bout any Yankees."

"Why, certainly." Peter slapped his knee and laughed a big bold laugh. "They tells me when the Missus heard of it, she bust out into tears. That wicked rail-splitter, she said, that *taaall* man. This is the beginnin' of the end."

"I seen soldiers on the road."

"Yessir, them boys goin' off'n fight the Yankees. But I tell you this, they ain't gonna win. Them Yankees comin' right on down make free men out'n all of us. Ain't that right, Ben?" He patted the ground beside him. "Here, Tom, set down. Have yerself a bite."

BY the time Ben and Peter had shared their lunch and let him drink some tinny-tasting water, Tom felt he had known them for a good long time, Peter at least, since he was the one who talked so much, and grinned so much, and laughed and slapped his leg. He was a loose-limbed wiry man, friendly and impulsive. Ben was shorter and more squarely built, with a large head and remote, contemplative eyes the color of dried leaves. He told no stories, offered few opinions, but was apt at any moment to break out in loud, enthusiastic prayer.

"Ben don't talk much, but he's a right fine hand at prayin'," Peter said. "I figure he could pray us out of near 'bout any sort of trouble."

"This Hiram, would he pay me?"

"Pay you? Sure. So why's you all fired up for gettin' paid?"

"Gonna save my ol' mother's price so I can buy her free." He waited, watching Peter's face.

"You been payin' no attention to me a-tall?" Peter said. "You wait, jest wait. Let them Yankees make her free, then you got your ol' mother and keeps your pay as well." He grinned, wadding up his lunch rag. When he had stuffed it in the satchel, he shook the last drips of water from his pannikin, held out his other hand for Ben's, and looped both on the string. "Come on along," he said to Tom, "we gonna get you fixed with Hiram for some payin' work."

CHAPTER FOURTEEN

AFTER Tom had vanished in the woods, Eugenia flicked the reins and urged the mule on up the road to Salisbury, the mule recalcitrant, as though it understood that it had lost the one man in the world who cared about its welfare, she in a daze of fear and indecision, half regretting what she had just done, half proud she had been bold enough to do it. Her thoughts, if thoughts they could be called, circled like a blind moth around her father. How was she to face him now? She had not thought this through, she told herself, she had acted on an impulse. She must go back, she must find Tom and take him back. But then an argument started up inside her head, circling and circling, singeing its wings on the imagined outburst of her father's temper.

At the outskirts of the town, she stopped and pulled her carpetbag from underneath the seat. Shading her eyes, she peered along the road ahead, and then the road behind—no soul in sight—then drew out of the carpetbag a large tobacco tin and opened it. Gold chips glinted in the early morning sun.

She had not planned to steal Papa's cache. She had come upon it unexpectedly one day when she was cleaning house. He had spent the night before sneezing in his sleeping loft, the noise reverberating through the tiny cabin like a series of explosions. After work that afternoon, Eugenia took a broom and climbed the ladder, intent on clearing out the dust. When she turned the corner of the mattress back, she discovered a tobacco tin that clearly did not have tobacco in it, since it rattled and was weighty.

So, she told herself when she had opened it, my father is a gold thief too, just like Tom or any of the Negroes who tuck it in their trouser cuffs or press it in their hair. Papa could not have pressed it in his hair, since he had hardly any left of it, but he had obviously made good use of his pockets. She took a handful of the nuggets, some as large as a spring pea, and let them run out through her fingers. So had he stolen them? He must have, yes, else they would be locked safely in the bank. How foolish of him, though, to keep it here with nothing but a string latch on the door. Even Tom, a slave, had sense enough to hide his gold behind the wall.

After that she had kept an eye on Papa's cache, to see if it would grow. Sometimes there was more and sometimes less, from which she gathered that from time to time he used it to pay off a portion of his debts. She never stole.

But she had stolen now. When Papa told her he could not afford to set Tom free, her mind had flown to it. How much could a passage to Australia cost? Surely this nest egg was enough to cover it? She stirred the nuggets with her finger, panic starting in her throat again. What had she done? What had she been thinking? She must take back the tobacco tin, right now, at once, before Papa discovered it was gone.

But no, she had to stay away all day, she had to stay away, she had to give Tom time. And yet giving Tom time to make his getaway meant giving Papa time to discover she had robbed him. So what to do? March in the door and say, Here, Papa, this is yours, I did not mean to take it? I do not know what I was thinking?

Tears came to her eyes because she knew full well what she had been thinking. She had been thinking about leaving him. She did not want to go to Australia, to this place called Kapunda. Even the name was ugly and repellent. She had traveled half across the state so Papa could fail at gold mining. She would not travel half across the world so he could fail again in some godforsaken copper mine.

With a snap, she closed the tin, stuffed it back into her carpetbag, flicked the reins, and turned the mule and cart around. She climbed down onto the road and whacked the mule across the rump. Surprisingly, it started up, and she stood there watching it plod off the way they had just come, the cart crunching behind. Then she turned and set out walking into Salisbury.

MR. Spotswood came home that evening all fired up with plans. He had spent the day at Mr. Perrin's house with several of the single Cornish miners who, on learning of his plan to go to South Australia, had declared themselves hell-bent on joining him. The more they talked about it, the better the adventure seemed. Even Mr. Perrin became excited, declaring that, goddamit, he'd be in the thing himself if Miz Hedra were not so set on California. He produced a tintype of his brother, in a wide-brimmed hat, standing on the front porch of a low stone house, his wife and seven children arrayed below him, squinting on the steps. They looked prosperous and happy, although they did not smile.

The men passed the picture hand to hand, drinking gin and telling each other how Australia was a lucky country, everybody knew it, and they drank more gin and made their plans. From Gold Hill they would travel north by train to Salisbury, then east and south to Wilmington, then take a ship around Cape Horn and across the Pacific Ocean to Australia. Arrived in Adelaide, they would send a telegram to Mr. Perrin's brother and he would come and take them in his carriage to Kapunda. It would be the longest journey Mr. Spotswood had taken in his life and, not quite drunk, he felt light and youthful at the prospect.

Now he pushed open the cabin door and went in, hopping on one foot and then the other, pulling off his boots. He stepped into his slippers, bending to run a fingertip around the inside of each heel.

"Eugenie?"

Strange, the place was empty. He looked around the kitchen. No fire, no supper, not so much as a lighted lamp. Where was that girl? And where was Tom? He went out and looked up and down the lane, but it was empty too, so he came back in and lit the lamp. A note in Eugenia's hand was propped against it. He read it through and frowned. Female provisions? In Salisbury? What was this?

He went outside again and crossed the lane, padding in his slippers, but his hand was barely on the door when it swung back and Didema Ware appeared, tight-lipped and knowing. Suddenly he did not want to ask her anything, he did not want to know. But he was here now and Didema told him everything she knew and more.

Back home, he went to the table and stood looking at Eugenia's note. Where had she got the money to go shopping? No one had been paid in weeks.

And then his eyes turned up toward the ceiling. His crimson slippers climbed the ladder rung by rung. A moment later they climbed down again. He pulled a stool from underneath the table and sat down, the stool half skidding out from under him so that he had to snatch at it to save himself from falling. But no sooner was he safely settled onto it than his soul dissolved inside him. He seized Eugenia's note and ripped it into shreds.

"That black beast! That black beast run off with my daughter!" And he set his hands before his face, gasping and snorting at his grief.

When Didema Ware came knocking on the door next morning, all agog for news, she found him with a rope around his neck, hanging awkward and a little ludicrous from a rafter of the cabin. She sucked her breath in hard and set her hands akimbo on her hips.

"It goes to show," she said. "It surely goes to show."

She righted the stool Mr. Spotswood had kicked from underneath himself, picked up a crimson velvet slipper from the floor and wedged it back onto his foot, he swaying slightly at her touch. Then she went off, lustrous-eyed and purposeful, to report the matter to Miz Hedra.

IN Salisbury, Eugenia had spent all day going store to store clutching her carpetbag, although she made no purchases, stopping at notice boards to examine advertisements for runaways and announcements of sales and auctions to be held, caricatures of Mr. Lincoln that made him look demonic or demented, instructions where to sign up for the army. Her hair was damp with heat, perspiration ran in trickles from her armpits, her undergarments chafed between her legs.

Salisbury had changed since that lighthearted day she had come shopping here with Tom. Then it had been blue-eyed spring, now the molten heat of August smeared the air so that everything seemed out of focus. No pretty ruffled girls paraded underneath the spreading elms of Innis Street. No young men either, except a pair who, serious in military uniform, struggled up the street on brand-new crutches, a third coming behind, a winded-looking boy with one sleeve empty, glum disappointment on his face. They did not pay Eugenia any mind.

In the square, a red-faced fire-eater was making a speech below the newly invented flag of the Confederacy, from time to time hauling out a pocket handkerchief to mop his forehead, while sharp-eyed men of the militia moved their horses up and down behind the crowd. A feeling of confusion filled the air, a sort of nervousness, a wary watchfulness, and there seemed to be a lot of drunkenness about, fallen women too, Eugenia knew it from their boldness and the bright colors of their clothes, like the whores who used to slip onto the goldfield.

Late in the afternoon, she stepped into a coffee shop where the waiter seated her at a table by the window and went off with her order written on his pad. Eugenia glanced around and pulled the tobacco tin out of her carpetbag. Setting it on her knees beneath the tablecloth, she lifted the lid and slipped a handful of nuggets into the pocket of her skirt. Another glance around and she tucked it away again. The waiter came back with iced tea and a bun and she ate and drank, fanning herself with the napkin and watching the people going about their business in the street, slow walking, heavy with the summer.

A shadow fell across the window and a man was looking at her through the glass, his ratlike, sparsely whiskered face inches from her own. He wore a skewed black hat and a boldly brown and yellow checkered shirt, buttoned too tight at the neck. Eugenia jerked back and he raised a finger, black-nailed, bony, and lowering his head so that his nose and finger seemed to be one object, sighted at her down it with narrowed, close-set eyes.

"You," he said, his Adam's apple rising from his collar. Eugenia understood the word from the way he shaped his lips. "You," he said again, then dropped his hand and looked directly in her eyes. He smiled. He had no teeth.

His glance shifted sideways as though somebody had spoken. Eugenia turned to look. The coffee shop proprietor was making shooing motions in the doorway. When she turned back, the man was gone, but the incident unnerved her. Until now she had been fueled by her indignation at Papa, her defiant satisfaction at having set Tom free. Now uneasiness crept through the door and sat down with her at the table. To be a young girl here alone—anything could happen. She could be robbed, or carried off into the woods and raped, murdered, tossed into a ditch to rot, and not a soul would know of it or come after her to save her. Never before had she been away from home with no protector or companion. If only Tom were outside waiting with the mule cart and his gentle smile.

A tear dripped on her hand. She looked at it, a bright gem on the skin. Her skin, she could not bear to look at it. The sun-burned coarseness of it, not a trace of what once had been its pearly whiteness, the harsh labor it implied. And it was Papa's fault. All of it his fault. He had betrayed his wife and then he had let down his daughter.

Teacup unmoving in her hand, she stared out through the window with unseeing eyes, building up the angry story in her head. If Papa had not misbehaved with that slave Tilda, Mama would be alive today and she, Eugenia, would have someone she could turn to, someone to be her friend. She might even have a sister. What would it be like to have a sister? She tried to conjure up a sister for herself, but here came Didema Ware with her reporting eyes. A brother, then, a brother, what would that be like? Would it be warm and comfortable like Tom? She would like to have a brother.

And then it came to her. It was not just Tilda that Papa had sold, but Tilda's swollen belly too. Had he and Mama argued over it? Had they fought between themselves? Had gossip spread, Mama's friends mocked at her behind her back? She must have felt it. She must have been humiliated. Perhaps she gave Papa an ultimatum: her or me, she said, your dirty Negro mistress or your wife, how do you choose? He chose his wife, of course. What else to do? And sold the mistress with the child. *So do I have a brother somewhere in the world?*

No, it would not do. It was all nonsense, a wickedness of her imagination grown out of her bitterness toward Papa. But then she thought about the comfort Tom had been to her. If she could just have someone she could call her own, someone to belong to. If only Tom could be her brother.

The waiter coughed beside her, making scratching motions on his palm. The place was filling up with people, her table was required. She slipped her hand into her pocket and paid him with a tiny piece of gold, then rose reluctantly and went out into the street, regretting she had stayed so late, telling herself not to panic, not to panic.

But now Salisbury frightened her, the way eyes fixed on her and slid away, or did not fix on her at all, but then she thought about Australia and firmed her step and raised her chin and pretended to be confident, while her mind swirled and swirled around the question of what to do now, please God, what to do?

As she turned the corner from Main Street onto Innis, a man stepped out and blocked her way. He wore a skewed black hat and a boldly brown and yellow checkered shirt, buttoned too tight at the neck. He smiled, toothless, and jostled up against her, smiling, smiling, breathing whiskey in her face, snatching at her carpetbag. Now he had her by the arm, his fingers hard into her flesh, she gasping and half sobbing, "Help me! Help!"

Then she was on the ground, wrestling for her carpetbag. An enormous wrench and she felt the thief's grip snap. In one movement she was on her feet while he, slowed by whiskey, scrabbled on the ground. She wheeled away and would have run, but glancing up, found a row of faces turned on her from a veranda lined with chairs and tables. Above their heads a swinging sign: *Mansion House Hotel.*

It was a sign from heaven. In three strides she was up the steps and onto the veranda, the watching faces turning from the thief stumbling to his feet, to Eugenia, carpetbag in hand, gasping up the steps, to the thief fleeing down the road, and then back to Eugenia striding red-faced across the brick-paved floor, the hum of speculation following.

Ignoring all of them, angry with them all, she pushed through the foyer door and strode up to the desk, hesitated, swallowed, looked the clerk directly in the eye, and delving in her pocket, produced a chip of gold, which she plunked down on the guest book. A brief argument, another chip produced, and she followed a grinning bellboy upstairs to her room.

It was not until the door had closed behind him and Eugenia swung her carpetbag onto the bed that she realized it was lighter. No need to empty it, no need to strew everything across the counterpane, no need to rummage through her extra petticoat and drawers and stockings, her brush and comb and feminine supplies. No point in rushing down the stairs to beat on the front desk, and when the constable arrived, no point in pouring out her story, demanding he arrest the brown and yellow checkered man. He was long gone, the constable assured her, licking his pencil with a mobile tongue while he eyed her up and down. About this tin of gold. How did she come by it? Why had she been wandering all day about the streets? Yes, it had been noted. And what was she planning to get up to, a single woman alone in a hotel at night?

• • •

AND so it had been no use. The gold was gone, the thief was gone, the constable suspicious of her story. Indeed, she had been lucky not to have been taken in and charged with theft herself.

Now she could not sleep. A pulse throbbed in her neck. Her head felt tight. With the gold lost, she had no option but to go back to Papa. No, she could not do it. She could not face him. Perhaps he was already drumming up a hue and cry. At dawn, a search party with a warrant to arrest her would be riding up the road to Salisbury. She would be hunted down and hauled back in disgrace. She would be branded thief. Didema Ware would gloat. Papa would not believe she had repented. He would blame her and mistrust her, maybe he would even beat her. And then he would abandon her. He would go off and leave her in Gold Hill, alone and penniless. Oh, what a fool she had been, what a little fool!

Stop it. Do not be hysterical. There is some solution. Always there is some solution.

She tried to organize her thoughts, but they would not be organized. Every time she came to a conclusion, some other conclusion took its place. She should not have set Tom free; she should have. She should not have taken Papa's gold; she was entitled. She should have headed home this afternoon; she should have stayed right here. Tomorrow she should go back to Gold Hill; tomorrow she should look for work.

And there it was: she had come to a decision. She would look for work.

Her heart swelled and she fell to building up a plan. She could clean a house as well as any, she could sew. She could be a housemaid, no, a lady's maid, maybe a companion. But wait, could she not read? Did she not have a flowing hand? Could she not play the piano, sing, recite by heart a dozen Shakespeare sonnets?

She had not entirely forgotten these accomplishments. A little polishing, a little practice, and she could become a governess, a private teacher in some wealthy family. She would have her own room with muslin curtains on the window, and when her charges were tucked into their beds at night, she would have time to tend her hair, to smooth creams on her face. Her prettiness would blossom once again, and—this was best—because she was of a cultivated mind and swift in conversation, she would eat her meals with the family. When visitors came, she would be included in an evening of music here, a card game there, she would go to balls and dances once again, once again the gentlemen would vie for her attention. And one day, walking delicately down a stair, she would look down, and there, below her, standing glaze-eyed in the grand front hall, would be a man, a rich, dark, handsome man, tumbling into love with her.

She fell suddenly asleep, like a miner falling down a pitch-black shaft, and at the bottom, waiting for her with a mocking sneer, were the ragtag ghosts of fantasy.

She had taken a position and had a little room with muslin curtains. It was a pretty room, with pale pink wallpaper and pale pink roses in a vase. They were a gift and she had set them in the vase herself. A man had given them to her, the man who now was pushing through her door. It was the master of the house—it was Papa—coming at her with a winking leer. She was backing off from him, pinned against the wall, he toothless, breathing whiskey in her face, she slipping and scrambling up the long black shaft of sleep to where Tom was turning off into the woods, one hand held up and gold dust gleaming in his hair.

She came awake with a rush to find herself rigid, staring wide-eyed and unblinking at the ceiling, her heart pounding so hard the brass knobs on the bedposts rattled. Outside, light was growing in the window.

CHAPTER FIFTEEN

For five days Eugenia knocked door to door along the wealthy homes of Salisbury with no success. No one wanted her, not as a governess, not as a maid. Inquiries at businesses and shops yielded the same result. Her feet hurt and her head ached and her chips of gold were almost gone. If only she had slipped more into her pocket.

On the sixth day, leaving the hotel with calculations in her head of how much longer she could stay before the desk clerk called the constable to turn her out into the street, she heard the whistle of a train and stopped, indecision in her heart.

She had stopped outside a milliner's where she had inquired three times for work. Sample hats and bonnets filled the window, tulles and flowers and ribbons in a grand display. Eugenia stood gazing in at them, listening to the train hoot south, the sound lessening to the ghost of a sound, to the memory of a sound, to silence. Gradually the image of a woman rose out of the window's finery, a woman in a plain dull gown, a plain dull bonnet on her head, a worried face. The whole effect was shabby, grubby, desperate.

Now Eugenia understood why nobody would hire her, now she knew what her decision had to be.

AND now she waited on a hard bench in the sun, idly watching the activity around a half-built wooden structure on the far side of the tracks. In her hand she held a one-way ticket to Gold Hill, and from time to time tilted forward, peering north along the tracks for an approaching train, then tilted back. As another hour toiled around the platform clock, her figure gradually melted, her bonnet nodded in the heat.

To the south, a storm was building. When a train pulled in from that direction, it dragged a violent sky behind. The train sighed and clacked a little farther on, and sighed again, and stopped. Asleep, Eugenia did not hear it, did not hear the footsteps padding past, the footsteps stopping, coming back. Asleep, she was aware she needed to wake up, something crucial hinged on it. She struggled into consciousness, and saw beneath her bonnet brim a pair of ankles that she recognized. Every muscle in her body tightened, wrenching her straight-backed.

Before her stood Miz Hedra, the fat folds of her face quivering with disapproval. Behind Miz Hedra, Mr. Perrin and several of the other Cornish miners, their faces radiating disapproval of a different sort.

Eugenia's ticket fell out of her hand. She scrabbled after it. "Miz Hedra. Why Miz Hedra. Fancy that! Are you heading out for California? Is Papa with you?" She peered around Miz Hedra's bulk. "Where is Papa?"

• • •

SHE could not comprehend it. Miz Hedra was a liar. Eugenia fled out of the station with her mind in turmoil, hardly knowing where she went. She was aware of rapid movement blurred into a blank, of faces, voices, her own breath rasping in her throat, a strong hand on her arm propelling her.

When she came back to her senses, she found herself sitting in an office of some sort, weeping in her hands and hiccuping, the kind eyes of a spare, gray-whiskered man regarding her through wire spectacles across a desk. He seemed to be a man of standing and authority, perhaps a sheriff or a constable. No, he wore no uniform, just a small red ribbon fixed to his lapel. Perhaps he was a judge. She glanced about the room. It was anonymous and spare: a desk, two chairs, some papers on the desk, some boxes on the floor.

Eugenia felt it would be rude to ask her benefactor's name, sure that he had introduced himself while she was still in such a state of shock she had not absorbed the information. Whoever he might be, it seemed that she had told him everything about herself because now he said, "You must remember you did not intend it. You can perhaps be blamed for stealing gold from your papa, but not that he has hanged himself. And you did the right thing letting Tom go free. God would have willed it. It was a hard choice you had to make. King Solomon himself would have been perplexed by it."

King Solomon—so this man is a minister. The thought relieved her, as though God himself had come to reassure her and to comfort, to forgive her for Papa. *Oh, poor Papa.* But no, she could not think of him, not now, it was too much, if she thought about him now her heart would swell up and explode, she must set her mind on other, safer, things.

As though he read her thought, the man leaned across the desk and in a low voice said, "Miss Spotswood, you have become an abolitionist. The good Lord would approve of that. Here, take my handkerchief and blow your nose."

Eugenia snuffled into it. "An abolitionist?"

He glanced toward the door. "Hush, not so loud." His posture changed. He straightened, leaned back in his chair, hooked a finger in the armhole of his vest, and regarded her above his spectacles with a genial, forbearing, half-impatient look, as though her presence had been forced on him and he would handle it the best he could and then get rid of her.

Eugenia had heard nothing, but now a light tap on the door. As it swung open, the man said, "Oh," unhooked his finger from his vest, and let his face relax.

A smiling lady came into the room, a tea tray in her hands.

"Tea," the man said. "How kind."

He looked up into the lady's face and the smile that passed between them told Eugenia they were lovers. No, not lovers yet, the chase was still in progress. This lady also wore a small red ribbon fixed onto her breast—a lover's gift?—and Eugenia felt a flash of envy. *To love, to be in love.*

She waited for an introduction, but none was offered. Eugenia had the odd sensation she should know the lady's name, that she had been introduced before but somehow time had folded on itself and she had lost the folded part.

The man watched the smiling lady set the tray down on the desk and pour two cups of tea, and he dropped six lumps of sugar into one with a pair of tiny silver tongs. "Sweet tea," he said. "It will calm you."

The woman slid the cup and saucer toward Eugenia. "Drink up, dear, do what Dr. Kinney tells you." She turned back to the man. "If that is all . . ."

The door swung closed behind her.

Dr. Kinney. So this must be a hospital. Eugenia felt her heart lift, and sink again—*another hospital*—and lift. *Perfect, it would be perfect.*

She sipped her tea and found that Dr. Kinney had been right, the excessive sweetness soothed her. He took his without sugar, resting a sympathetic gaze on her above the rim.

"Dr. Kinney, please, is this a hospital?"

He set his cup onto the saucer. "A military wayside hospital, or it will be when it is completed. Did you not notice it while you were waiting for the train?"

"You mean the half-constructed building on the other side?"

"The same. I saw you on the station, sleeping on the bench. I felt quite sorry for you in the heat."

"You saw Miz Hedra, then?"

"I thought perhaps she was your mother come to force you to go home. I thought you were a runaway. Then, when the commotion started up—"

"You came to rescue me."

He pulled his mouth down, chuckling through his nose. "The white knight on his steed."

Eugenia laughed.

"Ah, that's better. Would you like more tea?"

"No, thank you. I would like to talk about employment at your hospital. I am a nurse. I took care of injured miners at Gold Hill, and others too, the sick. I am quite expert."

"We are but half constructed. We have no patients yet."

"Shelter, then? A cot to sleep on? Surely there is something useful I can do?"

Dr. Kinney drew in a deep breath and hunched forward in his chair, forearms on the desk, his eyes fixed on her face, assessing, contemplative, grave.

Eugenia shifted underneath his gaze. "If I have offended . . ."

"No, no." He nodded twice, and then again. "I think you can be trusted."

She watched him, waiting.

"I have a friend, a Mrs. Baker, an exemplary woman. I think perhaps she might provide you with a bed until we sort out what to do with you. Come, I will take you to her. Are you feeling strong? It's a good step to the carriage house." He rose and went to the window. "We must hurry if we are to beat this storm."

"Perhaps we should wait for it to pass."

He consulted his pocket watch. "It grows late. We must make a run for it, else we might both end up sleeping on the floor."

A humpbacked wooden bridge took them back across the tracks. Eugenia had seen it while she sat waiting on the platform, but for the life of her she could not remember crossing it. She looked along the platform to the bench where she had been sitting, but her carpetbag had vanished. A gust of wind threatened to tear her bonnet off. She turned her face away, clutching at it with one hand, with the other steadying herself against the rail. They crossed the farther platform and came out onto the street. No sooner there than the sky, which had been tumultuous and gray, blackened suddenly and everybody fled indoors.

"Hurry, we must hurry." Dr. Kinney seized Eugenia's elbow, lengthening his stride until she was half running. Even so, by the time they reached the public carriage house, thunder was rumbling overhead. As they set out, heavy raindrops started on the carriage roof, making the canvas jerk and jump above them, and by the time they reached the edge of town, a torrent was beating down on it. Despite all this, the horse continued bravely, perhaps, Eugenia thought, because it was accustomed to driving about to medical emergencies through every kind of weather.

• • •

THE rain had eased but still came down in a steady, soaking drizzle when Dr. Kinney pulled back on the reins and climbed down from the carriage. "We have arrived," he said, holding out his hand.

Eugenia tucked the loose ends of her hair into her bonnet, set her hand in his, and stepped into a puddle that came almost to her ankles.

Dr. Kinney laughed. "Sorry, we'll dry you out inside."

She put her hand up to the collar of her gown, clasping it tight to keep water from trickling down her neck, and trotted slip-slap after him through a picket gate and along a walk bright with the reflected glow of windows. She craned her neck, examining the house. It was a large, white, two-storied house with columns, a gallery above, and a wide veranda underneath, the sort of house she used to dream of when she dreamed about advancing in society. It had a strange, lopsided look, though, and even in the half dark she could see it had begun the slippage into seediness. Water gurgled from the eaves.

Then they were dripping water on the carpet of a spacious parlor, where Dr. Kinney introduced her to a woman perhaps approaching forty, with gray hair curling at the front, the rest pulled tightly back into a topknot high up on her head. She wore a gray gown and a short gray jacket with a silver brooch secured to its lapel by a loop of fine red ribbon. *So I was wrong about the lover's gift.* A kind and yet determined face. Dark, tragic eyes. Eugenia thought her beautiful.

"Well," Mrs. Baker said when they were introduced, "you surely look in need of refuge, like a stray cat hauled in from the rain. You have no bag? No baggage? Nothing but your own wet shivering self? We must dry you out and feed you something warm before you catch your death."

She tugged a bellpull on the wall and a Negro girl as tiny as a bird appeared. In a moment, Eugenia found herself spirited upstairs and plunged into a deep hot bath, the girl attending her without a word, for which Eugenia was grateful.

That done, she found herself dressed in a fine white cambric shift, which she presumed belonged to Mrs. Baker, and propped up in bed with a tray on which was a bowl of steaming black bean soup and a plate of biscuits. When the girl left, Eugenia set the tray aside, and slipping out of bed, retrieved the last few chips of gold from her gown pocket, looked around the room, then slid open the desk drawer and hid them at the back. Then she climbed back into bed.

She had eaten all the soup and was finishing off the last biscuit when the girl appeared again. She took the tray, and balancing one edge on her hip, scooped up the bundle of Eugenia's clothes.

"What is your name?" Eugenia asked.

The girl looked big-eyed at her, "Alouette," she said, and fled out of the room.

A moment later, Mrs. Baker tapped and came into the room, smiling and fussing about, straightening the drapes and Eugenia's pillows. "My dear, you're feeling well? You haven't taken cold? Would you like a hot brick for your feet? No? Then you're quite comfortable?"

Eugenia took hold of the coverlet's edge. "Yes, thank you, ma'am. I'm more comfortable than I have been in years." She sniffled, clinging to the coverlet. "I'm sorry, I do not mean to weep. I'm just so very grateful for your kindness, ma'am."

Mrs. Baker bent and touched her cheek. "Alouette calls me Aunt Baker. You may too, if you wish."

"But I . . . but Alouette . . ."

"Did you think she was a slave?"

"Why, no, yes, I . . ."

"She's an orphan, a sweet girl, a nervous little thing, but you will grow to like her." Aunt Baker raised one eyebrow, giving an inquiring nod. "Dr. Kinney says he thinks you can be relied on."

"Oh, yes, ma'am . . . Aunt Baker. I am most reliable."

"You can keep your mouth tight shut?"

Eugenia nodded.

"Dr. Kinney also says you are an abolitionist." Aunt Baker sat down on the bed's edge and took Eugenia's hands. "Eugenia Mae, are you an abolitionist?"

Eugenia heard herself assert she was. It seemed important.

"Then I take it you are for the Union?"

"I . . . do not know. I had not thought about it."

"Then think about it now, child. We are at war. Everybody must take sides, like it or not. You say you are an abolitionist. It seems to follow you must be for the Union."

"I think I am for neither side. I do not want a war. These last years I have seen too many dead and half-dead men. I have sat beside their beds and listened to their groans and watched them die in agony. And this was from their ordinary labor, from ordinary accidents that miners have. To go to war and tear each other up on purpose seems to me a sin. It is a sin against the love of God."

"Is it not a sin against the love of God to buy and sell his children?"

"You mean slavery? Did Dr. Kinney tell you about Tom?"

Aunt Baker nodded.

"I want Tom to be free."

"Then you must take the Union's side. The South will not relent."

"Did Dr. Kinney tell you about my father . . . what he did?"

"He told me everything."

A sob started in Eugenia's throat. "He was going to sell Tom. I did not want him sold, it was too cruel. And then Papa . . . I did not mean . . . oh, Aunt Baker, am I wicked? Am I wicked?" Suddenly she was in Aunt Baker's arms, weeping on her breast. She went on a long time, and when she had calmed to a sporadic hiccuping, and then to a long sigh and silence, Aunt Baker stood up, briskly smoothing down her skirts. "Come now, no more of this. They say suffering improves the soul, but I say too much dwelling on the past is self-indulgence, an excuse to sit with folded hands. The best cure for a sore heart is useful work."

Eugenia sniffed. "Yes, ma'am."

Aunt Baker hesitated, then seemed to come to a decision. "I am not offering to pay you, but I can give you food and a warm bed in exchange for your assistance."

"What would you have me do? Do you need a house-keeper?"

"I need a nurse."

"You have an invalid living with you?"

"Not exactly."

"I do not understand."

"Patience, patience. You must have a good night's sleep. We'll talk about it in the morning."

CHAPTER SIXTEEN

EUGENIA woke next morning to the sound of voices from below. She threw the covers back but could not bring herself to
rouse, and so sank back into the unaccustomed luxury of the
feather mattress. She had slept soundly, not so much as a dream,
and felt quite cheerful until she thought about Papa.

Then it all came back to her. Miz Hedra's fat face trembling
over her, her downturned mouth surrounded by grim flesh, her
spiteful Christian eyes, the way she seemed to wallow in the hor-
rifying details—how Papa's face had turned dark blue, how his
crimson slipper fell as they were cutting through the rope—and
Miz Hedra's accusation, "Your fault, it is your fault," the accusing eyes of Mr. Perrin and the Cornish miners back behind.

Eugenia's throat went tight. An enormous weight sat on her
chest. *Oh, Papa, why did you do it?*

But she knew why he had done it: from despair because his
daughter had run off with everything he had, because he could

no longer see into the future, because she had ruined him, because she was ungrateful, because he loved her. She would have to bear it always, all her life, the memory of that. And yet, when she thought about the way Tom looked at her, one hand held up, before he turned and vanished in the woods, she could not regret that she had freed him.

She felt herself ripped half apart between relief that Tom had not been sold and grief about her father. She owed her father loyalty and love, and she had loved him, she understood that now. Too late, she saw him as a man battered by exigency. Too late, she understood that a man cannot be blamed for what the heavens throw down on his head. From the moment they left Wilmington and set out for Gold Hill, she had railed at fate, bitterly complained it was not fair, that she, Eugenia Mae Spotswood, deserved better out of life. She had spent her whole time looking at herself, seeing no one but herself, her suffering, her humiliation, her ruined hopes for happiness. Not once had she considered how her father must be suffering, how his humiliation must have stung and stung and stung, how every day he must have dreamed of what was not, of what had been and was no longer. To have a wife die, to lose everything he owned. From his daughter he had needed sympathy and love. She had given him the bitter herb of spite.

And yet, she asked herself, does not everyone need love, even a slave? In that, Papa and Tom had been alike. Alike too in that they had no one else but her to love them. Why could she not have had them both? Why did she have to choose?

Abruptly, she pushed aside the covers and went to the window, examining a sky that told her nothing except that it would rain again. So had she slept all day? If hunger were an indication, she might have slept all week. She went to the commode, and having splashed water into the basin, proceeded to wash her face and hands and dry them on a towel hung at the side. That done, she examined her gown, which was spread across a chair, and finding it clean and dry and crisply ironed, pulled it on, tidied her hair, and set off downstairs.

The house seemed empty, yet at the same time had a sort of furtiveness about it, as though unseen people breathed behind the walls. A breakfast of eggs and ham and cornbread with coffee was set out in the dining room and Eugenia ate alone. Someone, a girl, was singing in the kitchen, the sound so soft Eugenia thought at first it was imagination.

The singing stopped and Alouette appeared in the doorway, wiping her hands on the corner of her apron. She smiled, dipping her head shyly. "I'm to take you to Aunt Baker."

"Wait, Alouette. I want to ask you something. Aunt Baker has hired me as a nurse, or so she says, but she refuses to discuss my patient."

Alouette glanced toward the window. "Not so loud."

Eugenia dropped her voice. "Why? Is this patient a secret?"

"Aunt Baker will tell you all about them."

"Them? There is more than one?"

"You must let Aunt Baker tell you."

Mystified, Eugenia followed her to a paneled office where they found Aunt Baker going through some papers. She wore a cotton housedress, light brown sprigged with pale green flowers, and a bibbed apron of plain calico. One errant curl bobbed and beckoned from her topknot every time she moved, making her seem younger than she had the night before.

"What's this?" she said, looking at Eugenia. "A long face still?"

"I'm perplexed by your intent, Aunt Baker. I am to be a nurse, you say, but I've seen no sign of any patient."

Aunt Baker did not answer. Taking Eugenia by the hand, she led her down a hallway, through the kitchen, where Alouette was now humming at the sink, out into a closed-in sunporch that ran from the back door of the kitchen along the full depth of the house. The door at its far end was open and through it Eugenia could see the high stakes of a kitchen garden.

Halfway down the sunporch, a large, gray-headed Negro sat on a stool beside a broad low drying table on which herbs were set out in a large flat metal pan. Above him on the wall, dried herbs hung in string-tied fragrant bundles. At Aunt Baker's nod he rose, moved the metal pan onto the floor, and with a great heave of strong arms, slid back the table to reveal what appeared to be the entrance to a root cellar. He hesitated, glancing back across his shoulder at Eugenia.

"Don't worry, she is one of us," Aunt Baker said. "Eugenia Mae is her name. She is a nurse. Eugenia, this is Henry."

Henry turned his head full round and looked Eugenia up and down, unsmiling, as though memorizing what she looked like. Then he hauled up one of a pair of heavy trapdoors to reveal a ladder going down to dimness.

Aunt Baker gathered her skirts and went in backwards. "Come, my dear," and she vanished out of sight.

Eugenia followed, more mystified than ever. The trapdoor closed above them and she heard the drying table scrape back into place.

At first she could see nothing, although she could hear raspy breathing and a low, continuous moan. The air was dank with mold and the musty, slightly rotten smell of old stored sweet potatoes and damp sacking, another, sharper, smell Eugenia recognized as coming from sheets damp with inadvertent urine, and that more disastrous human smell she also knew.

Her eyes adjusted to the flickering candlelight and she saw a large storage cellar with shelves lining the walls. On the shelves were various bottles and boxes and baskets, stacks of blankets, small wooden whiskey barrels set in rows. Below, lined along each wall, were cots, in several of which lay men apparently in various states of injury or illness. At the far end, a fireplace, empty, and tacked above it on the wall, an enormous Union flag.

Blood pulsed at Eugenia's temples, a hot tightness gathered in her head.

Aunt Baker's fingers closed around her wrist. "Careful, the floor is slippery. Alouette has given it a sluicing." And she started down the double row of cots, drawing Eugenia with her.

"Good morning, Jack." Aunt Baker folded back a blanket to reveal the bruised arms and bandaged rib cage of a man who appeared to have been severely beaten. "Eugenia Mae, this is Jack Hites."

"What happened to you, Jack?" Eugenia said, and he rolled his head to look at her but did not speak.

"He finds it hard to breathe," Aunt Baker said. "His ribs are in a bad way, broken, almost all of them."

"Who did this to him?"

"Governor Clark's state troops at High Point, for promoting what they called 'a rebellious disturbance' against the war." She set her hand on Jack Hites's shoulder. "Poor Jack, he's been well paid for his rebellion. Careful of the floor."

She led Eugenia on to where one eye in a bandaged head watched from the next cot. "This is Sam McFee. Hello Sam, and how are you this morning? Aha, a smile I see. You must be feeling better."

"Who's this?" Sam said, his suspicious one eye on Eugenia.

"Eugenia Mae," Aunt Baker said. "Be nice to her, Sam. She is a nurse. I do not want to frighten her away." She half turned to Eugenia. "A band of secessionists intent on impressing him into the army kicked him so severely in the head I fear he has been blinded in one eye."

Sam looked fiercely one-eyed up at her. "I'll see again, or someone's going to pay for it."

Aunt Baker laughed. "Sam's great complaint is that they have impressed his horse."

"I'm Hartnet Simpson, miss," came a voice from the next cot, and by the time they stepped across, Eugenia half slipping on a patch of damp, its owner was well into the story of how, at the Battle of Bull Run, a minié ball had got him in the neck and another in the groin, and so he had been bundled with some others on a train and carried here to Salisbury to be treated at one of the wayside hospitals. But, he told her, his voice rising in a mix of petulance and agitation, he had no desire to go back and be a Yankee target one more time, so the minute his groin was healed enough to bear his weight, he had hobbled off one night while the nurse in charge was dozing in her chair, made his way across a field of corn, and sheltered in a barn, where some Negroes found him and brought him to Aunt Baker, who, he said, was the best woman in the world beside his mother.

Aunt Baker said nothing through all this, but when Hartnet's flow of words ran out, she leaned down with a tender, lingering motion to adjust the bandage on his neck. A waft of that familiar smell came out of it. *So he will die. He will go rotten from the neck and die.*

"And these three—over here, my dear," Aunt Baker said, crossing to the other side. "These three who lie together, these are Friends, Quakers, good men, pacifists, and abolitionists. They will not fight, nor will they cease witnessing to their opinions on the institution of slavery. This one is Pennebacker Simms. He was strung up by his thumbs so long that not just his thumbs, but his shoulders too, were wrenched out of their sockets."

Pennebacker Simms did not respond to this account, just lay looking at a point above him with a dazed look on his face.

"Laudanum," Aunt Baker said.

She went to the next cot—it was where the moaning came from—and drew the blanket back to show a body swathed in bandages from neck to anklebone. "This is Thomas Sweazly. He was jabbed with bayonets. The wounds go inches deep all over him. I think his lung is punctured."

Thomas moaned as the weight of the light blanket came back down.

"There, dear," Aunt Baker said.

"And this last Friend who breathes so noisily is Jarvis Fowle. He was hung up by the neck from the rafter of his barn and left to slowly strangle. His voice box was damaged so he cannot speak, and his eyes forced clear out of his head. They are doing better now, although they bulge, and he cannot yet see out of the left."

Eugenia saw an image of her father strung up from the rafter, his pale blue eyes bursting from his head. She made a hissing sound between her teeth. "And you want me to take care of them?"

"I do, if you will agree to it. These men are war protesters, Union loyalists, dissenters, pacifists, call them what you will. They need a nurse, Eugenia. We must get them back to health before we spirit them away to safety. You've heard of the Underground Railroad that helps escaping slaves? Well, we are a sort of underground railroad for dissenters." She laughed, although she did not sound amused. "We help rebel Rebels, if you will."

"But where will these men go?"

"To Union lines, to their families if it is safe, or to hide out in the mountains. The Friends want us to get them to Ohio."

"And when they have all gone? What will I do then?"

"I do not doubt there will be others like them." Aunt Baker turned a sharp eye on Eugenia. "I assume you are a fair hand with a pen?"

"I have written barely a word since going to Gold Hill, but I have not forgotten how. Do you need a secretary too?"

"A scribe. We are writing letters to our North Carolina boys, encouraging them to desert, assuring them of our assistance. We have hundreds more to write."

"You speak of 'we.' There are others in this conspiracy?"

"Dr. Kinney, of course, and others too, a growing number, although I do not know how many. We call ourselves the Order of the Heroes of America, or more simply, Red Strings, after the harlot Rahab who hid Joshua's two spies. You know that story?"

"Yes, I've heard it read in church. Rahab was told to hang a red string from her window so when the Israelites came back to conquer Jericho, they would see it and she would be spared. Is it not strange, though, to name yourselves after a harlot?"

"We do not think about her harlotry, but about her steadfastness, as we are steadfast for the Stars and Stripes. When the Union takes the South, they will spare the Red Strings as Joshua's army spared the woman who had stood by them."

"But this is dangerous work. You could be slung in jail for it, or hanged."

Aunt Baker snorted. "Most of the men I'd fear have gone to war. As for the rest, they make a big to-do from time to time about the danger of conspiracies and the need to set up a patrol, but before long they yawn, they complain of being sick, or exhausted from exertion in the heat, and go back to rocking on their front verandas with a shot of whiskey and a fat cigar."

Eugenia laughed. "You make them sound quite harmless. Still, if you *are* discovered, would they not stop rocking and come after you?"

"Dr. Kinney is a city councilman, a man of influence, and there are others, Union men, who would protect us. Our greatest safety lies in keeping our mouths shut."

"What if I refuse to join you?"

"It is your decision, but I think you are a brave girl. I think you can live with a little danger for a righteous cause."

Aunt Baker's eyes were on her face. They were still standing by Jarvis Fowle's cot. Eugenia leaned to touch his arm, drawing her fingers across the rough wool of the blanket in a soothing motion.

"I do not know. I do not know."

Aunt Baker turned away and jerked a bellpull on the wall. In a moment the trapdoor heaved back on its hinge. "Go upstairs, my dear, where it is light and you can breathe fresh air, and think on it. If you decide to join us, come back down. I have an apron waiting for you right here on the shelf."

FOR an hour and more Eugenia paced up and down the upstairs gallery, or stood staring out toward the roofs of Salisbury. The sky had cleared somewhat and was now by turns bright and gloomy as clouds passed across the sun. A tall spire with a weather vane rose above the trees at the near edge of the town. Its tin roof glinted and then dulled. Below, the garden rustled.

Eugenia thought about the men downstairs, about the Friend who had been hung up by the neck. She thought about her father. Tears came and she brushed her hand across her eyes.

If she went to work for Aunt Baker, perhaps they would be caught. Perhaps they would be shot as traitors. A week ago, she had no thought in her head but preventing Tom from being sold. A day ago, she had nothing in her head but horror and remorse about Papa. It seemed a year, ten. She was a shocking person, a thief, a murderer, and now to be a traitor.

And yet Aunt Baker did not see herself as any sort of traitor. Red Strings they called themselves, did they? An inflammatory name for a conspiracy. She thought about the harlot, Rahab, how she had saved herself by playing traitor to her country. And yet she had done right, she had been on the Lord's side. Aunt Baker and her coconspirators were surely on the Lord's side too. They loved the Stars and Stripes, how could they be traitors?

A tear overflowed and trickled down around her nose to tremble at the corner of her mouth. She licked it off, so salty, and sniffed. She did not understand all the argument and politics about secession. She wanted two things only: for Tom to be a free man and Papa to be alive. And yes, she wanted one thing more: for this war to go away, just go away. She wanted everything, the war, Papa's death, his disastrous failure as a businessman, to be a dream, a waking nightmare, her imaginings about the slave called Tilda too. Perhaps if she went back to bed and slept and woke again, the entire mess would disappear and everything would be all right.

At this thought, exhaustion took her. Yes, she would sleep, she would go indoors and lie down on her feather mattress. But as she turned toward the door, Henry appeared behind it, smiling at her through the glass. Eugenia, in her distraction, fancied he was Tom. She gasped, setting her hand against her heart.

Henry pushed the door aside and came out with a steaming mug held in his hand. "Coffee?"

He did not go back inside, but stood beside her at the railing while she drank. He said nothing, just stood there, and at first Eugenia wished he would go away, but the strong brew revived her and she realized that his solid presence was a comfort. She pointed out across the trees. "What's that building, Henry, the one with the tin roof and weather vane? The one catching the sun."

"It's Maxwell Chambers's old cotton factory at the end of Bank Street. You've not seen it? You can walk from here to there in minutes. They're enclosing it and its grounds inside a palisade."

"What for?"

"It's to be a prison, a military prison."

"You mean for captured Yankees?"

"Yankees, yes. And for anyone the Confederacy takes it in its head to quarrel with, no doubt."

"Abolitionists?"

"Perhaps. I do not know. They do not share their plans with me."

Eugenia turned to look at him. "Henry, pardon me for asking, but I've never heard a Negro speak like you."

"I'm from Boston, the same as Adeline—Aunt Baker. We are old friends."

"She doesn't speak like you."

"She married south a good time back and has taken on the accent."

"Are you a Red String also?"

"We all are in this house."

"What about Aunt Baker's husband? Does she have one? She has not mentioned him."

"He died two years ago. That was when I came to Salisbury. I planned to carry her back home to her family, but she said she was no weeping widow and refused to come."

"She is a brave woman, then."

"She is formidable."

He took her empty mug and turned to walk away.

"Henry."

He turned back and looked at her.

"I'd be grateful if you would let me back into the cellar."

CHAPTER SEVENTEEN

⬥⬥⬥

IN Chapel Hill, the students from the university had gone marching off to war, the main street of the town lined four deep with well-wishers and sweethearts and brave, fearful mothers and teary-eyed secessionists. The new flag of the Confederacy had waved. Young ladies wept from sentiment for these young handsome marchers, with their smart straight backs and swinging legs, full of the truth and rightness of their cause, the conviction God himself was on their side. Old women wept as well, not out of sentiment, but out of memory of other times when men had marched to war and not come back.

Clyde Bricket, pushing through the crowd to catch a glimpse, was full of patriotic fervor. How he wanted to be with them! To take a gun and march and all the women cheering for him, waving handkerchiefs and weeping for his courage and his manliness. Pa had forbidden him to come to town today. You got a farm to run, he said, the likes of us cain't be messing with no war. What good is such a war to us? he said. Don't need no war, just need to be let be. And don't be thinking about running off, you're too blamed young to volunteer.

Clyde wanted Pa to volunteer, to get a uniform and be a hero, but Pa wouldn't, just hauled his suspenders up onto his shoulders and went off to slop the hogs. Nothing Clyde said moved him, the more he said the angrier Pa got, and when one day he came to him, his lip stuck out and truculent, to say Fred Hintner done gone off and volunteered, and he not yet sixteen, and Caleb Hirst, at fourteen years, gone off to be a drummer boy, Pa pulled back and swatted him so hard upside the head he knocked him down. Don't you understand nothin' I have said, boy? You ain't goin' to be no drummer in no army. We got a farm to run.

THE months went by, Pa going day to day about his crops and hogs and how much this year for tobacco and keep your mouth shut, boy, go mend the fence and when you're done with that, we got loose shingles on the roof, as if he'd never heard about no war.

But then Jeff Davis put out the Conscription Act. All men eighteen to thirty-five, it said, and Pa was only thirty-three years old. At first it was easy enough to step off behind a tree when Captain Burke came blustering down the road with his recruiters, but after a while Jeff Davis started to run out of soldiers to send off to the war and things got serious for folks like Pa.

One day Clyde came home for supper to find his father with a shovel underneath the chicken house. What you up to, Pa? And Pa said, Get another shovel, boy, we got to make a hiding place. What for a hiding place? Clyde said. Who's gonna hide under a chicken house?

It turned out Pa was, and did that very night, slept there with a blanket and a dish of food like some stray dog. Clyde was angry with him, and embarrassed, but when Captain Burke and half a dozen of his men showed up two days later, riding up onto their land no different from patrollers, searching not for nigras but for Pa, calling him a deserter, though he'd never been in any army, Clyde felt his umbrage rise and stood in front of them and lied right through his teeth until they went away.

And so Pa worked by day and hid by night, and he was not the only one, Clyde knew that for a fact from Amos, who went out in the woods and met with other nigras and came back, sucking his teeth and grinning, knowing everything that went on about the place, saying they was dozens of them, hundreds maybe, hiding out all over.

At least Pa had dug hisself a good place, good and deep, and lined it with old sacks so he didn't have to lie down in the dirt, and dug a tunnel to the chimney of the house so he could have a fire when it was cold. The smoke came out with all the cooking smoke, not a soul would know it. Clyde was proud of that. His pa had more sense than to go off fighting in a war that would do him no damned good at all, just get his head blown off, or his leg, which might be worse.

But then, one day when the recruiters came, Pa flying hell-for-leather for the chicken house, the hound dog, who was sleeping on the porch, saw him running past and got it in his head it was a hunt, so up he heaved and took off baying after him. The recruiters took one look at that there dog with his head stuck underneath the chicken house and his backside sticking up, tail going like he just trapped a coon, except it weren't a coon but Pa, and they knew right well what the situation was.

But Pa, who weren't no fool, while they were calling out to him from one side of the chicken house, was crawling out the other side and heading for the woods. By the time they hauled that fool dog out of there, and shouted a bit more at Pa, and Pa

did not appear, and then they went in after him, they found the
bird had flown the coop. Jest flown the coop, Amos told Clyde
afterwards, shaking with admiring laughter. Jest hightailed it
out the back o' there, he did, your pa, jest skinned into the woods
and got away. The boot is on the other foot, he said, which puzzled Clyde, who could not see that anybody's boot had anything
to do with it.

Now Pa needed a new hiding place. Amos said some of
those other fellers had dug theirselves deep secret caves, they
got trapdoors on the top and everthing, even chimneys coming
up through burned-out stumps, since guards out hunting for deserters wouldn't think a thing about a little smoldering, they'd
put it down to nigras who set light to trees to smoke the pos-
sums out.

That was when Clyde thought about the time Old Mary's
Tom had suddenly appeared above him on a slope by Morgan's
Creek. He figured it was Morgan's Creek because it was a big
one with a lot of stones. He had been frightened then, thinking
as how Tom was magic and had walked out of a tree, but he was
older now, and had more sense, he knew that nigra must have
had a den or cave to hide in. He thought that he could find it if
he tried. So he tied the hound dog to the porch rail and headed
off into the woods. All day he searched, and on the second day
got good and lost, but on the third day he walked right up to it
as if he had known all along.

He went back for Pa, and Amos came along as well, and the
three of them stood looking at it from the steep slope of the gully
opposite. Don't see nothin', Pa said, don't see no place to hide.
You got the wrong place, boy. But Clyde said, Jest wait here, and
he scrambled down the gully and across the creek and up the
bank and vanished. Then he stuck his head back out of the undergrowth, calling to the others to come see.

Pa was sure impressed. Done good, boy, he said, it is a right fine place to hide, you done real good. It was better than going off to war to be a drummer, making his pa proud.

Amos, on the other hand, was not so taken with the place. He curled his lip and sniffed and said, Them other fellas in the woods, they sure do make theirselves some fancy hideaways, dug out with a fireplace and all to keep them warm at night, considerable clever, yes indeed. And Pa, who did not hold with anybody being cleverer than him, or warmer either, said, Then do it.

They started work at once, no point hesitating, and by the next week's end had tunneled back behind and made a hole deep enough for a man to lie full length and sleep and almost stand, working with spades and grubbing hoes, catching the red clay in a bedquilt, then toting it off in buckets and a couple piggins to dump it in the creek, where the running water washed it off.

They fixed a barrel in the entrance so it would not collapse, and inside they cut a fireplace in the wall and made a flue straight up, and hauled a half-burned stump to set on top to be a chimney like Amos told them to. Inside the cave, they piled a thick soft carpet of pine needles, and made a bed by driving forked stakes into the ground and laying small poles side by side across them, with pine boughs running down the other way. On top they set a mattress made of sacks stuffed full of leaves, and a blanket, and the quilt they'd used for hauling dirt, well shook out. It was a good bed, anyone could sleep there. Clyde wanted to, but Pa said, Go on, get out of here, from now on you are my eyes, I am relying on you, which made Clyde even prouder than he'd been before.

Before they left, he and Amos hauled a fallen pine across the creek to make a bridge so Pa could get safely to his hiding place without wearing a betraying track into the slope. They jumped on it a bit to make sure it would hold and then set out back home, memorizing the way so they could bring food to Pa by night. Amos said they had to have a plan so Pa would know when it was safe to come out to the farm and work. So they made a plan that if Pa heard the two of them hog-calling, first one and then the other, it was okay to come out, but if he heard nothing, he had to creep down through the woods and peep out through the trees, and if the best red bedquilt was slung across the porch, he should go back and hide until someone came to fetch him.

It was a good plan, and it worked well until Old Mary fell ill with an arthritic fever and could not raise up off her bed to make the food. Which meant that Clyde and Amos had to cook, and work the farm, and take care of Ma, and Old Mary too, and carry food to Pa. But then Ma, who hadn't said one word nor turned a lick since Baby Sister died, got up completely unexpected from her chair one afternoon, and with a stern look on her face Clyde had never seen before, commenced to wrap a dishtowel round her waist and tie it at the back, and before long a kettle was bubbling on the fire with a good thick soup of fat middling and greens sending up its greasy smell.

Clyde and Amos ate their fill and when the light began to fail, Amos carried out a covered pail to Pa. He took a rod and line as well, slung across one shoulder, so if anybody chanced to see him they would think he was going fishing in the creek. Clyde stayed behind and helped Ma clean up, talking to her in an excited voice, not quite knowing what he said, he was so astonished by her starting up to work that way, and a little frightened too.

She said nothing through all this, and the times when Pa came home, she sat out on the porch like she'd always sat before, and stared in front of her. But when Pa was off and hiding in the woods, she roused herself and bustled about like any normal wife, soaking cornfield peas and husking corn and prodding sweet potatoes in the glowing coals with a pair of metal tongs. It is a miracle, said Amos, and Pa said, I'll be danged, boy, if you and Amos cain't cook good as any woman.

Within a month, Pa had two others living with him, one a real deserter, the other one Fred Hintner's pa, who said, God strike me dead, but I will never fight for that Jeff Davis who took my boy away and slaughtered him.

CHAPTER EIGHTEEN

❧

Plunged into the swamp of other people's need, Eugenia found Aunt Baker had been right: the best cure for a sore heart is useful work. *Do not think about Papa, do not think about Mama, or Tilda, or some imaginary child she might have had, put Tom from your mind.*

Morning to night she threw herself into her tasks, wrapping broken heads and kicked-in ribs, packing fevered men in compresses, dosing them with quinine, picking buckshot out of shattered flesh, setting dislocated thumbs and shoulders, soothing panic-stricken runaways. And despite the running sores, the running bowels, the coughing and the vomiting and the smell of rotting flesh, despite the early mornings when a patient stiffened and grew cold, she was surprised to find she came downstairs each day impatient to get started, loving it almost, this constant tussling with death, this urgent, urgent need to win, the triumph when she did.

At night, with Alouette or Henry supervising in the cellar, she sat at the desk up in her room, spread out notepaper and pen and ink, and wrote letters one by one to soldiers from North Carolina—*Come home, this is a rich man's war, a poor man's fight, come home, we will protect you*—drawing a line through the name of each recruit when she had finished with his letter. Inside each, she included a length of bright red string. *Wear this in your lapel.*

Two nights a week, a group of Red Strings gathered in the parlor, the murmur of their voices coming from behind the heavy door. Eugenia did not join them, although she grew to know some of the faces going in and out and to respond to the greeting "United we stand" with "Divided we fall." Aunt Baker said she might attend if she insisted, but there were things it was better for her not to know; it was best to keep the secrets of a secret society split between its members. From this Eugenia understood that the Red String hospital was known only to a few.

Sometimes, writing letters in her room with the burr of voices underneath her feet, she would think about the Red Strings planning their conspiracies in other parlors, other towns, maybe other states, and the sensation would come over her of being part of something larger than herself, her happiness and suffering just a small part of the happiness and suffering of a threatened nation. When a new patient arrived and she found he had deserted, she would draw her breath in hard and ask if he had got a letter from a Red String. The answer was not often yes, but when it was, she would look up at the Stars and Stripes slung on the wall and feel patriotic and expanded. Sometimes she would take his hand and kiss him, gently and a little dramatically, on the forehead. "I am your guardian angel," she would say. "I am going to make you well."

Behind her, Dr. Kinney's steady, reassuring presence, his uncanny way of showing up just when she needed him, his discreet, soft-footed vanishings and reappearings. And behind Dr. Kinney, like a solid bolster, Aunt Baker's stern, unflagging strength, with such a well of kindness underneath that no matter who came bleeding to her gate, the bucket would go down into the depths and come back full. Eugenia marveled, and modeled herself on her.

Henry too became a steady presence at her back. At first he had watched her with a dubious eye, as though expecting her at any moment to toss aside her bandages and medicines and go off in search of less demanding work, but as the weeks and months went by and she gave no indication of frivolity, his attitude began to change.

What finally cemented them together was the cellar chimney. Having been hastily dug out to join the chimney of the kitchen, it did not draw right, and from time to time the cellar would fill up with a bitter blueness, causing Eugenia's patients to burst out in coughing fits and their eyes to run. Then she would ring the bell up to the kitchen and Henry would arrive to lift back the heavy trapdoors and prop open the sunporch door. This would cause a rush of air up the stairway from the cellar and before long the blueness would turn clear again. This happened so often that she and Henry got the remedy down pat and the two of them developed the sort of easygoing camaraderie that collusion in a tricky project brings.

As for Alouette, Aunt Baker had been right about her too: Eugenia grew fond of her, although she never really grew to know her. Bright-eyed and chirpy, she hummed and sang about the house morning till night, took on the basest tasks with no word of complaint, was always at Eugenia's elbow when she needed her, and was never in the way when the need for solitude came over her. And yet she never spoke about herself or where she came from, always slipped away from questions with a smile, the sudden need to stir a pot or weed the vegetable garden. When Eugenia asked Aunt Baker for her history, Aunt Baker simply smiled and said, "My dear, if she wants to tell you, she will tell you," which Eugenia, thinking of Didema Ware, took as a rebuke. On the other hand, she found it comforting: she could trust Aunt Baker with her life, she knew it.

EACH morning Alouette and Henry stood together in the pantry, examining the shelves. Then Henry headed off to town, to see what was for sale that day and to jostle with the crowds that swarmed about the telegraph office and the *Carolina Watchman* building, clamorous for news. When he came home, full- or empty-handed as his luck might have been that day, Aunt Baker would sit down on whatever was available—a bed, a chair, the corner of a step, a stump out in the yard—and setting both her hands against her knees as though to brace herself for what would come, "What is the news today?" she would inquire, or, if he brought with him a copy of the *Watchman*, "What does the paper say today?"

At first, supplies could easily be found, although the price of coffee, sugar, and other luxuries had quickly grown enormous. Now, though, as eighteen sixty-one turned into eighteen sixty-two, with no end to the war in sight, salt rocketed from ten to fifteen dollars a sack to twenty-eight. The Northern blockade had begun to take its toll.

Each day Henry brought reports of new alarms about the lack of lamp oil, tallow, firewood, medicines, the soaring price of flour and meal. Meat of any sort became so hard to come by that even a pig's knuckle with its surface turning green was welcomed to the kettle Alouette kept stewing on the stove. Every spare minute they spent in cultivation of the vegetable garden, but the minute their little crop was harvested, here came the Home Guard, demanding rations for the troops. What remained of greens and turnips and sweet potatoes vanished down into the cellar as though sucked into the gullet of the earth.

Clothing, cloth, leather to make shoes, all fell into short supply, and Eugenia found herself presented with a problem: how to come by sufficient shirts and boots and coats and hats and trousers in which to clothe departing patients?

The Red Strings solved her problem by carrying off boots from the military boot factory and bolts of shirt linen or gray wool cloth from the military warehouses. Each time a bolt of cloth appeared, usually at night, Dr. Kinney's smiling lady friend appeared behind it. Eugenia knew her name now, Ruth Louise. She came cloaked and wrapped and bonneted, a couple of similarly furtive women at her back. Within minutes the bolt would be divided up and the three of them would vanish just as furtively as they had come, each with a length of cloth inside her cloak, which she would carry home and set to work on in secret, sewing clothes to dress Eugenia's patients. Many mornings Aunt Baker and Alouette appeared heavy-eyed and weary after cutting cloth and sewing all night long, their arms full of offcuts to be ripped and rolled into new bandages.

And so, as each new group of patients was ready to move on, new clothes would be produced, food bundled into packages, and one night, in the tiny hours, Henry would shepherd them up the ladder to the sunporch. Soon a shadowy figure would creep through the side gate, a pattern of soft knocking on the sunporch door, then the low voice of the guide giving them instructions for the journey west.

One night, standing with Aunt Baker at the gate, watching another group vanish into the darkness of the woods across the lane, Eugenia said, "Aunt Baker, I've never asked you this before, but I do wonder. Why is it you do this work?"

Aunt Baker twitched her shawl closer round her shoulders and took a long time answering. "My son. I do it for my son."

"A son? I didn't know you had a son."

"Henry hasn't mentioned it?"

"Henry doesn't mention anything unless he is obliged to."

"He died at the first battle of Bull Run. His head was blown off by a cannonball."

Eugenia drew a sharp breath, setting her hand against her mouth. "How do you bear it?"

"I do not bear it. I do not sit about and mourn. Instead, I work to save the sons of other mothers. That's why I became a Red String. That's why I do everything I do."

"You are a saint."

Aunt Baker laughed abruptly, pulling at the gate to test the latch. "His name was Conrad. He was a young hotspur and thought it was a nice big thing to get into the service. I said to him, 'But we are abolitionists, we do not hold with slavery. Why would you want to go off fighting to preserve it?' He would not listen, he simply would not listen. It was during the first glorious flush of war. Gala balls were being held, patriotic speeches made. Everybody was enlisting. Many of us tried to reason with our sons, but once a young man's blood is up for battle, only God can stop him, and God chose to stay his hand. I am no pacifist. We must fight when we must. And so I took to fighting in my own way, for the safety of other mothers' sons."

She turned, her breath brushing the fine hairs of Eugenia's cheek. "I'm not sure I am succeeding. There are so many dead, so many grieving mothers. But I'm sorry. I am preaching. The night grows chilly and you are fatigued. We must get you off to bed."

• • •

NOTEPAPER and ink were eaten by the war as well. When Eugenia's supply for writing to the troops ran out, she wrote in pencil on whatever paper came to hand. When no more pencils could be had, she sharpened a stick and held it in her candle and wrote to them in charcoal on the blank leaves of Aunt Baker's books. When all Aunt Baker's books were rummaged through, she looked around her in frustration. Where to get more paper?

It was then that she discovered God, or at least the Bible. Since Bibles could no longer be purchased from the Union— "The hardened Yankees have declared them contraband of war," an outraged letter to the editor complained—the citizens of Salisbury had formed a Bible Society and were busy printing their own. Volunteers were needed. Eugenia volunteered. Once a week, on Wednesday afternoon, she left her patients with Aunt Baker and set off for the printing office, coming home with a heavy swing to her skirts from the purloined paper stuffed into the pockets she had sewn into her petticoat.

How the printers kept coming up with paper she had no idea, but if a shortage threatened, the Bible Society called a prayer meeting and pretty soon more reams of paper would appear. Eugenia felt no compunction about stealing paper from the Lord. He seemed to have enough. And since he had stood aside while men were led into the path of danger, surely it was up to him to lead them out.

Aunt Baker, having given the matter its due thought, came to much the same conclusion. "My dear," she said, "if the Lord looks down and sees what you are up to when the printers' backs are turned, he will surely look the other way," smiling as she spoke, albeit warily, as if the recording angel might be taking down her words.

• • •

ONE afternoon, Eugenia left the printing office and set out for home. A chilly wind was blowing and she clutched her cloak around her with her arms crossed on her breast. Today she had succeeded in making off with more paper than usual and she walked slowly, exchanging signals with Red Strings she recognized from the meetings at Aunt Baker's—right hand, with third and fourth fingers closed, held up to the mouth, answered by a left forefinger to the corner of a left eye—nervously aware of the purloined freight swinging underneath her skirts.

Salisbury had become a noisy, bustling place, a constant turmoil of activity. Not only were troops garrisoned here to guard the prison, but the intersection of two railroads made the town a perfect place for the storage of government supplies, with more troops to manage and protect them. Workers in the military shoe and clothing factories—old men, one-legged one-eyed veterans, young boys, women—went back and forth in shifts. Whores, who seemed to multiply like flies, went about their trade, while drunkards and nefarious characters wandered the streets, picking pockets, begging from the passersby, leaving their filth behind them on the streets. Amongst them, dogs wandered in and out, pissing against walls and snuffling in discarded trash. Bits of dried-out dung and straw and scraps of paper swirled along the street, creeping into storefronts and tangling in fences. Here a bottle rolled click-click-click until a beggar picked it up and carried it away.

With all this going on, Eugenia went unchallenged through the streets, past the mob gathered to complain about high prices and extortion, the way the Yankee blockade made everything from sewing needles to scythe blades unavailable. Past the warehouses and train yards churning with insistent hoot and clamor, on toward the military prison where children shouted, tossing scraps of food across the palisade, and good Christian women lined up at the gate with tobacco and sweet potato pies to exchange with the prisoners for trinkets carved from wood and bone, where alarms real and imagined kept the guards and town authorities in a blather of harassment and concern.

As she put the prison at her back, and then the last house of the town, Eugenia grew more confident and lengthened her stride, her loaded petticoat bumping up against her legs. The wind blew stronger out here in the open, and although she walked with vigor, she felt a cold flush coming on her cheeks. She hurried on.

But now, approaching her, a horse, a man she seemed to recognize smiling at her crooked-mouthed. He wore the flattish, brimmed hat of a cavalryman and a heavy, dun-colored military cloak fell from his shoulders across the horse's rump. He held a musket in the crook of his left arm and with his right hand he controlled his horse.

"We meet again," he said when he got close.

Eugenia stopped, conscious of the heavy forward movement of her skirts, and stared at him, her memory sifting for his face.

Now he was right above her. "Miss Spotswood, am I right?"

She nodded, making as though to pass, but he moved his horse to block her. "Not so fast, there, not so fast." With one finger he tipped back his hat. "Happen you don't remember me—Ned Tarkel? You once complained to me about a tin of stolen gold."

Sandy hair straggled at his neck, the same sand color as his beard and eyes, his face intimate and goatish, that same look Eugenia remembered when he licked his pencil in the foyer of the Mansion House Hotel, his eyes traveling on her, up and down.

"Oh," she said. "You were the constable."

"Never did find that there thief of yourn. Evaporated clean away. Strange the way that happens." He pulled his hat back down and leaned toward her, speaking in a confidential tone. "So what've you been getting up to?"

Eugenia drew herself up tall and looked him in the eye. "I

am going home, sir. I have been doing the Lord's work for the Bible Society, and now I am going home for supper. I am living with—"

"I know who you're living with. I've kept my eye on you." He rocked back in his saddle. "You're living with that Yankee nigger, no?"

"I live with Mrs. Baker. Mrs. Adeline Baker. She is—"

"I know who Mrs. Baker is. The judge's widow." He hesitated, smirking. "Died a couple years back."

"You seem to know everything, sir."

He said nothing, just looked down at her with that half-leering smile, and then—*do not do it, do not do it*—he was reaching down his hand, offering to haul her up behind him on the horse, to carry her back home.

She stepped away. "Why, sir."

"Come, Miss Spotswood. I represent the law. I'll not hurt you." His voice became wheedling and he pushed his face toward her in its flat-brimmed hat. "You have no suitor, no young man, no one to walk out with?"

"No, sir." She saw his eyes narrow and light up. "But I am engaged, sir, to be married."

His face darkened and he laughed, an outward snort of sudden foulness. "Little lying whore."

Eugenia dropped her eyes, shivering so hard she could scarcely keep her jaw under control, and it came to her that she was truly frightened for the first time in her life. She had been nervous, fearful, sometimes had been close to panic, but this was new, this flat red of her rising blood, like a wall she had run into, robbing her of thought, of breath, of movement, like a dream of running, running, getting nowhere.

She did keep moving, though, her legs carrying her one step and then one step, getting nowhere still, because each time she took a step, Ned Tarkel's horse, while seeming not to move, was there in front of her, the rough cloth of Ned Tarkel's knee against her temple, his boot against her arm, a gentle, threatening pressure. And his voice, cajoling, mocking, imminent. She dared not look at him. His face insisted.

She wanted to be brave, to knock him from his horse and grind his leering face into the road, but she just stood there like a bird before a snake, and turned and turned into his horse, his leg, his triumphant male smell.

And then the roll of wheels, the hollow clopping of a horse's hooves on dirt, and Henry's voice. "Leave her be, Ned Tarkel. Leave her be."

Ned Tarkel turned. He gathered up his phlegm, a rough bubbling sound, and spat onto the dirt. "So it's the Yankee nigger come to save his little whore."

Henry ignored him, looking at Eugenia. "Come," he said.

And somehow, afterwards she could not remember how, she was in Aunt Baker's gig, Aunt Baker's horse rolling its shiny big black haunches up ahead. Beside her, Henry, his voice low and consoling, Ned Tarkel's coarse voice calling out behind, "You ain't seen the back of me yet, little nigger whore."

"Hush, hush," Henry said. "Ignore him, just ignore him."

"How can you bear it, Henry? How can you bear to live here when people treat you so? Why don't you go back to Boston? Why does Aunt Baker stay?"

"You know why she stays. As for me, I stay here to protect her."

"Protect? From whom? Is she in danger?"

"Perhaps. Perhaps not. You know her husband was a judge?"

"I didn't, not until today. Ned Tarkel told me."

"He sent Ned's father to the lockup. Five years for horse stealing. He died in there."

"I see."

Henry said nothing, flicking at the reins.

"Henry? What is it? What?"

He reached behind the seat. "Here, tuck this blanket round your knees. You are quite blue with cold."

"You have to tell me."

"All right then, I will tell you. The judge was shot. In his own garden. Murdered."

Eugenia drew her breath in hard. Somehow she had known this all along. No, not known, but sensed that deep beneath Aunt Baker's terse efficient surface, beneath her grief about her son, something other, something dark and wounded, thrashed. She half glanced across her shoulder. "The killer was Ned Tarkel? Why did he not swing?"

"There is no proof."

"It is too much. She has sacrificed too much."

"You must not speak of it to Adeline."

TWO days later, the Home Guard came and impressed Aunt Baker's horse. Five men came together. They did not so much as rap against the door or give notice of their intention, but simply set to at the barn like common thieves, and when they had failed to break the padlocked chain securing its door, took to ripping out the planks and tossing them about until half of one side was gone. They led the horse out, and when Henry ran out to prevent them, knocked him to the ground and spat on him, standing in a circle. Ned Tarkel was not with them, but Eugenia knew he was behind it, that he had sent them on account of her.

"Go back where you came from, Yankee nigger, afore we take and sell you like a nigger should be sold."

And Henry flat out on the ground, spittle running on his

face, and nothing, not a thing, Aunt Baker or Eugenia could do to help him, Alouette in tears behind. Then the five men rode off with the horse.

One day, said Eugenia's trembling blood, *one day, Ned Tarkel, you will pay for this.*

CHAPTER NINETEEN

⚭

TOM was now a turpentiner. Hiram, the crew boss, had put a roundshave in his hand and said he was a chipper. "Like this," he said, "and this, to make the sap run free," and showed him how to score a tree above the pouch to keep its pores from clogging with dried sap.

All day Tom went ahead of Ben and Peter, his footsteps muffled on the sandy trails, sinking the sharp curved knife into the long-leaf pines, just far enough but not so far that he would damage them. Young trees he scored down low, older ones above where they had been scored the year before. Sometimes an old tree had a makeshift wooden ladder propped against it and he would climb it to get above the old scores and make the new ones for this year. In some sections he carried the ladder on his shoulder because all the trees were old.

The work was hard and long, and yet he felt safe in this enormous forest with its sandy ridges and its throbbing swamps, its row on row of straight black trunks that seemed to go forever between solid-looking rays of sun. No patrollers came riding through with whips and guns, no militia drummed their heels across a dusty mustering ground, no overseer shouted in his face. While the gold mine had been a constant loud tumultuous racket, here his thoughts were broken only by the call of birds, the hum of insects, the occasional brief encounter with a poor white hunter or a Negro runaway.

The sand along the trails was whitish, sometimes tending into yellow, like gold dust spread across the forest floor. It made him want to run his hands down into it and scoop it up and hide the whole lot in his hair. Sometimes a pine snake reared up from the trail, hissing at him with its head gone flat, its tail vibrating like a rattler. Sometimes a gleaming green or golden beetle skittered off in front of him, a dragonfly with a quivering blue body and flashing, silver wings. Sometimes, from a thicket, a bird looked boldly at him out of one side of its head, then turned to look out of the other eye, as though it needed to look twice to make sure it would know him in the future. He drank from narrow streams of water clear as glass, and learned to carry in his pocket a hollow reed through which, if he felt out of sorts, he drank the rain caught in a pine tree's pouch, screwing his face up at the taste while he felt it cleaning out his liver and restoring him to health.

For the first time in his life, he found that he looked forward to the company of other men. His day's work done, he met up with Ben and Peter and they went fishing in the lake or trapped the quail that whistled *bobwhite bobwhite* as they scuttled through the undergrowth. They lit a fire and cooked, and talked into the night, sharing jokes and stories and complaints and rumors of the war. When the fire died down, they slept beside it on the ground, or if it rained, under crude shelters made of rusted iron sheets propped up with branches.

Small turpentiners' cabins were strewn throughout the forest, but they were squatted in by poor white families, men who toted guns and hunted in the forest, their cage-ribbed dogs slinking at their heels, their wives dried up, clay-chewing women with the shakes, their children wild and sly-eyed, running about half naked while their mothers scratched out gardens for a little corn, some cowpeas, collard greens.

Tom asked Peter why the turpentiners didn't hunt the poor whites out and take the cabins back.

Peter spat. "Don't want no trouble with them ol' good-for-nothin' trash. Mr. Avery, he know they here. He make a deal with them to keep a fire watch in exchange for living in a cabin, but they never does. Any fire starts up we beat it out ourselves. Don't pay them folks no nevermind. No point gettin' crosswise when the other feller's got a gun."

EACH Friday Tom was paid. At noon he waited for the mule cart to come by, loaded this time not with barrels but with other workers, materialized out of the forest like spirits of the trees, roundshaves and gum ladles swinging from their belts, calculations in their heads. Jammed together in the cart, they swayed and rattled down into the shallow valley where, as they approached, other mule carts joined them, heading toward the chimney of the turpentine distillery, which rose brick red between the trees, unfurling smoke into the sky.

The distillery was a wooden structure with the look of something improvised and hasty. It housed a copper still inside a red-brick furnace with an open wooden platform up above, and at each corner of the platform, four jake-leg posts holding up an angled wooden roof. On one side, on the ground, a stack of turpentine-filled barrels waited to be hauled down to the river. On the other side, a windmill clacked above a huffing force pump.

A wooden trough ran from a spigot at the bottom of the still to the clearing's edge, where it leaked above a lake of residue, deep red and glair, shot through with bluish greenish facets, like an enormous gemstone rising from the earth. And over everything, the smell of fumes that stung the eyes.

In the clearing around the distillery, in no discernible arrangement, were other buildings, all with the same rickety, half-ruined look: the cooperage, the sheds for storing split-oak hoops and timber for the barrels, the glue house where the insides of the casks were sealed, stables for the mules, the plantation store, the payhouse.

Payment of the men was supervised by one of Mr. Avery's sons, an arrogant young dandy by the name of Zebulon. On account of the twenty Negro law, he did not have to go to war, but came on Friday afternoon, the walnut handle of a Walker Colt jerking on his hip, to pay the workers, both the white men and the slaves who had made above their quota for the week. He brought with him a dignified old Negro whom he addressed as Uncle Phillip.

Master Zebulon did not speak directly to the workers, nor actually hand the money out. This was done by Uncle Phillip, who sat at a plank table outside the payhouse while Master Zebulon, coat turned back to show his pistol, watched across his shoulder, eyeing each man as he came, smacking his riding crop into his palm as though he would as soon lash out at him as pay him.

Since he was a subhire and not recorded on the books, Tom did not line up at the table, but waited out of sight for Hiram to come and peel off a few notes from his own week's pay. While the other workers lounged about the grounds of the distillery, or spent their entire week's pay in one fell swoop at the plantation store, Tom slipped back into the forest, made his way to where his gold was hidden in a hollow log, drew it out, wrapped the new notes with it, and then slid it back.

But one day a gray fox made its nest inside the log, so he changed his hiding place to a high-up hollow that had been carved out by a woodpecker, climbing up to it on one of the makeshift wooden ladders. He made a picture in his head of where it was so he would not forget, and did not keep his freedom paper there, but always in the pocket of his shirt.

The only soul he told about his hiding place was Ben, making him swear that he would use the gold to take care of his mother if he should come to a bad end. It was not that he distrusted Peter, just that he figured telling more than one was risky, and of the two, Ben, with all his praying, would be frightened the Lord would burn him up in hell if he did not keep his word.

FALL came. Hiram, the crew boss, took away Tom's roundshave and gave him a long, narrow-bladed axe, telling him he had to be a hacker now and open a new section of pines. Seven or eight slanted slashes like the whiskers of a cat down into the trunk a handsbreadth above the ground, then hollow out a pouch and notch the corners so the sap would flow toward the center.

Within a week, Tom was expert at laying on the strokes and spent all winter going tree to tree in a section from the track where the boy came with the mule carts, to the creek below the marsh, then along the ridge behind the creek, on down to the river, then along another ridge and back down to the road. He had to make one hundred twenty-five new pockets every day, and because of it he learned to count that much higher than he could before.

Spring came, and summer, and the pine sap flowed again, thick, sticky, golden as the sun. Tom traded axe for roundshave and once more became a chipper.

• • •

FOR the past few months, a Negro waterman named Robert had been making secret visits in the night to Mr. Avery's plantation. Robert used to be a flatboatman, poling barrels on the Neuse River, but now he lived in a town called New Bern, which he said had fallen into Union hands. Instead of poling barrels, he worked as an agitator for the Union army, going out into the countryside to encourage slaves to leave their masters. He brought with him a sense of boldness and reports about the war, how Abe Lincoln was all set to free the slaves, how runaways from the plantations crowded in the streets of New Bern and were given jobs so they could help to win the freedom war.

In the dim flicker of the firelight, he spoke of North and South, of the Rebels and the Yankees, the Confederacy and the Union, of generals named Lee and Grant and Sherman, one with the odd name Stone Wall, and another called Beast Butler. He spoke of battles fought in places Tom had never heard of—Fort Pillow, Cross Keys, Savage Station, White Oak Swamp, Bull Run—running the names easily off his tongue as if they were old friends. He said there were two presidents now, Abe Lincoln in Washington, who was for the North and figured he was for the South as well, and Jefferson Davis in Richmond, who was for the South alone and hang the North. He said the war was like a competition to see which one would win, and whoever did would be the boss.

Tom tried to understand his talk about secession but he could not get a picture in his head of what it looked like, although he did know that a war meant a crowd of people fighting with each other and a winner in the end. He figured if the Yankees won, it wouldn't matter if the hatted man had lied or not, his mother would be free.

Robert had a deep low voice and an almost white man's face, but with a head of hair as black and tightly curled as any Negro's. It made Tom shiver to look at him, he was so white, and yet at the same time so black, as though God had got confused when he created him.

"I can take you down the river to New Bern," said Robert. "You can be a free man, Tom."

"I already a free man. I got my freedom paper from Miss Genie."

Robert looked at him sorrowfully. "Ah, Tom," he said. "You think that freedom paper mean any sort o' tiny thing? The white man want you for a slave, he take you for a slave, freedom paper or no freedom paper. Why that paper of yourn might's well be a recipe for pickles or plum jam for all the white man care. You sit here on your backside, tellin' me you a free man, but I say, you want freedom, boy? You got to do somethin' about it. Freedom ain't some gift this Miss Genie lady give you. It ain't no gift at all. You got to hunt it down and catch it. You got to snatch it in your hand. Did no one tell you that before?"

Seeing he was getting nowhere with this line of argument, Robert shifted tactics. "You got a mother somewhere, yes? You think the good Lord want her die a slave? She goin' to if the South done has its way." His voice became cajoling. "Come on with me to New Bern, Tom, help the Yankees win this war. Think about your mother, boy. You want never see her face again on 'count o' you don't dare?"

Tom shifted uneasily, his face gone stubborn. "I can see about my mother my own self."

One night Ben looked up at the moon above the treetops, a corncob in his hand and his mouth half full of chewed-up corn. "Dear Lord," he said, "dear Jesus Lord, I hear you, and I gonna do it. Next time he come, I gonna do it."

Tom and Peter looked at him. "Do what?" Peter said.

"Gonna run. Gonna go on down the river with that Robert to New Bern, help them Yankees win the war. Yes, Lord, I gonna be a free man."

"You goin' do that, are you? Well," said Peter. And he went on spooning sorghum mash into his mouth.

Ben turned to Tom. "You comin'?"

Tom shook his head. "I'se a free man already now."

PETER left a few days after Ben. That night it rained. It rained all week and all the next. The swamps rose, and to keep from floating off at night, Tom climbed into the lower branches of a tree to sleep. When the water ceased to rush and settled down into the swamps, it massed with tiny wriggling shapes. Soon mosquitoes rose up every evening in a cloud. To keep them off, Tom rubbed his skin with gum so that he glowed like a man preserved in amber, and insects stuck against his arms and neck, waving their tiny frantic legs until they died. At night, when he went down to the lake and swam, the gum stayed stuck to him, and when he rose up at the water's edge, luminous fine algae slipped and shifted off him so that he seemed to be a bright god rising underneath the moon.

One by one the other turpentiners fled or drifted off or went with Robert to New Bern, and down at the distillery the Negroes vanished one by one. The whole world seemed on the move, the very woods seemed restless, as though the trees themselves would take off to join the Yankees. Even the poor white trash had gone, the women and the wild-haired children too, leaving their cabin doors aswing and their dooryards strewn with the detritus of their lives, old pots and kettles with the bottoms rusted out, a broken chair, a twig broom with no handle, a barrel with its sides sprung out.

From time to time the heavy boom of cannon resounded in the distance, and when an old branch gave way, cracking and smacking its way to earth, it seemed to Tom to be the sound of musket fire. Sometimes Miss Genie would come walking down the rows of pines, her arms held out toward him. "Tom, I am your friend, I love you. There, I've said it now." Sometimes the figure walking through the pines would be the hatted man, blood as thick as pine gum oozing underneath his hat. He would be telling something in a blurry voice and if the wind was blowing in the treetops, Tom would fancy that he heard his mother weeping. Behind the hatted man, he would see confusion in the air, unseen images of battle, the slap and roar of guns, and unhappiness would come down on his head.

On unhappy days he would think about Ben and Peter in New Bern, and Robert who had promised he would come to the landing dock in the dark of each new moon and look for him. Maybe he should go off down the river to New Bern and help the Yankees win the war. But after a while his head would get roiled up in confusion. "I'se a free man," he would say. "No call to run off anywheres," his voice loud and truculent, blurting out of him as if he would convince himself. Then he would slash a tree too deep, and slash again, and make a mess of it, and cry, with pity for himself and for the tree, which had not done him wrong. He began to watch the moon.

ONE morning Tom awoke with his decision made. Tonight he would slip off to the river in the darkness of no moon. He did no work that day, just wandered in the forest, kicking at the sand. Later, just before he left, he would go and get his gold.

The plantation bell began to ring at noon, the sound traveling easily through the dry, still air. The clanging made an agitation start up in Tom's head. It made him think of hard-faced men with muskets in their hands. It rang all afternoon. When at last it stopped, he set off to retrieve his gold. It was early yet, but he would wait beside the river, hidden in the undergrowth.

He had just started out, when he heard the padding sound of

hooves on sand and Uncle Phillip appeared out of a side trail with a rifle slung across his shoulder. "Hey, you there," he said.

Tom braced to run.

"Don't run," said Uncle Phillip. "I ain't goin' hurt you. I'se jest sposed to round you up."

"What you goin' do with me?"

"Show you to Mr. Avery, I guess. He wants to know how many turpentiners left. Cotton niggers been runnin' off, house servants too, so Mr. Avery, he makes a plan to round up everyone what's left and ship 'em west outa temptation's way, to near Raleigh somewheres or to Hillsborough. Soon's they hear that, all the rest jump up and run off, ever last one o' them 'ceptin' me and ol' Thrasher who got the rheumatiz so bad he couldn't jump up fast enough to go to heaven."

"Why you not run off too?"

"Figure I'se too old. I sposed to round up all the turpentiners."

"Ain't no turpentiners. They all gone."

Uncle Phillip spat. "You don't say so? Then I'll just round you up and take you in one man alone."

"I'se a free man," Tom said. "You cain't round me up."

"Gotta come back with somethin' and so far you's all I got."

"I'se a free man, don't belong to Mr. Avery."

Uncle Phillip unslung the rifle from his shoulder. "Come on now, you be good. I got this here gun and I sposed to show back up with somethin'. When Mr. Avery seen you, you can go along. Come on now, I ain't gonna hurt you, jest show you off a spell."

MR. Avery was waiting for them on his horse in the empty yard of the distillery. He was a big man, not young, but handsome, with a well-made wide straw hat and highly polished spurs. In one hand he held the reins, and in the other a silver-mounted, double-barreled shotgun. It was the first time Tom had seen him. He had seen his house once, when he was not used to the forest and broke out to a field of cotton with workers going down the rows in broken-down straw hats. Beyond the field, a high brick house with a side porch and a chimney at each end stood with an air of neat, clean confidence in a garden filled with flowers.

Thinking of it, Tom felt a strange and forcible emotion take him, as though a hand had seized him by the gut. It seemed to him he recognized this Mr. Avery, not his face, but the air he had about him of a man accustomed all his life to getting his own way. Now he had been crossed he wore a curious expression, half anger, half incredulity, with a little fear mixed in, enough to make him dangerous. It was the expression Mr. Morgan used to wear before he ordered up a whipping, and Tom felt a cringing sensation start up in his neck. He looked down at the ground. But then he thought about the freedom paper in the pocket of his shirt and lifted up his head, looking sternly at the air in front of him.

Mr. Avery did not look at Tom, but back behind him with a waiting air, moving his head from side to side and stretching out his neck as though expecting to see someone else appear out of the woods. When no one did, he said, one eye still on the trees, "Why, Uncle Phillip, I am disappointed in you. I know you are no woods rider, but is this all you could find?"

"They's all gone, marse. Ain't no more left. Jest this'n."

Blood crept up Mr. Avery's neck. He turned aside and coughed as though struggling to control himself. "This isn't one of mine. Who is he?"

"Some hire. Says he's got his freedom paper."

Mr. Avery's face swelled and the red flush on his neck crept up onto his jaw. "Who are you, boy?"

"Tom, sir. The crew boss, Hiram, he done took me on."

"Did he now? And where is Hiram?"

"Don't know, sir. Run off I guess."

"And the other turpentiners?"

Tom shifted nervously, glancing up at Uncle Phillip, who looked back down at him with a look of wry amusement on his face.

"Well? Don't just stand there. Answer me, boy."

"I'se all there be, sir."

"When did they go? Last night? This morning?"

"No, sir, I been alone awhiles."

"And why, pray, have you not run off with the rest?"

"I'se a free man, sir. Just couldn't make my mind up to it."

Uncle Phillip laughed, a low, unexpected sound. Mr. Avery swung on him, red now past the hairline. His voice, though, was even and controlled. "You knew about this, didn't you? You let them go. You closed your eyes to it. I trusted you, Uncle Phillip, and you have let me down." He jerked the barrel of his gun at Tom. "Well, then, we must make do with what we have."

"Cain't do that, boss, less'n he agrees to it. This man got his freedom paper."

"Does he indeed?" Mr. Avery held out his hand to Uncle Phillip. "So let me see this . . . freedom paper," dragging the words out in a scornful drawl.

Tom fumbled in his pocket and held it out.

Mr. Avery ignored him, holding out his hand to Uncle Phillip, who hesitated and then took the paper and handed it across. Tom's insides twitched. He felt proud and nervous and curiously exalted. It was the first time he had showed his freedom paper to a living soul.

Mr. Avery read it with a serious face. He turned it over, turned it back, and read it through again. He gave it a flick and let it droop against his thigh, looking at Uncle Phillip.

"This thing isn't legal. It's just a letter signed by somebody whose name I cannot read."

"Miss Genie signed it," Tom said. "Miss Eugenia Mae Spotswood. I belonged to her."

"Uncle Phillip," Mr. Avery said, "tell this foolish boy a freedom paper is a court certificate signed by a judge. That is the law."

Dismay rose up in Tom like sickness. He seemed to hear the hatted man: *They done made a law.*

"And anyway," Mr. Avery went on, "the date is clear. Did no one tell this boy he had ninety days to leave the state?" He flicked the paper. "This thing is a year old. Even if it were legal, he has overstayed his welcome. Uncle Phillip, take him in."

"Don't rightly like to do that, marse. Less'n he agrees to it."

"Agrees? Who are you to say he should agree? You let my Negroes wander off and tell me nothing of it, and now you tell me I must ask permission of this boy before setting him to do a few odd jobs? What has happened to you, Uncle? I have known you almost all my life. I've trusted you with my affairs. I've sat in the same church on Sunday and listened to the same lessons, sung the same hymns. You've always been a God-fearing man and a good servant. I've never had to punish you or whip you. But now you take it upon yourself to give me lectures, as though you have forgotten all civility. Or are you no longer in favor of civility, Uncle Phillip?"

With one finger, the old man tilted back his hat. "Guess the only thing I be in favor of is freedom." He gathered up his phlegm in a considering way and spat onto the ground. "And by the way, I ain't your uncle nohow, never were."

As Mr. Avery's gun came up, Tom turned and ran. He heard the explosion and the thump of Uncle Phillip's body falling to the ground. He did not look back, just ran without stopping until he was deep inside the woods.

• • •

HE had meant to run away, just purely run away, but his breath kept stopping him. His heart was jumping in his throat and his head felt as though it would explode. He stopped to vomit and it cleared his head, then headed on toward the river.

Almost there, he stopped again, sweat running in his armpits and his thoughts awry. There was something he must do, but he could not think of it. He beat his fist into his palm and shook his head. His gold, yes, that was it, he had to fetch his gold. He swung around and headed back the way he had just come.

At his tree, he stopped, looking about him for a ladder, but there was none. He ran on down the row of pines and came back with one slung across his shoulder. This he propped against the trunk and scrambled up, counting rungs, stopping on eleven, then thrust his hand into the hole. Withdrew it empty. Looked around, confused. Wrong tree, he must have the wrong tree.

But the next tree, which had a hole at the same height, was empty too, and the next one had no hole. He went along the row, then shook his head and turned the other way. But though he found a dozen holes, not one held any cloth-wrapped package, and the light was fading fast.

Frantic, he skidded back and forth, trying this tree and another until at last he flung the ladder down, sobbing now, wracking his brains for someone to whom he had let slip his hiding place, or someone who had spied on him. His mind avoided Ben, but when at last no other culprit could be seized on, he sat down with his back against a tree and cried into his hands.

NOW he was headed back toward the river. The sun's last afterlight had faded and there was no moon, but he knew the trails so well he had no need of it, running hard on the soft sand.

Soon he heard the low hum of the river up ahead, caught the slightly rotten smell of mud exposed, and heard the click of frogs.

He topped the steep embankment and hesitated, peering through the overhanging trees to the narrow strip of water down below. A fire glittered and he smelled food cooking. Voices murmured.

A great rush of relief came out of him, and without a warning shout, he went scrambling down the slope beside the wooden barrel chute.

Three figures, a woman and two men, squatted on the near edge of the dried-out mudflat, eating around the fire. At Tom's approach, all three swung upright, as though he had stepped on the hinge of a trap and it had sprung.

"It's only me—Tom," he whispered, the sound of his voice loud and traveling in the silence.

Robert said nothing, just watched him come across the mud, and when he was close, smacked his hand against his thigh. "Well," he said, turning his voice across his shoulder to the other two, "looks like we done got ourselves another Union man."

CHAPTER TWENTY

TOM had not been on a boat before. The sensation of it frightened and excited him, the way the water slipped and slipped away, the skidding forward across rustling dark, the muffled dip and thrusting of the pole. From low sedgy banks came sudden squeaks and splashings, and overhead, cypresses and water oaks locked branches across the narrow, twisting river, making the night so black that when he turned to his companions in the boat, he could not make out their faces.

The couple, Harriett and James, had with them a baby and a little child, boy or girl Tom could not tell, it was so dark. The boat rode heavy, the water just below his fingertips, and they had gone a long way before he brought his mind back onto Ben.

"Robert," he said at last, "that Ben, what he be doin' these days?"

Robert chuckled. "He doin' the Lord's work at the Baptist church, helpin' out the preacher. He runs the prayer meetin' every Wednesday night, and another one on Sunday. He can shout and holler to the Lord anytime he fancies and get paid for it as well."

"Oh," Tom said, and sat there puzzling on how a man could shout and holler to the Lord knowing he had stolen someone's gold. Ben must be very wicked after all.

Gradually the river widened, the overhanging branches drew back on either side, blackness gradually eased to dimness, and suddenly the sky turned silver, the water reflecting back the light. Robert's pole no longer reached the bottom and he let the current carry them along, steering with the pole's flat end. The air took on a salty smell, gulls dipped and wheeled, swooping to skim across the surface. To their left, a quick convulsion of the water, the beat of wings, and a gull passed low above them, gulping down its catch. A pinkish sun came to ride beside them in the water, the sound of bells and voices carried on the breeze. Harriett called out, "Hallelujah, Jesus!" and James's deep voice echoed, "Thank you, Lord!"

Tom twisted round and let his eyes run over them. Their hands were raised and their faces turned to heaven. "Thank you, Jesus!" "Hallelujah!" "Free at last!" they called into the dawn, their voices joyful and frightened all at once. They had bundles with them and they leaned against them, praising God.

The traders' wagon came into Tom's mind, the bundles and the children leaning up against them, their parents coming on behind, singing, singing, praising the God who had given them these children ripe for selling. He thought about the way he searched the faces of the parents for his father, although he knew he was not there, and about those other half-remembered children, his brothers and sisters, lost before he knew that he had lost them.

The baby and the little girl—he could see now it was a girl—were sleeping in their mother's skirts, and after a while she gave up on praising God and bent to kiss her children. James gave up too, and reaching across his wife's shoulder, touched the baby's head. The tenderness of his action caught Tom at the heart. He would like to have a family too, one that did not get sold away.

A churning sound, the hiss of steam, the thumping of an engine, and a paddle steamer cut across their path, making their boat lurch and heave. Robert shipped his dripping pole and the little girl began to wail. Tom clung to the boat's sides, staring at this monster, yet barely seeing it, his mind transported back to Gold Hill with its thump of engines, its hiss and sigh of steam. He saw Miss Genie's face look at him solemnly, her bare feet on the rocking cradle stepping side to side, saw her tight dark curls bent above a pail of newly peeled potatoes, her hand reaching for his.

A moment only, and he was back clutching at the boat, the little girl behind him quiet now, her mother murmuring. The sound of Robert's pole sliding back into the water and they continued forward, slipping up and down the sides of glinting swells. Before them, a watery expanse stretched out and out until it merged into the early morning mist. Tom twisted back to look at Robert. "Is this here the ocean?"

Robert shook his head but did not speak, intent on steering his way through a mess of light-draft steamers and flatboats and fishing boats and transports and gunboats and tugboats and small sailing boats and schooners with white sails flashing in the sun. Burned-out hulks lolled, half submerged, and the whole place rang with horns and bells and whistles, churning engines, the clank of rigging against mast, the shouts of Negro sailors.

Now they were at the wharf, now scrambling up a ladder into the early morning activity of a fish market where soldiers in blue uniforms, white women in hooped skirts, Negro women and old men bickered and bartered, hauling off the early morning catch. Turpentine barrels were stacked in open-fronted warehouses, bales of cotton at one end of the wharf. The spin and

slap of ropes, the roll of barrels, the steady chanting of the stevedores.

From here Tom could see that they were on a jutting point of
land where two rivers came together, one the narrow twisting
Neuse they had just traveled down, the other a wider, flatter
river whose far bank he could not see for mist. Just above the
mist, small precarious figures swarmed about a half-built bridge,
a spiderlike structure that traveled out across the water in a wa-
vering line and vanished, as though it had broken through to
some far, invisible, and longed-for place.

Tom felt a hand against his back and Robert's voice said,
"Let's get on with it," and he led his charges out onto a sand-
paved street where horses flicked their tails beneath broad spreading trees and carriages stood at the ready with their drivers
dozing in the shade. On past formal, tall brick houses, pillars
flanking their front doors, past white-painted wooden houses
sprawled behind their broad verandas, past shady gardens filled
with flowers. The trill of mockingbirds, the sharp red flash of
cardinals, the impudence of gulls.

Lounging on the steps and front verandas were blue-clad soldiers, buttons flashing on their coats, swords glinting at their
sides. These were the Yankees Robert had talked about so often
by the evening fire, the heroes who had come to free the slaves.
Tom wanted to call out to them and thank them, but they
looked at him as though he were not there.

The little girl whined that she was hungry and her mother
hushed her. "Not far now," Robert said. They turned a corner,
went down another tree-lined street, and stopped outside a garden lustrous with yellow and red roses. Milling outside the gate
and in the garden, and sitting with their bags and bundles on the
lawn and the veranda, were crowds of Negroes and some poor
whites too. Tom was amazed. He had never seen so many Negroes in one place before. He figured there were hundreds.

The gate stood open and Robert pushed his way through, Tom and his companions following him to a shaded spot where he left them sitting on the lawn, elbowed his way to the front door, and vanished inside the house. In a few minutes, he came back and told them they must wait and he would find some food, then went off again and before long came back with a fruit pie and lemonade. They ate and settled down to wait for whatever was going to happen, the children once more sleeping in their mother's skirts.

The scene seemed at first to be nothing but confusion, but gradually it became apparent there was order here. No one pushed or shoved or quarreled. The mood was jubilant and yet subdued. From time to time, a soldier in a white shirt and suspenders came out to the veranda and went back inside followed by a group of three or four. After another while he appeared again, gradually working his way through the assembled multitude. More people arrived outside the garden all the time and none of those who went in with the young soldier came out with him again. Tom had just begun to marvel at how many people must be packed inside this house when it occurred to him that houses have back doors.

The sun was halfway down the sky when their turn came. Tom had been dozing and his head felt thick and heavy as he followed Robert up the steps. Inside, the sound of voices behind walls, the clash of pans, the smell of cooking. The soldier in suspenders said his name was Private Mendell and that he was from Massachusetts. By the time he had finished saying it, he had shown them into a large parlor made into an office with a desk set squarely in the middle. Behind the desk sat a kind-faced man with heavy whiskers and a sweating forehead. This, Tom knew from Robert, was Mr. Vincent Colyer, Superintendent of the Poor.

At right angles to Mr. Colyer's desk, a smaller desk was set.

On it was a large book, open, and a pen and inkwell, the young mulatto clerk behind it tilted forward in his chair. Half a dozen chairs were ranged along the wall and Private Mendell told them to sit down. Then he jerked his head at Tom, who came to stand before the desk.

Mr. Colyer smiled and said his name was Vincent Colyer, which Tom already knew, and this, indicating the clerk, was his assistant secretary, Amos Yorke. "Welcome to New Bern," he said. "And what's your name?"

"Tom, sir."

"Last name?"

"Dunno, sir."

Mr. Colyer looked at him. "We don't have slaves here. You can have a last name if you want."

Tom opened his mouth to say Tom Morgan, then to say Tom Spotswood, but neither wanted to come out. "Guess I got no name but Mary's Tom."

Amos Yorke's pen hovered above the page. "Last name required."

Mr. Colyer laughed. "Tom," he said kindly, "you've got a right to a name of your own. You're a free man now you're in New Bern."

"I were free already when I come here. I been a free man for a year and more. Just don't have no last name."

"You can choose one if you like. Any name you want." Mr. Colyer spread his hands out in a generous motion.

Tom felt as though the whole world stared at him. He turned his head aside, shuffling his feet, and found Amos Yorke watching him and nodding. He looked back at Mr. Colyer, his body tensed.

"It's okay, Tom, it's okay," Robert's voice said close behind. His hand was on Tom's shoulder, a comforting sensation. "Go ahead, tell them any name you want."

Tom turned his head and whispered, "I'se a free man, you knows that."

"Sure, I knows that. No one's saying you ain't free. We all proud of you for that. Jest want you to have a free man's name. Tell you what, you so all-fired on bein' a free man, you go ahead and take it for a name. Tom Freeman, what you think o' that?"

Tom looked at Mr. Colyer, who said, "Freeman. Yes, a fine name, a fine name." He looked at Amos Yorke tilted on his chair, pen hovering. Amos Yorke looked him in the eye and nodded. Tom looked back at Mr. Colyer, "Yessir, it be a fine name, yes."

He liked the sound of it, and yet he didn't like the sound of it at all. It was some other man, not him, not Mary's Tom. Something made him glance across his shoulder. Robert stood behind him, smiling solidly, but it seemed to Tom that behind Robert was an empty space, as though his mother had just turned and walked away.

Robert turned his head, following Tom's glance. "Hey, don't you be runnin' off, now."

Tom turned back to Mr. Colyer, staring at him with the sort of look a man has when he has just seen a vision, blank and open-eyed and dazzled. He set both fists against the desk and leaned on them.

Mr. Colyer said, "Are you still with us, Tom?"

"Yessir. I'se here."

"Tom," said Mr. Colyer gently, "I think Freeman doesn't fit. You have to have a name that fits."

"Dunno what else to call it, sir."

"You say they called you Mary's Tom?"

"Yessir."

"Which means you're Mary's son, right?"

"Yessir."

"Then why don't you take Maryson for your last name? Tom Maryson. How does that feel to you? You think it fits?"

"Yessir, I'd say so, yessir."

Mr. Colyer took out his handkerchief and wiped his forehead. Amos Yorke scratched his pen against his book and read aloud, "Tom Maryson," and caught Tom's eye and smiled.

Tom felt a sob come in his throat, but now Mr. Colyer was asking how old he was, and when Tom hesitated, he looked up at him and said, "It's eighteen sixty-two now. September, eighteen sixty-two. Do you know when you were born?"

"No, sir. Awhiles back, sir."

Mr. Colyer smiled. "Never mind." He turned to Amos Yorke. "Write adult, that will do."

A few more questions, which Tom answered easily, and then, "Occupation?"

"Dunno, sir, dunno what that is."

"What sort of work have you been doing?"

"Been a turpentiner, sir, been livin' in the woods."

"You can find your way about the woods pretty well, then?"

"Pretty well, I reckon."

"Are you a brave man, Tom?"

Tom considered, thinking of his panicked howling in the gold mine. "Figure I scares easier 'n some, but I tries to be a brave man."

"How would you like to be an army scout?"

"And wear a uniform with buttons?"

"I'm afraid not, no. Negroes aren't allowed to join the army."

"How I be a army scout then?"

"You'd be on what the army calls civilian duty. Almost all the Negroes here work for the army, doing one thing or another."

"What else they be 'cept scouts?"

"Mainly laborers, building the fortifications around the town, or the bridge across the river. Some of them are cooks, or servants to the officers."

"Don't want to be no servant."

"No, I can see you don't. Well then, the best job for a turpentiner seems to be a scout, since you can find your way about the woods and are accustomed to a lonely occupation."

So Tom said he'd be a scout and Amos Yorke wrote it by his name. Mr. Colyer smiled and shook his hand. "We have a school here, Mr. Maryson. You can learn to read and write. Would you like to be signed up?" And Tom, dazed by all the questioning, agreed.

CHAPTER TWENTY-ONE

Spring, eighteen sixty-three. Clyde's pa and his two friends had been discovered. A party of Home Guard, out hunting for deserters in the forest, had fallen clean through onto them. It had rained for weeks, and the ground had softened, needing only some heavy weight to press down on it to make it give. Which it now had, a couple of the guardsmen tumbling down amongst the men below. Struggling for a footing, they were surprised to find the earth erupt around them and three wild-eyed fiends rise out of it and flee into the woods, knocking down two other guardsmen on their way.

The captain, with the quick instinct of a hunter, swung up his gun and fired after them. Someone was hit, he knew it from the scream, but all three went thrashing on. Shouting, Stop! Stop or I shoot! he bolted after them, his men hard at his heels, shooting and hallooing as they came. They lost all three, but Pa took a bullet in the lung, and though he made it out of there, kept moving by pure cussedness, and his friends did all they could to save him, it was hopeless.

Clyde and Amos dug his grave and Ma stood beside them at the graveside, Old Mary too. Old Mary sang a funeral hymn in her deep surprising voice:

> *Weep not for me, you standers by*
> *Who now beset me round,*
> *For in the grave I now must lie*
> *Until the trumpet sound.*
>
> *My flesh is like the clay or dust*
> *To which it must return.*
> *My spirit must return to rest,*
> *The place from whence it came.*
>
> *I must be gone for ever more*
> *And leave you all behind*
> *Until the day of Dread is come*
> *And judgment to mankind.*
>
> *When Christ majestic in the clouds*
> *Shall judge the world abroad,*
> *Let saints and angels cry aloud,*
> *Rise Dead and meet the Lord.*

Clyde cried, and Amos hiccuped in his throat, pulling his sleeve across his nose. Ma didn't cry at all, just stood there staring into the grave with that new stern face of hers. After they shot Pa, they had come and stole his horse, they said the army needed it. They were set to take the mule as well except Ma came at them with a pan of boiling water, so they didn't take the mule.

Clyde wished Uncle Benjamin was there, since he was a preacher and could have said the words about Pa's body to the ground and his spirit to the Lord the way they said it for a proper burial, but Uncle Benjamin had been took and put into the army. He did not want to go. I am a Union man, he'd said, but they said if he opened up his mouth and said that one more time, they would hang him for a traitor. I will not fight, he said, I am a man of God, my business is to save men's souls, so they made him be a chaplain.

When the singing was all done, Pa's two friends came out of the woods with shovels on their shoulders and stood beside the grave with their hats held in their hands. Then they put their hats back on and set to work filling in the hole. It was only fair, they said, since Clyde and Amos dug it. When the dirt was piled up good and high, they swung their shovels back onto their shoulders and prepared to go off into the woods to dig another cave.

You be joining us before too long, Fred's pa, Mr. Hintner, said. You better start out watching for yourself else fore you know it you'll be fighting for the big man's nigger like the rest.

But I ain't yet seventeen, Clyde said.

Like I say, you better watch out for yourself.

Clyde turned his head and spat onto the ground. They have shot my pa, he said, and they have stole his horse. Danged if I will fight for them. They cannot make me do it.

They'll make you if they catch you, boy.

Clyde hooked his fingers in his waist and hitched his pants up with a swaggering motion. I ain't goin' to fight for any big man, no sir, I am not. A hesitation came across his eyes while he tossed about inside his head for something brave and dangerous to say. Why, he said, I'd go off for the Yankees afore I'd fight for them.

Fred Hintner's pa looked down at him from underneath his

hat. He said, I know a feller who can help you get that organized. And Clyde, who had not thought to really do it, just said it out of spite and sorrow for his pa, said, I just might if'n I weren't needed here by Ma.

Then Ma, for the first time in his life he could remember, opened up her mouth and spoke. Go on, get outa here, she said, go on and do it. You ain't no good to no one squattin' in a hole.

Chapter Twenty-two

Tom lived with Robert now, and another scout named Charley. The new bridge across the Trent River had been completed, and on the farther bank a town had grown, clustered about the railroad line, of tents at first, then makeshift huts, and with time, more houselike little houses with tin roofs and porches and gardens in between where corn grew almost to the eaves.

Robert's was a simple frame house two rooms deep with a shady, low, if somewhat shaky, wood porch at the front where climbing roses grew in pink and white profusion, sending out their fragrance like unexpected gifts. Every morning they were wakened by the rattling progress of the train that set out at first light, bristling with soldier talk and rifles, to patrol the line from New Bern to the coast. Tom would open his eyes to see Charley's silent figure, already fully alert and ready for the day, outlined in the window. It gave him a sense of well-being, the same sort of feeling he used to have when he was a child and would wake to see his mother's figure moving in the dimness of the cabin back on Mr. Morgan's place.

Charley was as tall as Tom, but too thin for his bones and angular. Big-knuckled hands hung off his arms as though attached by accident, and when he sat down on a stool, he seemed not so much to sit as to fold down, his long knees shifting back and forth as though they never would get comfortable. He had a smiling, easy way with him, although he rarely spoke, and when he did it was important. He and Tom shared one of the bedrooms while Robert had the other to himself, a condition he intended to remedy as soon as he could persuade a pretty young mulatto by the name of Rose to marry him.

A large black cat shared the house with them. It had appeared at the back stoop one day with a struggling bird between its jaws and when the door was opened, boldly took up residence. When it was not out hunting, it prowled room to room behind them, backing off from any outstretched hand, watching everything they did with calculating yellow eyes. They called it Rebel Cat and made it swear allegiance to Old Glory. Tom, sitting with his feet up on the porch rail, a glass of lemonade in one hand, Webster's blue-backed *Elementary Spelling Book* in the other, and Rebel Cat sprawled out at watchful ease beside him, figured life was grand. The only thing that bothered him was Ben and what to do about his stolen gold.

Down at the Baptist church, they had given him new pants, and a shirt and jacket that fit him pretty well, a new hat too, which at first would not fit on his head, but fit fine after they shaved him. The barber wrapped his head up in a hot wet towel and set to stropping his knife, lifting the towel from time to time to test how soft his hair and whiskers were. When he was satisfied, he held onto Tom's nose and lathered him up with a shaving brush like Mr. Spotswood's, then set his knife low on his neck and drew it up across his jaw and up his cheek and all the way across his head and down the other side. Then he wiped the knife on a towel and drew it up again, going on until Tom's neck and face and head were smooth as glass. It was a splendid luxury.

Shoes turned out to be a problem for a while. The shoe man whistled through his teeth. "Where you get them feet?" But after some rummaging beneath a table, he produced a box of discarded army shoes and found a pair that fit, not new, he said, they had come off a dead man, but since he died a hero in a battle they were lucky shoes.

At the Baptist church Tom had discovered Ben, who lived in a room at one end of the stable. Ben told him Peter was now field servant to a corporal in the Massachusetts Forty-fifth and invited him to come along to prayer meeting. Tom felt awkward and refused, and Ben seemed hurt, which made Tom puzzle even more about his soul, because he seemed to be a good man. When he was not running a prayer meeting, he spent his whole time helping the ex-slaves who crowded into New Bern every day, loaded up with babies and bundles and enormous piles of bedding.

They came on rowing boats and flatboats, floating down the river like great clots of waterweed, or by twos and threes with Robert or some other waterman. They came fleeing through the swamps, their masters' hound packs baying after them. They came by mule and ox cart and by foot along the dusty roads, or just materialized out of the woods, hollow-eyed and skinny, their possessions in bundles on their heads. Each time Union troops went out to forage or to tear up railroad trestles or to fight a battle, they rose up from the rice and cotton fields and followed them back to New Bern.

The Yankees called them contrabands, since they were spoils of war, and Ben was ready with his arms held out to all of them, offering a roof, a meal, a cot, a blanket for the night, guidance on where to go for work and housing, where to get new clothes and treatment for their blistered feet and the fevers of their children.

When their earthly needs were met, he held his arms out to their souls and they crowded to his meetings at the Baptist church, where they shouted, "Hallelujah, Jesus!" and sang and danced until the windows rattled in their frames and the night resounded with the music of thanksgiving. Every one of them loved Ben. Tom could not understand why he would steal.

ONE Wednesday night, while the prayer meeting was making a great stomp and clapping in the church, Tom crept into Ben's room at the far end of the stable. He looked around. The room was sparse to bareness: a tiny table with a candlestick, a stool, a cot. Underneath the cot, half visible below a hanging edge of blanket, a wooden locker with a hinge. Tom's heart began to race. He glanced around, then bent and dragged it out. No lock. He turned his head across his shoulder, listening. Just the ruckus from the church. Flipped up the lid. The locker was full up to the rim with Bibles.

On his knees, he rooted through them, stacking them around him on the floor, but nothing, no gold, only Bibles. He flipped the blanket up and peered beneath the bed. Nothing still, not even dust, and nothing wedged between the mattress and the slats that held it up.

Someone laughed out in the yard. In a second, he was stacking back the Bibles, shoving back the locker with his foot, the locker catching in the blanket, dragging it half underneath the cot. He jerked the blanket back and flung it out across the mattress, but it wound itself around his arm, and then he flung too hard, let go too soon, and the whole thing slithered off the farther edge beside the wall.

Scramble on the cot, retrieve the blanket, fling it out again, this time getting it placed right. Now smooth it down, yes, good, the near edge hanging so.

But now the mattress held two indentations where his knees had been, the blanket sagging into them. Nothing for it but to jerk it off again, and hoist the mattress up and shake it into shape, a cloud of fine straw spraying out into the room. Set it down now, carefully, and spread the blanket back.

He rose and looked at it. The bed was fine, but what to do about the straw? A broom? He looked around, sweat running in the small of his back, dripping from his temples. But now a swell of hallelujahs from the church, and then, above it all, a high clear single voice, as though in accusation. Tom spun away and fled out of the room. Not three steps into the yard and here came Ben toward him, hand outstretched, his face alight with welcome. "Well now, if it ain't Tom," he said. "Come on along and help me tote some Bibles over to the church."

TO Tom's surprise, he enjoyed the crowd and bustle of Ben's prayer meeting, the exuberant singing of the hymns, the thumping syncopation of the freedmen's dancing feet, the way the women's headwraps bobbed and fluttered like a crowd of brightly colored butterflies, the glint of candles on the men's newly shaven heads. Little children on their mother's laps clapped their hands, swaying to the music, while older children danced around the edges, wild with a new happiness they did not understand.

Ben did not stand out front directing as preachers generally do, but moved among them with his Bibles, pressing them into their hands, murmuring, and touching arms and backs and shoulders, setting his hand against a forehead, blessing, making a low continual praying in his throat. This man a thief? It seemed impossible. Tom, a Bible clutched against his chest, watched him in a glow of certainty that he was innocent, and in a twist of fear that he was not. He did not go to prayer meeting again, and when he saw Ben on the street, he said he was too busy, his spare time was taken up with school.

He loved to go to school. At first he had been doubtful, and when the teacher, a young lieutenant from Massachusetts, came along the row handing out spellers, he said, "Scusee, sir, I think I likely got signed for schoolin' by mistake."

The teacher stopped, balancing the stack of blue-backed spellers on his forearm. "Why's that?"

"Ain't got much head for learnin', sir. On 'count o' bein' a simpleton."

"Who told you you're a simpleton?"

"Why, sir, de entire world since I were a little chile. They say I ain't got nothin' in my head."

"Nothing in your head, eh?" The teacher smiled down at him. "We've got just the tonic for that here." And he put a speller in Tom's hand and went on down the row.

For several evenings after that, Tom went along to school expecting to be dosed up with the tonic for his head, but after a while he came to realize that it had not been medicine on a spoon the teacher meant, but a different sort of tonic, one that came out of the pages of his speller. Rows of words ran down each page, with sentences beneath them showing what they meant. From these sentences, Tom learned a lot of things he hadn't thought about before, like, "The chewing of tobacco is a useless habit," "It is almost impossible to civilize American Indians," "A patriarch is the father of a family," "A toothbrush is good to brush your teeth," although it bothered him to learn that "Wars generally prove disastrous to all parties."

"Next page," the teacher said, and started down the "ow" words in the primer. "Ow-l, owl," he said, the class repeating after him not quite in time, so the word sounded like a moan.

"The owl has large eyes and can see in the night," said the sentence underneath.

Tom felt as though he had a starving belly in his head that had just discovered food. Every evening and every Sunday afternoon he sat above his blue-backed speller, bringing to the lines and dots and squiggles an amazed and almost reverent attention. He saved his pay and bought a book called *Uncle Tom's Cabin* off a sutler's cart, because it was the same name as his own. He struggled with it and the Bible Ben had given him turn and turn about, then set them both aside, promising himself that one day he would master them, and saved his money up and bought a book with pictures that helped him understand the words.

It was called *Aesop's Fables* and he liked it because it had sayings underneath each story like the sayings in his speller: "Be on guard against men who can strike from a distance," which he thought a good thing for a scout to keep in mind, "Sorrow not over what is lost forever," which made him feel both sad and comforted about Miss Genie, "Do not attempt too much at once," which made him feel he had been right to set aside *Uncle Tom's Cabin* and the Bible. He fervently agreed with "Better starve free than be a fat slave," but "Two blacks do not make a white" he puzzled over, since there were no people in the story that went with it, only animals.

He learned to read the stars and knew now which one was the freedom star. At night sometimes, when he was coming home from school, he would turn his face up to it as though it were a friend. And when an owl turned its head to look at him with gleaming golden eyes, he didn't think that it was any sort of holy ghost. It did not say "Ho," or "Ho, ha," to warn him or to not warn him. It just said it for itself. Tom felt pleased he understood this now, and yet when he saw that head turn on the rigidly still neck, and felt the golden eyes, he could not help but shiver, as though they looked into his soul.

When he had practiced reading a bit more and got the hang of how to figure out new words, and the others in the class could do it too, the teacher started teaching them to say the words the way he said they should be said. "Re-peat after me," he said. "Re-peat." And when they didn't get it right, he tapped his pointing stick against his desk. "You have to speak correctly. You can't talk nigger now you're free."

"But that's the way I talks," Tom said.

The teacher, who had had another word ready in his mouth, let it drop out as a little groaning sigh and said instead, "Tom, Tom, what language are we speaking here?"

Tom looked at him. He looked around the room, but all the other students were looking at the teacher, waiting to find out.

"We're speaking English," the teacher said. He tapped his pointing stick. "Re-peat after me. Eng-lish."

"Eng-lish," they said.

"You know what talking nigger is?" the teacher said. "It's ignorance. When you can speak correctly you will not be ignorant. That will be the proof."

And so they all repeated and repeated and repeated until he laughed and said they'd all turn into Yankees pretty soon.

Then he taught them how to read a map. Tom had never seen a map before. It fascinated him. He could see the way the world was and which way was north. He looked for Chapel Hill and found it, and found Gold Hill, and Salisbury too. Down-the-River he could not find, so he put his hand up and asked the teacher to show him where it was.

The teacher looked uncomfortable and said that it was not a town as Tom had thought, but a word for being sold. This made it even more difficult for Tom to think about his father than it had been before. Try as he might, he could not remember what he looked like, not his face. He did remember his big hands, big fingers on big hands. If he closed his eyes he could see them gripped around the supervisor's throat. His father must have loved him, to risk his life like that, but he had been a child back then and it had not occurred to him.

Next time the teacher brought the map to school, Tom asked him where Australia was. "It isn't on this map," the teacher said. "This is just North Carolina. Australia is in the antipodes."

"How far be that?"

"How far *is* that. Re-peat."

"How far *is* that?"

"Well, Tom, I'm not sure. A good long way."

Tom was not satisfied. He would have liked to know how far a good long way might be. If it were not too far, perhaps he could go see Miss Genie when the war was done.

Next day the teacher came to class with a large round melon and a charcoal-ended stick. He made a mark on one side of the melon and another on the other side. "This is New Bern," he said, "and over here is Australia."

It did not look so far to Tom, maybe he could walk it, but then the teacher said, "There's an ocean between here and there," so that put paid to that.

When they could read a map, the teacher started up a separate class for scouts and made them draw their own. He said it was important for a scout to learn to draw a map so he could show the army where things were.

"What things?" said Tom.

"All sorts of things," the teacher said. "Where the enemy is camping, where he's pitched his tents and stacked his guns, where he's built breastworks to defend himself, what roads he's traveling on and which direction, where bridges are that we can burn, where railway tracks and trestles are unprotected so we can send out men to rip them up," going on and on with things that could be put on maps until Tom's head began to hurt.

"I cain't do all that," he said.

"I *cannot* do all that. Re-peat."

"I *cannot* do all that."

"Of course you can. Come here. Now look at this. See in the corner of the map, these little pictures? That's called a legend. This one with the straight line and the little crossing lines is a railroad. Find a railroad for me on the map. That's right. Now, find a river—this blue wavy line. Yes, that's the Neuse. So far so good. And what's this a picture of? A tree? Not quite. There's three of them. That means a forest. Find a forest on the map. Good man. Now, tell me if the river is north or south of the forest."

Tom considered. "South."

"No, no. You're looking at it upside down. Turn the map the other way."

And then it happened. The world swung upside down inside Tom's head. He saw the Avery plantation, saw himself rushing tree to tree, following the picture in his head. But the picture was the wrong way round. Uncle Phillip getting shot had got his brains all tumbled. He knew exactly where his gold was hidden now, he knew for sure. And he knew Ben had not taken it.

"Tom?" the teacher said.

Tom grinned. "It be on the north."

"It *is* on the north. Re-peat."

Tom was walking home from school that night when something else occurred to him: he was not a simpleton, not anymore. This realization came to him not suddenly, but like a slow turning of the head, as though he had heard a soft tapping on the door and gone to answer it half hesitant, unsure of whether he had heard a knock or not. But when he opened it, understanding stood on the stoop. It filled his head and ran out through his limbs and down into his feet and burst out of his throat, making him run shouting through the streets, not words, just shouting, happiness and wonder flooding out of him, lighting up the night. And no one paid the least bit of attention. New Bern was accustomed to freedmen going wild with joy.

CHAPTER TWENTY-THREE

A T first the army sent Tom out on spying missions with an
experienced scout by the name of Abraham Galloway, a
bold handsome fellow with a quick mind, an air of easy confidence, and a studied way of speaking that made white men trust
his judgment and even the most incorrigible of freedmen treat
him as a leader. He had about him both a fervor and a flippancy
that at its heart was serious, as though he knew what the world
was all about and did not think too much of it. When first he
came back south, he told Tom, the Union army hadn't taken
New Bern, and he had scouted down the coast to find places
where the troops could come ashore. "If I'd led them wrong," he
said, grinning wickedly, "you and I would not be sitting here today. So listen up, do everything I tell you, and you'll be all
right."

He turned out to be a demanding and yet patient teacher, and
Tom, who had gone out on his first mission in such a state of

trepidation he could barely breathe, found he had a talent for this sort of thing. Not only could he move through the woods as silent as any animal and stay still in one place for hours without falling off to sleep or letting his attention slip, but he could judge distances from sounds and make maps inside his head of camps and trenchworks, roads and bridges, and carry them back to Union lines, where he would draw them on a piece of paper, or take a stick and draw them in the dust.

Galloway he admired intensely, and wanted to be like him, but he was too much in awe of him to become his friend. "Are you named Abraham for Mr. Lincoln?" Tom asked him one day when they were sitting with their feet cooling in a creek.

Galloway laughed. "No, for Abraham out of the Bible. He was a great Israelite patriarch."

There was silence while Tom felt pleased with himself for knowing what a patriarch was. He was just about to ask what an Israelite might be when Galloway turned to him. "Tom, what do you want out of this war?"

Tom leaned back on his hands and watched the turkey vultures circling. "Guess I want to make my mother free."

Galloway narrowed his eyes, looking at Tom's upturned face. Then he reached back, took his shirt by the collar, and pulled it off across his head. "Yes, we both want that," he said, his voice muffled by the fabric. "I've got a mother still a slave in Wilmington." He stuck his head between his knees and splashed water on his neck. A pattern of scars covered his back, not whipping scars as so many of the freedmen had, like maps of battle etched into the flesh, but a pale pink marbling of the skin.

Tom was riveted. "Where'd you get those scars?"

Galloway half glanced across his shoulder, water dripping off his hair. "From turpentine. The fumes."

"You were a turpentiner?"

"No, I ran off on a freighter out of Wilmington, ten years

ago it must have been. I hid between the barrels. The fumes got trapped inside my clothes and burned my skin. My legs are like that too." He rolled up one leg of his pants to show the same pale marbling.

Tom sucked his breath in. "That hurt a good bit."

"A good bit, yes, but I was only sixteen then and figured it was worth it to be free." He rolled his pants back down. "Still do."

And he went on to tell how, on that voyage, he had almost died, the fumes from the turpentine corroding his skin so badly that by the time the ship reached Philadelphia, he half starved and his throat raging from both thirst and fumes, his legs would barely hold him. Hearing voices, he rose up unsteadily between the barrels where he had spent the last four poisonous black days. Lucky for him the stevedores were Negroes, and in the last moments before he lost consciousness he knew he was being taken somewhere safe. Two days later, he woke up with a roiling start that almost threw him from the cot on which he lay.

A white woman was bending over him, asking with one eyebrow raised if he had decided to come back to life. She wore an apron and a plain cap covering her hair, but he knew at once she was no maid or nurse, and he was right. She was a Philadelphia abolitionist, her house a stop on the Underground Railroad for runaways coming by the sea route from the South. She hid them in her attic and in secret rooms. Galloway she nursed back to health on a cot beneath the staircase, in the closet where the brooms were kept. She never told her name, and made him swear upon his life never to ask it, nor to venture out onto the street, or speak to strangers, or even to the others in the house, who, silent as himself, came and left during the time he was recovering. In exchange, she would send him on to Canada when he was well. He swore, and eventually she sent him on.

In Canada, he joined up with some others and between them

they started a relief society for runaways, a newspaper as well, and organized a militia to protect fugitives coming overland along the Railroad from Ohio, to prevent them being chased after and shot, or to keep the houses where they stopped along the way from being raided. Some of these guards were trained in Canada, and for the rest, someone was sent across the border with smuggled arms to train them where they were.

Tom listened to this story with an intense expression on his face. "How'd you get to eat in Canada? They paid you for this work?"

Galloway shook his head. "Earned my living as a brick-mason. A dollar seventy-five a day." He laughed. "Figured I was rich."

"I heard of people like you up in Canada, helping runaways. It's good work you did. But why come back here to be nothing but a scout?"

"A scout is good work too. It helps." Galloway turned to Tom, his face gone serious. "You know what I really want? What I came back here to do? I want to make the Southern Negroes into Yankee soldiers. That way they can fight for themselves, not rely on someone else to free them."

"The Yankees won't allow it, Mr. Colyer told me."

"They will, though, mark my words."

GALLOWAY was right. In January of eighteen sixty-three, Mr. Lincoln put out the Emancipation Proclamation. In May, a call went out for volunteers to join a colored regiment. But no one joined, or hardly anyone. One man in New Bern, another out in Beaufort County, eight more in New Bern. The recruiting agents held meetings and put up signs and accosted freedmen on the street. But the freedmen were leery about how they would be treated in a white man's army whose soldiers, on the whole, seemed to regard them as only slightly more advanced than savages. And what if they were captured by the Rebels? Would they be prisoners of war? Would they be sold as slaves, or shot as traitors? All sorts of questions bothered them. And so, although their heads were for the notion of enlistment, their feet were hard to move. It took a month to get a hundred men.

One evening, Galloway showed up on Tom's front porch. He had never come before and Tom, who had been sitting in the half light with his speller, jumped up in a fluster as though a dignitary had appeared. Because of it, he did not think to ask Galloway to come inside and they talked together in the dimming light, Tom still with his speller in his hand and Rebel Cat, who had leaped onto the porch rail, turning his yellow eyes from one man to the other.

"You know that fellow Edward Kinsley," Galloway began, "that recruiting agent down from Massachusetts? He's asked me to help sign up freedmen for the army."

"But I'm already working for the army."

"No, no, I'm not here to recruit you. I want your help with an idea I've had. I need a big man I can trust to make it work, someone who can look menacing and dangerous."

"Guess I'm not much good at fighting."

"You wouldn't have to fight." Galloway glanced around him at the neighbors going back and forth. "Can I come in?"

THE next evening, very late, Edward Kinsley answered the front door of the house where he was staying to find an enormous black man with fists the size of Sunday roasts insisting that he follow him. He hesitated, but since no one was about to help him, and since the fists, which were very black and powerful, flexed and unflexed in the manner of a boxer getting ready for a bout, he took the risk and followed.

Tom led him through dark and darker streets, Kinsley stepping nervously behind, wishing he had brought a weapon, until
they stopped before a house in a dead-end street so dark he
could make out only the angle of a roof against the sky. The
door scraped back, but instead of the expected flood of light,
the inside of the house was blacker than the street. Figures were
inside, he could not tell how many. No one spoke.

Someone, from the strong feel of it the fellow who had led
him here, took him by the arm and guided him up a stairway,
then up another stairway so narrow that his elbows caught
against the walls, to an attic room crowded with the smell of
bodies and the expectant sound of breathing. He stood completely still, listening with all his might. The scraping of a match,
a flaring sound.

Then the swaying flicker of a candle casting giant shadows
on the walls, and he was looking at a room jam-packed with
freedmen, all of whom seemed huge, and none of whom looked
sympathetic. In front of him, a little to the left, stood Abraham
Galloway, pointing a revolver at his head.

And so negotiations started: equal pay with black troops
from the North, rations for black soldiers' families, education
for their children, a Union promise to make sure ex-slaves captured by the Rebels were treated not as runaways or traitors, but
as prisoners of war.

Kinsley hesitated, sweating. Although a fervent abolitionist,
he had no authority to make such promises, especially ones involving what the Confederates might do. Galloway's face took
on a glowering look. The big man with the fists like roasts
breathed at his back. The entire room breathed menace. And no
one knew that he was here. He promised everything.

"It may not be the be-all and the end-all," Galloway said
when Kinsley had been released onto the street, "but it's a start."

In the days that followed, enlistment fever seized the freedmen of the town. Volunteers turned up at the recruiting office by the hundreds. They jostled on the front veranda and crowded in the street, slapping Kinsley on the back and cheering him when he went in or out, singing patriotic songs and heckling anyone who seemed reluctant, the women pushing their men into the sign-up lines, refusing to take no for an answer. Ben went to be a chaplain, Tom and Charley went for foot soldiers, although they went on being scouts, and Robert went on doing for the army what he did before but getting paid a good deal better. It seemed that every freedman in the town was putting on a smart blue uniform with shiny buttons and going out to drill and learn to shoot a gun.

Up till now, Tom had not had a gun, not one of his own. Sometimes when he went out on a mission, he had been handed a revolver in case he needed to protect himself, but he had never fired it and had to hand it in when he came back. Now he and Charley were issued ancient muskets and told that they could learn to shoot with Company A, North Carolina Colored Volunteers.

A sergeant took them to a field and drilled them over and over until Tom would hear his voice intrude into his sleep: Lower musket to the ground! Handle cartridge! Tear cartridge! Charge cartridge! Draw rammer! Ram cartridge twice! Return rammer! Cast-about! Prime! Cock hammer, point the rifle! Fire! With the practice in the field and then the practice in his sleep, Tom soon learned to go through these steps in twenty seconds, as required, and fire three aimed bullets in a minute. They almost never hit their targets, though, which made him glad he was a scout and not a soldier.

CHAPTER TWENTY-FOUR

AFTER the encounter with Ned Tarkel, Aunt Baker had forbidden Eugenia to continue with her thievish enterprise at the Bible printing office. Eugenia begged and pleaded, but with no success, and then she went to Henry.

"Please, Henry, you must make her let me go, you must. I'm running out of paper. I cannot let the likes of Ned Tarkel stop me writing to the boys."

But Henry backed up Aunt Baker. "And anyway," he said, "we have so many patients these days we cannot spare you, not even for one afternoon a week."

Eugenia fumed and fretted. She went back to Aunt Baker. "Your patients need you here," Aunt Baker said.

Back once more to Henry, who was in the garden splitting logs. He swung the axe down—whack!—and left it trembling in the chopping block. Then he set one foot on the block, one hand on his knee, and leaned toward her, holding her eyes with his own. "Adeline needs you here."

It was then Eugenia realized it was not so much that her patients needed her, although they did, but that Aunt Baker dared not let her from her sight. Aunt Baker did not dare? It was something she had never thought about before, and since she could not go out and face Ned Tarkel down, her imagination made him monstrous. The world took on a different cast. Up till now she had played at being a heroine, or so it seemed to her. Each time Henry read out another of Governor Vance's proclamations calling woe down on deserters, she had fancied every one of them had a letter in her handwriting tucked inside his pocket, and danced about the kitchen as though she were the total cause of the governor's frustration. Now each time Henry helped a new patient down into the cellar, she was tremblingly aware of the threat that rampaged through the countryside behind him, that rode its horses through the streets of Salisbury, leering from Ned Tarkel's face, a threat that any day might come battering on Aunt Baker's door.

At night, Ned Tarkel's face seemed to hover in the dark outside her window and got mixed up in her dreams. On the night she used the last page of her purloined paper, she saw her father hanging from the rafter of the cabin with his crimson slipper fallen and his blue tongue lolling out. She ran to save him, but when she got up close she found he wore Ned Tarkel's goatish smile. "No more writing letters to the boys."

But then the Southern army lost at Gettysburg, and Vicksburg too, and writing letters didn't matter anymore. Confederate soldiers, looking about themselves and seeing what the generals refused to see, that their enterprise was doomed, were hightailing it for home with no need of encouragement. They hid in caves and hollow trees inside the woods, and under barns and buildings. They pulled out their front teeth so they could not bite cartridges, feigned every sort of illness, and shot off their own toes. In outlaw gangs they roamed the central Piedmont, looting and doing battle with the law, fled east to join the Union at Beaufort or New Bern, fled west to join the mountain bush-wackers, or journeyed on across the border to the Union lines in eastern Tennessee. Captains and colonels took out advertisements in newspapers ordering their companies and regiments to come back and do their duty, but they did not come.

Now all Eugenia's time was swallowed by her patients, this one with a bullet in his gut from a running battle with impress-ment officers, this one blinded by exploding gunpowder from a failed attempt to fire a bridge, this one dug out of his cave and trampled on by horses when he ran, this one tarred and feath-ered and left swinging by his ankles in a tree all through a light-ning storm because he had organized a peace meeting in his barn, this one run off from the army, hunted down and roundly beaten, then run away again to hide, barn by root cellar by corn-crib, on his way west to the mountains, this one with a tape-worm partially expelled that, hauled out of his body, measured thirteen feet, this one with his feet so ruined from marching in tight boots that the bones showed through his flesh. Once a woman came, the only time, frightened into miscarriage by the Home Guard hunting for her husband, and finding him inside the chimney, where they lit a fire and held her arms behind her back while she listened to him suffocate.

It was high summer, eighteen sixty-three. The days were long and hot. At first the stone walls kept the cellar cool, but as time went on, heat sneaked down like a mist, subtle, heavy, weighing down the atmosphere and making sick men too lethargic to care about recovery. Eugenia dared not throw back the trapdoors for fear of sudden visitors. Instead, she and Henry hung water-soaked blankets from the ceiling beams and wrapped the patients in wet towels and sat beside them fanning, sometimes through the night.

More and more she abandoned her soft mattress in the up-stairs bedroom, choosing instead to spend her nights dozing fully dressed beside some groaning patient's cot or straw-stuffed pallet on the floor, always half alert for the demands of her charges calling out for bedpans or their mothers or laudanum to dull the pain. *Miss Genie, please Miss Genie.* She hardly noticed how she grew thinner all the time, how her gown grew looser on her body. She never looked into a mirror anymore, and grew ac-customed to less food, never thought about new gowns or shoes or bonnets.

When laudanum could not be had for any price, she dosed her patients up with whiskey, sometimes not knowing if their sore heads and vomiting were due to drunkenness or illness. She tore up all the drapes and curtains in the house for band-ages, and made Aunt Baker sacrifice her petticoats. Her patients were all she thought about. Her world closed down to them. She became, in a sense, deranged by pity, obsessed by an urgent need to save one more, and then one more, and one more after that. It seemed to her a sort of reparation, a redemption al-most, as though with each one saved she saved Papa. *But Papa cannot be saved. He is forever gone.* She could not think of that, she must make them better, make them better, do not let them die.

And when they died, and they did die despite her, she stood by Henry at their hastily dug graves out in Aunt Baker's meadow and mourned as if they were her own. These funerals were brief and furtive, taking place in early morning dimness or at night, with no songs or incantations, just a whispered prayer and the hurried scraping of shovel against dirt. When they were done, no marker was set up, no stone left to mark the grave. These mounds of soil were treacherous, like raw announcements to the sky of their activities, as though a field of spies were growing out there in the soil and one day would rise up to betray them.

Henry dragged across them garden trash and broken tools and discarded household goods to hide the turned-up earth until the weeds had time to take it over, as though the men buried there never had existed. Eugenia, though, remembered every one of them, keeping in her head the long roster of their names. Sometimes she would go out to the garden, and turning her face up to the sky, recite their names aloud—Simon Wimmie, Jackson Warren, Frank Matthias, Hardy McDonald, Lawrence Hughes, Johnny Keller—chanting them slow and solemn like a prayer for absolution. And when Ned Tarkel rose outside the window of her mind, leering and rattling at the pane, she snapped the shade down in his face.

AUNT Baker's front door clicked. A footstep sounded in the passageway. Eugenia, who had been boiling bandages, poking at the noxious-smelling mess with a long-handled metal spoon, said, "Henry's home."

Alouette, who was straining an infusion of boiled dogwood bark, an alternative for quinine, through the toe of an old stocking, set down her work, and wiping her hands on her apron, swung toward the door as he came into the room with that day's copy of the *Carolina Watchman* in one hand and a small sack swinging from the other. She reached for the sack.

"What is it? Flour? Is that all you could get your hands on?"

He handed it across. "Five pounds from Mr. Gaines, poor man. Some soldiers' wives terrorized him so badly that when he saw me coming he raised his hands above his head as though it were a holdup. The women are getting desperate, he says. They are panicked that the army's new whiskey distillery will swallow all the town's supplies of corn, and they're frantic about flour as well. He says they went mill to mill last afternoon, forty or fifty of them, with more trailing on behind, threatening the millers, accosting traders on the street, accusing them of speculation. Morriss Brown, John Euniss, others. Jeremy McCubbin padlocked his door and nailed a notice to it saying he was not responsible for anybody's grain he had stored there."

Henry laughed shortly. "Willy Frankford told them he had nothing in his store. 'Take me,' he said. 'I'll go anywhere you please. My own body is all I've got left to give you.' They forced a barrel of molasses out of Hartwell Sprague, out of David Weil a sack of salt. They rushed into the railroad depot with a handcart, screaming threats, several with carving knives, and carried off ten barrels of flour waiting to be sent off to the troops. Then they went off quarreling amongst themselves about how they should divide it up."

He set the *Watchman* on the table. "Where's Adeline?"

"Here I am." Aunt Baker came into the room, a bundle of twigs in her arms. She set them on the hearth, and pulling out a chair, readied herself for news. "What does the paper say today?"

Henry sat down too, shook the paper out, and spread it on the table. "Governor Vance says deserters won't be shot if they return to duty."

Aunt Baker snorted. "Won't be shot? Who is he, God, to say who will be shot and who will not?"

"He means that *he'll* not have them shot."

"What else does the paper say?"

Henry ran his finger down the page. "*The train on the North Carolina railroad ran off the track near Salisbury last night. Quite a number of passengers were on board, among them General*

Lovell of the Confederate States Army, on his way south. We learn that the lock on the switch was broken open by some scamp and the train thrown off by that means. The hammer and chisel were found close by the switch with which it was broken. How lost to all the finer impulses of human nature must the man be who would deliberately contemplate the destruction of a large number of human beings who had never wronged him. Such a person is a fit associate for the fiends beneath. This we hope will be a warning to our authorities to be more vigorous in guarding the town."

He stopped, looking at Aunt Baker. "Are the Red Strings responsible for this?"

"If so, I know nothing of it."

Henry grunted and turned back to the paper. "*We learn further that it is the habit of a certain class of our population to hold meetings nearly every night, where the 'carrying on' is said to be very extensive. Who superintends these gatherings we know not, but they should be stopped. At this time, all should be on the alert and anyone appearing suspicious should be made to give an account of himself.*"

Aunt Baker stood up, holding out her hand. "Here, let me look at that." She took the paper to the window, where she tilted it toward the light. "Hmm," she said, and "hmm."

"This could go badly for us," Henry said. "We could all end up in the prison down the road."

Aunt Baker frowned and shook her head. "Do not say such things."

"What shall we do?"

"Nothing. We will go on as before and wait for this to pass."

But the *Watchman* would not let things be. Something must be done, it trumpeted. A patrol must be set up "for the arrest of persons engaged in treasonable conspiracies."

Abruptly, the red strings in lapels and bodices vanished off the streets of Salisbury. One after another, letters were published in the paper from fearful citizens disclaiming membership in the Order of the Heroes of America, or claiming they had been duped into joining in the first place, swearing they had not understood that they were giving aid and comfort to the Yankees.

Aunt Baker took the red string off the latch of the side gate. The secret meetings in the parlor stopped. Visitors stopped coming to the house.

They waited. Nothing further.

AND then a message came from Dr. Kinney's Ruth Louise: Dr. Kinney had been impressed to be a surgeon in the army. Aunt Baker told Eugenia in the passageway and then went into the kitchen to tell Alouette and Henry, who were setting out the patients' meals.

Eugenia followed her. "What do you think, Henry? Do you think they took him on account of us? Do you think we are suspected?"

Henry hesitated. "There's something all of you should know."

"What?" Eugenia said.

At the stove, Alouette made a rattling with her spoon inside the kettle. Aunt Baker became very still.

"I think someone is watching us. Watching the house. He hides behind the bushes on the other side of the road. I went after him last Wednesday, and again this morning, but both times he was gone before I got to him."

"You think it is Ned Tarkel, don't you?" Eugenia said.

Henry glanced toward Alouette, who stood with her back toward them, furiously stirring at the kettle. He nodded.

"You should have spoken sooner."

"I didn't want to frighten you. I'm not even sure it *is* Ned Tarkel."

"Still, you should have told us."

There was silence, just the scraping of the spoon and the swishing of the liquid in the kettle, Alouette's head bent over it so that steam rose at each side of her neck like a pair of ghostly hands.

Aunt Baker went across to her. She slipped an arm around her shoulders, turning her. With one finger, she tilted up her chin and looked into her eyes. "Child, you must not panic," she said softly. "Ned Tarkel is a coward. Henry will take care of him. We will all miss Dr. Kinney, but I do not think he is suspected. He has been impressed because the army needs more surgeons, that is all."

Alouette, her eyes fixed on Aunt Baker's, nodded, but her entire body trembled.

Aunt Baker pulled her close and held her for a moment, then, as though Ned Tarkel's name had not been mentioned, she said in her usual firm voice, "Go on, child, back to work with you."

Later, in the cellar with Henry, Eugenia said, "I did not understand Alouette was so fearful of Ned Tarkel."

Henry shook a clean sheet out across a cot. "She has her reasons."

"She is afraid for Aunt Baker?"

"Yes, and for herself."

"But why would Ned Tarkel care one way or the other about Alouette? Why would he hurt *her*?"

Henry tucked the corners of the sheet under the mattress.

"Henry?"

He straightened, sighing. "You remember I said there was no proof Ned Tarkel shot the judge?"

Eugenia watched him, waiting.

"Alouette saw it happen through the kitchen window. They would not let her testify."

"What should we do? The poor girl is beside herself."

"Alouette is tougher than she looks. She will recover."

BUT Alouette did not recover. Her brightness became brittle and her eyes took on an inward cast. She ceased to sing about the house. She did not eat. Her birdlike body grew skeletal. One morning, as the sun came shimmering pink and silver up the kitchen wall, she huddled on the hearth beside the stove and drew her legs up, staring at the floor and shivering.

"It is nothing," Eugenia said, examining her anxiously. "A light fever. It will pass."

"It is nervousness," Aunt Baker said. She crouched by Alouette and took her in her arms. "Come, little one," she said, and rocked her like a child.

Henry hauled quilts into the kitchen and made a nest for her beside the fire. He made a cold compress for her forehead and heated up a brick to warm her toes. He fed her whiskey but she choked on it and so he made her drink hot water in which sweet potatoes had been boiled. He sang her songs, humming when he lost the words, and held her hand and called her "little Lette" and told her stories to distract her. All to no avail.

At last Aunt Baker said, "We must get her out of here. We must send her north to Boston where she can feel safe. My sister Belle will take her in. Would you like that, little one?"

A sigh came out of Alouette and she began to weep. "There, child," Aunt Baker said.

And so one night the shadowy figure of the guide appeared out in the garden and Alouette was spirited away. Eugenia stood a long time looking out into the darkness after them, and when

Aunt Baker came to ask if she would go to bed, she said, "Who is he, this guide? Are you sure he will take care of her?"

"He is a mountain man, the best there is, a Red String through and through. I would not trust Alouette to any other."

"What is his name?"

"There is no need for you to know."

CHAPTER TWENTY-FIVE

CLYDE had been fighting for the Yankees for a good long time before it occurred to him that if they won the war and all the nigras got set free, he could not be a slave catcher like he'd planned, not even a patroller. He did not understand how he had got himself in such a situation. One minute he'd been hitching up his pants and bragging by his father's grave, the next he was a private in the Yankee army, shooting at fellers he had no business shooting at. And yet if he didn't shoot at them, they would surely shoot at him, and kill him, so there was nothing for it but to shoot them first.

Sometimes, in the beginning, he thought he'd creep across the lines one night and turn into a Rebel, but then the Rebels got theirselves beat up so bad at Gettysburg he figured maybe that weren't such a fine idea. In the year since then, hardly a night went by but one more Rebel crept across the Union lines and gave himself up for a pair of shoes or half a loaf of bread, which made Clyde think they would surely lose the war they were such yellow-bellies, he would rather be a Yankee winner anytime.

He thought some more about the nigras going free and figured after all it would not be so bad. Uncle Benjamin, before they made him be a chaplain, had told him if the nigras only could get free, they would rise up in a bunch and head on back to Africa, where they came from in the first place. They are longing for their homeland, he told Clyde, and showed him an advertisement about it in a newspaper, along with the advertisements for deserters from the Rebel army. Homeland Liberia, it said, which was in Africa, and underneath there was a picture of a ship sailing on the ocean. Any nigra who was free and had the money for his passage was allowed to go.

Clyde asked Amos if he'd like to go to Africa if he was free, but Amos only shook his head and laughed. What you do say, he said, and went off to chop wood.

Clyde thought that if he were a nigra, he would go. He would just save his wages up and go. It would be a grand adventure, going on a ship like that. He might be frightened when he started out, but it would be a grand adventure, better than staying on a farm his whole life long.

When he joined the army, he had sat around a good while doing nothing, and after they began to fight he had been considerably frightened, sometimes he could not sleep at all because of it, which meant he was plumb fagged out when he had to fight next day.

Being frightened did not mean he was afraid to fight, although at first he had been, he had vomited and even run, but now, although he was still frightened almost all the time, he had gotten used to it. The cannon boomed so loud you could not hear the Rebels' high thin screaming coming at you through the smoke, anyways not much, and he had developed a way of keeping his head straight and squinting up his eyes so that he only saw far enough in front to keep from stumbling. If you looked straight at the soldiers coming at you with their muskets and their bayonets, you were done for like a rabbit frozen by the shadow of a hawk.

The trick was not to see them, just to run after the flag and shoot and shoot, trying not to breathe too deep so as not to suffocate from powder smoke, trying not to listen to the minié balls crying through the air like souls of dead men flying up to heaven. And when you got up close, you'd be done for if you didn't have a bayonet. You could swing a bayonet around and yell and keep the other feller off you, and if you got lucky you could stick him through. Or you could belt him with your musket butt.

He had told the quartermaster he would like to have a pistol, but the quartermaster said be thankful for a Springfield it will fire a good long way, which was true, although you did not always know if you had shot an enemy or if it was the feller next to you who did it, you could not know for sure unless you got him close. Which was why Clyde only knew for sure that he had shot one enemy. Ran right up behind and shot him in the head. He might have shot some others, and he thought he had, but he could not tell for sure, mostly they were too far off and everyone was shooting and people falling down all over, so if he did they didn't count. It was the ones you knew for sure that you could notch into your musket. It was his second battle when he shot the enemy for sure. He did not know how many he had stuck through with his bayonet enough to kill them, up close things got so confused that all you cared about was getting out of it alive.

Now it was the spring of eighteen sixty-four and here he was in this place Spotsylvania. Tomorrow there was going to be another battle, that's what everybody said, but you couldn't know for sure until the trumpet sounded and the sergeant came and shouted in your face. A storm was up, making it hard to sleep, all that belting on the outside of the tent, and the wind gusting and whooping, making the canvas billow and cave in and billow up again, and water rushing so that even though he wrapped himself in his oilcloth he was soaked, and the other soldier that he shared the tent with shouting, Holy Mother! Holy Mother! every goddam minute. His name was Brian. He was Irish and had come across the ocean on a ship, they recruited him right off the dock in New York City. I came here to find a better life, he said, and look at what I got.

But Clyde thought being a soldier was exciting, better than a farmer like his pa. Maybe he would go off for the army when the war was done and be a full-time soldier. He could go all over, anywhere there was a war, and see everything there was to see and kill a lot of enemies. He would be a corporal pretty soon, he figured, and a sergeant after that, and tell everyone below him what to do. They would do it too, a sergeant had authority, he could have them shot if they refused. He could not be a lieu-tenant, since he had no horse, but a sergeant was pretty well high up. Why, if it weren't for Ma needing a place to live, he would sell that farm right smart the minute he got back. As he thought of it, he flinched. If Pa could know his boy was thinking thoughts like that, he'd surely take and clap him good and hard upside the head again. Tomorrow he would shoot another en-emy for sure.

BUT he didn't shoot another enemy. Rain was still slashing down, and though he heard the popping of percussion caps, he did not hear many shots. He didn't fire one shot himself, al-though he tried. His powder was all wet, the others' too. Still, they made it to the Rebel earthworks, an army of mud men plastered to a wall of mud, then slipped and slithered down into the trenches, thigh deep in water, blinded by the rain. That was when he got taken prisoner with some others.

When Clyde heard the way his captors spoke, he understood the trouble he was in, since they spoke the same way he did. It made him furious, and homesick too. He wanted to tell them, Hey, I am from Carolina, I am a friend. On the other hand, he wanted to bash their heads in, every one.

When they asked him who he was, he lied at first and said he was from Maine, but they did not believe him. They stole his hat and jacket, almost ripping off his arm to get his jacket off. After that, they bucked him down with his hands tied around his knees and his musket shoved through underneath them, and stuck a bayonet close up in his face and said they would slit his nostrils if he did not tell the truth.

So then he told the truth, that he was from Chapel Hill and had never joined the Rebel army, which meant he could not be a deserter, but then they said that they would hang him for a traitor. They did not hang him, though, they had to go and fight, and so they put a guard on him, and the others they had caught, until they could get back to deal with him.

While he was waiting for them to come back, sitting in the mud with water sluicing off him, Clyde thought about his situation. He figured the Yankee soldiers with him were all goners, and he might be a goner too. At first he thought he might run off, trusting to the rain to hide him. They had pulled his musket out from underneath his knees and he worked the ropes around his hands and pretty soon they loosened. But by now the rain had eased, and although a mist rose up and clung to everything, it was not dense enough to hide a running man.

So then he thought he'd best make up a story. He just might get shot unless he thought up a good story. He figured he would tell them he'd been tricked into the Yankee army and was waiting for his first chance to escape. Maybe he would cry a bit and say, Thank God you have saved me, now I can join the Rebel Cause. But then he thought about how every night these Rebels slid out of their trenches and their rifle pits and came slinking with their hands above their heads to give themselves up to the Union pickets, half naked most of them, their canteens clicking at their waists, with no ammunition for their guns, or no guns at all, and every one of them half starved, and he thought when they came back to deal with him they might not believe he was a Rebel at his heart. He sat and worried on it, getting angry in his head and trying to make his story better.

They never did come back to deal with him, maybe they got shot, and pretty soon a Rebel lieutenant came along and before long after that Clyde found himself in a line of prisoners slipping and sliding down a road so churned by horses' hooves and wagon wheels it was like wading through a bog. They were taking them to Salisbury, back in North Carolina. A jail was there, the others told him when they stopped to rest. It was for Union prisoners of war, everyone had heard of it. They said he should be glad to go there and shut up his complaining since he could sit the war out now and go back home alive.

But Clyde did not want to sit the war out, he wanted to shoot a lot of enemies and be made a corporal and then a sergeant and tell privates what to do. He could not shoot anyone if he was a prisoner. So he kept his eyes out and his wits about him, waiting for an opportunity to straggle back and drop out of the line.

Now it was the second day of marching, early morning, the sky hung low and gloomy, thick mist rising up to meet it underneath. Clyde realized he could not see the front part of the line, and when he turned around, could not see the guards behind. The road had narrowed, dense mist-filled woods pressing close up on both sides. He tensed, readying himself.

But before he made his move, they were turning off the road and scrambling down a cutting. An enormous sigh came up from down below and Clyde realized they were heading for a train. It was now or never. As he came out of the cutting, sliding down the last steep section on his rump, he scrambled sideways and behind a bush.

The next thing he knew, something smashed him so hard upside the head he fell down on his back. It was one of the rear guards, like a ghost above him in the mist, hissing in his teeth. He raised his musket one more time, but Clyde flung up his arm and the blow caught him fair across the elbow, setting him to yelping like a dog, and the guard screaming at him, You damned Yankee, I will kill you, God help me, I will kill you!

He did not do it, though, just took him by a fistful of his shirt and jerked him up and shoved him down the slope, Clyde stumbling and swaying dizzily, past a row of cattle cars and up onto a flatbed carriage of the train. Up ahead, the engine gave another sigh, then shrieked and jerked and started down the track, the prisoners huddled up and clinging to each other for fear of falling off, coughing and spitting in a cloud of burning, soot-filled smoke.

Clyde sat hunched over with his legs sprawled out, jolting back and forth, watching the woods spin sickeningly by, his elbow throbbing and his other hand against his smashed-up head. It hurt inside his brain, the way it used to when Pa took out for him. He did not miss Pa, he realized. He had been a mean man, yes indeed.

ARRIVED at Salisbury, the train groaned to a halt. The guards stood up on the flatbed, waving at their prisoners not to move. They sat in silence, the train wheezing and sighing, blowing steam out sideways on the tracks. On one side of the train, across the tracks, were fields and scattered buildings. In one of the fields, a Negro woman stopped pushing on a plow and waved at them.

On the train's other side, across a brief expanse of hard red ground, a high stockade fence with a walkway about three feet from the top and a row of armed guards looking down at them. A commotion farther down the train, a whistle blast, the grating sound of doors slid back, and a double row of men came shuffling and stumbling along the platform. Some wore parts of uniforms, some not so much as a shirt. None of them had shoes.

Without a glance at Clyde or his companions on the flatbed car, they straggled by, some limping or hopping, some leaning on each other's shoulders, some crying and moaning, others staring stoically ahead. Guards came with them, decked out in a strange mixture of Confederate and Union uniforms, chewing tobacco and shoving at their prisoners as they bustled them along.

A shout and Clyde and his companions were tumbling off the flatbed's side, lining up behind them. Another shout and they were at the prison gate. It swung back with a rickety, protesting sound. As he went toward it, Clyde looked up the palisade at the sentries with their guns. They looked back down at him.

Rebels. He would shoot the lot of them if he had half a chance. And he wouldn't be a prisoner for long. Ten days, that was the agreement between North and South, ten days and he would be exchanged. They had whupped those Rebels good already, they would not last, everybody said it. Clyde wanted to get back so he could see them go down the last time. His mouth fixed in a sneer. Ten days, that was all.

CHAPTER TWENTY-SIX

TOM and Charley were a team now. Together or apart, they sneaked inside the Rebel lines, reporting back the numbers of round tents and wall tents and how many men there were in each. They counted rifle stacks and cannons and measured forts by counting their own footsteps, and reported on positions of rifle pits and breastworks, what sort of freight was going up and down the railway lines and where the lines were vulnerable to attack. A dozen times they had been almost caught by pickets, Charley lost the top of his right ear to a bullet, and twice they had been hunted through the woods by hounds.

Before they went out on a mission, Charley always made Tom kneel with him and pray. "Oh, God," he would say, "we are going into mortal danger. Preserve me and my brother Tom," and although Tom figured it was up to him and Charley to watch out for themselves, it made him feel as though he had a sort of family.

One day, Robert paddled Tom and Charley up the Trent River early in the morning. A Rebel camp was on the other side of Trenton and the plan was for the two scouts to go in disguised as pipe and pipe tobacco vendors and bring back information on its strength. Robert pulled his boat into the reeds where he would wait for their return and watched them set off carrying a pair of flat display trays on their backs and bundles of their wares. They had done this sort of thing before. When they got closer, they would hide their muskets and set up their trays with the straps around their necks and lay out the pipes and packets of tobacco. The Rebel camp was quite a distance off and they traveled steadily in silence, each man thinking his own thoughts.

Tom was thinking about Rose, who had married Robert at the Baptist church eight months before. Ben had come back from the field to read the service and when it was done Rose moved into the cottage with everything she owned held in one hand. She had gleaming golden skin and generous red lips, and despite a small physique, enormous energy. Morning to night she talked and bustled, laughing and teasing and organizing everyone.

Charley followed her about, obeying orders, laughing at her jokes, hanging on every word that fell out of her mouth, looking bashful when the word that fell was praise for him. And yet she could be sharp and temperamental, from time to time flouncing to the bedroom for a sulk, which mercifully did not last long. Tom thought she was well named, brilliant as a rose yet with a thorny underside.

Since marrying her, Robert had gone about with a permanent grin planted on his face, full of talk of family and how Rose would have eleven or twelve babies before it was all done. Rose, who had begun to swell up almost as soon as they were married, laughed and said he'd better save his money if he wanted her to have eleven more. She was a cook, and earned a fine income selling pies and cakes and fish stews and casseroles to the Union soldiers in the camps around New Bern. Sometimes Tom went with her to help wheel the cart, to make sure the Yankees treated her the way a lady should be treated, and as she got more cumbersome, to make sure she did not tumble into one of the stinking refuse pits surrounding every camp.

He envied Robert, not for having Rose so much as for the babies. He would like to have some babies too. He would like to have his mother, and his father back from Down-the-River, and his brothers and sisters, those ghostly shadows at the edges of his memory, and some children of his own. He would need a wife, of course. What sort of wife? A wife like Rose? No, Rose was a nice girl and very pretty, but she was too raucous for his taste, too prone to sing and dance and make the whole house rattle with her laughter and enthusiastic worship of the Lord. Too prone, too, to tell everybody, not just Robert, exactly what it was they ought to do.

What sort of wife, then, would be good for him? He thought about it traveling through the woods, and after a while fancied that he saw a woman's swinging skirt, and heard the padding of bare feet across a floor. He screwed his face up, trying to bring the image into focus, but could not make a picture in his mind. He and Charley had just picked their way across a swamp, knee deep in slush, and were climbing up the sandy ridge beyond, when he realized the barefooted woman in the swinging skirt was Miss Genie.

It could not happen, he knew that. Miss Genie had said she loved him, but she would not want him for a husband, she would laugh at him, and maybe tell her father, who would get riled up and have him taken off and strung up from a tree, or whipped. Anyway, the pair of them had gone off to Australia to be copper miners. He would not see Miss Genie anymore.

He would like to see her, though, and tell her he was not a

simpleton. He would like to sail across the ocean and appear—
rap, rap—at her door. "Good day, Miss Genie," he would say,
pulling off his hat and speaking carefully the way the teacher at
the school had taught him, "I came to tell you your Tom's not a
simpleton." And she would look at him with wonder, then reach
and seize him in her arms and kiss him on the mouth.

The ambition of it made him laugh out loud. He snatched off
his hat and smacked it against his thigh, the sound of it like a
gunshot in the silent woods.

Charley stopped abruptly and looked back. "What you doing, boy?" he hissed. "You fancying to get us killed?"

Tom pulled an apologetic face. "Sorry," he mouthed, and set
his hat back on with an exaggerated show of soundlessness.

Too late. A Rebel picket appeared out of the woods. Although neither Tom nor Charley wore a uniform, their black
faces and their guns and skulking attitudes told the picket all he
needed. "Damnation! Nigger spies!" He jerked his rifle up. Tom
and Charley turned and fled. Behind, a shot rang out. The picket
shouted for the dogs.

It was the third time Tom had been hunted by a pack of
hounds since he had been a scout. The first two times panic
seized him by the head and yanked him through the woods, tripping over stumps and fallen trees and into holes, flailing at overhanging branches, skidding on slick needles, whooping, and half
vomiting with fear. If Galloway had not been there to guide him,
he would have blundered on until he got himself trapped in a
gully or floundered into swampy ground so dense with over-
growth he could not break through. This time, though, cast
upon his own resources, a cool hard urgency took hold of him.
He must get Charley safely back to camp.

The hounds had not yet found their trail, he could tell it from
the way their baying broke, and then went high and hesitant,
and then went on, and broke again. He and Charley had tossed

their trays and packs of merchandise aside and now ran fast with just their muskets in their hands, splashing through every swampy patch and puddle they could find to break their scent.

The voices of the hounds took on a lower, steady note, and Tom knew they had found the trail and it was time for action. A dense copse lay ahead and to the left. He swung toward it, Charley close on his heels. Inside the copse, they primed their guns and waited, panting, for the hounds to come within their sights.

And here they came. The two scouts fired together, the combined explosion tossing such a fright into the hounds that they collapsed onto each other in a pile of agitated legs and flopping, terror-stricken jowls. Tom could not tell if either of the shots had hit their mark, but by the time he had reloaded and raised his gun to aim, the hounds were bolting back the way they came, trailing behind them a panicky high yipping.

They waited. Nothing but far crashing and then silence. So they set out again, intent on putting so much distance between themselves and their pursuers that even if the hounds recovered from their fright, they could not run them down before they reached the river.

When they could run no more, they rested, and then ran again, the urgency of their flight diminishing with every stop. At last Charley swung his arm up. "Whoa! Enough!" and they went on at a slower, steady pace, laughing and congratulating each other on their escape.

Too soon for congratulations. They were trotting on the ridges through the swamps when they heard the bay of hounds again, and men's voices shouting. At first Tom thought they had been overtaken, but then he realized these men were on horseback. A stray band of Rebels scouring through the woods had come upon them quite by accident.

No thick copses to use for hiding here, so each man slipped

behind a tree, and when the hounds appeared, let fly. One dog went down silently. Another spun around to snap at its flank, then sank onto the ground and lay glaze-eyed and whimpering, while the remainder of the pack milled about long enough for Tom and Charley both to load and fire again. They were so close it was hard to miss, but miss they did. The dogs ran off, and by the time their owners rallied to advance again, Tom and Charley were well off into the swamps, running for their lives.

Tom's hat was gone and he ran as he had run so long ago when he was hunted through the woods by Morgan's Creek. But this time he was not afraid. His heart sang and the sky above him sang. Heat gathered in his body, raging like a furnace stoked and pumped with bellows to a white-hot flame. Reaching up in midstride, he ripped his shirt away, and ran and ran, stumbled and fell down, and rose, and stumbled on, both shoes vanished in the sucking mud, his pants so thick and heavy with the stuff he scrambled out of them, flung them aside, ran on until he saw the river spread before him, and Robert small and distant, growing larger every moment on the bank, his boat behind him on the gleaming grinning water, dancing with his two fists punching at the air, Tom shouting now across his shoulder toward the sound of Charley coming on behind, *"Come on! Come on! We're going to make it!"* the two of them in nothing but their undershirts and drawers, limbs pumping hot and easy and triumphant, bolting through the howling swamp with viscous brown mud flying up behind like wings.

THE next week, in shirts and pants and hats dug out of the boxes at the Baptist church, and brand-new military boots that creaked, Tom and Charley went out on a long, looping expedition that took them northwards to the border of Virginia, then back along the north–south railway line through Goldsboro to Warsaw. Almost a month passed before they got back to New Bern. Now, as they approached it late one afternoon, the town seemed to be on fire. Black smoke hung above it in a heavy cloud and from as far as two miles out they could smell camp filth festering in the stifling heat.

Before long, they began to pass groups of townspeople fleeing down the road, hauling their possessions on carts and wheelbarrows, those who still had mules or horses of their own in carriages and wagons piled high with lamps and mattresses and sacks of food. A family on foot had stopped to rest. Tom and Charley paused to question them. It was the yellow fever, they were told. It had struck the town with such rapidity and force that already hundreds had been buried and more were dying every day. Tar fires had been lit on every corner, the wooden buildings on the wharf at Craven Street torn down because they harbored pestholes mantled with green slime, the rank vegetation around the outskirts of the town cut down and dried and burned to dissipate infection in the air, but still the pestilence raged on. These unfortunates themselves had lost a father and a sister and a child.

It did not occur to either Tom or Charley not to go back into town. They had a report that must be made, and they would make it. Earlier that year the place had raged with smallpox and they had lived through that. They did not doubt they would survive the yellow fever too.

But as they came into the main street and found it silent and deserted, save for the ghostly smoke-wreathed figures tending to the corner fires, a sort of premonition came into Tom's head, a nervous tautness of the brain. He sent Charley on to report at camp while, half choking and with tears streaming down his face, he went to see if all was well at home.

What he found along the way made his stomach tighten and the blood pulse in his ears. On every house, at door or gate or tacked onto the upright of the porch, was the warning white flag of the fever. Not a curtain stirred. He crossed the bridge and found the freedmen's village just as silent and white-flagged. As he approached the corner of their lane, a cart turned out of it, piled with bodies. He snatched his hat off and stood aside for it to pass, wanting to vomit, to cry out, because the faces jolting past, blood-red eyeballs of the fever staring, belonged to neighbors, friends. He looked for Rose and Robert but did not see them.

The cart rounded the corner and swayed off down the road, a lone dog coming mournfully behind. Tom stood looking after it, then drew in a long breath and went on until he reached the picket gate. No sooner had he pushed it open than the door flew back and Rose fell into his arms. "He never saw her, his first baby and he never even saw her."

ROBERT had been dead a week. Rose had given birth alone, the child a tiny nameless girl. Now they were on the road, Tom and Rose and Charley and the baby fleeing from the pestilence together. Charley had made off with a horse and saddle and some ammunition from the military camp. No one seemed to care or even notice, so consumed were all the soldiers with their dying and the dying of their fellows. He brought the news that Abraham Galloway had snatched his mother out of Wilmington and brought her to New Bern where she had caught the yellow fever, her son now in a fever of alarm that by bringing her to freedom he had done her in.

He also brought the news that Mr. Lincoln had been re-elected and that, in Atlanta, the Rebel army had skedaddled out of town ahead of General Sherman and his men, the whole place in a panic about what would happen next. Tom knew about this

General Sherman. He had red hair and the Rebels said he was a wicked madman.

It was a sweltering hot day of eighteen sixty-four, the sky the fierce blue of early fall when the leaves have just begun to turn but the atmosphere still clings to summer. The air smelled of dust, and of the smoke that hung like spirits of the dismal dead above the town behind. Rose and her baby traveled on the horse, with Tom in front and Charley bringing up the rear, both with muskets at the ready. Rebel Cat swung in a sack between Tom's shoulders, watching the passing countryside with enigmatic yellow eyes.

Tom's plan was to go back to the Avery plantation, where he would recover his gold—he was certain he would find it—and search out an abandoned white trash cabin to take over till the war was done, which he figured wouldn't be too long since everyone was sick of it and wanted to go home. Then they would strike out for Chapel Hill. What they would do when they got there, he had no idea, except that he would scoop his mother up into his arms. All of them would stay together, he was bent on that.

He walked mourning down the road, his mind on Robert, who had been his friend. Sometimes, glancing back at Rose, he felt such pity he could hardly bear it. She had made a cradle for the baby from a blanket tied by its ends about her waist and neck, and seemed to wilt above her, weeping helplessly and softly, "Oh, my man, my man, my man." Charley, loping on behind, scanning the woods on either side for enemies, let his gaze rest on her from time to time, his face expressionless.

Eventually the rhythm of their forward movement soothed Rose into silence and Tom began to think about the future, wondering how he would earn a living back in Chapel Hill. Perhaps he could use his gold to buy his way into a business, a blacksmith, maybe, or a wheelwright. Maybe even buy a farm, or a

store with big glass windows at the front and a fine display of—
what? Top hats, maybe, or embroidered waistcoats. On the
other hand, maybe he could start a restaurant and Rose could be
the cook.

He thought about what Robert said to him that day before
he fled the turpentine plantation: "Freedom ain't no gift. You
got to hunt it down and catch it. You got to snatch it in your
hand." Once the war was over, maybe freedmen could snatch
anything they chose inside their hand. Maybe they could take up
with ladies who were white. He half smiled to himself, thinking
about showing up on Miss Genie's doorstep in Australia with
Rebel Cat yowling and disgruntled on his back.

They traveled slowly, and as the sun slipped down behind the
trees and a low fog started from the ground, Tom realized he
had underestimated how far they had to go, and made prepara-
tions in his mind for a night beside the road. Food was stuffed
into the saddlebags, enough to last two days, and blanket rolls
were roped onto the horse's back. At this time of year the nights
were cool but not unpleasant. All they needed was a safe, protected spot.

But before he could choose a place to stop, they rounded a
curve and there, off to the left, was the Big House of the Avery
plantation. He had seen it only once, but even though the garden
had grown up with weeds and the house looked, from this distance, sad, he knew for sure it was the one. It seemed to be abandoned.

Closer inspection proved him right. The doors and windows
all stood open and the rain had beaten in so that the floor of the
front entryway had warped, the planks lifted up and curling at
the edges so that they had to tread carefully to keep from tripping. Apparently someone had tried to burn the place down by
setting fire to the curtains in the parlor, but the fire hadn't taken

and all that remained was some scorching of the wall and the half-burned curtains, which had mildewed, as had the wall and floor below the open window. What little furniture had not been looted had been ripped and torn, although not completely wrecked, and in the kitchen, dishes had been smashed against the walls so that the floor was thick with broken china. Amongst it all, a pine plank table stood on four stout legs.

Upstairs, rain had come in through the windows and the mattresses smelled of mold. But they were mattresses, Rose said, and could be aired. She seemed quite cheered, and while she set to work sweeping up the debris in the kitchen with a pine bough, Charley went in search of firewood and Tom went off to scavenge through the smokehouse and the barn and other out-houses to see if anything was left to eat. He came up with noth-ing, but as he stepped out of the corncrib, a buck stood in the middle of what once had been a lawn, just stood there looking at him, balancing its antlers like a gift. Even when Tom raised his gun it did not flinch.

They ate well that night, and in the morning Tom left Rose with Charley and set out to find his gold. He had dreamed the forest had burned down and he was wandering empty-handed amongst fallen, blackened stumps. But no, although the distill-ery was nothing but a ruin overgrown by vines and climbing weeds, the forest stood. He went directly in, following the map inside his head.

An hour later, he arrived back at the house, calling out to Rose and Charley. They were in the kitchen and he went through and set his bundle on the table. "Come here. Come and see."

It was all there, even the paper money, which by now was not worth much. Charley made a whistling inhalation of his breath and Rose, her baby in her arms, leaned over it, admiring. She damped the tip of one finger with her tongue, set it in the gleaming dust, and held it to the light. It sparkled on her finger. She set her fingertip against her baby's forehead, the child staring up at her with unfocused baby blindness.

"For luck," she said.

Charley laughed, a low sound of delight. "Will you just look at that?" Because the color of the gold dust was the color of the baby's skin. And so they named her Baby Gold.

CHAPTER TWENTY-SEVEN

INSIDE the Salisbury prison compound, Clyde was seriously
worried. He had been here for months now and not one soul
had been exchanged, unless you counted as exchanged the ones
who had gone to heaven, or to hell for wickedness, for cursing
or for fighting or for stealing or for beating other people up. The
place was crowded, a vast expanse of ragged half-starved men,
he figured thousands. Not so much as a roof above their heads,
although there were buildings, hospitals and quarters for the
guards and such. The biggest building had been a factory of
some sort, but now it was a hospital, full of men lined along the
walls to die.

The first few nights he slept on the ground and watched to
see what other people did. A few of them had tents and he tried
to get in under one of them, but it was so crowded under there
that when one man turned in his sleep all the others had to turn

as well and pretty soon they shoved him out. So then he thought, ten days, not so bad, I can sleep out on the ground ten days.

After that it rained for three days straight, and three nights too, and the prison yard became a bog and stank with all the putrid smells that come out of a man. When Clyde lay down to rest, he sank up to his ears and feared that if he fell asleep he would just drown in shit.

So he thought he'd make himself a dugout, the way the others did. Their holes were all across the prison yard, some with two or three men together, peering out of them like wild beasts from their lairs. He knew how to do it, since he had done it with his pa, although he did not have a spade or grubbing hoe, just a case knife, which made it slow, and no bedquilt, which meant he only had his shirt for hauling off the soil. He made a low wall around the entrance to keep the rain from flooding in, although after a while it leaked down through the ground. At least his wall kept dead rats from washing down, or maggots and other such disgusting things.

Having two or three men in one hole together meant that one was always there to guard it when the others were away, and it was company at night as well. Before Clyde started digging, he asked a couple of others if they would share with him, but no one seemed to take a fancy to his company, and so for a while he shared it with a nigra, which was better than not having anyone at all.

The nigra's name was Caesar and he reminded Clyde of Amos, Pa's hired slave back home, he had that same slow way of talking. He had been a sailor once and could tell about what it was like to sail a ship out on the ocean. And he could sing, you could hear his singing come from underneath your feet when he was down there on his own. When people heard it they did not try to steal the hole.

Caesar had jumped ship in Baltimore, but was caught and

hauled to Salisbury. Having been a sailor all his life, he did not take well to prison, so one day he tried escaping. He hid himself amongst a pile of bodies waiting on the dead cart to be buried. He planned to let them bury him as well and when they went away he would dig himself back out. He asked Clyde to come with him, but Clyde said it was foolishness, pure foolishness, they would have to leave their clothes behind since everyone was buried naked, how would they escape, would they run naked through the mountains all the way to Tennessee? And anyways, guards were at the cemetery. But Caesar figured he would wait till night to dig back out. He figured since he was so black no one would see him in the dark. He would get clear away and find some slave somewhere who would help him. But when they picked him up and slung him in the pit the breath came grunting out of him, and so they knew he was alive and shot him dead.

This story, carried back into the compound by the guards, was talked over and opined on by one man to another until someone telling someone else was overheard by Clyde, who slammed his fist into the dirt wall of his hole and swore. For a while he fought off muggers trying to take his hole away from him, but got beat up so bad he thought they'd kill him in the end, so he gave it up to them and went back to sleeping on the ground with rain coming down all over him, and lightning cracking so close overhead he flinched as though a sniper had him in his sights. He missed Caesar singing in the night.

More prisoners came crowding every day. Some said they came from someplace called the Libby prison up in Richmond, others from a prison called Andersonville down in Georgia. All of them were pulled down and depressed, not one with the least idea of why they had been moved, nor did they care, they were so sick and starving fit to fall down in their tracks. A good number went directly to the hospital, which meant that they were goners, hardly anyone got out of there except to be tossed in a pile beside the dead house wall and then swung naked up onto the cemetery cart and hauled off and tossed into a pit.

Clyde had seen that cemetery. He had volunteered one time to be on burial detail for an extra ration, which he did not get, and had seen what it was like. All those bodies slung every day into the pit together, it was pitiful. He had to shovel dirt across them, full into their faces, it was right pitiful, and the bad smell made his stomach turn. After that he had to help with sorting the dead men's clothes so they could be handed out to someone else to die in. They crawled with graybacks, but there was no pot big enough to boil them in.

It was after that he got the diarrhea, not all the time so he was not sick to die, although he knew he'd lost a lot of weight. He knew that for a fact. He'd been going by the commissary building where there was a platform scale out front, and climbed up onto it and weighed himself. Eighty pounds, he must be skin and bone. He pulled his shirt up, looking at his ribs, and pulled it quickly down again. He could not understand why he had not been exchanged. He asked a guard, but the guard just spat and said, You get any closer to the dead line, you sorry little rat-faced Yankee shite, and I will shoot you. He would have too, and no one to either know or care, they were all too busy stealing some other feller's cornmeal ration straight out of his mouth, or making plans about digging tunnels to escape.

Everybody talked about escaping, everybody. Most of them did not try it for fear of being shot, or for fear the bloodhounds would come after them and rip their throats out. The bloodhounds were caged up outside the gates and spent all night howling when the moon was up. Each morning, the guards walked them round the outside of the stockade, you could hear them out there baying when they thought they'd caught a scent. Perhaps if he had gone with Caesar he could have warned him not to grunt. Perhaps they could have found a creek to run along and hide their scent. Perhaps they could have got away. He wished Caesar wasn't dead. He was just a nigra, nothing much, but Clyde had liked him pretty well, and no one else would be his friend, he could not understand it.

THE weather had turned cold. Last night when he lay down to sleep, the mud cracked under him with ice. His pants and shirt froze onto it and someone stole his shoe. He would have got the other one, but Clyde woke up and kicked him good. After that, he could not sleep because his shoeless foot was hurting with the cold. He bent his leg and twisted up his toes and sucked on them. It did no good. Once he would have thought one shoe was not much good to anyone, but now he felt right glad for it and wished he had a pair. Maybe if he went about very early in the morning, he could steal one from a corpse. But everyone was hunting for a pair of shoes, an extra coat, a blanket, and he got shoved out of the way by bigger men.

He did not intend to die, he would not do it, he would stay alive. He had eaten mice, he ate a cat leg once, stole it from another prisoner's boiling can, and he had eaten roaches, and picked graybacks from his hair and eaten them.

One day he turned in some prisoners who were digging a tunnel underneath the palisade. They were muggers anyways, bad types, they were no good for anything. The guards shot them for it and Clyde got half a loaf of bread. He ate it all at once in case someone snatched it off him, and it made him sick, being only half baked with the corn inside raw and hard and sour. They had put lime in it to make it rise, but it did not rise and the lime brought on his diarrhea again. There was no outhouse he could go to, not even a slop bucket he could use, the men just crouched down where they stood. The pit along one fence was full of it, washed there by the rain since you could not use the pit directly. It was part of the dead zone and if you went too close, the sentry up above would shoot you. The best you could do was not shit too close to anybody's hole if you did not want to be beat up again.

He went and crouched under an oak tree, groaning and looking up the trunk for a piece of bark low enough to reach. If he could get a piece of bark and a little bit of firewood, he could boil the bark and make some tea, which would help to keep his bowels from griping and flooding all the time. But the trees had been peeled as high up as a man could reach standing on another's shoulders, and so he crouched there dolefully, thinking about the tunnel diggers he had given up. He wished he hadn't done it now. He wished he'd asked if they would let him help them, he could do it, he was good at digging, and maybe they'd have got away, the lot of them. He wondered where they came from. One was from the South, Clyde could tell it from his accent. He had fallen on his knees and called out for his mother just before they shot him. Ma, he had called out, Oh, save me, Ma.

Thinking on it, Clyde felt his bowels twist again. Maybe that boy came from some farm hereabouts, which would mean he was a kind of neighbor. He was nothing but a Rebel, one of them deserters, he was no good for anything. They'd said Pa was a deserter, though, and Uncle Benjamin as well. Maybe that boy's pa had been shot too, maybe his ma was all alone with just a nigra to take care of her.

For the first time since Clyde left home, a thought occurred to him. What if Amos had run off? Slaves were running off all over, everyone knew that. What if Ma had no one to chop wood or tend the farm or go out hunting in the woods? He wanted to get up to his feet and hike his pants up, but every time he thought that he was done, his gut wrenched and he had to crouch back down. Pa's friends would take care of Ma. They would not let her starve. But what if them Home Guard fellers had found their cave and shot them too?

He was sweating and felt hot all over. He thought any second he would fall down on his face. He set one hand on the ground and leaned on it. His head felt dizzy and his tongue felt like a swollen dead thing in his mouth. His insides were coming out again. He felt himself slip forward and heard a voice say, Ma, oh Ma, I need a drink of water.

And there was Ma, sitting in her slat chair on the porch, staring at her cradle full of flowers. And here came Old Mary with a wooden bucket from the pump. She set it on the step and went inside and came back out. In her hand she had a ladle made out of a gourd. She dipped it in the bucket and turned and smiled at him and poured the water on the ground. That there's for Tom, she said. And then the dream came back, the one he never could get shed of. He saw the red drop gather on the bottom of Tom's heel, and then the little spurt of dust.

When he came to, it was snowing and somebody had stole his pants, stole them right off his body. His last shoe gone too. No, here it was, he had it in his hand, he must have clung on to it hard. He twisted down and pulled it on, looking at himself. A sad and sorry sight. Nothing on him but one shoe and a shirt, and his own shit frozen onto him. When he raised his head and looked about, he realized he'd been lying there a good long while because the snow was thick enough to hide the mud. Everyone who could had vanished underground. Others were huddled together under the old factory building, others under leafless trees, others marching, marching, back and forth, trying to keep from freezing, others holding out their hands to catch the snow and eat it. Still others, those who had gone mad, just went on wandering and talking to themselves the way they always did.

His pants had not been much protection from the cold, but without them the north wind cut right through him. He pushed himself into a sitting position, his head shrugged back into his neck and his knees drawn up to his body, and rubbed his legs ferociously. But his skin was too sensitive and painful to be warmed by friction, so lowering his chin between his knees, he wrapped his arms around his legs, looking bleakly at the red spots across the insides of his thighs. He had not noticed these before, and after a while shifted his rattling numb jaw to examine his calves and the outsides of his thighs. They were the same, the sparse stiff hair, the tiny rings of inflammation at each base. Goddam! he said, Goddam! He stood up unsteadily, favoring his painful toes, but then he realized he could not feel them anymore. He could not feel that leg at all, the left one. He gave in then, and went to stand in line outside the hospital.

The wind was banking snow against the wall, and around the feet of the men in line. Clyde stood with one hand on the wall for balance, and tilting back his numb leg, held on to the ankle with his other hand. This kept it out of the snow but the wind was just as cold so after a while he let it drop. He tried to keep his teeth still, what was left of them. He'd lost three more the last few days, and figured pretty soon he'd have none left at all. He had the scurvy, he was sure of it, he could tell it from the red spots on his legs.

The line moved sluggishly, the men behind him and in front coughing in their hands but silent otherwise, some with pus-weeping rashes on their chests and arms from having burned themselves with heated nails or bits of wire to make it look as though they had the smallpox. This would get them from the main compound to the smallpox camp outside, where they figured it was easier to make a getaway. Clyde did not believe this. Once you started to the hospital, it was the beginning of the end, everybody knew it. But he tried not to think of that. He tried to think about a plan for getting out of here. He would die, he knew that now, if he did not get out.

The orderly stuck his head out of the door and jerked his neck, frost puffing from his mouth. You next, he said, and Clyde went in.

The doctor looked at him. He hardly bothered with Clyde's toes, although he gave him a piece of torn-up bandage he could wrap them in. He looked at the red spots on his legs and said, Pull up your shirt, and when he saw the way his ribs showed through, he shrugged.

It was that shrug that did it. Clyde knew it meant the end, there was no hope for him. He hobbled from the hospital, past the dead house where a pile of bodies waited to be hauled away, then stopped and came back and stood staring at them staring back at him with frozen, pallid eyes. This one had been eaten from the ankle to the hip by graybacks, his legs so rotten with the sores the bones were coming through. This one had died of scurvy. He lay with his mouth open, not one tooth left in his head. This one had the swollen knees and feet of breaky-bone disease, the legs up to the knees dark blue as indigo. Several had no hands or feet. They had rotted off with gangrene. Others had the sinews showing through where rotten flesh had fallen off.

Once Clyde would have vomited at such a sight, but he'd lived with it for so long he'd built a wall behind his eyes so that he saw it without seeing. Now it was as though a window opened in the wall and he saw himself as he would be soon, lying right here in this pile, frozen with his flesh half rotted off.

He looked across the prison yard, at the still expanse of snow where no smoke crept up from the prisoners' holes and makeshift chimneys like it used to do when firewood could be had. There was little of it now, what there was fought over and carried off by the strongest and most violent men. Those left without froze one after the other. Curled inside their holes, they were pried out by the first to get to them, intent on ripping off their clothes, the rags of the dead added to the rags of the barely living, grayback infestations added to the infestations they already wore. Then they would take over the dead man's hole and, in their turn, freeze.

Clyde looked behind him and to either side. No one paid attention. No one would miss him when he was dead and gone. He wished he'd gone with Caesar. Before he'd finished thinking it, he'd pulled his shirt across his head, twisted off his shoe, and tossed them both in through the window of the dead house out of sight. Then he stretched out on the pile of bodies.

Being on top of the pile meant he was the first to be slung onto the cart. He willed himself not to grunt and was absurdly pleased when he did not. What he had not counted on was the weight of the bodies slung on top of him, pressing his face down onto slats oozing with putrescence. By the time the cart was fully loaded and the team of horses strained forward and began to move, he was sure he'd suffocate. He felt his gorge rise and swallowed hard. If he vomited he'd surely drown in it. He struggled with his head and neck and managed to turn his face into a pocket of foul air.

He heard the driver speaking to the sentry on the gate, heard the gate swing back, and then clack shut behind. At once he started on a harder struggle, one less likely to succeed. Between now and when they turned into the cemetery, he must somehow slither backwards out of here. He had fallen with his right arm flung out and his hand against the wagon's side. This gave him purchase, and he pushed out and back with all the strength left in his body. The bottom of the wagon was slick with dead men's fluids and before long he moved an inch, another inch, another, the cart rattling below him at what seemed a breakneck pace. Another inch.

And now his feet were paddling in air. Now his left hand

found the back edge of the wagon. Pulled. And pulled again. And pulled. Slick and slithering, like a new foal falling from a mare, he fell onto the ground. He lay a moment stunned, then eased his head up, waiting to be shot, and watched the cart go creaking off ahead.

No one shot him, no one called. He looked up at the walk-way on the palisade, but was so close he could only see the un-derside. He listened for a footstep up there. Nothing.

He turned the other way and looked across the railroad. No one was about, just pure clear snow and an open field over-grown with frozen weeds. Do it now, he whispered, run. And he hauled up off the ground and ran, stumbling and picking himself up and running on, listening for the baying of the hounds, wait-ing every second for the shot, and ran, and no shot still, perhaps the sentries were huddled up against the cold and paying no at-tention, and ran on still, his chest hurting and his ears hurting and his good toes hurting with the cold, and he thought that any minute he would freeze stock-still, and ran and ran, his naked bottom twinkling white across the whiteness of the snow.

CHAPTER TWENTY-EIGHT

"THIS one is done for. He is already dead," Aunt Baker said, looking at the body just hauled down the stairs. She turned back the blanket in which Clyde was wrapped and looked him up and down. "Nothing but a sack of bones, frozen clean to death."

Eugenia came across and looked at him. She set her ear against his chest, one finger in the air. "No, his heart is beating, barely. We must warm him up."

"He's too far gone, poor fellow. Frozen as a stick, nothing but a waste of blankets."

"For shame, Aunt Baker. While there is life at all, the slightest flicker, we must try to fan it to a flame. Here, take this bowl, get hot water from the kettle and some cloths. We'll cover every inch of him with compresses until we thaw him out. Fetch whiskey too, and a clean dipping rag so I can drip it in his mouth. If he dies when he is thawed, so be it, but I'll not have one of my patients dying frozen."

"Well, now," she said an hour later, "will you look at that? I do believe he moved his lips." She bent her head down to Clyde's mouth. "Phew! This boy has scurvy. His mouth smells like a cesspool." She inserted a cautious finger between Clyde's blue-black lips and prized his mouth open. "There, look at that. Half his teeth already gone. And will you look at his gums? We may have saved him today, but he'll die tomorrow if we don't get some wholesome food into his body. Aunt Baker, do you have some soup warm?" She turned back to Clyde, wiping her fingers on the corner of her apron. "What I would not give to lay my hand on half a sack of lemons."

"HIS name is Clyde, he tells me, and he wants to go home to his ma," Eugenia told Aunt Baker later on that day.

"He is coherent, then?" Aunt Baker clapped her hands. "Well done, Eugenia Mae, well done!"

"He also tells me he's from Chapel Hill. Is that not a great coincidence?"

Aunt Baker looked at her inquiringly.

"Remember Tom, my boy at the Gold Hill mine, the one I freed?"

"Yes, yes, of course. You said he was from Chapel Hill. A great coincidence indeed. Perhaps it is an omen. Something good, of course," she added hastily. Her face turned serious. "But what's the matter? The prognosis isn't good?"

Eugenia frowned, tipping her head at Clyde, who appeared to be sleeping. Going to the foot of the cot, she turned the blanket back to show the wad of bandages around his foot.

Aunt Baker pulled her mouth down, wrinkling her nose. "The frostbite, it has mortified?"

"Hush. Come upstairs."

Eugenia pulled the bell and the pair of them went to stand

looking up the ladder, waiting for the sound of the drying table scraping back across the floor.

"Henry," Eugenia said as he handed her out into the brightness of the sunporch, "we have another task for you. Not a pleasant one, I fear."

Henry released her, then handed up Aunt Baker, and while she shook her skirts into position, stuck his head into the trap and shouted, "Back in a minute, boys. Behave yourselves down there," his voice echoing up out of the flickering dimness. Then he turned to Eugenia. "What is it, this new unpleasantness? Not another amputation?"

"I'm sorry. I know how much you hate it."

Henry drew his hand across his eyes, turning to Aunt Baker. "Is there no other doctor we can call?"

"You know there is not. With Dr. Kinney gone, there's no one we can trust. We'd be done for if some strange doctor went whispering out of here. No, we must do the job again ourselves."

Henry looked back at Eugenia. "It *must* be done?"

"It must."

Henry's face wrinkled in distress. "He will die without?"

Eugenia took him by the arm, looking up into his face. He looked sideways down at her. "Henry, I know you are kind-hearted, that you recoil from making this boy suffer any more, but we must come to a decision here. If you are too squeamish, I must do the job myself and you know I'll botch it. I do not have the strength to saw the bone."

A long sigh went out of him. "I have no choice, then. I will do it."

THEY did it that same day, with Clyde stretched on the bench used for this purpose in the space beside the ladder. A pair of ancient bedquilts was suspended from the ceiling to hide proceedings from the other patients, of whom there were at present nine lined along the walls. Sounds could not be hidden though, and what was going on was clear enough.

Aunt Baker, at the head of the bench, held firmly to Clyde's shoulders, while Eugenia leaned hard on his good leg with one hand, and with the other held the lamp, moving it at Henry's whispered, "Lower. Higher. A little to the left," watching in a sort of daze, transported back to the Gold Hill hospital where she and Tom had held down miners while they were relieved of limbs.

She looked at Henry's downturned face, at the concentration on it, the determined movement of his hands. He cut around the leg first with a carving knife honed to a fine edge on a rasping stone. The shocked flesh seemed almost to welcome it, the slice was done so fast. For an instant Eugenia saw the bone, pale and helpless looking, then the sharp hard spray and the thick black welling up, the sickening metallic smell. Clyde, half drowned in whiskey, struggled and cried out, then, like a creature caught in a hunter's trap who knows he must give in because he has no recourse, passed into unconsciousness. The saw worked with a damply swishing sound.

A moan ran cot to cot behind them, punctuated by a low sobbing from the far end of the cellar. "Oh, no," a young voice said, "oh, no, please no," over and over until the operation had been done.

Eugenia poured a slug of whiskey on the stump, clamped a wad of cloth around it and pressed down hard. "You may not like it, Henry, but you are becoming quite an expert."

Henry said nothing. He wrapped the rotten foot in a piece of sacking, and with it swinging from his hand, climbed the ladder, set his shoulder against one of the trapdoors, and heaved. A shaft of light fell into the dimness, brighter than the lamp. Eugenia looked down at Clyde's bloodless face. *He will die of this.* She felt a hard lump come into her throat. *He will not die. I will not let him.*

"Here, let me help you with the bandage," Aunt Baker said. "Yes, that's it, good and tight."

When Henry returned, he brought with him a steaming bucket and a mop, and when he had lifted Clyde back to his cot, where he lay completely still with his arms straight at his sides, set about cleaning up. The other patients were silent now, except for the sobbing boy. Aunt Baker took a jar of whiskey from the shelf, poured a good quantity into a cup, and went to crouch beside him. Pretty soon the sobbing turned into a snore.

ALL afternoon and night and all next day and week, Eugenia sat beside Clyde's cot every moment she could spare from tending to her other patients, holding his hand and murmuring, propping his head on a bolster to spoon soup into his mouth, catching the runoff in a wad of cloth beneath his chin, while he lay there with his mouth hung open like a dead thing, his eyes unfocused, flickering with the flickering shadows flung by the fire onto the wall.

I have lost him, she would tell herself one minute, and the next, no, I have saved him. Then she would set a wet cloth on his forehead, or a hot one if he were shivering, looking in bemusement at the close-set eyes and ratlike face, the mouth already fallen in from lack of teeth, making him look like his own grandfather. His nose was sharp, his chin peremptory and weak, his ears like the two handles of a jug. He was nothing, she knew that, a piece of flotsam tossed up by the war. If she had met him in Gold Hill, she would have dismissed him as another worthless cracker. Here he was her patient and she would fight for him.

And so she sat with him and held him down and soothed him when he raved. Sometimes his eyes grew large and he called out,

"Ma, oh save me, Ma!" Other times he thought Eugenia was his sister who was dead, or that he was back in prison, flinching from rats and muggers, clutching her arm and begging her for food, for water, for a rag of cloth to wrap his frozen foot, holding panic-stricken conversations with men who seemed to want to kill him, shivering and sweating all at once. Or else he was once more running for his life, his breath wrenched out of him in thudding gasps, twisting his head across his shoulder, whimpering and praying, "Please, God, not the hounds, don't let them send the hounds."

Day after night he stormed and ranted and exploded with horrors Eugenia could hardly imagine, of death and misery so soul-blasting it drove men mad. How much of what he said was true and how much was delusion, she could not tell, but he was like a man come back from the dead to make report of hell. She had fought for other patients before this, many of them, but the battle for this boy was the battle of all battles, as though she fought not just with death but with the Devil himself, and it seemed to her the Devil was Ned Tarkel. All would be lost if she let Ned Tarkel beat her now.

And then one day Clyde turned his head and looked at her and smiled. "An angel, my sweet Lord, it is an angel come to rescue me."

It was then Eugenia knew that he would live. She called Aunt Baker to come see. Aunt Baker leaned above him. "I declare, Eugenia Mae," she said, "you have brought him back to life by nothing more than willpower. So, young man, are you feeling better now?"

Clyde ignored her, his eyes fixed on Eugenia. "Angel, my sweet angel out of heaven."

And so he started to recover, Eugenia spending more time with him than she should in fairness to her other patients because as his leg recovered his tongue recovered too. He was like a toothless, garrulous old man determined to tell everything he'd ever done before it was too late. Eugenia was fascinated, not with Clyde himself, but with the images he put into her mind of Chapel Hill, although he never mentioned anyone called Tom. She told herself she was not making him a favorite because he was, in some sense, redolent of Tom, and a hundred times stopped herself from asking if perhaps he knew him or might know of him.

And then one day Clyde mentioned ol' Sam Morgan and all her senses came alert. Had not a Mr. Morgan been Tom's owner? Yes, she was sure of it. But Clyde's remark had been a casual mention only, one name in a group of farmers who had shipped tobacco somewhere to be sold.

And so she prodded him. "Was he very old, this old Sam Morgan?"

Clyde looked puzzled for a moment. Then his face cleared and he grinned, showing his black gums. "Ol' Sam ain't old at all, it's just, it's just . . ."

"A nickname?"

"It's what Pa used to call him. We got ourselves a hire from ol' Sam."

"A boy to work the fields?"

"Nah. Amos, he does that. We got a broken-down old woman to keep house for my ma. She weren't a bad old woman, Old Mary were her name. Made me a cake one time, she did. I never had a cake before. She made sweet sticky stuff called . . ." He screwed his forehead in a thinking way.

"Frosting?" Eugenia said.

"Frosting, that was it. She took some blueberries and put them through a flour sieve and mixed the juice with it and turned it blue. She let me stick my finger in the bowl and have a taste. Sweet and sour together it were, best thing I have ever ate."

"You seem to like her quite a lot."

Clyde made a spitting sound. "She were just a nigra."

Eugenia wanted to press him about Mr. Morgan's other slaves, but that dismissive spitting sound prevented her.

The healing days went by. Clyde forgot Eugenia was an angel and clutched her hand, begging her to marry him. Eugenia deftly freed herself, saying neither yes, which would disappoint him in the future when she took it back, nor no, which would disappoint him now. It was a good sign, though. Once a man was well enough to fall in love, he was past the point of dying. So many of these men had asked to marry her she had lost count. Once or twice she had been tempted, when it seemed they might have property or wealth, but who knew what the war would do to property and wealth? Clyde, toothless cracker that he was, was like a prize won in her contest with the Devil and Ned Tarkel. But a prize that is a life can easily be snatched away, and so she must be vigilant. No harm must come to him, not now, or all her efforts would have been in vain, Ned Tarkel, with his leering eyes, the winner after all.

CHAPTER TWENTY-NINE

ANUARY, eighteen sixty-five. Henry came down from the gallery to report the sky above Salisbury was full of smoke. "I'll go see what's happening," he said. He jerked his coat from its peg on the kitchen wall and pulled it on, wrapped a blanket round his shoulders, and went crunching off, the white cloud of his breath preceding him, his boots vanishing and reappearing in the snow.

Three hours later, he came back with news of a fire amongst the government buildings. The factory that manufactured military shoes had lost ten thousand dollars' worth of leather, although how much had been burned and how much made off with by enterprising thieves could not be determined. The Commissary had been gutted, the Quartermaster's Department lost equipment both to fire and thievery. The office of the *Carolina Watchman* had been threatened too, but its equipment had been saved and enough of it returned for the editor, undaunted, to promise a paper would be published in the morning.

Published it was, waving its accusing finger at "a band of incendiaries in our midst who are universally odious to the community, as well as disloyal to the South." The police were going house to house in search of property "mislaid" during the fire.

"They will find nothing here," Aunt Baker said.

"I doubt they'll come here," Henry said. "They'll concentrate on houses in the town."

"Still, we must be careful. Henry, you stand watch upstairs on the gallery. Eugenia, see that all the cloth is hauled down to the cellar. Take everything. The thread. The needles. Check the floor for scraps. Take the biggest cooking pans into the cellar too, and the knives and cleavers and the serving ladles, and the extra bowls and cups and spoons. Make sure your patients understand they must be quiet, and be ready to put out the cellar fire. I'll see to the rest."

The day went by, then Sunday, and no searchers appeared. On Monday, Henry went to town in search of news.

Within the hour, he came breathless down into the cellar to report a band of prisoners had escaped last night, perhaps as many as a hundred. Authorities were searching thoroughly this time, every house both in the town and out.

"They'll be here at any minute. Put out the light. Smother the fire. And keep your patients silent. Not one sound. I'll let you know when it is safe." Then he was gone, the trapdoor thudding closed behind him, the drying table scraping into place.

Eugenia hurried to the fire, and taking up a bucket of old ashes, smothered it. She blew the candle out. "Not one word, one sound," she whispered to the sudden darkness, "or we shall all be lost. But pray, boys, pray silently."

Stay calm, she told herself, stay calm.

But she found panic rising in her throat. What if they were caught, what if they were caught? Had she hidden all the sewing? If the searchers set eyes on gray Confederate cloth the jig would certainly be up. Had Aunt Baker thought to bring the row of sheets in off the line? And what had happened to that pan of bandages she had been boiling?

Silence now, nothing but breathing in the dark. And then the sound of boots overhead, of doors and closets slammed, of fists smacked into walls in search of hollow places, the kitchen door crashed back against the sunporch wall, the thud and crunch of feet approaching. Now the drying table would scrape back, a lamp would flash into the cellar.

A murmur back behind her.

"Shh."

A cough. Another cough.

"Hush. Shh."

But now she coughed herself. Dear God, the place was filling up with smoke. She had not put the fire completely out. Blindly, she swung around, but everything was blank, the sound of muffled coughing like a message pounded on a drum. *Dear God. Dear God.*

Then more footsteps and the trapdoor groaning on its hinge. "Be brave," Eugenia murmured, and turned to face her captors.

A pair of legs came down the ladder and Henry stood before her, holding up a smoke-swirled lantern, peering at her underneath. "I'll help you get the place aired out."

The cellar broke out in a flood of sobs and violent coughing. "They are gone now?" "We are safe?"

THE air was clear now, both trapdoors flung back, the cellar chilling rapidly. Henry was busy laying a new fire, Aunt Baker going cot to cot, checking on the patients, reassuring them.

Eugenia left them to it and climbed the ladder, intending to go outside and breathe fresh air. At the top, she swung herself across the lip and out onto the sunporch. It did not register at once, Ned Tarkel standing there before her, smiling, a pistol held nonchalantly in his hand. "We meet again," he said, and glancing toward the open trap, "What have we been getting up to here?"

No time to shout a warning. No time to vanish back into the cellar and swing shut the doors. No time to run. He had her by the hair now, pistol at her neck, forcing her back down.

Aunt Baker met them at the bottom of the ladder, hands behind her back, neck bent, an attitude of penitence. "So, Ned, you have found us out."

Ned Tarkel's eyes went back behind her to the Union flag slung on the wall, then dropped to Henry, who had risen from the fire, a log of stovewood in his hand. Eugenia felt Ned's hand twist sharply in her hair, saw his pistol swing out to the front. She raised her foot and brought her heel down sharply on his instep.

The shot went wild, the sound of it enormous in the tight space of the cellar, as though the earth had blown apart. The floor came up and hit Eugenia in the face. And then confusion, someone cursing, someone screaming, a crash, another crash, and Eugenia looked up to see Ned Tarkel grappling with Henry. Aunt Baker was behind him, a cleaver in her hands, swinging it above her head, and in almost the same movement, down. The lantern flickered as Ned's skull split neatly down the middle with a popping sound. He stood a moment, holding on to Henry, then he fell.

Silence, every patient who was conscious watching big-eyed. And then Aunt Baker's voice, busy, practical, efficient. "Come, Eugenia Mae, we must clean up this mess. We do not need our patients' sensibilities offended any further."

Eugenia, struggling to her feet, heard her own voice say, "But I wanted to be the one to kill him."

"Oh, no. He was mine. This one was always mine." Aunt Baker wiped the bloody cleaver on her apron and set it on the operating bench. "Henry, we must dig another grave. I'll fetch the shovel."

A choking noise came from Clyde's cot. Half dazed still, Eugenia went to him. He clutched her hand so hard she thought the bones would break, with the other grabbing at his throat, his face screwed tight, eyes rolling in his head.

"Henry, help! He's having a convulsion."

Henry, busy hoisting Ned Tarkel's corpse up the ladder, called back down, "It's just hysterics."

Aunt Baker, close behind him, turned. "We've got no time for that. Whack him. Go on, whack him hard."

So Eugenia reached back with her free hand and whacked him, the sound of her palm against his cheek ringing through the cellar like a whipcrack. Clyde gave a great hiccup and clapped both hands to his face. "Oh, Miss Eugenia."

"Do you feel better now?"

Glumly he conceded that he did.

"I'm sorry I had to hit you, Clyde." Although she had, in an odd way, enjoyed it. "Go to sleep now. Behave yourself."

She turned away, and taking up the mop and bucket from the corner, set about cleaning the floor, wrinkling her nose at the slick unwillingness of Ned Tarkel's brain to be disposed of. So concentrated was she on her task that she barely heard, behind her, someone snicker in the cellar's dimness. "Think I'll have me some hysterics."

And then Clyde's snarl, "Shut your stupid yapper, you, or I'll come across and shut it for you."

"How you gonna do that, baby boy? Come hopping on one leg to beat me up?"

A ripple of mockery went up and down the cots and another, older voice said, "Enough, boys, that's enough. He was just frightened. No call to persecute him for it."

"Ooh, he's a frightened little boy," the first voice sang.

"Shuttup! Shuttup!" Clyde's voice escalated into shrillness.

Eugenia spun around. "You, Clyde, leave it be!"

Clyde made a whimpering, offended sound. "I want to go home to my ma."

"You will when you are ready."

"But I cain't do it on my own. I cain't do it with one foot."

Eugenia felt impatience rise. An urge came over her to take another whack at him. "If you will just stop sniveling, I'll take you home myself." She turned abruptly and followed Henry and Aunt Baker up the ladder.

THE spring of eighteen sixty-five approached. Sherman and his bummers rampaged northward through South Carolina, looting and burning as they came. All North Carolina's regiments were marshaled under General Johnston and sent east to stop him in his tracks. Salisbury, which had been full of troops, emptied out, leaving a mere handful of five hundred or so men to guard both the prison and the huge new stocks of government supplies shipped south before the southbound General Grant and north before the northbound Sherman.

The town was in confusion, full of refugees from South Carolina fleeing out of Sherman's path, filling up the houses, their porches and verandas, sleeping in barns and in the shelter of the railroad depots, eating up the stores of food and Salisbury's fund of charity.

A few months earlier, in September, the *Carolina Watchman* had reported President Davis's speech in Georgia complaining that two-thirds of the Confederate army was absent without leave. If just half these would return, he begged, just half, the South could win the war. He went ignored. Confederate soldiers fled the army by the hundreds every night. Authorities at home gave up on hunting for deserters, and so they went back to their families and waited for the war to end.

In October, North Carolina's Governor Vance mourned in a letter to a friend, "What does this show, my dear sir? It shows what I have always believed, that the great *popular* heart is not now and never has been in this war. It was a revolution of the politicians not the people."

In February, General Lee wrote to Governor Vance, "The divisions from which the greatest number of desertions have taken place are composed chiefly of troops from North Carolina." On the same day, he wrote to J. C. Breckenridge, the secretary of war, "I regret to say that the greatest number of desertions have occurred among North Carolina troops, who have fought as gallantly as any soldiers in the army." In March, he wrote to his beleaguered president, "I do not know what can be done to put a stop to it. I cannot keep the army together unless examples are made of such cases."

But the dam was well breached now, and in Salisbury the prison guards even gave up on hunting after escapees. Embarrassed by the death toll, fearful of postwar retribution from the North, and with a leery eye on General Stoneman advancing from the west, the town was in a panic that if action were not taken they would be discovered with five thousand and more diseased, half-starved, half-naked, half-dead Union prisoners on their hands. The better part of valor was to get rid of them. And so, contingent by contingent, all the prisoners who could walk were being marched in columns through the town and east to Goldsboro, where they would be shipped by rail to Wilmington to be exchanged. The sick came after them, hobbling, leaning on each other, dragged along by friends or hauled in blankets to the Salisbury station, where they were loaded onto cattle cars and sent north to Richmond in Virginia.

Because of all this, Eugenia's flow of patients dwindled, the few she had recovered and went on. Now Clyde alone was left, first crawling, then hopping clumsily about the place on his one foot, grabbing at furniture and door frames, sliding along walls, skinny as a piece of fence wire, grinning with the few teeth still in his head.

THE last frost passed. Crocuses poked up their purple and gold heads. The weather brightened and the sky turned blue. Dogwood and redbud and azaleas broke out into blossom. Birds flew in and out of them with twigs and bits of fluff. Henry hauled what was left of the whiskey out of the cellar and slid the drying table up against the wall for the last time.

Aunt Baker set Eugenia to planting early vegetables and had Henry bring the last sack of turnips, and another, smaller, one of sweet potatoes from the barn and set them in the kitchen, where she rationed them even more severely than before, using even the half-rotten ones for soup.

They had no eggs, since all the chickens had long ago been taken by the army, no milk, since the goat was gone, and no mule to plow the meadow. Henry might have pushed the plow by hand, but it had been impressed, for what Eugenia could not imagine, a moving army does not have time to till the ground, and she could only think it had been another instance of Ned Tarkel's spite. Yet she was grateful for it in a sense. It would have seemed a desecration to grow corn out of her dead patients, and as for eating it, her mind balked at the thought. And so Aunt Baker's meadow stayed a graveyard, its headstones pink and blue and golden wildflowers trembling in the wind. Ned Tarkel did not lie beneath them. Henry had buried him out in the woods.

A knot of lightwood was nowhere to be found these days, and with the price of firewood up to forty dollars a cord, Henry spent a good deal of his time in the woods, foraging for fallen trees dry enough to burn. He chopped them into lengths, dragged them home, and stacked them by the barn, where he took them one by one and chopped them up for stovewood, while Clyde sat nearby on a log, sunning himself and offering instructions. Before long Henry tired of him, so he invented a pair of crutches from a couple of V-ended branches, padded their tops with pieces of old sacking, and told Clyde to get up off his backside and learn to walk.

At first Clyde was resentful. He did not need a nigra to tell him what to do. But after he began to get the hang of it and had made a few turns around the yard, he figured it was not such a bad idea, that even nigras could have good ideas, and that since Henry was half again as big as him and had two feet, he may as well let him be boss, it wasn't like it was an insurrection.

Pa had got ahold the wrong end of the snake about nigras always wanting to make an insurrection. Mostly they just wanted a good feed and no one getting after them to pull their tails, the same as him. Pa had been wrong about a lot of things, he figured. He thought about Old Mary who had always been so kind, and figured he'd done bad to turn Tom in that way. He thought about how Pa had made a snorting noise and said, If that ain't frippery, when he saw that cake Old Mary made with all the pale blue sticky sweet stuff on the top. Old Mary paid him not a bit of mind. She put a knife into Clyde's hand and said to close his eyes and make a wish, then he could cut the cake. Back then he wanted more than anything to be a slave patroller just like Pa, but these days he didn't want to be like Pa at all, although he thought that, after all, it might not be so bad to be a farmer and take care of Ma.

Since he grew old enough to think about it, Clyde had always thought that Ma was Strangely Silent out of mourning for her baby girl. Now it occurred to him she had refused to talk because she did not want to talk to Pa. Perhaps she was afraid that if she offered an opinion he would clap her upside the head the way he did to his own son. Perhaps she was afraid of him, maybe even hated him.

The more he let his mind go down this track, the more important it became to Clyde to know exactly what it was Ma used to think about all those years when she was sitting in her slat chair on the porch, staring at the flowers in the cradle. Perhaps when he got home she just might tell him if he asked her kindly. With Pa dead and in the ground, she might become a real ma like other people had. The thought both fascinated and appalled him, for its warmth and hominess, and for its disloyalty to Pa.

With these thoughts running through his mind, Clyde spent hours each day swinging his crutches up and down the yard, getting his strength up, so he said, to travel home. Before long, he tossed one crutch away and lurched triumphantly, and a little defiantly, up and down on his good leg and the remaining crutch. Inside, he learned to thump his way up and down the stairs, the whack and clatter of his passage a continual advertisement of where he could be found.

"From now on you are doomed to be an honest man," Aunt Baker laughed, "since you cannot creep about behind other people's backs," at which Clyde took offense, thinking she had accused him of dishonesty, and it took her the best part of the day to coax him back into good humor.

Chapter Thirty

WHEN Eugenia climbed out of the cellar for the final time, she had felt like an animal just come out of hibernation, blinking in the light. Despite the war and all its shortages, the world felt safer, and after a few days she could not believe she had spent so many months in the half dark with nobody for company but sick and dying men.

All day she worked in the kitchen garden with her head bare to the sun, humming and singing the way Alouette had always done, pulling weeds and readying the soil for greens and runner beans, foraging for overlooked potatoes. With a sensation almost voluptuous, she sank her hands into the living soil, neither thinking nor not thinking, but floating in a sort of waking dream, one day merging into the next as though time had run into a blockage, the way a flowing river runs into a beaver dam and stops, its currents puttering about, letting whimsy take it as it may.

The sensation of sunlight on her skin was an almost unbearable delight, and she rolled her sleeves up and turned back the collar of her gown, and when she could be sure no one would surprise her, sat with her back against a stump, her skirts drawn up above her naked knees and her face turned to the sky. She could not get enough of it, the warmth, the light, the two gold discs that gleamed and shimmered on the insides of her eyelids. Sometimes she felt an urge to rip off all her clothes and throw herself facedown, like the heathens she had read of worshiping the sun god. She wanted to be wild. To make an offering. To hang flowers around her neck and paint her breasts and dance. She did none of this, however, just went on with her digging and her weeding and her careful planting of the tiny seeds, tender new life springing up beneath her hands.

One day Clyde came clopping like an old horse down the path to break in on her ruminations. "My pa," he said, his voice unctuous and instructive, "my pa, when he were on this earth, saw to it that my ma always wore a hat out in the sun. He said as how the female skin is very sensitive."

"Well, I am not your ma, and you can keep your pa's opinions to yourself. It's about time you went home, young man."

Clyde flinched away. He was not ready. He would go next week.

Eugenia, crouched amongst her seedlings, watched him stumbling back along the path. She had seen tears start in his eyes and wanted to call out to him, to tell him she was sorry, he had taken her by surprise, she had not meant to be unkind. But ever since Clyde had made the turn away from death and started on the journey back to being Clyde, he had been getting underneath her skin.

Her mood turned suddenly morose and she spent the afternoon without once humming or breaking out in song or turning her face up to the sun. In fact, she rolled her sleeves down and shook her hair across her forehead, because Clyde's remark about the female skin had made her think about her own, how very white it had been when she first came up from the cellar, and how quickly it was turning brown. Before long at this rate, she would turn completely black.

This thought brought her to Tom. She sat back on her heels, adding up the months since she had seen him turn away and head into the woods. Three years, eight months. So long? And yet it seemed a day. When she left him by the roadside, she had wept, promising herself she would think about him every day forever. Foolishness that was. When she came to work here with Aunt Baker, she had determined she would put him from her mind. And she had succeeded, had she not, until Clyde came? It seemed she had. And yet it seemed she thought about him all the time. So was she in love with him? She had fancied once she was. But she had been young then, and these years of war had been a hundred.

She stood up, stretching, looking off across the lane toward the woods, and for a moment fancied she saw Tom standing there, one hand raised in farewell and gold dust gleaming in his hair. What would he think of her if they should ever meet again? Would he recognize her even? Her nature had changed greatly since Gold Hill. Then she had been a selfish, whining child. Today she was another person, someone, she hoped, better, someone kinder. And if this war had changed her, surely Tom had changed as well. What was he like now he was free? Had he made it all the way to Canada? When the war was over and he came back south, would he look for her?

She thought about Henry and Aunt Baker, how they were solid for each other, friends, like a brother and a sister. It would be a fine thing to have a friend like that. But these were foolish thoughts, the notion was impossible. Tom had gone on the way her patients went, leaving her behind.

• • •

A week went by, another. Clyde became shy and secretive about his stump, and developed a clever way of folding the bottom of his pants so it could not be inadvertently revealed. When Eugenia asked to check it, he refused, coy as a young girl with budding breasts, and everywhere she went he came stumbling after her, skittishly refusing help.

One morning, the four of them were eating breakfast at the kitchen table. Henry had been to town and was telling them the news from the shabby half page of what these days passed for a newspaper. "The Presbyterians are calling for a prayer meeting. The South is going up the spout."

"Why? What's happened?" Eugenia asked.

"Richmond has fallen to the Union. President Davis and his family and all his government have fled."

Aunt Baker peered at the paper upside down. "You don't say so. What else has happened?"

"General Sherman is in Goldsboro, reported to be getting ready for a move on Raleigh, where the citizens are all aflutter waiting their turn to be knocked into next week."

"And what of General Stoneman?"

"Who knows? First they tell us he's heading this way, then they say he's turned north into Virginia, then that he's vanished, and today the word is that he's appeared like an avenging angel in Winston and Salem."

"Has there been bloodshed?"

"It seems not, or not much, since they put up no resistance."

"Perhaps we'll get off as lightly here," Aunt Baker said.

"The prison is our problem. It will count against us."

"But it's almost empty now. By the time he gets here there'll be nothing left to see but buildings and a palisade."

"Don't forget that escapees have tongues. They'll have

reported their disgraceful treatment. Salisbury surely has a reputation and Stoneman will be well aware of it." Henry consulted the paper again. "It says here he has a force of at least fifteen thousand, maybe as many as sixty thousand." He grunted. "Fifteen or sixty, there'll hardly be a fight, and they say he can be as cruel as Sherman when his dander's up. Please God he doesn't burn us."

Clyde, who up till now had been paying more attention to his bowl of turnip soup than to the conversation, clapped his hand against the table. "Then we're in for it?" he demanded, his voice bristling with anxiety.

"We won't jump that ditch until we come to it," Aunt Baker said.

Eugenia looked across the table at him. "Calm down, Clyde. What's come over you these last few days? Last week you were perky as a flea, this week everything is a catastrophe. We're Unionists, have you forgotten that? And you were once a Union soldier. They'll hardly set you up against a wall and shoot you for it."

He looked gloomily at her. "It would be a mercy."

"Come now, let's be cheerful," Aunt Baker said. "It'll not be long before this hellish war is over and we can get some decent food again." She screwed her face up, looking down into her soup. "I'm so tired of eating turnips."

"Clyde," Eugenia said, "what do you mean it would be a mercy?"

Clyde clenched his hands together on the table. "I have a strong desire to see my ma before I die," he said, his voice so soft he seemed to be speaking to himself.

Aunt Baker reached to pat his hand. "You will not die. You mustn't say such things."

"I say only what I know."

Henry shifted on his chair and caught Aunt Baker's eye. A low thrill of alarm went through Eugenia. "What is this, Clyde? What do you know?"

"I know this war has killed me."

"You speak out of depression."

He shrugged. "I'se cheerful as I ever were, but I am rotting."

"No. Your leg has healed."

"I tell you I am rotting."

"Show me."

He shook his head.

"Don't be stubborn, boy," Henry said. "If you won't show it, I'll show it for you."

Reluctantly, Clyde heaved his leg onto the table and rolled up the bottom of his pants.

Eugenia, on her feet now, leaned across. "Turn it to the window. No, a little more this way." She took the stump and turned it to the light.

Clyde winced, saying nothing. On the bottom of his stump, at one end of the scar, a dark greenish patch about the size of a man's thumbnail tapered to a thin line running several inches up the inside of his leg.

"Aunt Baker, Henry," Eugenia said, "what do you think?"

"Above the knee this time," Aunt Baker said. She became practical and bustling. "Come, Henry, we'll do it here on the kitchen table. I'll set a pan of water on to boil. Eugenia, fetch bandages and whiskey. Henry, bring the saw."

Clyde jerked his leg down off the table. "No, keep off me, all of you."

"But you must," Eugenia said, "you must or you will die."

"Then die I will. I cain't bear the pain a second time. And after that, what then? A third time, and a fourth, until I don't have nothing left to cut away?" He set his head on his hand

and began to cry. "Oh, Ma! If I could only see my ma before
I die."

Helplessly, they watched him, glancing at each other, then
turning back to him. Eugenia felt a tearing in her heart, not pity,
more like anger, with Clyde because he had not spoken and now
demanded sympathy, and with the war as well, with fate, with
the God of love who had withheld his hand of mercy from this
wretched boy. Ned Tarkel's leering face rose up before her and
her heart began to pound. She felt a sense of suffocation. Had
Ned Tarkel, after all, won the battle for this last of all her patients? She wanted to jump on Clyde, to swear at him, to hold
him down and amputate his leg by force. No, no, she should be
kind, to plead, persuading him, but fury choked her into silence.

"Come, Clyde," Aunt Baker said, "don't cry. If you don't
want the surgery, we'll not force it on you. Here"—she mo-
tioned to Henry, who handed her a dishrag—"wipe your nose
on this."

Clyde snorted into it and hiccuped. "You take me for a
coward."

"We take you for no such thing," Aunt Baker said. "You've
been a brave boy, Clyde, but God has not been kind. You have
some time left, though, time enough to see your ma. Henry, are
the trains still running?"

"Surely you—" Henry began, but stopped when Aunt Baker
shot him a meaningful look Eugenia could not interpret.

"They must be," he went on. "When I passed the station this
morning they were sending off another load of prisoners, those
who were too sick to move before. And there are still some left.
The guards are back and forth between the prison and the station every day with more."

"I cain't go on no train," Clyde said. "I cain't. Them guards
might recognize me. And anyways, I got no money for a ticket."

"I have a little money held back for an emergency," Aunt Baker said.

"But we ain't got no cart to haul me to the station. I cain't get there one-legged."

"No matter. Henry will take you on his back."

"And at the other end? How will I get home?"

"We'll send a message to your ma to meet you."

"Ma cain't read. The station is too far. And she won't have no mule. The army will have stole it."

Eugenia's fury broke. "Clyde, you are impossible. You beg to see your ma, yet you set every roadblock you can think of in the way."

"Hush, hush," Aunt Baker said. "Henry, since Clyde objects to going on a train, could we find some other sort of transportation?"

"I doubt it," Henry said. "Every horse and mule and cart and carriage for miles about has long since been impressed."

"They had horses at the prison," Clyde said. "For the dead cart."

Eugenia snorted. "Very suitable. We send you home to die upon a horse that pulled a dead cart."

"*Send* me? Alone? With no one to take care of me?"

"Chapel Hill is not so far," Aunt Baker said. "It won't kill you to take a little journey on your own."

"But Miss Genie said as how she'd come with me. She promised it."

Eugenia swung on him. "You are a wicked boy to lie like that."

"I ain't lying, I ain't lying. You promised me when Aunt Baker whacked that feller with the cleaver."

"Ned Tarkel? Why do you have to drag him into this?"

Clyde's voice went tremulous and stubborn. "It were when Aunt Baker whacked him that you promised me."

"I did no such thing . . . oh . . . I had forgotten. You were sick to die back then. Now there is no need."

"But I am dying *now*."

Eugenia smacked her hand down on the table. "That is your own choice. My job is to make you well. That you would choose to die absolves me of responsibility." And she jumped up and rushed out of the room.

ALTHOUGH these days she rarely went beyond the garden, Eugenia's agitation drove her striding off along the trail her patients used to take into the woods behind their guide. She had not explored it before, and did not explore it now in the way of someone taking pleasure in a journey. Instead, she plunged along as if she were pursued, shoving back encroaching vines and undergrowth with her bare hands, oblivious to thorns and stinging nettles. Her mind was in a tumult, raging against Clyde. She had risked her life for that little runtlike piece of uselessness, and now he would take sides against her with Ned Tarkel. *How dare he pay me back this way, how dare he? To let himself rot willingly, how dare he do Ned Tarkel's dirty work?*

It was not until the trail crossed a clearing by a pond that she stopped her forward rush, pulling up so suddenly that her head jerked on her neck. She turned and went down to the pond, where she crouched, weeping now, and drank, and splashed her face and cooled her scratched-up hands. A low tumble of rocks rose at one end of the pond and she made her careful way around the marshy edge and climbed up on them and sat. "Control yourself," she said aloud. "Calm down."

She sat a long time there, chin in hands, watching the reflected trees and the small mud-colored fish suspended in their branches, forcing herself into a sort of acceptance of Clyde's fatal decision, telling herself it was his life to throw away or not as he saw fit, there was nothing she could do, that when he died it would mean nothing more than that another of her patients had died, it would not mean Ned Tarkel had won anything at all.

The light changed and suddenly the fish were striped and barred, a golden flush along translucent sides. Eugenia glanced up at the sun and rose, brushing her hands against her skirt. She must go back, Aunt Baker would be worried. But as she rose, turning down her head to pick her way, she saw an image of her mother's grave, the way rocks were piled on it against dogs and other foragers, and it came to her that she was standing, not on a stray rock pile in the woods beside a pond, but on a grave. Whose grave? Nausea rose, then a feeling half bitter, half triumphant. *Ned Tarkel, I am standing on your grave.*

CLYDE met her at the entrance to the woods, his skin a peculiar greenish color in the reflected light, as though he had begun to rot all over.

"Henry's been out searching for you. Aunt Baker is beside herself."

Eugenia went to brush past him, but he took her by the arm. "I been worried. I been worried about you."

She laughed. "Better you should worry about Clyde."

"You promised you'd come with me."

"Leave it be, Clyde. I'll not undertake a journey just to watch you throw your life away."

"I am not a coward."

"Then have the amputation."

"You promised you'd come with me."

She strained away from him. "Will you not let me go? My head is throbbing. Let me go."

• • •

"AH, there you are," Aunt Baker said when Eugenia came into the kitchen. Her voice was casual, but her relief was clear. She and Henry were sitting at the table with a letter spread between them, two pages of what, even from a distance, showed itself to be an educated hand.

From time to time a letter would arrive from Aunt Baker's sister Belle with another letter folded into it, written by her for Alouette. The news thus far had been good. Alouette's health had improved, was better now, she loved Aunt Belle, was employed in useful work sewing uniforms for soldiers, something she was skilled at, although these days she stitched at dark blue cloth instead of gray.

"Another letter from your sister? How is Alouette?" Eugenia asked.

"She says she does not want to come back south."

"But when the war is done . . ."

Aunt Baker shook her head. "She does not want to come. She had a hard life here until . . ." She stopped, one hand spread on the table and her eyes on Henry's face.

"Until you saved her," Henry said, and slid his hand across the table until their fingers almost met. He did not look into Aunt Baker's face, but kept his eyes fixed on their hands. Aunt Baker's eyes were on them too.

And it seemed to Eugenia that something almost visible passed between the black hand and the white, something powerful and protective, almost holy. It was like a moment in a church before the altar, like the time she went one early morning to the beach in Wilmington and saw a fog bow arched above the sea. She had heard of such a thing before but never seen one, like a thick white rainbow in the early light. All around was thinner mist, the beginnings of a horizon in the distance, and as she watched, low sun came glimmering across the water and turned the fog bow into an arch of pure light.

Henry slid his hand back. "I'll do anything you want," he said, and Eugenia understood he and Aunt Baker had been discussing what they would do after the war. She took a chair beside Aunt Baker. "Clyde says you've been looking for me, Henry. I'm sorry I ran off like that. I cannot bear to go to Chapel Hill and watch him die without a fight."

"I'd not let you," Henry said. "The roads are full of bushwhackers and starving soldiers going home. They would not hesitate to rob a woman and a cripple traveling alone, or worse."

"And yet you're prepared to let Clyde go alone."

Henry frowned. "It's his own choice. I've warned him of the dangers. Anyway, if he's killed along the way, it might be a mercy. And perhaps his mother would prefer to think of him as a hero killed in battle rather than a boy who died of rot because of stubbornness."

"Now, Henry," Aunt Baker said, "that's frustration speaking. Eugenia, my dear, Clyde is a selfish boy, and much too devious to let himself die easily. When he said he'd not have the operation, I took it for self-pity and am ready every moment for him to change his mind. Henry and I have agreed it's best to play along with him. When he stands facing the journey with death waiting for him at the end, he'll think again, I have no doubt of it. It may be at the last minute, but Clyde will save his own life if he can. As for you, you have a life of your own to think about, a future. You must decide what you will do with it."

Eugenia sighed. "I suppose you might be right. What will *you* do, Aunt Baker, when the war is done?"

Henry made a hemming sound. "If you'll excuse me, I have a task to do." And he slipped out of the room.

Aunt Baker watched him leave, then turned back to Eugenia. "I'll go back to Boston, to my family and to Alouette. Don't look so surprised, my dear. I've done what I stayed here in the

South to do. And I am tired, Eugenia, very tired. I need some time to breathe."

"Henry will go with you?"

Aunt Baker nodded. "We'd talked a little about starting up a Negro school, but now Alouette tells us she will not come back, and although Henry would agree to anything I ask, I know he's stayed away too long. He is my good, dear friend, and has been my rock for these past years, but now it is enough. Boston is his home. He longs for it." She half turned to Eugenia. "You'll come with us, of course."

"I . . . I had not thought of it."

"You have no family, my dear. We would like to be your family."

"You have been a mother to me."

"I would like to be."

The sun was falling through the window across the corner of the table. Eugenia moved her hand into the triangle of light, and moved it out again. "Boston seems so far away."

Aunt Baker spoke again, her voice lighter now, less confident. "I did not think you'd need persuading." She touched Eugenia's arm. "But, my dear, there's no need to rush to a decision. Think on it. Give yourself some time."

LATE that morning, Henry's head appeared in the kitchen window. "Hey there, Clyde, I have a horse here for you. Not much of one, I admit, but the best horse willing to work for anyone called Clyde. I even managed to secure a saddle."

They looked up to see a broken-down, old, gray-jowled, swaybacked rip looking one-eyed in at them. Aunt Baker went across and eyed it back, her face doubtful. "Can he make the journey? Can he carry anything at all?"

"A good feed of new grass—the yard out here is full of it—and he'll be ready for any sort of transportation."

"Does he have a name?"

"If he does, I do not know it."

"Then we shall call him . . . what shall we call him? We shall call him Transportation." She turned to Clyde. "Come, Sir Galahad, don't sit there looking glum. Come and meet your valiant steed."

THAT afternoon, Henry rigged up a pair of saddlebags from the last of the Confederate cloth while Aunt Baker boiled up sweet potatoes and wrapped them into packages. Eugenia refused to have anything to do with it, but went outside and yanked weeds out of the ground as if each one was a mortal enemy, while Clyde sat on the back stoop watching her with a stubborn, piteous, curiously calculating look and Transportation ate his heart out in the yard.

They ate supper upstairs on the gallery, Henry and Aunt Baker chatting cheerfully about Clyde's departure in the morning, reassuring him that death by rotting wouldn't be so bad, it was a better way to die than some, Henry with his saw cleaned up and ready in the closet beside a stack of bandages and the last half cask of whiskey, Aunt Baker watching Clyde's face for signs of giving in.

Eugenia was silent, one half of her mind angry still with Clyde for his pigheadedness, the other half swinging between Tom and Boston. She thought about Tilda too, and about her fantasies of a brother somewhere in the world. She had never talked about this to Aunt Baker, had not had time in these last years to dwell on it herself, but in recent days, with leisured hours working in the garden, she had found the questions that had always haunted her were haunting still. In the morning, she would put everything before Aunt Baker. It would relieve her, and perhaps Aunt Baker could advise her how to put it all behind her and go on, perhaps to Boston.

But next morning, before the sun was fully over the horizon, Eugenia was wakened by the sound of gunfire from the north. Not stopping to pull on her gown, she leaped from her bed and rushed out to the gallery, closely followed by Aunt Baker, also in her shift. Henry was already there, straining out across the rail.

"What is it? Has Stoneman's army come?" Aunt Baker said.

Henry raised a finger. "Hush," his voice drowned by the sound of running feet and shouts from down below, "The Yankees are upon us! Bar your doors, the Yankees are upon us!" And a clutch of soldiers swinging rifles and sabers and revolvers backed hastily along the street.

"Thank God," Aunt Baker said. "At last it is the Union."

Clyde came clattering on his crutch. "What? What is it? Are we dead?"

"Don't be silly," Eugenia said. "I think we are at last delivered. Our brave protectors retreat as though the Devil himself has come to town."

"My horse!" Clyde wailed. "The Yankees will impress my horse."

No sooner said than a mob of Federals swept past in a great clatter of hoofs and rattling of swords and the shouting of strange oaths. Their caps were gone and they stood whooping in the stirrups, urging their horses to a breakneck speed. Several shots rang out.

On and on they came, it seemed for hours, bringing with them clouds of agitated orange dust, making the house shake with the thunder of their passage. When the last of them had gone by, headed toward town, Aunt Baker set her hand against her heart, backed up to a chair and sat down suddenly. "Oh, my!" she said. "Oh, my! I had not expected there to be so many."

Henry leaned farther out across the rail, his face turned after them. "Not sixty thousand, though. Fifteen seems more likely."

"Enough to steal my horse," Clyde said. He hobbled to the rail and peered suspiciously into the garden, as though expecting to find some Yankee bummer hidden in a bush. "They'll be back, you can be right sure of it."

Eugenia swung toward the door. "Then we'd best hide Transportation."

"Where? The barn is all tore up."

She shrugged. "Why, in the house, of course. I'll tie him in the kitchen." She hurried downstairs and outside to the garden. "Come, Transportation." And she led the bewildered horse through the sunporch and on into the kitchen, where she tied him to the table leg. "Stay still," she said, and left him looking one-eyed about himself, twitching his left ear in consternation.

"What now?" Clyde wailed when she reappeared upstairs. "What shall we do now?"

"Come," Aunt Baker said, "we must get out the red string." She hurried off and came back with a bundle. "Take a piece each and fix it to your breast. And now a long one we can tie here to this post and let it dangle down. Yes, yes, like that, that's good. And now for downstairs." She turned and headed for the stairs. "Here, Henry," she said, when everyone had clattered after her, "one for the front door, one for the front gate. And here Eugenia, for the back door and the side gate. I'll hang one in the kitchen window. Oh, I wish we could just drape the house."

"What about the flag," Eugenia said. "The Stars and Stripes? Should we get it from the cellar? We could drape it off the gallery upstairs."

"No, that would be too blatant. If some Rebel saw it, who knows what he might do? Red string is more subtle, the Union men will get the message."

"Do you really think they'll treat us kindly on account of it?"

"I do. I do most earnestly."

Clyde, who had been looking increasingly perplexed, said, "But these are Yankees. I don't understand."

"That's because you don't know the story. Eugenia, Henry, off you go. Clyde, stay here and help me make some breakfast."

THEY were sitting over the remains of a meal of sweet potatoes and rye coffee, watched by the perplexed one eye of Transportation, and Aunt Baker was explaining to Clyde the story of Rahab and the spies, when the sound of hooves came along the road and stopped outside the house. Aunt Baker, her cup almost to her mouth, set it back on the table with a slow deliberate motion. Clyde moaned low in his throat and reached for Transportation's bridle. Eugenia and Henry both sprang for the window, knocking into each other in their haste.

Outside, a band of Union soldiers had dismounted and were busy looping their reins around the pickets of the fence. Their tunics were unbuttoned and their neckcloths hung limp and frowsy as old rags. They seemed to have a conference, then one of them, a tall red-bearded corporal, came lurching up the walk, drawing back his tunic to set his hand on the butt of a revolver. A monstrous thump on the front door.

"Bummers," Henry said. "And drunk into the bargain. No doubt they've raided Jack Hall's groggery, and every other groggery in town as well."

"They wasted no time at it," Eugenia said. "They look drunk as lords."

"I'll get the door."

"No, your black face will be a complication. Let me go. Drunk or not, they will respect a lady." He started to insist but she had already left the kitchen in a swirl of skirts.

She had barely turned the key when the door pushed open and the corporal thrust a hairy fist below her nose. "Out of my way, you Rebel bitch." When Eugenia would not budge, he drew back and jammed his fist under her jaw, tilting her head until she looked up at the ceiling. With the other hand, he seized her by the throat and had commenced to strangle her when Aunt Baker's voice behind them said, "Corporal, desist!" her tone so commanding that he dropped his hands and stood looking at her stupidly, spittle drooling from the corner of his mouth.

"We are Union people, Corporal, Red Strings, if you have heard of us, and have spent this entire war nursing back to health dissenters from the Southern cause. For that you will respect us."

Aunt Baker's hair was coming loose, her face was gaunt, her forearms thin as copper sticks, and yet the corporal quailed before her.

"You have heard of us? President Lincoln himself is a Red String, so they say."

He turned to look at his companions in the street, then turned back, swiping his fist across his mouth. His uniform was powdered red with dust.

"Call off your men. We'll have no pillage here," Aunt Baker said.

For a moment Eugenia thought he would obey. He stepped toward her, stepped away, stepped back, and then away again in a little dance of indecision. His big green teeth bared themselves, then hid inside his beard, then bared themselves again.

From the street, someone shouted, "Yo, there!" and the whole band began crowding up the walk together, stumbling and getting tangled in their swords.

Aunt Baker set her feet apart and her hands upon her hips. "Call them off, I say."

Now the men were climbing up the steps of the veranda, now milling at the door, shoving in their faces. Eugenia, certain they were done for, felt her heart begin to race, but as the first one set his heavy boot inside, Clyde appeared, his face pale as death, and stood before them on his one good leg, brandishing his crutch.

"You all get on outa here. I am a Union soldier."

They stopped, staring at him. One of them laughed.

"I am a Union soldier," Clyde repeated, close to tears. With his voice shaking but completely clear, he went on to describe what had happened to him in the war, how he had run off to join the Union army and been taken by the Rebels. "I were in that goddammed wicked prison down the road," he said. "I were starved and froze and I have et cockroaches and graybacks and my teeth fell out and someone stole my pants and then I hid my-self, buck nekkid, on the dead cart and run off and these here people took me in, half dead, and brung me back to life. They are good Union people, you should let them be."

The corporal turned his head toward Eugenia. She held his stare. He turned toward Aunt Baker. "Come on, boys," he said across his shoulder, and they were tumbling back along the path, slapping each other on the back and spitting in the bushes.

Well, Eugenia told herself, there might be hope for this boy as a human being yet. "Why, Clyde," she said aloud, "you may be worth saving after all."

Clyde, half silly with agitation, said darkly, "They'll come back, you mark my words. They'll steal my horse, they will steal Transportation. I got to get out of here. I can slip off by the north."

"Contain yourself," Eugenia said.

"You *will* go?" Aunt Baker said. "You do insist on it? Well then, if you must, you must, but you must wait for dark." She turned away, turned back. "We would all be happy if you changed your mind. Will you not change your mind?"

But Clyde would not.

Chapter Thirty-one

∾

About midafternoon, the smell of smoke, and a heavy pall came across the sky, dense brown billows roiling from the center of the town.

"What now?" Clyde moaned. "Are they burning the place?"

Aunt Baker turned on him. "I think you should not go. I think you should wait. Why will you not wait? Why will you not have the operation?" She flung away and left the kitchen, coming back contained. "Forgive me, Clyde. You want your mother. I understand, I do."

Henry set a finger alongside his nose and slipped off to see what was going on. An hour went by, during which time Clyde had him shot full of holes, strung up by the neck, and carted off to prison, all at once. Then Transportation fouled the floor and both he and Clyde were banished to the yard to supervise each other while Eugenia and Aunt Baker scraped the droppings up and tossed them out the window, then went down on their hands and knees to scrub the boards. That done, they sat down at the table.

Another hour went by. Clyde came inside and looked at them and went outside again. Aunt Baker set a pan of turnip soup to warm. She sat down at the table. Clyde came in and out again. Eugenia went to the front gate and looked along the road. She came back to the kitchen and sat down. When the sky began to turn from brown to ghastly yellow, she and Aunt Baker looked at one another. Then they both got up and went outside to look along the road.

And here came Henry, hauling a handcart piled with new shirts and military coats and underwear, several large packets of coffee, a smoked side of bacon, a half barrel of biscuits, and the news that the government depots had been broken into by the Yankees. What had not been carried off by poor whites and whores and Negroes had been fired, which was what accounted for the smoke.

"Four entire squares of burning clothes and food and medicines and bales of cotton, it's a crime. When I left, a posse was heading for the arsenal and railroad buildings, intent on setting fire to them as well."

As he spoke, a terrific explosion rocked the air.

Aunt Baker clapped her hand against her heart. "I suppose that was the arsenal."

"I suppose it was." Henry tumbled his booty onto the table. "Here, Eugenia, try on this new coat. It's not made for a lady but better than no coat at all. Where's Clyde? Oh, there you are. Here, take this shirt and coat. And here"—handing him a bright red pair of drawers and undershirt—"quit moaning and get yourself decked out to greet your mother. I'm sorry not to have some boots, but I arrived too late." His voice took on a worried tone. "I wish I'd managed to secure a gun to send with you."

"What happened to that Ned Tarkel feller's pistol?"

"I threw it in the pond. I did not think it was a good idea to keep it. Now I wish I had."

"I pray he will not need a gun," Aunt Baker said. "But what's happening in the east? Has there been a battle? Will it be safe for him to leave or will he run flat into Stoneman's army?"

"They were fighting for the railroad bridge across the Yadkin River, but the Rebels held them off and now they've given up. I heard they tore the tracks up all the way back to Salisbury, so it's a good thing Clyde has Transportation. You still have him, don't you? No, don't start prognosticating doom, Stoneman's army is getting ready to head west out of town. By the time we've eaten, it should be safe enough for you to head off to the east."

Fortified by bacon and real coffee, Clyde's spirits rose. Aunt Baker cut thick slices off the bacon and wrapped them with some biscuits while Henry strapped on the makeshift saddlebags and loaded in supplies. Late in the afternoon, Eugenia looked up to see flames shooting above the trees from the direction of the prison. She ran inside and stuck her head into the kitchen. "Clyde, come see!"

He came hobbling with a distraught expression on his face. "What? What is it now?" When he saw the flames and realized where they came from, he clutched her arm and burst into tears.

"Come now, this won't do. You should be rejoicing."

He gave a great sniff. "I will save my rejoicing for when I clap eyes on my ma."

Eugenia's anger with him had died down, but when he turned a pair of doglike eyes on her, she felt irritation rise again. She turned back into the house and went looking for Aunt Baker, who was sitting at the kitchen table, looking meditatively down into a steaming cup. When Eugenia appeared, she said, "So, my dear, our conversation has been quite delayed. Have you given thought to Boston? Here, sit down, let me pour you another cup of coffee."

"I've spent every minute we were not having an emergency thinking on it."

"And what is your decision?"

"I'd like to come with you, I'd like for you to be my family, I'd like to be your daughter, but there is something else I'd like to talk with you about. A foolish thing, but for a long time now it has confused and bothered me. I would like for you to give me some advice."

Aunt Baker said nothing, just looked kindly and inquiringly across her cup, and before she knew what she was doing, Eugenia found all her old nighttime fantasies tumbling into words. "And so, you see," she said, "I have this feeling, this sensation of a brother, a half brother, somewhere in the world." She flushed. "Sometimes I think of him as Tom."

Aunt Baker set her coffee down and sat making patterns on the table with her fingertip. "Tom," she said at last. "I have wondered if you still think fondly of him."

"I know it's foolishness."

"Not foolishness, my dear. Sometimes, when a great loss happens, such as losing your papa, the mind will seize upon the object closest in nature to what has been lost, or the person closest. It's a way of keeping going in the world. When my dear husband died, and then my son, I also seized on something real and close and tangible."

"Other people's sons."

Aunt Baker nodded. "You see, I'm not the saint you think I am. I'm just a grieving woman clinging on to what I can."

"And me? Do you cling to me as well?"

Aunt Baker smiled. "You're different. You are more like me, I think. I do not cling to you. I do not think you would allow it.

And yet I love you in a way I loved none of those poor boys because you *are* like me. You're a strong woman, Eugenia Mae, and will make your own decisions. I cannot make you come to Boston with me, or even love me."

"I love you, I do love you."

"Yes."

"So what of Tom . . . I mean this person I think about as Tom, this half brother?"

"My dear, has it not occurred to you that this child you think of as your brother might not be your brother after all?"

"My sister, then? Or has the whole thing been foolishness, a fever of the brain?"

"Have you never wondered why your mother had no other child but you?"

"Yes, many times. I asked Papa, but he would not discuss it."

"These strange half dreams you speak of . . . perhaps it might be simpler than you think. Come, Eugenia, I do not want to say it straight. I want you to arrive at it yourself. After all, such things happen all the time."

Eugenia's hand went to her hair. She seemed to feel again the wrenching of the brush and heard Mama's voice: "Such curl, it is unnatural." But now it seemed to her that the emotion in that voice was not impatience, but distaste. Acid came into her throat. Was that how it had been? Was her mama not Mama at all, but Tilda, a slave who let, or had been forced to let, her master take away her child—*why look, it's white, no one will know*—and give it to his childless wife? And had Mama resented it? Had the woman she had called Mama, the woman she had longed for all her life, hated her so much that she had died of it? Was that how it had been?

"My dear, you're trembling." Aunt Baker leaned across and set her hand on Eugenia's knee. "Eugenia Mae, look at me."

But Eugenia could not. She did not want Aunt Baker's eyes

on her, her sympathetic, practical, blunt gaze, regretted telling her, regretted speaking her night fantasies aloud, as if by speaking them she had brought to life something she could not control. All these years she had been playing with a notion, something spun from air, but now it was outside her, something apart, like an animal released that crouched before her, eyeing her, making up its own mind which way to leap. She thought of how Ned Tarkel's Home Guard spat on Henry, not a thing that he could do. If it should be like this . . . if she should be the one . . . Tension grew inside her like a head of steam inside a kettle until she felt about to burst.

I must get out of here. I must get out.

"Aunt Baker, I am sorry. I need to get some air."

OUTSIDE, she ran slap-bang into Clyde, almost knocking him down. "Oh, Clyde, I'm sorry, I am sorry. What are you doing lurking about here?"

"I ain't lurking. I am guarding my horse."

"It's about time you went off on him."

"You're still angry with me."

"No, I'm not."

"You're upset then."

"Go away, Clyde. Go on, be off with you to Chapel Hill."

A sly look came across Clyde's face. "I'll have the amputation if you come with me. Doc Berryman will do it."

"Rubbish. Whoever Doc Berryman might be, he's certain to be off at war, or dead. You're a little fool not to let Henry do it here."

"I don't trust no one else to do it so I do not rot again. Doc Berryman's the best in Chapel Hill, everybody always said so. I aim to have him do it if you'll come with me and help me to be brave."

Eugenia began to shake along the insides of her thighs. *Tom is not there, he is not there, you know it for a fact. He is driving for a fine hotel in Canada. He has a top hat and a fancy waistcoat and is right this minute picking up another guest. He is not in Chapel Hill.*

Clyde's hand fastened on her arm. "I swear I'll have the operation if you come."

"You are a cruel boy, Clyde. Let me go."

AUNT Baker was still sitting at the kitchen table when Eugenia came back in. "I must apologize again. I seem to get upset so easily these days." She clasped her hands together, not looking at Aunt Baker's face. "I have decided to go with Clyde to Chapel Hill."

"No, I'll not allow it."

"He says he'll have the amputation if I come. He says a Doctor Berryman is the only one he trusts to do it right."

"He would *blackmail* you?"

"He'll not have it if I let him go alone."

Aunt Baker frowned. "I knew he'd change his mind, but I thought he'd have the operation here. Eugenia Mae, I've said before that Clyde is selfish. He's playing on your kindness, and your upset of mind."

"He stood up for us against the bummers. We owe our skins to him perhaps."

"And perhaps I am a wicked woman, but I'm not sure it was *our* skins Clyde had on his mind. Why he wants you to come with him to Chapel Hill, I do not know, perhaps he is attached to you, but by making this demand he shows he has no concern about your life. That he has settled on a surgeon is proof he intends to have the operation whether you go with him or not. I told you he would save his own life if he could, and he will do it, but I'll not agree to let you go to Chapel Hill."

"What's this about Eugenia going to Chapel Hill?" said Henry's voice behind them, and Aunt Baker told him what had happened.

"So let him blackmail," Henry said. "I've warned Clyde the journey is too dangerous, but he ignores me. He can take his own life in his hands, but he is not taking yours. You may go later if you want, when the war is done and everything is settled and the roads are safe, but to go now would be foolhardy."

"But I need to know he's done it. I need for him to live. It's important to me. And the longer he delays, the more he rots." Eugenia spun about and paced in agitation up and down the kitchen. "We must find someone to protect us on the road. What about the guide, the one who used to lead the boys across the mountains?"

"Tandy Cavin?"

"So that's his name. You would not tell me if you did not think the journey not so dangerous after all."

"I concede the war is almost over, but the danger is not past."

"My dear," Aunt Baker said, "sit down. You are upset. I'm sorry I upset you. We must discuss this calmly."

"You said yourself I would make my own decisions, and I have made one. I will go."

"Go where? You will go where?" And Clyde was in the room.

"To Chapel Hill. I've decided to go with you."

Aunt Baker began to speak and stopped. She looked down at the floor and sighed, then looked back at Eugenia. "Then we must get you ready for your journey. No, Henry, she has made her mind up. She will go."

Henry, who had planted himself before Eugenia, readying himself for speech, let his breath out in a rush. He took her by both forearms, and pulling her toward him, kissed her fiercely on the forehead. "Go then, stubborn woman. We'll make of it the best we can." He released her, and turning to Aunt Baker, said, "I'll go hunt out Tandy Cavin."

Aunt Baker set her hands on the table, preparing to stand up, but as she did, something happened to her face, a sort of slippage. She drew a breath and stiffened up her spine.

NOW it was Eugenia and Clyde's turn to vanish in the night behind the shadowy figure of the guide called Tandy Cavin. They did not head into the woods as Eugenia's patients used to do, but in a northeast loop through backstreets made darker by the sheets of flame roaring upward from the center of the town, punctuated by bursting shells and ammunition. Eugenia led Transportation, Clyde riding mournfully above her, certain that at any instant they would be challenged. But no, they made it out of town, the great cracking conflagration falling steadily behind.

They traveled all that night and made as good time as they could with such a horse, but early in the morning heaven opened and rain fell down in torrents. Hiding in the woods protected them but slightly and so they set their minds to plodding through it, Transportation stumbling from time to time, Clyde clinging to the slippery saddle and whining in his throat, Eugenia with sore feet and aching legs, half blinded by the rain, half wishing she had not set out on the enterprise with such a baby, and Tandy Cavin silent as a rock in front.

For an hour or more they traveled through the storm before it faded off behind them and the sun appeared. Now Eugenia got her first clear look at Tandy Cavin. He was a tall man, sleepy-eyed but sharp-eyed, mountain-skinny, wiry, a loping man, taciturn and leather-vested. When he took his hat off to shake it free of water, his stringy dark hair stuck up at the back as though he'd slept on it. He carried a Kentucky long rifle as casually as if it were part of his body, propped on his shoulder like a shovel or a fishing pole. From time to time he turned to look at them, although he said no word, and had barely said a word all night, but it seemed to Eugenia that something rose off him, a sort of emanation, a sort of certainty of who he was and what he was about that would make men think twice before confronting him. He will do, she told herself, yes, he will do.

The sun was weak and sickly, and although it shone all day, it was not warm enough to dry them out, so they camped that night and went the next day waterlogged and shivering, Eugenia encouraging Clyde on while privately worrying over what would happen if he caught a chill. She had no medicine, not even whiskey, and doubted that his weakened constitution could bear up under an illness. Still, she put a brave face on it and jollied him along, telling him they were already halfway there, or nearly there, or would be nearly there tomorrow, although she had no idea how far they had come or how far there was to go.

The day after found them drier although Eugenia's underclothes felt clammy and had begun to smell suspiciously of mold. The road was full of Rebel soldiers, or what had been soldiers, they were so pitiful and ragged, and bewildered-looking too, as though some great surprise had overcome them and they did not know how to deal with it. Cautiously, Eugenia watched them pass—gray-faced, exhausted men in twos and threes and solitary, some no more than children, others lined and wrinkled with premature old age, paying no attention to the clear, damp spring day, to the dogwood blossoms lacing through the woods, or the yellow pollen floating from the pines so that they seemed to travel on a golden road. These were the boys she had spent the war trying to help. She ought to pity them, but she found they frightened and repulsed her, with their skinny shanks and bleeding feet and what clothes they had left on their bodies hanging in sad rags, their blank defeated stares. She was afraid one of them would take it in his head to make off with Transportation, but perhaps because the horse was such a scarecrow of a thing himself, no one seemed to think he might be better off on Transportation than on his own two ruined feet.

A couple of them stopped when they were camped next night and asked for food. Eugenia gave them each a biscuit and a slice of bacon, receiving in exchange the information that General Lee had signed a truce with General Grant, which cheered her, that President Lincoln had been shot dead by an assassin, which she dismissed as a canard, and that General Sherman's troops had taken Chapel Hill, the place was full of Union cavalry, which filled her full of trepidation. Tandy Cavin listened silently.

Next morning they set out again, Eugenia wondering aloud as they packed up their things if they should turn back to Salisbury until the whole business of the war had been resolved, Clyde whining that he did not care, he did not care about no war, he wanted nothing but to see his ma. Eugenia turned to Tandy Cavin to ask him his opinion, but he had already headed off.

Toward noon that day, a solitary man who looked half wild or half mad came plodding up the road toward them with his hair and beard all every which way and his head turned down. He wore a rifle slung across his back and ignored them as he passed, but a little distance on he shouted back at them, "Stop, hey, stop there, you!" and came at a run to seize the bridle-rein out of Eugenia's hand, a bold but unwise move, since Tandy Cavin, in what seemed to be a single movement, turned and shoved him so hard in the chest he fell backwards, cracking his head sharply on the road.

"That'll learn you," Clyde said, while Eugenia gazed in

startlement, first at Tandy Cavin, who had resumed the journey, then at the groaning soldier at her feet.

"That'll learn him not to take my horse," Clyde said.

"What will we do with him? The poor fellow's head is bleeding."

"He ain't your patient. He is a criminal element. Pass me up his gun. The cartridge box and caps as well." He examined the rifle, the grin on his face disappearing when he shook the cartridge box. "Goddamit, not a one." He tucked the box into his bedroll with the cap box, also empty, and shrugged. "Got me a fine gun anyways. It is in good condition."

"We can't just leave him here."

Clyde looked fiercely at the soldier, who, with one hand to his injured head and the other pushing at the road, was attempting to get up.

"Mr. Cavin, Tandy, stop," Eugenia called.

He did not turn. Instead, he raised his right hand, tilted it back behind his shoulder, and then jerked it forward. Eugenia stepped out after him without another word.

Toward sundown they were challenged by a pair of Union pickets. Eugenia thought Tandy would back off and was looking about her for a trail into the woods, but instead he took his hat off by the brim, and beating it gently against his leg, looked mildly down at the two men. He said something Eugenia could not hear, and one of the pickets answered. Tandy spoke again, and the pickets stepped aside.

"Fine horse," one of them said as they went past, and laughed.

Then they were jostling into Chapel Hill, along what Clyde said was Franklin Street, the main street of the town, and here was the Baptist church, here was Mr. Ruffin's hardware store, now empty with a broken windowpane, here Miss Caroline's ladies' clothing store, empty but with windowpane intact, here the university, its grounds aswarm with blue-clad men on horse-back and on foot, here the courthouse and post office, here the road to Uncle Benjamin's house. Before long, they turned right onto a side road, traveling through woods, then open farmland, and then woods again, on through a flat wet singing marsh and up a steepish hill and down again, out onto an old stone bridge across a creek.

"This here is Morgan's Creek," Clyde said. "It ain't far now. We will be home by dark."

CHAPTER THIRTY-TWO

A few weeks earlier, Tom had woken to a swarming sound like bees. He lay a moment, listening, then pushed the covers back, and going to the window, threw it up and stuck his head into the morning. Not bees, but battle sounds, coming from the west, the heavy roar of cannon, the rolling of a drum, the sharp rattling of muskets, once what sounded like the distant screaming of a horse. He pulled on his pants and went downstairs.

Rose was at the parlor window, Baby Gold at her breast, watching Charley, who was standing in the yard, his head cocked and a listening expression on his face. He looked across at them. "Close by Bentonville, I reckon."

All morning they listened, at first nervous that the armies might be coming their way, then, as the afternoon drew on, debating with each other about who was getting the advantage and whether either of the armies would head their way when it was done.

The sound of battle faded with the fading of the light and next morning Tom left Rose and Baby Gold with Charley and set out through the forest to investigate. The day was fine, as had been yesterday, but for weeks before the sky had done nothing but rain, turning the swamps to quagmires from which dozens of small creeklets ran away. He slogged along, up to his ankles in the sticky bog, then up to his knees, his waist, slipping and sliding, grabbing at the stiff dense blackjack thickets to pull him up onto a sandy ridge before descending to another patch of marshland on the other side.

He had begun to think of turning back when suddenly, in all directions, the long-leaf pines were stripped of bark, their naked-looking trunks so pitted by grapeshot that in some places he could see right through, branches littering the ground beneath them, cut off by bullets as neatly as if they had been sawed. All around, in the open and in thickets and in the swampy woods, lay abandoned guns and knapsacks and canteens, and sprawled, already stinking corpses, their faces blackening beneath the sun. Here a barefoot man half clad in a blue uniform, here a young boy, just a child, in Rebel rags. The place smelled of rifle smoke and peach blossom, and fog hung above the swamps. Inside it, the ghostly figures of a burial detail hauled the dead off one by one, the calls of birds mingling with the muffled clink of shovels.

Tom skirted around them, collecting ammunition pouches on his way, and came out on firmer ground behind a farmhouse from which a deal of noise was coming, screams of what seemed agony, and shouts, a curse that ended in a roar, from time to time a thump. He crept around to the front yard, where he was confronted by half a dozen turkey vultures ripping and tearing at a pile of human arms and legs, the steps and porch littered all across with more.

"Yah! Get on there!"

The turkey vultures hunched their heads into their shoulders and went on with their meal.

"Yah!" He stamped and waved his arms, advancing on them, but it was not until he was almost close enough to touch them that they turned away and took to their reluctant wings.

A leg flew out the window, landing at his feet. It had a strong calf, muscular. Tom's gorge rose. It had just registered on him that the farmhouse had been turned into a field hospital, when a voice behind him said, "You, boy, help me load this wagon," and he found himself tumbling limbs into a mule cart, some of them already rotten, the flesh soft and breakable, turning liquid in his hands, while the disappointed turkey vultures circled overhead.

"Who won this battle?" Tom asked the corporal who had impressed him.

The corporal snorted whiskey in his face. "Who you *think* won? Gen'l Sherman doesn't lose."

"Sherman? Last I heard he took Atlanta."

The corporal went on loading arms and legs. "Burned it down. And we burned a good deal more since then." His voice took on a bragging tone. "Burned our way all across Georgia to Savannah, then headed on up here. Did in all sorts of towns. Columbia was best. Had ourselves a *fine* time in Columbia. The niggers met us in the streets, arms full of wine and whiskey and champagne and beer and . . . oh, anything we wanted. It was a fine drunk we had ourselves that night. Rolled cotton bales out on the street and burned them. Burned that city too, right down to the dirt it stood on. They had it coming on account they started up this war. Got me a nigger woman underneath a stair that night, and a pair of silver candlesticks. One fine time it was, the best of all."

He grinned and heaved. A leg thumped on the cart. Another leg. "I tell you this. A house will burn, but turpentine burns better. We found barrels of the stuff stacked at river landings on the way up here. And distilleries—oh, my! And then there are the forests. I have seen forests burn, but nothing burns like Carolina long-leaf pine."

He threw his hands up in the air and made a whooshing sound. "Burned from the border almost up to here. Middle of the day the smoke so thick you'd think it was the middle of the night." He shrugged. "But now they tell us leave all that stuff off, this state is sympathetic to the Union." He shrugged again, looking about at the litter on the ground. "Not that you could tell."

Tom eyed him up and down, assessing. "You did all that, did you? Where are you and General Sherman heading off to now?"

Abruptly, the corporal swung to look at Tom with small-eyed red suspicion, an arm dangling from his hand like an extension of his own. "Who's asking? Who are you, anyway? What you doing here?"

"Just came to do my bit for these poor . . ." Tom indicated with his hand.

"Then get on with it and stop your mouth." The corporal swung his extra arm onto the cart. "Don't stand there gawping. I said get on with it." And he made a trumpet of his ass.

When the cart was well piled up, the corporal, who had fallen into a truculent silence, said, "Take it to the pit. It's that-away." He pointed up the track and Tom set off driving the mule. At the first turn he glanced across his shoulder, jumped down from the cart, and gave the mule a smart slap across the rump. The creature drew its lips back, snarled, then gathered up its legs and bolted down the track, the cart with its macabre load jolting behind. Tom watched it for a moment, then slipped off into the woods. Before he went back to Rose and Charley, he wanted to discover which way the army was headed, and so set out to overtake it.

A little farther on, he saw ahead of him a cloud, pale red and lucent, with wreaths of smoky darkness rising on the east and west. And then a growing stench, of shit and sweat and that peculiar acrid smell of herded animals, then a sound like rolling thunder, low down and growing steadily the closer he approached. Before long it resolved itself into the roll of wheels, the creak of wagons and the tromp of hooves on dirt, voices in a low cacophony, the tap-tap of a single drum and a sort of cadenced humming. He recognized what he was hearing—an army on the move—but when he topped a rise and saw it, he was astonished at its size. It seemed to spread horizon to horizon.

Numbers rattled through his head. A thousand, ten thousand, a hundred thousand. He could not begin to guess. Troops on foot tramped through the fields at each side of the road as far as he could see. On the road itself, carts and wagons churned the clay, loaded up with sacked and bagged and barreled and boxed-up supplies on which perched chickens, geese, and turkeys, squawking and gobbling, making their opinions known, while hogs and sheep and cattle milled behind them and around, their herders shouting, tugging, cursing, threatening with sticks, the shaking earth churned up with dung of every color and consistency, turning it into a fetid quagmire where ambulance wagons with canvas tops swayed and cried and moaned.

Mounted troops moved on the road as well, many hauling dilapidated cabs and carts and buggies behind lame mules and sickly, straining horses, here a cart pulled by a team of one mule and one goat, and not one soldier either mounted or on foot with a full suit of clothes, some with hardly any clothes at all. They were patched and holed and shredded, their heads bare to the sun, or with handkerchiefs twisted about them, or topped with obviously purloined hats—tall black silk top hats crushed into extraordinary shapes, old-fashioned fancy hats of fur, some with no tops or no brims, or neither. Some men had small animals for pets. Here a squirrel perched on a swaying knapsack, a coon trailing on a string, a fighting cock balanced on a forearm. Filthy faces, skinny filthy naked chests and skinny naked knees and arms, bloodied muddy feet, and floating over all of it the smell of whiskey.

They seemed cheerful enough, though, which Tom figured was the whiskey, shoving and laughing amongst themselves and singing, off-key, "John Brown's Body," mixed with "The Star Spangled Banner" and "Johnny Comes Marching Home Again," from which Tom concluded the corporal must have told the truth about them being winners of the battle back in Bentonville. That these were Sherman's troops, he had no doubt.

His fear had been that they would head for New Bern, which would put the Avery plantation in their path, but now, calling up a map inside his head, he figured they were bound for Goldsboro. It was time he headed back. He glanced up at the sun—it was starting its descent—and unease took him, increasing as the world turned shadowy and glum. His pulse quickened and he broke into a run, thinking of the time he and Charley had fought off a band of bushwhackers, shooting at them from the upper windows of the house, and another time had fended off marauding Negroes who came whooping and demanding in the middle of the night. That time, Rose had poured boiling water on their heads and they had gone off caterwauling. But what if they had come again? What if Rose and Charley had been taken by surprise?

The sky began to roll and threaten up above the trees and he ran faster, skidding on needles damp and slick as ice, scrambling in and out of swamps, thorns and thickets lashing out at him and tripping him, tearing at his clothes, his hands, his face, clutching at his hair. The sky fell down with a roar.

THE storm had passed as suddenly as it had come and now the moon looked through the treetops, bathing everything in soothing light. Tom felt his breath slow and his pulse slow and his feet become steadier beneath him. He was almost home, he recognized the woods. Here was the creek, its stepping-stones gleaming in the moonlight, its water gurgling peacefully. He stopped to drink and soothe his damaged hands, and then went on, calling, "Rebel? Rebel?" because the cat had come to meet him as he often did, mewing his greeting. Soon he would wrap himself around his leg and arch his back, and when Tom bent to stroke him, he would flick his tail and hum his welcome song.

But although the mewing was close by, and now in front of him, Rebel Cat did not appear. Tom stopped, looking about. "Rebel? Where are you, boy?" And then it wasn't Rebel. It was Baby Gold, upside down inside a bush and mewing like a cat. Beyond her, Rose, her skirts tossed above her head, sprawled out on the ground.

Tom scooped Baby Gold into his arms and ran to kneel by Rose, turning down her skirts. The moon shone on her face. Her eyes were open and she seemed to smile. Tom's heart went away, and with it everything inside him, every thought and memory. He was a creature with no bones, no substance, nothing but a long, continuous sigh.

Then Baby Gold turned her head toward her mother, mewing, and he reached out and closed the brightly staring eyes. He rose, calling softly, "Charley?"

He did not see him at once. The house confused him. Somehow it had taken on a different shape. Then he realized half of it was gone, the front part nothing but a chimney and a pile of sodden ashes from which blackened timbers threw their arms against the sky. That was when he saw him. Dead too, oh dead, facedown in the long grass, his arms flung out toward the woods. Tom saw it all: the struggle and the desperate flight to rescue Baby Gold and Rose, then the blast from behind lifting him, the forward pitch, the drop. Baby Gold was silent, looking at the moon.

IT was morning by the time he had dug their grave and buried them, together, face to face, to give each other comfort. He piled the grave with stones to keep out animals and stood beside it, leaning on the shovel, and it seemed to him he heard his mother's voice, that sad hymn she used to sing when someone died: *Weep not for me, you standers by . . .* just that one line, repeated and repeated.

Rebel Cat had reappeared and was crouched in the grass by Baby Gold, body tense, yellow eyes aglint, following Tom's movements. When Baby Gold began to mew again, his tail twitched at the tip, but he did not look at her, just went on watching Tom as he stuck the shovel upright in the ground and bent to pick her up.

A jay veered overhead, the path of its flight a blurred rush of defiant blue. Behind it, swooping and pecking at its back, the gray shriek of a mockingbird.

DAY to day Tom went so stunned with grief he could do no more than care for Baby Gold. His time was taken up with feeding her and washing her and hanging her rag diapers out to dry. When she cried he clung to her with panic in his heart, as though she might at any moment follow Charley and her mother to the grave. Baby Gold, though barely six months old, seemed to understand that he too needed comforting and clung to him as tightly as he clung to her. Rebel Cat, with the eerie perspicaciousness of cats, watched by her side.

Every day clots of Rebel soldiers went along the road, plodding wearily toward their homes. For the most part they passed by, taking the house to be a burned-out ruin, but one evening Tom heard footsteps coming through the yard to the back of the house. He snatched up Baby Gold and bundled her into the larder, whispering, "Hush, hush, not one sound." Then he answered the door with his musket in his hands.

Three men stood there, ragtag, shoeless, gunless, drenched with rain and mud-caked to the knees. Tom expected them to challenge him, but they seemed to be lost souls, unsure of themselves or their own place in the world, much less the place of an upstart Negro squatting in the ruins of a white man's house. They wanted food, they said, a bed, the kindness of a shelter for the night. Tom hesitated, half inclined to shoot them, but then pity took him and he agreed to let them use the barn.

For the first time since Rose and Charley died, he busied himself with the needs of someone other than Baby Gold. He boiled up soup, and while the soldiers squatted in the barn and ate, clambered up the ruined staircase of the house to haul down what was left of mattresses and quilts. One of the soldiers, the tall one with blond hair, started out to be considerably snarlish, but once he had hot soup in his belly he seemed to have no more energy than his companions to care about the proper way the world should be.

That night Tom learned General Lee had given up, and General Sherman was chasing General Johnston's army west toward Raleigh, beyond which, only a few miles away, lay Chapel Hill. The war was over, the deserters said, or so close to over they had no inclination to be risking their necks further for a failed cause.

After they had settled in the barn to sleep and Tom had

barricaded himself inside the house, he sat down on the kitchen floor with his back against the wall and Baby Gold sleeping in his lap, and talked to Rebel Cat.

"I been considering," he said, "the notion of us going on to see about my mother."

CHAPTER THIRTY-THREE

Eugenia and Clyde had arrived at Bricket's farm at dusk, Clyde excited as a child, calling out, "Ma! Ma!" as they turned onto the rutted track leading to the house, leaving Tandy Cavin back behind them in the shadow of some woods. Tandy had shaken his head at Clyde's excited invitation to a meal, turned his eyes away from Eugenia's words of gratitude, and in his low-voiced unloquacious way, given her directions on how to get in touch with him when she was ready to go back to Salisbury. As Ma appeared on the front porch, a thin suspicious presence, and stood staring with a broomstick in her hands, he vanished. One second he was there, the next was not, as though by some feat of magic he had turned himself into a tree.

"Who's there?" Ma called. "Who is it?"

"Ma, it's me, Ma. Don't you recognize your boy? I come back from the war."

She came down the step and watched as they approached.

When they got close and Clyde slid down from Transportation, she said, "Well now, I see you've given up a leg, but at least you got yourself a horse."

"Ain't much, but I got me a fine gun."

Eugenia had expected Ma to seize her son and weep and kiss him, but Clyde did not seem disappointed. He stood before his mother, grinning, while she examined him all over, making comments on the odd assortment of his clothes, his skinniness, his lack of teeth. Eventually he stopped grinning long enough to say, "Ma, this here is Miss Eugenia."

Ma turned to Eugenia with a narrow-eyed, suspicious look, as if she might have come to carry Clyde away again.

"I'm Clyde's nurse," Eugenia said.

"Come on and set," Ma said, and turned toward the house.

A man was sitting on a slat chair on the porch. The wide brim of a black hat cast a shadow on his face. Clyde came up the step holding out his hand. "Hey there, Uncle Benjamin."

Uncle Benjamin held out his hand, not quite connecting it with Clyde's, at the same time turning his head in a peculiar, half-sideways movement that Eugenia recognized.

"Well, praise the Lord," he said. "Young Clyde has come back home. Son, you can help me plow the field. That boy Amos has run off."

"But Uncle Benjamin," Clyde said.

Uncle Benjamin took off his hat and hooked it on his knee, and Eugenia saw the ruined face, the blasted sockets of the eyes.

"Uncle Benjamin," Clyde said. "I will surely do that."

"We done made acorn tea," Ma said, and an old Negro woman came out to the porch carrying a tray. "This here is Old Mary."

THEY ate squirrel stew for supper, Uncle Benjamin telling proudly how Ma had trapped the creatures her own self, Ma demanding to know everything, just everything that had happened since the day Clyde went away. When she heard about his rotting leg, she drew herself up stiff-backed on her stool.

"We'll get Doc Berryman to cut it off, oh yes, indeed we will. The good Lord saw fit to send my boy back home alive, I ain't about to let him stand and rot."

Clyde said, "Ma, I plan to do it, but I think I just might purely die of all that sufferin'."

"Son," Ma said, "lookit your uncle Benjamin, that man has suffered more than you."

"Yes'm," Clyde said.

Then Uncle Benjamin told how he had gone to be a chaplain in the army and ended up a gunner, and how the gun exploded in his face. "But praise the Lord," he said, "I still got two good legs."

When the sky grew dark, Old Mary went off to her cabin and Ma took Uncle Benjamin's hand and led him toward the bedroom.

Clyde said, "But Ma."

"Clyde," Ma said, "it ain't your business what I do."

Uncle Benjamin turned back, screwing up the socket of one eye in what Clyde took to be a wink, and then Ma shut the door.

Eugenia, exhausted, had stretched out on Clyde's cot. He came to stand above her, leaning on his crutch. "I ain't sure what to think o' that."

"Of what?" Eugenia said, already half asleep.

"Of Uncle Benjamin and Ma."

Eugenia yawned. "It ain't your business, listen to your ma."

Clyde turned away, and hauling the red bedquilt outside to the porch, wrapped himself in it and settled down to sleep. "Well, I'll be dogged," he said. "Uncle Benjamin and Ma."

He thought about it all next day, watching Ma with Uncle Benjamin, the way she touched him all the time, the way she laughed when Clyde saw not a thing to laugh about, Uncle Benjamin being blind and all, how was he to earn a living now he could not ride about preaching to the damned, and wasn't it a sin what he and Ma were up to when the bedroom door was closed?

That evening after supper, Clyde and Uncle Benjamin went to sit together on the porch, Uncle Benjamin with his arms along the arms of Ma's slat chair, and Clyde perched on a stool. Ma was washing dishes with Eugenia, who had promised him she would not leave until he had his amputation.

Clyde looked out into the dark and said, "Uncle Benjamin, ain't you and Ma afraid of hell?"

Uncle Benjamin put his hand up to his eyes and said, "Afraid of *what*?"

Clyde flushed. "I didn't mean . . ."

They sat in silence, Clyde watching the dark and Uncle Benjamin, his head half turned, listening into it. After a while Uncle Benjamin cleared his throat and said, "Son, it's not a sin, it is true love."

"It ain't?" Clyde said. "It is?"

"Your ma and me, we've always been in love, ever since the day I came down here from Norfolk."

Clyde said nothing.

"Your ma says I should not tell you this, not yet. She says it will be too much of a shock."

"Ain't much can shock *me* anymore."

"Well then, I'll tell you. Your ma and me, we're planning to get married. Just thought we'd wait and see if you came home. Figured we should ask if such a thing would bother you."

Clyde looked out at the dark and it came to him that this was why Ma never spoke to Pa. He felt absurdly pleased, and guilty too, but mainly pleased. He figured Uncle Benjamin would make a better pa than Pa, and waited to feel guiltier.

Uncle Benjamin turned not quite to Clyde. "So, son, does it bother you?"

Clyde grinned. "I reckon not."

DOC Berryman showed up next day, a fat-jowled man too old for war, with faded pale red whiskers and no hair at all. A pair of round wire spectacles kept slipping down his almost nonexistent nose, which he twitched constantly to keep them from completely falling off. He sat down on the step and ordered Clyde to roll his pants up, and when he had examined the stump from every angle, pressing it here and there and asking if it hurt, he coughed twice and applied a hand to his domed head, feeling it carefully all over as though looking for some information on how he should proceed. Then he clasped his hands and hunched forward, forearms on his knees, unclasped them, and pressed one finger to a spot just above his right ear. "We've had a little setback here, young man, a little setback." He stood up, turning up his face and wrinkling his nose to adjust his spectacles. "I'll send my man to get you in a day or so."

Several days went by. Eugenia helped about the place or wandered in the sunshine or picked berries in the woods. While they had been traveling, the wildness of her need to leave Aunt Baker's house had been taken over by the strange wildness of their journey, blocking out the conversation that had catapulted her onto the road with Clyde. Now, berry can in hand, she felt it circling round her, tapping at the window of her mind. She wanted to keep it out, to keep the drapes drawn and the shade tight shut, but she knew that one day she must face it, either to dismiss it finally as nonsense, or to accept it as a question she would have to live with all her life.

Cautiously, she drew the drapes back and took hold of the bottom of the shade. She thought of Alouette and how Aunt

Baker rocked her in her arms as though she were a cherished daughter. She thought of Tom, how she had loved him. But to be black, to have black blood herself. It seemed as though a monster stood outside the window, leering in at her with Ned Tarkel at its back. She tugged the shade and let it rise a sliver. Applied an eye. No monster, no Ned Tarkel. She drew her breath in, drew it in some more, let the shade up with a rush.

And looked out at a future world she did not know how to understand, a world of liberated slaves. To liberate, what could it mean? She had known free blacks in her life, but even some of them had slaves. To be black, like Tom, or partly black—like her?—how would that be? The North had made a declaration, of war to keep the country unified, of freedom for the man with the black face, but no one had said what that would mean, how black and white would live.

Could Tom come home and live like any other man? Could he sit on a white-railed veranda, rocking, with a mint-flavored whiskey in a crystal glass? The thought both frightened and excited her.

At that moment, Old Mary came onto the porch and emptied a pan of steaming water over the rail onto a clump of dusty nettles at the corner of the house. On her way back inside, she straightened something leaning on the wall beside the door. It was Clyde's crutch.

Eugenia's contemplations flew out of her head. She ran inside, where Ma and Uncle Benjamin were sitting at the table shucking corn.

"Where is he? Where is Clyde?"

"Doc Berryman's man done took him," Ma said, picking corn silk off the sleeve of Uncle Benjamin's shirt. Neither of them seemed the least concerned.

"But I must find him," Eugenia said, handing the can of

berries to Old Mary. "Where are they doing the operation? I promised Clyde I would be with him."

Ma stood up, produced a clay pipe from her apron, and set about stuffing it with tobacco from a can. "Doc Berryman knows what he's about."

"He needs a nurse. I've always been Clyde's nurse."

Ma drew a burning twig out of the fire and sucked the flame into her pipe. She coughed, picking tobacco off her tongue. "Ain't no call for that. Doc's got a fine nurse of his own."

"But Clyde needs me. He's always needed me."

Ma looked at her. Smoke leaked around her teeth. "He don't need you no more. He's got his ma."

Eugenia felt something in her wilt. She turned to Uncle Benjamin. He seemed to feel her movement, and reaching for his cane, got up and felt his way out to the porch, where he arranged himself in the slat chair. Old Mary crept out after him.

Ma watched them go. She looked back at Eugenia. "Not that we ain't grateful to you, Clyde and Benjamin and me, for what you done. You are a good woman, that I cain't deny, but let me put it to you plain. We are poor folks here, the bummers have took even what we had, and you are eating up our rations, doing no one any good."

"Oh, I'm sorry, I am so sorry." Eugenia fumbled in her pocket. "Here, this is for you. It's gold, a few small pieces only, but it's all I have, and the price is up so high these days . . ."

Ma's nostrils flared. She drew away, looking at Eugenia's outstretched hand as though something nasty festered there. "Ain't asked a guest for payment yet in my whole life, and don't intend to start. It's time for you to go on home." She stuck her pipe into her mouth and sucked ferociously.

Tears came behind Eugenia's eyes. Go home? But where? To Boston with Henry and Aunt Baker? To Canada in search of

Tom? She thought about her patients, captive in the cellar, how they had needed her and loved her, and for a moment she was sorry the war was almost done.

Ma coughed, blowing out a gust of smoke. "I ain't intending to be cruel. It just is best if you go on back to your own folks, thems as is responsible for you."

Eugenia drew in her breath to say I have no folks, I have no home, no one is responsible, but then she looked into Ma's eyes and saw there fear that she would stay where she did not belong, like the last man to climb onto a loaded raft, sinking everybody on it.

"I'll go today."

Ma touched her arm. "Tomorrow will do fine."

OLD Mary was crossing the yard when Eugenia went outside, and it occurred to her that she would ask her if she knew anyone who might have heard from Tom, his mother maybe. She called, "Old Mary, hey there!" but the old woman didn't hear and went on. Eugenia followed, past the empty hog trough, along a trodden path between long grass, across a rattling wooden bridge above a creek, and down another path to a swept yard surrounded by a low fence made of twigs stuck in the ground and bound with twine. Old Mary moved aside a section of the fence, pulled it back in place behind her, and went on toward a cabin in the center of the yard. Eugenia hesitated, then gathered up her skirts and stepped across the fence.

"Old Mary!"

Old Mary, who had reached the doorway of the cabin, turned. Her expression was neutral, neither welcoming nor hostile. She glanced behind Eugenia, then looked back at her face.

"Excuse me," Eugenia said, suddenly breathless, "I was wondering if you might know someone by the name of Tom who once belonged to Mr. Morgan."

Old Mary reached down and back behind herself, pressing her hands against the uprights of the door. In that motion, Eugenia saw Tom the day her father brought him home to her. She saw him backed against the wall, his hands pressed up against it as though to push a hole through which to run away. This old woman's motion was not one of flight, but of protection, as if she would prevent Eugenia from entering her life.

"Mary," Eugenia whispered. "Are you Tom's mother, Mary? Have you heard from him? Do you know where I can find him?"

The old woman's expression changed to one Eugenia recognized, that secretly triumphant look slaves wore when one of them has run away and no one knows a thing about it. "Ain't no point hunting after him," she said. "Slavery days be almost done."

"He's not my slave. Not anymore."

"Then you best forget him."

"Mary . . . can I call you Mary? Mary, you don't understand."

"I understands all right. I spent my whole life understanding. They done took away my man, done took away my children one by one, so's here I am, an old woman all used up and not a soul to care." She made an impatient brushing movement with her hand. "And you cain't call me Mary, no. You can call me ma'am. Go on, get out o' here. I got no truck with you."

Eugenia blinked. Old instincts rose, and with them anger at this woman's impudence. She turned and strode away, but had not yet fully crossed the creek when she stopped, her heart thumping and her head hot and tight. She looked down into the water. It was a little creek, not much more than a trickle. A row of jars floated in it, tethered to a tree trunk by a string. Some sort of liquid was in the jars, a pale amber color. Herb tea perhaps. They bobbed and swirled, making a gentle clicking one against the other.

Eugenia set both hands on the rail, which swayed beneath her weight, and watched them. Herb tea, a curative, a medicine, a salve. She watched them click. No other sound, just the trickle of the water and the clicking of the jars.

As she calmed, Old Mary's face rose up before her, hollowed out with loneliness and sorrow and hard work, and it seemed to her she wore the same face as the woman Tilda who might be her mother. Light played through the leaves, glittering off the surface of the water, turning the row of jars into ungamely golden jewels. She thought of Tom, of how the gold dust glittered in his hair, telling herself, *No, do not be foolish, he is not here, he is not in Mary's cabin, he is not anywhere about.* And yet the sense of him close by seemed palpable.

Once again she heard Old Mary's voice: "You cain't call me Mary, no. You can call me ma'am," and sudden admiration rose. The pride of her, such spirit, after all that suffering. Eugenia turned. She would go back to her and apologize, make her be her friend.

But when she got back to the cabin, Old Mary wasn't there. The door stood open like a challenge, and although Eugenia wanted to go in, although she reached and set her hand against the jamb, she could not do it. The place was empty, she could feel it. There was nothing here for her.

She sank onto the step, and with her hands against her face, rocked back and forth, like a mother comforting a child. A sigh came sobbing up her throat and she began to weep, loudly, unrestrainedly, in a way she never had before, going on a long time, hardly knowing why she wept, but in a strange way loving it, that sensation of release, like the sudden freedom of a bird held in a cage who beats and beats against the bars until one day the door flies open and he staggers in amazement up the sky.

At last she quieted, exhausted and replete, an aftermath of

trembling inhalation shaking her from time to time. Then the sense of someone watching, and she lifted her head to see Old Mary sitting on a turned-up pail beside the step, not three feet away, just sitting there, hands clasped in her lap, regarding her.

"Ain't that bad, child," she said.

Without intending to, without considering inside her head, with no feeling of embarrassment or shame, or wondering if she would be judged or condescended to, Eugenia said, "You see, I think my mother might have been a slave. My father died before I had the chance to ask him." And when Old Mary shifted on the pail the way a woman does when she is settling in to hear a story, she went on and told her everything.

When she had done, Old Mary was silent for a while, eyes narrowed, head tilted to one side in an assessing way. When she spoke it was as though a judgment had been rendered.

"This here Tilda, she had wrong done her."

"I don't know if it's true, I really don't. I could have just imagined it."

Old Mary's mouth went hard. "I had seven children once. I grieves for them."

"But *Tom* will come back, I know he will come back to you, he swore he would."

"And you, child?"

In that moment Eugenia knew what she must do. She must go back to Wilmington. She must find out about her mother. She must find out who she was. That was the important thing. All her life, as far back as she could remember, that had been what pulled and pulled at her, that dreamlike knowing, that urgent, urgent need to understand, that fear. Well, she must face it now. She must sweep her arm across the window and look clear-eyed at what looked back at her. Tomorrow she would get in touch with Tandy Cavin and send him back to Salisbury with a message for Henry and Aunt Baker.

. . .

NOW she was walking down the road away from Chapel Hill, the small bundle of her possessions in her hand. She had asked directions of a captain on a horse, who had told her the train station was a good walk thataway, and pointed off along the road toward the eastern sky.

Eugenia slipped her hand into her pocket, fingering her last few tiny bits of gold. It was enough—she hoped it was enough—to pay her fare to Wilmington with some left over to support her until she could find paying work. All around were drunken soldiers, singing, laughing, dancing in the road. As she passed, one and another called to her, flirting, begging her to dance with them, filling her with news. The Rebels had surrendered, a treaty signed at some farm just out of town, the Bennett place, they called it. General Sherman and General Johnston had shaken hands and signed the paper in the kitchen of the farmer's home. The war was over, done, they told her, offering her whiskey and a kiss.

She smiled, brushing past them and the Negroes who were also thronging in the streets, drunk too, on freedom and loud enthusiastic plans to go off searching for lost families. Somewhere out there Tom was coming back home to his mother, she could feel it, but she did not want to be here when he came, it was not time for that. It seemed to her that all her life she had been only half a person, that out there somewhere in the world her other half was waiting. She moved ahead as though she walked toward herself.

AFTERNOTE

Tom was a real person. I discovered him while reading Kemp P. Battle's *History of the University of North Carolina*. What little is known of him—how he ran off to the woods and was flushed out, shot in the legs below the knees, and sold—is told in a few brief sentences on page thirty-one. After that he disappears, as though he never had existed. Everybody needs a story, it is what makes us human, and it grieved me that Tom did not have one. So I set out to follow him and discover what his story might have been.

THE ROAD FROM CHAPEL HILL

by Joanna Catherine Scott

DISCUSSION QUESTIONS

1. Early in the novel, a resentful Eugenia is talking with her father about their situation. When he gives thanks that her mother is not alive to see how far they've fallen, she says, "Why, sir, I am alive." What does her shame about their new status say about her character? How would you have reacted in a similar situation?

2. In Gold Hill, Eugenia is coerced into service as a nurse to injured miners. Later, living with Aunt Baker, she willingly nurses deserting soldiers. What do you think drives her now? How much of her passion is guilt over the death of her father and her role in it?

3. Would you characterize the love between Tom and Eugenia as romantic, or is it more complicated? When Eugenia notices that Tom is in pain on the rockers, she persuades her father to change his duties. Why do you think she feels pity for Tom and not her father?

4. After Mr. Spotswood buys Tom for Eugenia, Miz Hedra begins to refer to her as "Miss Hoity-Toity." Would you call this a reflection of Miz Hedra's disdain for slavery, her jealousy of Eugenia, or something else? Do you agree with Eugenia's assessment of Miz Hedra as a hypocrite?

5. The theme of freedom runs throughout the novel. In what ways is Tom, despite his slavery, freer than Eugenia? In what ways is Clyde, a free white boy, enslaved?

6. All three protagonists have some issue with their fathers. Discuss the ways in which they handle them.

7. When Eugenia asks Tom how he thinks it feels to be white, he says, "Don't rightly know, Miz Genie. Angry, mebbe," and Eugenia realizes that, despite her show of affection, he can tell she's angry with her father. What else do you think Tom sees in her? In what ways is Tom the most perceptive character in the story, despite being called a simpleton?

8. Clyde spends much of the beginning of the novel planning to become a patroller and runaway-slave catcher. Instead, he winds up fighting for the North and losing these ambitions. Discuss the instances in which Clyde shows himself to be more of a man than he was at the outset of the novel. In which ways is he still a boy?

9. After her father kills himself, Eugenia is rescued from destitution by Dr. Kinney, who places her with Aunt Baker. Do you believe that all Eugenia needed to become a better person was a strong mother figure? How do Alouette, Henry, Aunt Baker, and Eugenia fill the gaps in each other's lives to form a family?

10. Are there any parallels between the story of Rahab and the Order of the Heroes of America (Red Strings)? Between Jericho and the South?

11. In the turpentine plantation, Robert tells Tom, "Freedom ain't some gift this Miss Genie lady give you . . . You got to hunt it down and catch it. You got to snatch it in your hand." How does this affect Tom's perception of freedom? How do the three protagonists go about snatching their own freedom in their hands?

12. Eugenia battles to save Clyde from death, even going to Chapel Hill with him to ensure he has his leg reamputated. Why does she need him to survive so badly? Why is Clyde so desperate to go home, despite the dangers of the journey?

13. Why do you think Scott called this novel *The Road from Chapel Hill*? How does the town of Chapel Hill serve as an anchor to the story?

14. This novel is rich with minor characters. Which of them appeals to you, and why? What impact do they have on the direction of the story?

15. Toward the end of the novel, Eugenia learns a shocking secret about herself. How did the author allude to it all along? How did Eugenia's subconscious awareness of it affect her perception of herself?

16. Scott subtly captures the split attitudes of Southerners, especially North Carolinians, toward the war between the states. In what ways have Scott's images and depictions come to inform, challenge, or even contradict your previous notions?

17. Tom was a real person. In fact, Scott dedicates the novel to him. How does this affect your reaction to him, and to the novel as a whole?

18. At the end of the novel, Eugenia, a stronger woman, is walking off the page in search of her mother and her future. How do you think her story and Tom's might have continued?